40903   8/1   £28-20

Library of
Davidson College

VOID

A Festschrift for
Native Speaker

JANUA
LINGUARUM Series Maior 97

Studia Memoriae
Nicolai van Wijk Dedicata

edenda curat
C. H. van Schooneveld
Indiana University

A Festschrift for Native Speaker

Edited by
Florian Coulmas

MOUTON PUBLISHERS · THE HAGUE · PARIS · NEW YORK

410
F418

ISBN: 90 279 3498 3
© 1981, Mouton Publishers, The Hague, The Netherlands
Printed in the Netherlands

82-1770

Native Speaker: La Bocca della Verità

Preface

The making of this book was an exciting experience. In January 1979 a first announcement about the *Festschrift* was circulated. The response to this invitation to contribute has surpassed my best expectations, and I wish to thank all those who encouraged me to pursue the plan although they felt unable to contribute. I am particularly grateful to the authors of this book, because, from working with their manuscripts, I have learnt so much about the notion of what it means to be a native speaker. In the hope that this will also prove to be true for others, the book is presented to the critical reader. It is respectfully dedicated to those who made me a native speaker.

F.C.
April 1980

Contents

Florian Coulmas
Introduction: The Concept of Native Speaker — 1

PART ONE EPISTEMOLOGY AND HISTORY OF LINGUISTICS

Victor H. Yngve
The Struggle for a Theory of Native Speaker — 29

Th. T Ballmer
A Typology of Native Speakers — 51

Jacob Mey
"Right or Wrong, my Native Speaker." Estant les Régestes du Noble
Souverain de l'Empirie Linguistic avec un Renvoi au Mesme Roy — 69

Kenneth L. Pike
Wherein Lies 'Talked-About' Reality? — 85

Asa Kasher
Minimal Speakers, Necessary Speech Acts — 93

PART TWO METHODOLOGY

H. Schnelle
Introspection and the Description of Language Use — 105

Esa Itkonen
The Concept of Linguistic Intuition — 127

Jon D. Ringen
Quine on Introspection in Linguistics — 141

Konrad Ehlich
Native Speaker's Heritage. On Philology of "Dead" Languages — 153

PART THREE FIELD WORK: TECHNIQUES AND ETHICS

Eugene A. Nida
Informants or Colleagues?   169

Werner Kummer
Malinche, Patron-Saint of Informants?   175

Hartmut Haberland
A *Minimum Morale* on how not to Listen to the Native Speaker   195

PART FOUR GRAMMAR: THE STRUCTURE OF INQUIRY

Bennison Gray
Parallel Structure and "The Failure of Modern Linguistics"   203

John Hinds
The Interpretation of Ungrammatical Utterances   221

Adam Makkai
What Does a Native Speaker Know about the Verb KILL?   237

Bjarne Ulvestad
On the Precariousness of Linguistic Introspection   245

D.H. Whalen
The Native Speaker and Indeterminacy   263

Dieter Wunderlich
Linguistic Strategies   279

PART FIVE ASPECTS OF LANGUAGE ACQUISITION AND USE

Walburga von Raffler-Engel
The Native Speaker in his New Found Body   299

John O. Regan and Alan L. Ziajka
Observing the Native Doer: Prelinguistic Behavior among Infants and Young Children   305

Contents xi

Ton van der Geest
How to Become a Native Speaker: One Simple Way 317

Florian Coulmas
Spies and Native Speakers 355

Tohru Kaneko
On Translatability 369

David R. Olson
The Literate Native Speaker: Some Intellectual Consequences
of the Language of Schooling 379

List of Contributors 391

Index of Names 393

Index of Subjects 398

FLORIAN COULMAS

Introduction: The Concept of Native Speaker

A COMMON REFERENCE POINT

This book is an attempt to review and rethink the methodological foundations of the study of language. Its point of departure is the *native speaker*. As there is no way of doing linguistics without taking account of him, he can be conceived of as a common reference point for all branches of linguistics. Hence, the basic problem is not whether or not the native speaker plays a part in the study of language, but rather how this undeniable part should be defined. Where should he enter the process of acquisition of knowledge about languages and language, and what should be his task? The individual chapters of this book combine to discuss this question which touches the very heart of linguistic methodology. While the chief concern of their authors is the nature of language, the focus of the book as a whole is on the nature of linguistic analysis. It is thus a contribution to the reflection of what linguists do and of the task that they set for themselves.

In different subdisciplines of linguistics the relation between data and theory is subject to different factual and methodological constraints and hence has to be defined differently. The difficulties the native speaker has in grasping abstractions about his own language have different implications for the grammarian, the psycho- or socio-linguist, the historical linguist, the epistemologist, the computer linguist, the methodologist, the applied linguist, etc. Yet, the native speaker is more or less closely related to the object of inquiry in any kind of linguistic research. Moreover, linguists of every conceivable theoretical orientation agree that the concept of the native speaker is of fundamental importance for the field. This is clearly reflected in the literature, where this concept is so often made use of by linguists stating the principles or aims of their analytic work.

1. Data must come, directly or indirectly, from native speakers of the language under study (Hoijer 1958:573).

2. The informant . . . is a familiar and necessary part of the study of any living

language, whatever its position in the world. The informant is not a teacher, nor a linguist; he is simply a native speaker of the language . . . (Robins 1964:364).

3. A complete scientific description of a language must pursue one aim above all: to make precise and explicit the ability of a native speaker to produce utterances in that language (Halle 1962:64).

4. The goal of a theory of a particular language must be the explication of the abilities and skills involved in the linguistic performance of a fluent native speaker (Katz and Fodor 1962:218).

5. One way to test the adequacy of a grammar proposed for L is to determine whether or not the sequences that it generates are actually grammatical, i.e., acceptable to a native speaker (Chomsky 1957:13).

6. A grammar is . . . *descriptively adequate* to the extent that it correctly describes the intrinsic competence of the idealized native speaker (Chomsky 1965:24).

7. Semantic tests are one source of behavioral data for which a theory can be made to account. More narrowly then, it should predict certain native-speaker responses for given tests (Bendix 1971:406).

These are but a few quotations that bear witness to the significance of this key concept of linguistics. The authors may not always mean the same thing when they use the term "native speaker;" but despite irreconcilable differences between its more often than not implicit definitions, they obviously find it hard to dispense with it. No linguist could reasonably disclaim that his descriptions and analyses somehow relate to the speakers of the language that he studies, or to the human species as such, if he happens to be concerned with universals of language – however abstract this relation may be. Language simply doesn't exist but as a part of the human condition, hence we cannot even begin to study it without referring to a human being who is capable of providing us with the material of our investigation. Notice, however, that the native speaker's role is not restricted to that of a data source. (We will come back to this point below, pp. 6-13.)

The universal acceptance of the concept of 'native speaker' implies of course neither universal praise, nor agreement as to how to handle actual native speakers. Consequently, not every chapter of this book is a eulogy of the native speaker. But all of the authors strive to further our knowledge of reliable research methods, and, in so doing, shed light on some of the aspects of his multiform character.

He is praised by some as the (to date) "unsung hero of linguistics" (Nida) and applauded as being the only reliable source of linguistic knowledge, while he is attacked by others as a "king with no realm," (Mey) who is utterly corrupt. Some deplore the fact that so much attention is paid to the native speaker, and others say it is too little. Linguists are of necessity concerned with

Introduction: The Concept of Native Speaker

the native speaker, but the answers as to what he actually is or what it is that linguists should try to describe and explain are as diverse as their theoretical inclinations. One obvious answer is that linguists should describe *what the native speaker says* and try to discover patterns according to which his utterances can be systematized. A competing view states that *what the native speaker knows* in terms of language is what the linguist is after and what he should try to model. Still another position contends that linguists cannot do justice to their subject matter if they fail to explain *what the native speaker does*. We may thus observe that the respective conception of the native speaker as well as one's notion of what is and what is not interesting about him is very indicative with regard to the whole theoretical approach that one favors in the study of language.

Consider the following definitions of language:

1. a recursive formal mechanism that relates strings of types of sounds (or visual marks) with meanings and can thus be reconstructed by logical means;

2. a social phenomenon, a mode of action and interaction where people utter meaningful strings of sounds relative to communicative purposes which are in turn related to specific situational circumstances which the utterances serve to transform.

Considering the fact that proponents of both 1. and 2. (and many other and similar definitions) claim to be concerned about the native speaker, it wouldn't seem an unjust reproach to state that he is merely a protean "front man" (Gray) of the school that whoever refers to him happens to adhere to. It may thus not be altogether unreasonable to charge this concept with obscuring rather than clarifying fundamental differences. However, it is my conviction that this is too rash and too negative a judgment which ignores the fact that 'native speaker' is an indispensable component of the conceptual foundations of all of linguistics, relative to which its subdisciplines place limits on the range of their respective topics. Granting that the native speaker is indeed referred to with respect to a great variety of problems and different parts of his anatomy, we cannot ignore that he is also a unifying link enabling theoreticians of antagonistic views to identify a common ground on which they can dispute their differences, and reminding students of different linguistic subdisciplines that they do have something in common and that their explanatory models should hence be interconnectable.

AUTHENTICITY

The question as to what procedures to follow in gathering data on a language is not a trivial one. Obviously, not all utterances made in a language can qualify as data on which a sound description can be based. The linguist must be careful not to let his analysis be biased by data that are exceptional or unnatural. But how can he know in advance what is exceptional, unnatural, or deviant?

Languages are spoken by more than one speaker if they are spoken at all. With only one speaker left, a language such as for instance the Californian language Plains Miwok, is practically extinct, because he has nobody to talk to, and self-talk wouldn't keep it alive for long anyway. English has about 300,000,000 speakers and is thus one of the major languages of the world. Juang, a Munda language spoken on the Indian subcontinent has only 13,000 speakers,[1] but the problem remains essentially the same: far too many for a linguist to deal with. Which one (or which ones) of them should he choose as his informant(s)? A choice has to be made, if only for reasons of economy.

There are other reasons, too. Not every speaker meets equally well the demands of a linguist trying to assemble a good corpus. There is no doubt that linguistic skills vary individually. The linguist is thus not only faced with the problem of how to eliminate exceptional or unnatural utterances from his corpus; an equally important issue is to select a speaker who is able to provide him with the data that he wants, i.e., with the greatest amount of information about the language.

The above questions are hard to answer, and, as will be shown below, an appropriate answer depends to some extent on the language under investigation. However, one part of the answer is generally agreed on. Only those speakers of a language qualify as potential informants whose *first language* it is. No matter whether the data of linguistic analysis are considered to be actual utterances or statements about utterances or both, the regularities that these utterances or statements follow must have been acquired in the course of primary socialization with the acquisition of one's mother tongue. In short, speakers who can serve as data supplier have to be native speakers.

By this criterion all the speakers of a language who have learned it as a second language, however fluent they may be, are excluded from the population out of which the linguist must make his choice. In the case of English, this amounts to a drastic reduction by 50,000,000, i.e., one sixth of the 300,000,000 speakers of English that Voegelin & Voegelin cite. Yet, the remaining 250,000,000 are still enough of a problem for the linguist to cope with. Obviously, nativeness is only a minimal requirement, and by itself cannot solve the problem of how to select an appropriate informant. Language is a very democratic achievement in that practically nobody is deprived of it. Hence, even the additional requirement that the speaker must not be demented does not lead to any further significant reduction of the number of potential informants.

Placing other restrictions on the native speaker is much more difficult, because to say that speaker$_1$ knows his language better than speaker$_2$ in any reasonably well-defined and non-trivial sense of 'knowing one's language well' involves a host of conceptual and ideological problems. One way out of this dilemma is simply to say that anyone can do the job, any native speaker that is. But this only means to disregard it (see pp. 3 ff., 13 ff.).

Minimal as it is, the nativeness requirement rests on theoretical assumptions. It presupposes a qualitative difference between first and second language. It is only the first language that counts. While this requirement cannot guarantee that unnatural and exceptional utterances are excluded from the corpus, it does guarantee that the data are not distorted by interfering regularities of another language, or at least this is what it is designed for. The native speaker is thus seen as being the gate keeper of authenticity, because, as Samarin (1967: 57) rightly observes, the ultimate judges of naturalness can only be the speakers of a language. "Internal evidence cannot be used by the investigator for making an independent evaluation. He must depend on his informants" (*ibid.*).

It is interesting to note that the nativeness criterion is maintained across theoretical boundaries and contrasts. The quotations in section 1 witness significant differences regarding the conceptual status of 'native speaker' which will be discussed in more detail below (section 3). Within the framework of field linguistics, the native speaker is a human being who is able to give information about his or her language. In theoretical linguistics, by contrast, he often figures as an abstract idealization. Yet, notwithstanding these fundamental differences, the speaker whom the linguist is concerned about is invariably claimed to be a *native* speaker. He is the one who can legitimately supply data, and his language is what grammatical analyses are meant to account for. Thus, nativeness is *the* one universally accepted criterion for authenticity.

Such superficial consensus cannot obscure the fact that the issue of how to single out *the* native speaker remains on the agenda of pressing problems that linguistic practice cannot afford to ignore. Particularly salient are the following two questions. First, how do actual native speakers relate to the (an) ideal native speaker? For a satisfactory answer to this question it is essential to secure a mutual understanding among linguists about their subject matter and about the relation between observation and theory. Second, granting that nativeness implies authenticity, it is not clear how differences between native speakers should be accounted for, and whether or how they should be reflected in the theory of language. In dealing with this problem, Ballmer distinguishes various kinds of speakers and proposes "a typology of native speakers."

RELIABILITY

Pursuing further the question of how to select a native speaker for linguistic analysis, we have to consider the native speaker's reliability. With regard to what does the linguist depend on him, or, to put it differently, what exactly is it that the native speaker is supposed to do? Further, on the basis of an explicit answer to this question, what kind of native speaker can best render the required services?

The first question can be rephrased as follows: What are the data of linguistic analysis? There are at least three answers that can be advanced separately or in combination.

(i) The data of linguistic analysis are natural speech, i.e., utterances of native speakers to be recorded with pen and paper or tape recorder by the linguist. The utterances should not be produced expressly for the linguist, rather they should occur in unelicited texts. "Only texts ... can serve as the basic core of data from which an adequate analysis can be made" (Nida 1947: 146).

(ii) The data of linguistic analysis are judgements over utterances. These utterances are partly recorded and partly construed by the linguist himself, who then presents them to the native speaker in order to test the limits of the grammar. Data of this sort reflect "the intuitions of native speakers of the language, most importantly their judgements of the acceptability of sentences" (Greenbaum 1977: 4).

(iii) The data of linguistic analysis are judgements on the adequacy of grammars proposed for the language under study. They are obtained by presenting the native speaker with sentences that are generated by the grammar. (Cf. quote 5. on p. 2 above.)

While in gathering data of the sort mentioned in (i) attention is limited to what is publicly verifiable, (ii) and (iii) appeal to unobservables, that is, to speakers' intuitions. In all three cases it is however important to decide whether any speaker can be relied upon to provide the desired data or whether the linguist should rather turn to "native expert speakers" (Hill 1961). Are all performers equally competent? This is a significant point, because as testified by (i) - (iii), the native speaker may enter the analytic process at both ends (cf. Maclay & Sleator 1960: 275). His utterances are the raw data forming the basis for the discovery of the grammatical system (i). Next, his judgements operate on systematically manipulated utterances, the (classical structuralist) idea being that he makes decisions as to whether two given items are the same

Introduction: The Concept of Native Speaker 7

or different (ii). Finally, native speaker judgements may also function in the evaluation of alternative grammars for a given language. The informant is supposed to assess the sentences generated by a grammar, and he is expected (and credited with the ability and authority) to reject all ungrammatical sequences (iii). Grammars should map and explain the intuitions that underlie these judgements. This is the view widely accepted in contemporary mentalist linguistics.

Intuitions about the acceptability of sentences are now recognized by most linguists as important data (cf. Itkonen's paper). In so far, Chomsky's critique of the empiricist rigorism of structural linguistics was fairly successful. However, whose intuitions the linguist can safely trust remains an open question.

This problem has quantitative as well as qualitative aspects. The quantitative ones are discussed in more detail below (pp. 13 ff.) and hence only briefly touched upon here. The aim of a grammar to provide insight into the linguistic capacities of the native speakers is often interpreted to mean that it should predict all and only those sentences which the speakers of the respective language might accept as grammatical. This is an unattainable goal, if only because grammaticality judgements vary from speaker to speaker. Hence, in *writing* a grammar some idealization is inevitable, and this should cause no discomfort, not even to the most uncompromising empiricist, because no science can do without idealizations. Chomsky is right when he says that "opposition to idealization is simply objection to rationality" (1979:57). But this does not in principle resolve the issue of who should be entitled to supply the data.

The relationship between linguist and native speaker (data supplier) is a qualitative one, and it is a fundamentally important relationship, because it clearly is of great consequence for the analysis. Who then should be the linguist's native speaker? There are three options which are worth discussing.

1. *Anyone.* Every native speaker has the ability to make himself understood throughout his speech community. Hence, anyone's language must comprise a generalizable portion of the language of this community. One might argue that, on this ground, anyone is a reliable data supplier. A grammar which is modeled to match the intuitions of an arbitrarily selected (nondemented) speaker will inevitably contain certain idiosyncrasies, but it will also contain rules which will be found valid throughout the speech community if subjected to empirical testing. Obviously, the linguist who favors this option cannot make very strong, empirically founded claims as to the generality of his grammar, even though it may in fact be characterized by a high degree of general validity.

2. *A naive informant.* A person without formal or informal training in

linguistics whose reactions to linguistic stimuli are studied can be considered a naive informant. Rather than lessening the qualification of the native speaker, naivety must be seen here as an additional requirement, because it excludes a certain group of speakers. To favor this option means to rely on the advantages of ignorance. What are these advantages, if any?

Firstly, if the informant lacks any understanding of the problems under investigation, he is not in a position to try to make his answers conform to the researcher's wishes or expectations, unless the questions are phrased in such a way that the informant can guess the desired answer. Secondly, natural speech is not normally guided by much metalinguistic reflection. There is no way of knowing in how far reflecting upon one's language influences one's own language use. The choice of a naive informant might thus be a wise move to avoid unnatural distortion of the data.

There are of course also difficulties in working with naive informants. It may be hard to convey the idea of rejecting or accepting a sentence to begin with. Furthermore, the linguist will often find it difficult to tell whether a sentence is rejected on syntactic or semantic grounds or because it violates some norms of usage. In solving these problems, the linguist depends largely on his own ingenuity. He cannot hope to get much help from his informant.

3. *A sophisticated informant.* To overcome linguistic naivety, a speaker has to be able to make his language an object of thought and to take it out of the realm of the automatic. To the extent that he has the ability to reflect on his language he is a sophisticated informant, the obvious alternative to the naive informant. Nida strongly advocates the use of a native speaker with some linguistic background whom he considers "the linguist's colleague."[2] Some obvious advantages of the sophisticated informant are the following. He is sensible of the problems and can help the linguist to discover peculiarities of his language. In making unsolicited contributions he can facilitate the testing of hypotheses. And, as he understands the linguist's task, he can think of low frequency items and structures. Ideally, he can judge the systematic relevance of distinctions that the linguist has discovered or believes to have discovered. The assistance of a sophisticated native speaker may thus enable the researcher to find much sooner a plausible organization of his data than when depending on a naive informant.

The pitfalls that the linguist must be careful to avoid in working with a sophisticated native speaker are equally apparent. It is not an empty metaphor to say that the sophisticated informant has lost his innocence. Once he begins to wonder whether an utterance is "right or wrong" he is liable to become a victim of the long recognized and often commented on problem of the gap between linguistic norm and practice, i.e., the problem that informants' reports often tend to reflect the norms they aim at rather than their

Introduction: The Concept of Native Speaker

actual practice (cf. esp. Labov 1971, 1972). The native speaker's linguistic awareness may hence turn out to be a mixed blessing.

Undoubtedly, many other considerations could be brought to bear on the selection of a native speaker according to the above mentioned options, and it is unlikely that a definitive decision can be made once and for all. In discussing the respective pros and cons we have ignored so far the question of what language it is that the linguist wants to study. It was tacitly assumed that the native speaker speaks a language other than the linguist's language. Whether or not this condition should hold is, however, a crucial question. It is particularly important with respect to the first option: 'anyone'. For the claim that anyone is a reliable data supplier does of course not imply a random choice. Rather, those who favor this option typically make a very specific choice: They choose themselves. The real issue here is therefore whether the linguist is eligible to be his own informant; or, to put it differently, whether introspection should be admitted as a reliable method to acquire linguistic knowledge. Is the linguist a reliable native speaker? Anttila (1972: 349) gives a very concise statement of the problem:

Once you have linguistic training, you spoil your native intuitions as a normal naive speaker, and you cannot write a psychologically real grammar for a normal speaker. Linguists are not normal speakers when they write grammars. On the other hand, if you are a naive speaker, you cannot write grammars at all.

Anttila's observation can hardly be questioned, nor can it be ignored as unimportant. In my opinion, one of the major methodological conflicts in contemporary linguistics is centered upon this issue. On the one hand, it is commonly agreed that there are no data whatsoever which are observer-neutral. Hence the exclusion of the linguist from the role of the native-speaker-data-supplier does not by itself guarantee a corpus of 'pure' data. Furthermore, it is not unreasonable to credit the linguist, if not with privileged access to his internal linguistic knowledge, with a greater sensitivity to linguistic problems than the layman native speaker usually has. This seems to be Chomsky's position.

Admitting that not everything that is functional in one's internal grammar is available to introspection, Chomsky characterizes the task of a scientific grammar as follows: it

attempts to specify what the speaker actually knows, not what he may report about his knowledge (1965: 8).

For generative grammarians this requirement does not disqualify intuition as the data of linguistic analysis. Quite the contrary is the case:

The problem of the grammarian is to construct a description and, where possible, an explanation for the enormous mass of unquestionable data concerning the linguistic intuition of the *native speaker* (*often himself*) (op. cit.: 20), emphasis added).[3]

The ultimate aim, however, is to construe a theory of competence, i.e., a theory of how language is conceptually represented in the mind. A theory of this sort is an abstract model of an idealized native speaker. Clearly then, the native speaker leads a double life in Chomsky's work. As a data supplier he is a real person of flesh and blood, i.e., the linguist himself; as a possessor of linguistic competence he is an idealization. To question the legitimacy of this twofold character is not to question the legitimacy, or even necessity, of idealization in writing grammars. The point at issue is merely whether the linguist should be, at the same time, the subject and the object of research, i.e., whether his idealizations and abstractions should be based on his own intuitions. Ulvestad, in his chapter, presents evidence from syntactic research based on a large corpus of data that witness the precariousness of the native speaker linguist solution. One problem is that "the enormous mass of unquestionable data" referred to by Chomsky are not considered to be so unquestionable by everyone who has seriously dealt with the evaluation and classification of linguistic data. A number of empirical studies have demonstrated that acceptability judgements are not the kind of thing that one can take for granted on a common sense basis (e.g. Maclay & Sleator 1960, Hill 1961, Quirk & Svartvik 1966, Spencer 1973).

Hill (1961) put some of the sentences of *Syntactic Structures* to empirical testing and obtained responses that sharply disagree with Chomsky's predictions. His study was dismissed by Chomsky (1961) on the ground that in his experiment the instructions to the subjects were too vague. This was admittedly a weak point in Hill's investigation. However, similar results were reached in other investigations whose challenge is hence much harder to answer. Maclay and Sleator performed a study on informant reactions under neatly controlled empirical conditions. Observing that informant reactions are influenced by a variety of factors, they come to the conclusion that

> native speaker responses to language [are] a complex research problem in its own right and not merely a question of casually submitting language materials to any handy informant (Maclay & Sleator 1960: 281).

Furthermore, they feel obliged to deny the claim that masses of linguistic data can be taken as self-evident or unquestionable:

> Very little can be assumed in advance about responses to language, and even the most obvious predictions need to be checked empirically (op. cit.: 282).

Introduction: The Concept of Native Speaker

The same problem is taken up by Spencer who pointedly relates it to the relation of linguist and native speaker. "Do native speakers share the intuitions of linguists?" This is the question to which he has devoted an equally accurate empirical study (Spencer 1973). He comes to the conclusion that they don't and that linguists who rely solely on their own intuition "may not be analyzing the common language of the speech community" (1973:83). Ross came to similar results in his attempt to delineate the boundaries of English where he reports "fairly clear differences between linguists and normals" (1979:156).

The question now is how such findings ought to be interpreted and what consequences should be drawn. The most radical solution is to outlaw the personal union of linguist and native speaker altogether — the methodological position tirelessly advocated by Labov. He explicitly states that "linguists cannot continue to produce theory and data at the same time" (1972:199), because acceptability judgements or self-report and actual behavior do not necessarily coincide. A less uncompromising stance is taken by Bolinger who refrains from voting for a ban on introspection and intuition, although he somewhat teasingly declares that

> intuition is so important to generative grammarians that one could almost call them the psychologists of language[4] (1968b:204).

Bolinger questions the "priority of introspective evidence" that Chomsky (1965:20) feels compelled to concede, and his reasons seem very persuasive. It is inevitable

> that we are influenced by the case we want to prove (Bolinger 1968a:35)

and

> if a slightly unusual utterance is inconvenient, it is hard to escape the temptation to think it worse than it really is (*ibid.*).

The justification of Bolinger's warning against placing too much trust in linguistic data that consist only in introspective experience of the linguist is plainly testified by the following quotation from Katz (1966:281).

> Counter-examples cannot appear in linguistic experience because they would not count as linguistic experience.

A more elaborate discussion of the obvious danger of circularity and irrefutability of linguistic theories construed according to this maxim is advanced in Gray's chapter. Schnelle is concerned with a classification of the notion and function of introspection in linguistic analysis, and so is Ringen. They both formulate conditions under which introspection can be a legitimate tool of linguistic analysis. This is also one of the problems that Itkonen tackles in his discussion of linguistic intuition and its relation to empirical science.

There seems to be wide agreement that generalizations over introspectional data indeed constitute a serious problem which should not be pushed aside under the pretext that it is not the task of a formal grammar to predict actual speech behavior anyway. It is interesting to note that this problem is recognized as such not only by radical empiricists but also by those scholars who do not wish to deny introspection its proper place in linguistic analysis. Labov has always taken seriously the dangers of the researchers's incapacity to suppress his desire "to make things come out right," pointing out that there are hence "undoubtedly unconscious factors which lead investigators to find examples which support their own arguments and not to find counter-examples" (Labov 1971:444f.).[5] If this is right, the possibility that grammaticality judgements by linguists are impelled in a certain direction cannot be rejected too light-heartedly. Variation is reported on a large scale in a number of studies on what is and what isn't found to be grammatical (cf. e.g. Bolinger 1968a, Greenbaum 1977, van Dijk 1977), and this obviously is another important point concerning the native speaker's reliability. Hinds in his chapter approaches the problem of "investigator bias," his main concern being with the interpretation of ungrammatical utterances. For those trying to understand how language works they are, he argues, of great explanatory value. Philosopher Hilary Putnam once pointed out that

> to reject the problem of accounting for the use and the understanding of deviant sentences is to reject one of the most interesting problems in linguistics (Putnam 1974:84).

The pertinence of this claim is eloquently underscored by Hinds who gives an analysis of the structural relations enabling us to understand ungrammatical utterances.

Another salient point about acceptability judgements, which can again only nourish our distrust in the native speaker's reliability is the fact that these judgements are affected by a number of variables that are difficult to control. Bolinger (1968a) draws our attention to the problems arising out of the presentation of decontextualized sentences for assessment, and van Dijk continues along similar lines to demonstrate that

> our intuitions about sentence boundaries seem to be very unreliable indeed as an empirical base for a (sentence) grammar (1977:47).

The presentation of isolated sentences (strings) creates serious problems for the

Introduction: The Concept of Native Speaker

whole methodological approach that rests on acceptability judgements, because it inevitably introduces some degree of arbitrariness into the analysis. Whether individual speakers rate unusual sentences as acceptable or deviant depends on their inventiveness to think up an appropriate context and on their tolerance.[6] This sort of individual differences in finding a possible context and hence a possible interpretation for a sentence (Greenbaum 1977:9; Nida this volume) again cast doubts on the reliability of intuitive judgements of individual speakers. Should only highly imaginative speakers' judgements count as evidence, or should their judgements rather be considered as idiosyncratic extensions of the possibilities of the grammar that underlies the common language of a speech community?

If one of the aims of grammatical research is to give an account of a given language which is not totally independent of those who speak it, these and similar questions cannot be neglected, because they affect the answer to the more general question to what extent and under what conditions intuitive judgements over utterances can serve as data of linguistic analysis. Eventually, even theories with a minimal data base, theories, that is, of the kind that generative grammars are supposed to be, will not be able to evade this issue by insisting on the necessities of idealization.

To sum up the discussion in this section of what reliance we can place on speaker intuitions, we cannot credit the native speaker with much reliability, no matter whether he or she is a linguist or a normal. This should not be seen as a reason to dispense with speaker intuitions and self-observation. However, only a careful balance of introspection and empirical testing can obviate the risks inevitably involved in working with intuitive data: investigator bias and individual differences in linguistic skills and imagination.

REPRESENTATIVITY

It was argued in the preceding section that there are serious reasons why linguists should not trust completely and uncritically the native speaker's intuitions of well-formedness. His reliability was shown to be undermined in principle by a variety of factors. The question of his representativity and, more importantly, the representativity of a grammar that is based on his intuitive judgements touches upon a related issue.

The problem of representativity arises for those who treat the native speaker as an ideal as well as for those who deal with a real person. As a matter of fact, it is a complex problem involving a number of related issues.

First of all, there is the problem of idiolect. What part of a language is represented in an individual organism? How does it relate to the part represented in another organism? For those linguists who work with living native speakers these are questions concerning the validity of the data, and by consequence, the empirical adequacy of the theory derived thereof. For those linguists on the other hand, working with the ideal native speaker, the problem is what it is that a competence model represents. According to Chomsky's (1965) well-known definition, the ideal native speaker is a speaker who knows his language perfectly. How does he relate to an actual speaker and to an actual speech community? Chomsky's stipulation that he lives in a "completely homogeneous speech community" implies the very powerful claim that individual differences do not constitute part of the *explanandum* of linguistic theory. They can be legitimately ignored. What is disturbing about this decision is *not* the idealization involved here. The point is simply that we do not know exactly what it means to know one's language perfectly. Does this kind of unconscious knowledge represent the sum of the linguistic abilities of all members of the speech community? Is it the smallest common denominator? Or is it a generalization of the abilities of one individual, i.e., the native speaker-linguist? The well-known "in my dialect/idiolect . . . " arguments seem to point toward the latter possibility. Clearly, the linguistic abilities of individual speakers are both less and more than what is implied in Chomsky's conception of competence; less, in that a real speaker can never exhaust the recursive possibilities of a language, and in that an individual speaker's command of a language cannot equal the whole language as a social fact; more, in that no grammatical model can represent all of the facets of what a speaker knows about his language. Hence, the problem of how individual speech habits, however ideal they may be, relate to the description and possibly explanation of a language remains to be solved.

There is no doubt that rationalist competence models greatly enhance our knowledge about language and its procedural or, as Chomsky has called it, creative nature. However, the relation of these models to language as represented in individual people's minds or brains is fundamentally unclear. This is further evidenced by the fact that the status of the abstractions employed in these models for the description of the ideal system underlying linguistic form is somewhat ill-defined. Is the analysis correct according as its parts correspond to patterns that are in some way inherent in the object, or is it correct according as its predictions about the forms of utterances are correct, independent of any relevant correspondence between the formal symbolism the analysis consists in and the speaker's mental or neurophysiological processes and structures? In other words, in what sense do the parts of the formal symbolism represent anything at all, and if they do, what is it that they represent? Schnelle in his paper observes that transformational generative grammars contain elements, such as e.g. rule ordering, that represent nothing at all (see below p. 118). Elements of this sort cannot combine to create a structure which is isomorphic with that of the object. Structures containing such elements are imposed on the object rather than detected in it. Schnelle's proposal is that linguists should strive to map and make statements about the mental structures that constitute knowledge of a language and by so doing overcome the inadequacies of linguistic models which cannot relate the regularities of language to the concrete processes of the organism by which these regularities are brought about. Ultimately, this may lead to the abandonment or redefinition of the tradition-inspired distinction between competence and performance whose problematic and often criticized character (e.g. Bever 1970, Labov 1972, Hymes 1974, van Dijk 1977, Yngve this volume) is now widely acknowledged.

Another point concerning representativity is this. Given that the native speaker's knowledge of his language is what linguists should try to model, how much of what he knows is to be accounted for and what can be disregarded? This question seems to be particularly upsetting in the study of meaning where it is often very difficult to determine the semantic core and range of linguistic items. The theoretical demands of the respective model seem to be the only criteria setting the limits of how abstract the relationship should be allowed to be that holds between the meaning of a lexical item as specified in the dictionary and the use that speakers make of it on the basis of their knowledge. A passionate argument against any kind of conceptual reductionism for the sake of a consistent semantic theory is presented by Makkai in his exemplary attempt to show what a native speaker knows about the verb *kill*. Again, the competence-performance dichotomy is under fire, indirectly at least, because, that the many-sidedness of what speakers know of lexical items cannot be integrated into the theory is due to the formal constraints of a competence theory to model language as a consistent and determinate system. Indeterminacy in language is the topic of Whalen's paper. Showing that the determinacy of linguistic structure is a fundamental assumption of most modern theories and, taking a stand against it, he advances evidence as well as arguments why and how future descriptions of language should account for conflicting consistencies. Actual inconsistencies in native speakers' relations or intuitions should not be sacrificed on the altar of simplicity or idealization.

If a grammatical description represents a native speaker's knowledge of his language, how representative is the description relative to the language as a structured whole? This was the question guiding the discussion in this section, and a final issue which should not be kept silent about in this connection is the fact that it can hardly be answered indiscriminately for all languages. How do languages differ with respect to the generalizability and hence representativity of individual speakers' intuitions? We cannot answer this question here, but we can put it on the agenda of empirical linguistic research. It is a fairly reasonable assumption that languages vary with regard to intra-linguistic variability. As Gray rightly remarks in his chapter (see below p. 203 ff.), there is indeed an important difference between obtaining the English language from one English informant and obtaining the Tagalog language (as Bloomfield has done it) from one Tagalog informant. Most native speakers of English are subject to systematic exposure to particular views about the grammar of their language during the years of education. Moreover, English has a century-old written tradition while Tagalog lacks this kind of historical corset. Thus, as opposed to Taglog, English is a highly standardized language. That schooling may play an interesting role in shaping native speaker intuitions is not a farfetched supposition, which is discussed in detail by van der Geest. It would indeed only be surprising if language education should have no effect at all on a given language as a social phenomenon. Differences in standardization are obviously only a matter of degree, but they should not be left unaccounted for. To conclude, if there are any such differences and if they have a bearing on the representativity of individual speakers' judgements, this is surely a fact which is significant both for the field linguist and the theoretician. The former has to take into consideration another point in selecting his informant(s), while the latter has to account for the fact that the validity of introspective evidence may vary from language to language. Clearly then, the representativity problem remains a source of acute discomfort for linguists who reflect on the status of the results of their research.

VARIATION – NECESSARY OR CONTINGENT?

In justifying idealization as a necessary part of rational conduct in intellectual work, Chomsky (1979: 57) states that,

when you work within some idealization, perhaps you overlook something which is terribly important. That is a contingency of rational inquiry that has always been understood. One must not be too worried about it.

Is variation in language one such terribly important thing which was overlooked by idiolect grammars based on introspective evidence? Has the attempt to eliminate from the analysis non-pertinent factors led to the exclusion of a very pertinent, even essential factor? Is the homogeneity postulate a caricature rather than an idealization? Clearly, these questions epitomize a major methodological clash in contemporary linguistics.

In mentalist linguistics the conception of language as a formal system to be accounted for by means of a consistent and determinate algorithm resulted in the desire to obtain a uniform corpus on whose basis such a model could be construed. The easiest way to obtain a uniform corpus is of course to restrict one's attention to a single idiolect thus admitting the construction of a theory with minimal data base.[7] The methodological weak point of most formal grammars is hence that, strictly speaking, the model only holds for an idiolect but is tacitly assumed to hold for the language as a whole. The only possible methodological justification for this procedure has been to discredit variation as a performance phenomenon.

If it is true, as many scholars (notably Bailey, Hymes, Labov, Weinreich) claim, that variation is not a contingent imperfection of language which can be tolerated in communication but rather a central aspect of linguistic competence, then abstraction from variation appears in a somewhat different light. It is not justifiable — either on tactical grounds or in principle, because the incorporation of systematic variation must be considered then one of the crucial challenges of linguistics.

I need not recapitulate here this dispute between empiricism and mentalism in linguistics. The antagonistic positions are sufficiently familiar and are well-documented elsewhere (e.g. Chomsky 1968, Labov 1971, Bailey & Shuy 1973, Ross 1979). I would like, however, to discuss briefly two aspects of linguistic variation which are important for a proper definition of the native speaker concept.

The native speaker is affected by variation in two ways. One is that he shares certain grammatical rules with some members of his speech community and not with others. The other one is that he experiences variation in the acceptability/grammaticality of sentences and in the confidence he feels about his judgements. It is important to note that these two types of variation are really different and not merely two expressions of the same phenomenon. While the first kind of variation is a statistical matter existing only relative to a speech community, the second is a phenomenon subsisting on the level of idiolect. I may find a sentence perfectly acceptable although I hardly ever use the rules underlying its construction. And, on the other hand, I may produce on occasion sentences which range low on my own idiolectal acceptability scale. Most formal grammars fail to account for variation of either kind.

Attempts to overcome this deficiency come from two directions. The most advanced proposal of how to deal with intra-speech community variation is Cedergren and Sankoff's concept of variable rules, "where the predicted relative frequency of a rule's operation is . . . an integral part of its structural description" (1974: 334). Thus, optional rules are given application probabilities. The development of this type of rules has grown out of sociolinguistic research. The concept of degrees of grammaticality, by contrast, has originated in the study of formal grammar. The fact that a binary notion of grammaticality fails to accomodate speakers' intuitions concerning the questionable status of many sentences was recognized early in the history of transformational linguistics (cf. e.g. Ziff 1964), although without being of much consequence. More recently, Lakoff (1973) advanced a proposal to replace the discrete boundary between the grammatical and the ungrammatical by a 'fuzzy grammar' whose well-formedness is considered a graded notion with values ranging on a continuum from 1 to 0. Lakoff claims that variability with respect to well-formedness is an aspect of linguistic competence. Every sentence generated by a fuzzy grammar is therefore simultaneously assigned a well-formedness degree. However, this degree is an idiolectal value reflecting the relative acceptability of a sentence for an individual speaker. The interesting question arising if we look at both kinds of variability is this. How do rule application probabilities and well-formedness degrees interact? Or, to put it differently, is intra-idiolectal variation in well-formedness subject to systematic variation throughout the speech community? Ross' (1979) experiment seems to support this hypothesis. However, his data are very limited, and a definite answer to this question will only be possible on the basis of extensive empirical (observational and experimental) research. Eventually, every attempt to reduce the discrepancies between ideal and real native speakers and hence to advance the empirical adequacy of linguistic theory will have to incorporate both aspects of linguistic variation as well as their possible correlations.

NATIVENESS AND NATIVITY

Variation in language necessarily directs our attention to the integration of language and culture and to the native speaker as a social being. However, he is a biological being too, and for all that we know, language is both a social and a biological phenomenon. Hence, there is yet another undertone that resonates when talking about native speakers and nativeness: nativity. Without a few remarks about the biological conditions of language this essay would be even more incomplete than it is bound to remain anyhow.

In acquiring the language spoken in his environment, the native speaker partakes of the sociocultural inheritance of his speech community; in acquiring any language at all, he partakes of the biological inheritance of his species. Accordingly, the locus of language can be found in the community or in the species, and hence in every individual. Although it seems clear enough that these are complementary rather than opposing views, the emphasis placed on the search for the variable features of language on the one hand and on the invariant ones on the other has provoked considerable ideological dispute between their adherents ranging way back to the very beginnings of Occidental science. The two statements, 'Language is brain work' and 'Language is social work' can hardly be considered mutually exclusive. Yet, observations relating to either of them are not uncommonly put forth to challenge the other.

Introduction: The Concept of Native Speaker

In itself, the former statement does not imply that language is innate, but this is what it is taken to mean by mentalists. It is interesting to note, in passing, that this *mentalistic* stipulation eventually leads to a *materialistic* question, i.e., to the quest for the material, i.e., neurophysiological conditions of language. On the basis of our knowledge to date, we cannot but notice a tremendous inferential gap between theoretical statements about language and neurophysiological correlates. However, neurolinguistics is a rapidly developing and increasingly interesting subdiscipline of the study of language (cf. Whitaker & Whitaker 1976-79). Whether or not it will substantiate the innateness doctrine in any specific way remains nevertheless an open question. Our understanding of the physiological prerequisites of speech are quite advanced; but they supposedly have no bearing whatsoever on the innate nature of language.

The nativists claim that certain aspects of *knowledge* are inborn. Conceptions as to the content of innate ideas range from so-called analytic truths to moral principles. The idea that the abstract foundations of language are among these universal dispositions of the mind is relatively new, having come to prominence chiefly through Chomsky's reinterpretation of rationalist philosophy. Obviously, the doctrine of innate (unconscious) knowledge favors certain scientific methods; most importantly, it favors deductive over inductive reasoning. This is clearly one of the implications of nativism that give reason to controversy. The general assumption is that every normal human being is equipped with the innate ideas of language as such. If there is an invariant faculty of language, it must be deducible from individual performance. More empirically inclined scholars disagree since they tend to pay more attention to the varieties of language. Reconciliation between these opposing views is difficult, because the dissent is based in conviction rather than knowledge. The fundamental disagreement concerns the question of what it is that linguists must ultimately strive to explain: observable behavior says one, innate ideas claims the other.

The arguments that nativists advance in support of their claim are threefold:

— language is species-specific;
— language is too complex to be acquired by experience alone;
— languages share universal properties.

An additional point is that language is not only restricted to the species but also acquired and used by practically everyone of its members. Every normal human being growing up under normal circumstances with at least minimal exposure to language invariably becomes a native speaker. He is, in this sense, born to speak. The multiple problems involved in the human capacity to acquire language as conceived in psycholinguistics and learning theory are given a critical appraisal by van der Geest. In how far this disposition is based on innate, environmental, and developmental factors and exactly how they interact we do not know. However, despite its lack of precise correlation with linguistic analysis, the innateness hypothesis is interesting enough to warrant separate comment.

If the innateness theory is to be given a meaning other than metaphorical, the improvement of linguistic theory in accordance with internal criteria so that the theory can gain consistency, elegance, simplicity, etc., won't be enough. We don't know anything about the elegance or simplicity standards of the brain, and, at present, there is no way of telling the significance of metatheoretical principles, such as e.g., 'the simpler the better,' in terms of brain functions. Hence, providing that substantiation of the innateness hypothesis is recognized as one of the superordinate tasks of linguistics, the improvement of linguistic theory must be judged by external criteria, too. One such criterion is reduction of the correlational gap between linguistic abstractions and neurological abstractions.

To date, native speaker and native brain possessor are theoretically not highly integrated. However, in the light of the innateness hypothesis, any statement about universal properties of language implies fundamental claims about how the brain works. A model of the native speaker as a naturally gifted language possessor will therefore have to aim at providing an interpretation of (a) the functioning of a grammatical algorithm and (b) the organization of the mental information storage and retrieval system in terms of cerebral functions.

PERFORMANCE AND EXPERIMENTATION

Returning for a moment to the problem of introspection, it is obvious that the biological dimensions of language are beyond self-report in much the same way that other functions of the nervous system resist introspective discovery or explanation. Language must be considered to reside as some sort of structure inside the human head, but this surely doesn't mean that we can know anything of the actual processes going on in our heads when language is produced or processed. We have all experienced, for instance, the 'tip of the tongue phenomenon,' yet, the misdirected search strategy or the neural pass that is temporarily blocked and thus doesn't allow us to retrieve a word which we are nonetheless sure to have stored somewhere in our memory defy conscious access. It is therefore not a very promising procedure to ask ourselves, or any other speaker, questions such as, e.g., 'how do you retrieve an item from your mental lexicon, and how do you integrate a new one?' or, 'how do you proceed in order to find out whether a given string of words is

Introduction: The Concept of Native Speaker 21

well-formed or deviant?' From the answers we get to such questions we cannot expect to learn much about the processes going on in people's heads; and this is true for mental processes almost as much as for neural ones.

The relations between brains and intellectual processes are among the greatest mysteries of man's knowledge of himself (cf. e.g. Toulmin 1972). They are equally intriguing for the neurologist, the philosopher, and those linguists who are aware of and interested in the mind-body problem in terms of the human endowment with language. In order to answer questions of the kind exemplified in the previous paragraph, i.e., in order to find out how language is represented in the mind and to detect the neural correlates of mental structures and processes, the scientist must try to find methods to outwit our limited access to these structures and processes. It is here that his ingenuity and fancy is most important.

A large portion of psycholinguistic research consists in conducting various kinds of experiments. The researcher must take pains to devise tests whose reliability is not vitiated by improper input data, inadequate test instructions, or interference by uncontrollable subject participation. In this instance too, science is an interactive process, and the native speaker plays again a crucial part in it: he is the subject of the experiments. His task is very different here from that of a data supplier for grammatical descriptions or grammar evaluations. While he must be aware of the problem at least to some extent in order to give acceptability judgements, many psycholinguistic tests are devised in such a way that the subject is unaware of the problem which they are meant to elucidate. The data obtained from tests that measure, for instance, memory span, frequency in word associations, or the time necessary for certain retrieval, recognition or sentence completion tasks, etc., are pretty worthless in themselves. Only the conclusions drawn from them can yield any new insight. Test data are only significant in as far as they are interpretable with respect to a theoretical hypothesis (cf. Wunderlich's paper). The subject must cooperate in the experiment but need not know anything about the hypothesis. In some cases, elicitation techniques are designed expressly in order to avoid conscious interference of the subject.

Typically, experimental results can be interpreted differently if viewed against the background of different theoretical assumptions. Moreover, their interpretations can differ in quality. Psycholinguistic tests usually involve some sort of controlled task specific linguistic performance or non-verbal responses to linguistic stimuli. The conclusions drawn from the performance data thus obtained are of two kinds: (i) conclusions about those parts of performance which cannot be observed; (ii) conclusions about competence. The latter ones are to be integrated into a formal account of the knowledge that a person's language capacity requires, whereas the former relate to the psychological processes which function in putting that knowledge to use. It may not always be clear from the beginning whether the one has any bearing on the other, and, moreover, it is not unlikely that, as we learn to understand better the relations between them, a redefinition of the conceptual relation between *competence* and *performance* becomes necessary. This, however, is the nature of scientific concepts.

THE MULTIFORMITY OF NATIVE SPEAKER

Native speakerhood is one of the most human traits of man. This century has witnessed impressive progress in the language sciences that try to come to grips with this unique endowment of our species. New disciplines have evolved, and the old ones have undergone thorough changes. They all bear testimony to the multiformity of *homo loquens* and to the difficulties of detaching language from other properties and abilities of man.

The concept of native speaker occupies a central position in the study of language, and it gives reason to reflect on how to set the limits of its realm. What part of human abilities is to be accounted for by linguistic theories? Science is dependent on abstraction and idealization and hence can often not refrain from conceptual reductionism. No individual discipline can frame a theory of the native speaker that comprises the totality of his complex nature. A scientific account is therefore also dependent on interdisciplinary cooperation. The chapters of this book testify that the need for cooperation is perhaps more characteristic of the linguistic disciplines than of any other science.

The native speaker is not only a possessor of the species specific faculty of language. He is a member of a particular speech community and as such a speaker of various dialects. He is also the speaker of his idiosyncratic variety of language. He/she is a man or woman, child or adult, and his/her speech varies accordingly. Thus he has the ability to realize sameness and difference on various levels of language (cf. Pike's paper). Further, he is a communicator, a social being that makes use of other modes of communication which may harmonize or interfere with language (cf. von Raffler-Engel's and Regan/ Ziajka's papers). Being a speaker, he is also an actor, a performer of speech acts (cf. Kasher's paper). He has thoughts and wishes and intentions; and he has the knowledge of how to convey them through linguistic means. He has at his disposal the abstract rules allowing the generation of an infinite variety of utterances, but he is also subject to concrete, i.e. bio-social, limitations in following those rules. It is not very clearly understood, so far, how these limitations relate to the rules and to the universal principles underlying the uniformity in language ability.

An integrated model of the various dimensions characteristic of language

Introduction: The Concept of Native Speaker

as a bio-socially conditioned structure must be the ultimate aim of linguistic theory. In approaching this aim, the language sciences depend on cooperative efforts setting out from different directions while being aware that the objective is the same. The chapters of this book are meant to elucidate the multiple functions the native speaker plays in this scientific endeavor.

NOTES

1. All figures are taken from Voegelin & Voegelin 1977.
2. A similar position is taken by Samarin who gives a detailed account of the qualities desired of a "good informant" in field linguistics (Samarin 1967, chapter 3).
3. This view is echoed by Lyons who, however, clearly indicates the dangers that are involved. He states that

    the linguist . . . may of course be his own informant if he is describing his own language; but he must be on his guard against the danger of producing for description a corpus of material which includes only such sentences as satisfy his preconceived ideas about the structure of the language (Lyons 1968:138).

4. Chomsky probably does not find this characterization too bothersome, because he, as is well-known, views linguistics as a part of psychology (cf. e.g. Chomsky 1968:24, 1975:37, 160).
5. According to Paul Feyerabend's philosophy of science, this desire is not only natural but is and always has been an essential ingredient of every scientific endeavor. Every means to further the break-through of a scientific idea or theory is in principle admissible. However, not many linguists are known to adhere to Feyerabend's "myth of anarchy in science," not openly or consciously, that is. (Cf. Feyerabend 1975).
6. Cf. van Dijk's (1977:44) example, *John thinks with a knife,* which, if judged in isolation simply seems to violate a selection restriction: if however a question such as, *What has the postman been murdered with?* is supplied as a context, it is a clearly elliptical and hence acceptable sentence. Individual fancy is, no doubt, an important factor. Putnam (1974:82) reports the sentence, *Pepper doesn't sneeze me.* which was uttered in conversation by an extremely language conscious speaker who had stated only a few minutes earlier that *sneeze* could never be used as an intransitive verb.
7. For an interesting discussion of the role of data minimization in competence theories see Pylyshyn 1973.

REFERENCES

Anttila. R. (1972). *An Introduction to Historical and Comparative Linguistics.* New York: Macmillan.

Bailey, C.-J. N. & Shuy, R.W., eds. (1973). *New ways of analyzing variation in English.* Washington, D.C.: Georgetown University Press.

Bendix, E.H. (1971). 'The data of semantic description.' In Steinberg, D. and Jakobovits, L.A., eds. *Semantics. An interdisciplinary reader in philosophy, linguistics and psychology.* Cambridge University Press, 1971, pp. 393–409.

Bever, T.G. (1970). 'The cognitive basis for linguistic structures.' In J.R. Hayes, ed. *Cognition and the Development of Language.* New York: Wiley.

Bolinger, D. (1968a). "Judgements of grammaticality." *Lingua* 21: 34-40.
Bolinger, D. (1968b). *Aspects of Language.* New York: Harcourt, Brace & World.
Cedergren, H.J. & Sankoff, D. (1974). Variable Rule: Performance as a Statistical Reflection of Competence. *Language* 50(2): 333-355.
Chomsky, N. (1957). *Syntactic Structures.* The Hague: Mouton.
Chomsky, N. (1961). Some methodological remarks on generative grammar. *Word* 17: 219-239.
Chomsky, N. (1965). *Aspects of the Theory of Syntax.* Cambridge, Mass.: M.I.T. Press.
Chomsky, N. (1968). *Language and Mind.* New York: Harcourt, Brace & World.
Chomsky, N. (1975). *Reflections on Language.* New York: Pantheon Books.
Chomsky, N. (1979). *Language and Responsibility.* Sussex: The Harvester Press.
Dijk, T.A. van (1977). Acceptability in Context. In Greenbaum, S., ed. (1977). *Acceptability in Language.* The Hague: Mouton.
Feyerabend, P. (1975). *Against Method. Outline of an anarchistic theory of knowledge.* Atlantic Highlands, N.J.: Humanities Press.
Greenbaum, S., ed. (1977). *Acceptability in Language.* The Hague: Mouton.
Halle, M. (1962). "Phonology in Generative Grammar." *Word* 18 (1-2): 54-72.
Hill, A.A. (1961). 'Grammaticality.' *Word* 17: 1-10.
Hoijer, Harry (1958). Native reaction as a criterion in linguistic analysis. In Eva Sivertsen, ed., *Proceeding of the Eighth International Congress of Linguists.* Oslo: Oslo University Press, pp. 573-583.
Hymes, D. (1974). *Foundations in Sociolinguistics. An Ethnographic Approach.* Philadelphia: University of Pennsylvania Press.
Katz, J.J. (1966). *The Philosophy of Language.* New York: Harper.
Katz, J.J. & Fodor, J. (1962). "What's wrong with the philosophy of language?" *Inquiry* 5: 197-237.
Labov, W. (1971). 'Methodology.' In W.O. Dingwall, ed. (1971). *A Survey of Linguistic Science.* University of Maryland.
Labov, W. (1972). *Sociolinguistic Patterns.* Philadelphia: University of Pennsylvania Press.
Lakoff, G. (1973). 'Fuzzy grammar and the performance/competence terminology game.' *Papers from the ninth regional meeting of the Chicago Linguistic Society,* pp. 52-57.
Lyons, J. (1968). *Introduction to theoretical Linguistics.* Cambridge, Mass.: Harvard University Press.
Maclay, H. & Sleator, M.D. (1960). Responses to language: Judgments of grammaticalness. *IJAL* 26: 275-282.
Nida, E. (1947). 'Field techniques in descriptive Linguistics.' *International Journal of American Linguistics* 3 (3): 138-146.
Putnam, H. (1974 (1961)). 'Some Issues in the Theory of Grammar.' *On Noam Chomsky: Critical Essays,* ed. G. Harman. Garden City: Anchor Books, pp. 80-103.
Pylyshyn, Zenon (1973). The role of competence theories in cognitive psychology. *Journal of Psycholinguistic Research* 2: 21-50.
Quirk, R. & Svartvik, J. (1966). *Investigating Linguistic Acceptability.* The Hague: Mouton.
Robins, R.A. (^{2}1971 (1964)). *General Linguistics. An Introductory Survey.* London: Longman.
Ross, J.R. (1979). 'Where is English?' *Individual Differences in Language Ability and Language Behavior,* ed. C.J. Fillmore and W. Wang. New York: Academic Press.

Samarin, W.J. (1968). *Field Linguistics. A Guide to Linguistic Field Work.* New York: Holt, Rinehart & Winston.

Spencer, N.J. (1973). "Differences between linguists and nonlinguists in intuitions of grammaticality-acceptability." *Journal of Psycholinguistic Research* 2: 83-98.

Toulmin, S. (1972). The Mentality of Man's Brain. In A.G. Karczmar, J.C. Eccles, eds. *Brain and Human Behavior,* Heidelberg, New York: Springer.

Voegelin, C.F. & Voegelin, F.M. (1977). *Classification and Index of the World's Languages.* New York, Amsterdam: Elsevier.

Whitaker, H.A. & Whitaker, H., eds. (1976-1979). *Neurolinguistics,* 4 vols. New York: Academic Press.

Ziff, P. (1964). 'On understanding "understanding utterances".' In J.A. Fodor and J.J. Katz, eds., *The Structure of Language: Readings in the Philosophy of Language.* Englewood-Cliffs: Prentice Hall.

PART ONE

Epistemology and History of Linguistics

VICTOR H. YNGVE

The Struggle for a Theory of Native Speaker

ABSTRACT

Throughout the history of linguistics, language has been the object of study. But most linguists are interested in people. Yet Native Speaker has never really had a theory of his own in spite of the best efforts of all those who have labored on his behalf. The story of the struggle starts with the ancients. It moves on through Rask, Schleicher, Osthoff and Brugmann, Paul Saussure, Bloomfield, Sapir, Gardiner, and Malinowski. It currently involves us all. Human linguistics offers a theory in which Native Speaker is no longer known only through language: he becomes the object of study. Linguistics then becomes a natural science, fulfilling the promise of Rask and the other pioneers.

It was a cruel accident of history that the Ancient Greeks divided philosophy into three parts, for in so doing they separated the theory of language from people, and thus it came about that from the very beginning Native Speaker was deprived of what should have been his birthright, a linguistic theory of his very own. In the face of this denial and humiliation, the usually loquacious Native Speaker has remained remarkably silent, and those linguists who have come to his defense have had to swim against the tide of tradition.

From the very beginning of the history of the discipline, the major organizing force has been a quest for the essence of language, to use Roman Jakobson's apt phrase (1971). In consequence of this, Native Speaker has often been treated rather shabbily in public as a nonperson, merely a rather imperfect reflection of his language, a means to an end at most, a lowly servant who knows his place and speaks only when spoken to. Yet running just beneath the surface in works on grammar and language one can often discern an interest in Native Speaker himself, a genuine interest in people and how they communicate, an interest that has usually been repressed. Most linguists have been in the habit of averting their eyes as if ashamed to look at real people, or as if they thought it not quite a polite and dignified thing to do. But people are the source of all our linguistic data; it is important to study them and to try to understand how they communicate. In these pages I intend to explore some chapters in the history of the struggle for a proper theory of Native Speaker. I will then report on my own effort to reconstruct his birthright.

THE BIRTHRIGHT DENIED

Among the Greeks it was the Stoics who were most responsible for developing the philosophical foundation of linguistic thought.[1] In their view philosophical doctrine was divided into three parts, physical, ethical, and logical. Of these they placed particular importance on the logical part, which contained a theory of knowledge. For them the logical part was central because it considered how one arrives at truth, and without it ethics and physics could not express themselves. In placing particular emphasis on the logical part of philosophy they developed a body of logical and linguistic theory that was a remarkable achievement for the third century B.C., and was destined to survive in its major outlines right up to the present day.

The logical part of Stoic philosophy contained dialectic[2] and rhetoric. Both dialectic and rhetoric were treated in terms of the signifier and the signified, a semiotic conception that was to appear again and again in many influential works. Rhetoric was the science of speaking well on matters set forth by plain narrative; dialectic was the science of correctly discussing subjects by question and answer. It contained the nascent disciplines of grammar, logic, and epistemology. It provided a bridge of linked theories that reached all the way from the sound of the voice at one end through logic and truth at the center to the external reality at the other end. It was a breathtakingly elegant conception.

The relation of the sound of the voice to logic was conceived of as given in a series of levels. The first was a level of phonetic substance called *phōnē* (voice), which was defined as a percussion of the air, or the proper object of the sense of hearing. While the voice or cry of an animal is just a percussion of the air brought about by natural impulse, man's voice is articulate and capable of expressing thought.

The second level was a phonemic or phonotactic level called *lexis* (diction). Diction is voice reducible to writing. The difference between voice and diction is that whereas voice is just sound, diction is articulate, that is, segmented. The elements of diction are the 24 letters (phonemes). The Stoics carefully distinguished three senses of the word *gramma* (letter): 1. an element of diction – a genuine phonemic concept, 2. its written character, and 3. its name, as 'alpha'. The Stoic phonology included a fairly sophisticated classification of speech sounds.

The third level was a grammatical or syntactic level called *logos* (speech, that which is spoken). Speech was defined as voice that issues from the mind and is semantic or signifies something. The difference between diction and speech is that speech is always semantic, whereas diction is asemantic. To illustrate this point they cited a nonsense form (*blityri*) as an example of diction but not speech. Ambiguity arises when the same representation at the level of diction may be understood in two or more distinct senses at the level of speech. Their example involved a difference in word segmentation as well as meaning, quite parallel to the familiar *a name : an aim.* The elements at the level of speech were the five parts of speech: common noun, proper noun, verb, article, and conjunction.

The three levels – voice, diction, and speech – belong to the part of dialectic that treats the signifier. The part that treats the signified also had several levels, the first of which was a semantic level called *lekton* (speakable, capable of being spoken). It was a level of meaning, content, inner form, or logical deep structure. The levels of speech and lekton are connected by a relation of signification. Thus at the level of speech the common noun, the proper noun, and the verb are defined in terms of what they signify at the level of lekton, but the conjunction and the article are defined syntactically in relation to the other parts of speech. At the lekton level one finds the highly developed Stoic logic. Here are propositions, predicates, the concept of case, the reflexive, the active, passive, and middle voices; interrogation, inquiry, imperative, adjurative, optative, hypothetical, vocative; assertions, truth and falsity, denial and affirmation. Here we find the remarkably sophisticated Stoic logic, which went way beyond Aristotle and was not matched until modern times.[3]

Now notice first that the Stoic conception seems remarkably modern. This is because modern linguistics is built on essentially the same foundation, inherited through an unbroken tradition. Second, notice that Native Speaker has been overlooked. This happened because the Stoics had their eyes on the highly idealized planes of knowledge, truth, and logic. If one looks more closely, one finds that Native Speaker is kept discreetly in the background by such devices as the impersonal *we.* Thus in discussing complete and incomplete lekta, it is explained that *graphei* 'writes' is incomplete, for we inquire *Who?* Whereas *graphei Sōkratēs* is complete in itself. The *we,* who inquire, inconspicuously covers Native Speaker.

People were treated not in the logical part of philosophy, but in the physical part. Here were included, in addition to cosmology and other matters, the study of sound waves, biological and medical topics, and topics related to the eight parts of the *psychē*, that is, the five senses, the power of speech, the power of reasoning, and the generative and reproductive power in us. Much of the Stoic lore on these topics has been improved or superseded by modern scientific advances. The Greeks did understand that sound consists of waves in the air spreading in concentric spheres, and cited as an analogy the circular ripples in a pond when a stone is tossed in.

The cleavage of philosophy into three parts by the Greeks separated the study of speech sounds from the study of sound, and even today there is influential opinion that acoustic phonetics should not be part of linguistics.

It separated logic from the power of reasoning, and even today philosophical logic is taken as separate from the psychology of reasoning. It separated the study of speech and language from the study of the human power of speech. Today it is Native Speaker who, by his communicative behavior, gives evidence of the remarkable human power of speech, but the evidence is taken from him like a confiscatory tax on the poor and applied to further glorify the palace of grammar. Those linguists who have protested and tried to understand the power of speech so as to provide Native Speaker with his own theory have found themselves bucking a powerful tradition. Consequently their efforts have been misunderstood or ignored.

How can we account for the fact that the Stoic architecture of linguistics has survived for so long a time, and for the fact that its influence is so all-pervading even today? Again we owe it to accidents of history. The Greeks felt a need for a standard language over the newly won empire to take the place of the many Greek dialects and to serve as a standard of Good Greek for native and nonnative speakers and writers. Normative grammar was developed to fill this need. It took the Stoic dialectic as a philosophical foundation probably because the Stoics had pushed the philosophy of language farther and more successfully than had any other school of philosophy. It also accepted the methods of literary scholarship and textual analysis developed contemporaneously by the Alexandrians. Here were concepts of analogy and methods of collating texts that had revealed recurrent sames and differences and had led to the working out of Greek inflectional patterns.

Then it happened that the Stoic philosophy was particularly influential in Rome. As Rome came to ascendancy, the Greek grammatical tradition became a Graeco-Roman grammatical tradition, and Latin normative grammars were written on Greek models. Latin remained the language of scholarship throughout Europe right up to the modern era: Newton published in Latin. As a result, grammars on this model were studied in grammar schools for over 2000 years, and the Stoic philosophical preconceptions have entered our everyday language to the point where they seem completely obvious and unquestionable. Thus it has come to pass that grammar lives and the tradition has turned our eyes from people. Even the efforts of those who have protested the influence of traditional grammar in linguistics, or who have wanted to focus instead on people and how they communicate, have in spite of themselves been overly influenced by the powerful current of the very tradition they were protesting.

NATIVE SPEAKER IN THE HISTORICAL-COMPARATIVE ERA

At the end of the eighteenth century and the beginning of the nineteenth, informed opinion held that the study of Sanskrit and the comparison of ancient and modern languages could reveal something of the natural history of mankind. As preliminary results were obtained, it began to be held that the study of language could be a natural science. Rask,[4] for example, had said that language is a natural object and the knowledge of it resembles natural history. Invoking Linnaeus and Newton, he said that it is the highest triumph for the application of philosophy to nature when one can find out the true system in nature and show that it is the truth.

By the middle of the nineteenth century, August Schleicher, the leading theoretician of his day, set about to lay the foundations of a science of linguistics and to choose a name for the new discipline. Following Bopp and the other pioneers he focused on the comparative method as a means for historical reconstruction, an application of the Alexandrian recurrent sames and differences with a new twist. He summed up the method in the striking phrase (1848:5) "das Nebeneinander des Systems in das Nacheinander der Geschichte" (the juxtaposition of systems into the sequence of history). Schleicher was the first to actually draw family trees of languages (1860, 1861), although the family metaphor had been used on occasion for many years. He has with good reason been called the father of comparative linguistics.

In trying to conceive of linguistics as a science, Schleicher ran into a problem. He was influenced in the beginning by the then prestigious philosopher Hegel, who had laid down a distinction between disciplines dealing with *Natur* and disciplines dealing with *Geist* (spirit).[5] Under *Natur* fell the physical and biological sciences and the study of primitive and illiterate man. The phenomena here were considered to be lawful and ever repeating in cycles like the eternal motions of the planets or the repeated song of the lark. Under *Geist* fell history, the rise of literate civilizations, and the free will and self-consciousness of a people. The phenomena here were supposed to be involved with striving, becoming, freedom, and eternal change, hence not lawful. Where should language fall?

Schleicher put language under *Geist* in his first major work (1848) because it had a history and a becoming. But he soon (1850) retracted this as an error because language and language change seemed lawful. He drew a distinction between philology, which used language as a means to penetrate into the condition and life of a people and therefore fell under *Geist,* and linguistics, which had language itself as its object and fell under *Natur*, being a part of the natural history of man. Philology could only exist where there was a literature, but linguistics found the languages of the illiterate American Indians, for example, of the highest interest. Schleicher then put phonology and morphology in linguistics because they were lawful. Syntax belonged more on the side of philology because it depended more on the thought and will of the individual. Style depended completely on the free will of the individual. Thus for Schleicher grammar became lawful and language became an organism obeying natural laws like the other organisms of nature — animal, vegetable, and mineral. The idea that language was an organism apparently posed no problem in the beginning. The ancient Greeks, among them the Stoics, even thought of the world as a living being (*zōon*), rational, animate, and intelligent. Thus language was accepted as the legitimate object of a scientific linguistics, and Native Speaker as a human, the only real organism involved, was deported to another discipline, and with him were banished the difficult problems of syntax and style.

The acceptance of language as an object of study, and with it the traditional apparatus of grammar, brought in from the normative tradition preconceptions of a uniform language. Schleicher's family trees assumed, as was later realized, perfectly uniform languages and sudden splits. Schleicher (1850:21ff.) classified in terms of language classes, language stems, language families, languages, dialects, and subdialects (*Mundarten*), each related to the next as genus to species. But he did not carry his classificatory splits beyond the subdialect. Then how did he account for individual variation? He of course knew (1850:24) that everyone speaks differently. Individual variation he laid to style, depending on the free will of the individual, hence in the realm of *Geist* and conveniently outside the domain of scientific theory.

The result of all this was simply that language, grammar, and the tradition were enthroned as lawful and scientific, whereas individual variation, style, and some of the aspects of syntax, which appeared difficult from the point of view of grammar, were conveniently attributed to Native Speaker with his free will — again an institutionalized rationalization for discriminating against him and depriving him of the possibility of having a linguistic theory of his own. Shortly before his untimely death, Schleicher tried to meditate between his concept of language as an organism and Native Speaker as an organism (1865). Schleicher was a careful thinker and a clear writer confronting some very difficult problems. Had he lived longer, he might actually have come around to a theory of Native Speaker.

Interest in Native Speaker continued, nevertheless. Schleicher himself had visited Lithuania in connection with his comparative studies. He had heard Native Speaker was there and he wanted to obtain evidence from his own mouth. And although family trees were presented in terms of uniform protolanguages and their splits, they were then regularly reinterpreted in terms of people. For example, Fick (1871:1045ff.), on the basis of comparative studies and the reconstruction of protolanguages, tried to trace in geographic and temporal detail the splittings of bands of people and their wanderings, carrying their languages with them.

As time went on, there came to be greater appreciation of the importance of individual variation and the role of the individual in linguistic change, but language and grammar, enthroned, still imposed a strict discipline on linguists. Soon a protest movement grew to the point of open rebellion in the neogrammarian manifesto. Osthoff and Brugmann (1878:iii) proclaimed that "*Languages* were indeed investigated most eagerly, but *the man who speaks much too little*" (original emphasis; quoted from Lehmann (1967:198)). They pointed out that language is not a thing that leads a life of its own outside of and above human beings, but it has its true existence only in the individual, and hence all changes in the life of language can only proceed from the individual speaker: it was not the Greek language which dropped final *t*, but those among the Greeks with whom the sound change started. They called for more research on the psychological factors which are at work in sound changes and innovations, and particularly in the operation of analogical formations. That their manifesto is remembered more for its position on exceptionless sound laws than on its call for an increased study of Native Speaker reflects the selectivity of the tradition in its focus on uniform languages.

The neogrammarians and their followers did actually turn more attention to the psychological factors in Native Speaker, but the psychology of the day could not properly support the effort. Experimental psychology itself had just been born; the intellectual foundations of the discipline remained unclear; and the introspective methods used were often questionable and inconclusive. Nevertheless the next several decades found leading linguists interpreting their results in psychological terms, and although many keen insights were obtained, they were hard to substantiate scientifically. Much of the psychologizing amounted to little more than sheer speculation. One of the soundest thinkers of this era was Hermann Paul, who stated the program of linguistics precisely as obtaining an understanding of the Native Speaker:

The most special task . . . seems to be that of showing how the single individual is related to the community; receiving and giving; defined by the community and defining it in turn; and how the younger generation enters on the heritage of the elder (1889: xxx).

This early statement of the task before us is hard to fault from the point of view of the struggle for a theory of Native Speaker.

The trouble was that the traditional methods of recurrent sames and differences in texts had been developed for elucidating the grammatical structure and comparison of languages. They were ill-suited to investigating the single individual and his relation to the community, and no adequate nongrammatical methods, either psychological or sociological, were at hand. Consequently the psychologizing of the neogrammarians as a scientific enterprise on behalf of Native Speaker rested on inadequate foundations.

NATIVE SPEAKER IN THE ERA OF EARLY STRUCTURALISM

In the early decades of the twentieth century, structuralism and descriptivism amounted to a counterrevolution which reenthroned grammar. Native Speaker was tolerated, however, but he began to be systematically ignored by members of the official court. This era was characterized by a drive for law and order and for sound methodology. Native Speaker found himself an innocent victim of the increasingly strict and repressive atmosphere.

Ferdinand de Saussure prophesied, "Linguistics, having accorded too large a place to history, will turn back to the static view of traditional grammar but in a new spirit and with other procedures" (1916:119; 1966:82-3). These procedures were the procedures of classical grammar, and they were "absolutely above reproach" (1916:118; 1966:82). Saussure laid great stress on the theory of the sign, which in his hands became a relation between sound-image and concept, but later in his *Cours* (1916) he switched to the Stoic terms signifier and signified.

Saussure was interested in people, but he was not about to study them. The famous illustration of the two heads talking to each other was designed to show just what he was not going to study. His basic distinction between *langue* (language) and *parole* (speaking) cut at precisely the same point as Schleicher's distinction between linguistics and philology, between *Natur* and *Geist*. He was willing to conceive of a linguistics of *parole*, but, he said, "I shall deal only with the linguistics of language" (1916:39; 1966:20). So much for speaking. How about Native Speaker? "The activity of the speaker should be studied in a number of disciplines which have no place in linguistics except through their relation to language" (1916:37; 1966:18). Send him into exile!

Yet in spite of these strong statements Saussure did concern himself with Native Speaker. After carefully distinguishing language as a system of signs from speaking and from Native Speaker, he then engaged in the dubious practice that has frequently occurred, both before and since, of shoehorning linguistic signs into the head of Native Speaker: "both terms involved in the linguistic sign are psychological and are united in the brain by an associative bond. This point must be emphasized" (1916:98; 1966:65-6).

This kind of ambivalence about Native Speaker is seen again and again in the literature of linguistics even up to the present day. First it is carefully explained that a theory of language is different from a theory of Native Speaker, and this makes good clear sense in the light of the distinctions that were drawn by the Greeks and have been drawn by all major theoreticians since. Furthermore it seems clear that the method of recurrent sames and differences in text are grammatical methods designed for elucidating the structure of language. They are not psychological methods designed

The Struggle for a Theory of Native Speaker 37

for elucidating the structure of people. But then, linguists *are* really interested in people, it seems, and they can not resist the temptation to conceive of a grammatical theory as simultaneously a psychological theory. But this, in my opinion, is absurd and has always been absurd. Lingering doubts about the legitimacy of the practice probably accounts for the inconsistent treatment of poor Native Speaker: he is treated like an illegitimate child who is sometimes loved, sometimes disowned.

Leonard Bloomfield agreed with Saussure's criticism that neogrammarians such as Hermann Paul neglected descriptive language study in their focus on linguistic change. Abandoning his own earlier psychological approach he added

The other great weakness of Paul's *Principles* is his insistence upon 'psychological' interpretation. He accompanies his statements about language with a paraphrase in terms of mental processes which the speakers are supposed to have undergone. The only evidence for these mental processes is the linguistic process; they add nothing to the discussion, but only obscure it (1933:17).

Elaborating his edict that Native Speaker was to be officially ignored, he said

We do not understand the mechanism which makes people say certain things in certain situations, or the mechanism which makes them respond appropriately when these speech-sounds strike their ear-drums . . . . These mechanisms are studied in physiology and, especially, in psychology . . . . In the division of scientific labor, the linguist deals only with the speech-signal (r........s); he is not competent to deal with the problems of physiology or psychology (1933:31-2).

But of course the stimulus-response psychology of that era was not equipped to study the linguistic mechanisms in people, and the speech-signals which alone the linguist should study were simply sound waves in the air, as Bloomfield had just explained.

According to Bloomfield, the study of language could start without special assumptions in physiological and acoustic phonetics. However, in (1933: 76-7) he said

laboratory phonetics does not enable us to connect speech-sounds with meanings; it studies speech-sounds only as muscular movements or as disturbances in the air . . . . On this plane we find that speech-sounds are infinitely varied . . . . The phonetician finds that no two utterances are exactly alike . . . [he] cannot tell us which features are significant for communication and which features are immaterial.

In other words, the linguist was supposed to confine himself to studying the sound waves, leaving the study of Native Speaker to other disciplines, but the most careful instrumental study of sound waves could not reveal the traditional recurrent sames and differences in sound with which he aimed to operate.

Then he pointed out (1933:77)

> The fact that two utterances of the syllable *man* with different pitch-schemes are 'the same' speech-form in English, but 'different' speech-forms in Chinese, shows us that the working of language depends upon our habitually and conventionally discriminating some features of sound and ignoring all others.

Notice how as with the Stoics, Native Speaker has been covertly introduced. Bloomfield, however, is immediately overt about it, "The difference between distinctive and non-distinctive features of sound lies entirely in the habit of the speakers."

But if, as Bloomfield says, the difference lies entirely in the habit of the speaker, why can't we count reports of same and different as evidence about the structure of these habits — as evidence about the linguistic structure of Native Speaker? The thought may never have occurred to Bloomfield, for he knew where he was going. He aimed to use the Alexandrian methods of recurrent sames and differences to elucidate the Stoic structure of language as a relation between sound and meaning. Native Speaker became only an instrument used for eliciting the sames and differences he attributed to language. Bloomfield's goal, accepted from the tradition, was to study language, not Native Speaker. He had perfectly good evidence about Native Speaker and apparently did not realize it. Instead, as always, the evidence was confiscated into the treasury of language for supporting the ancient rites of grammar writing, even though the old normative function of the rites had been largely set aside by linguists.

Native Speaker was highly valued in this era as an informant if not as an object of study. He became the indisputable source of data. This was one of the proudest periods in the history of linguistics, for accurate data was highly valued and the problems of observer bias and systematic error were kept well in mind.

Throughout this era, however, protesters against the narrow fixation on language and grammar could not be silenced. As early as 1929 Edward Sapir had written

> It is peculiarly important that linguists, who are often accused, and accused justly, of failure to look beyond the pretty patterns of their subject matter, should become aware of what their science may mean for the interpretation of human conduct in general. Whether they like it or not, they must become increasingly concerned with the many anthropological, sociological, and psychological problems which invade the field of language (p. 214).

Sapir was ever a champion of a broad view of linguistics, a view that very much included Native Speaker.

The Struggle for a Theory of Native Speaker

Some years later, Gardiner (1932: 5-6) proposed what he considered a novel and superior approach:

> The problem which I am setting before myself may best be indicated by a comparison. Suppose an intelligent boy to be inquiring how the telephone or the wireless works . . . . Could a like question be profitably put to the ordinary philologist? . . . I have searched high and low without finding the problem either stated or systematically handled in this way . . . . The problem here to be studied is, accordingly: How does speech work? And if now we ask ourselves by what method this problem should be tackled, the procedure of other sciences at once affords the answer: By the study of concrete, particular examples. . . . This then, is my method: to put back single acts of speech into their original setting of real life, and thence to discover what processes are employed, what factors involved.

Gardiner's book was decades ahead of its time. It is only recently that such methods have commanded much attention.

Then in 1937, Malinowski saw that linguists were faced by a dilemma. He said,

> Once we recognize . . . that 'language is a form of activity, a mode of human behavior, perhaps the most important' . . . the question arises: Can we treat language as an independent subject of study? Is there a legitimate science of words alone, of phonetics, grammar, and lexicography? Or must all study of speaking lead to sociological investigation, to the treatment of linguistics as a branch of the general science of culture? If the earliest and most fundamental function of speech is pragmatic — to direct, to control and to correlate human activities — then obviously no study of speech except within the 'context of situation' is legitimate.

Such voices went largely unheeded by the establishment. Language remained the object of study as it always had been. Grammar remained the preoccupation of linguists, and they rejoiced in their structuralism and descriptivism, and in their rigor. They tried to keep linguistics untainted by considerations of meaning, and they excluded Native Speaker from the councils of theory.

NATIVE SPEAKER IN THE ERA OF LATE STRUCTURALISM

There comes a point where history is so recent that it is not really history. It will fall to later generations to sort out the important threads in what is certainly a rapidly proliferating literature. I will mention here only a few points that seem significant in relation to my own interests. But since my own interests are centered on Native Speaker, it will provide at least one fix on our star.

In the early 1950's an effort was started in an interdisciplinary area called

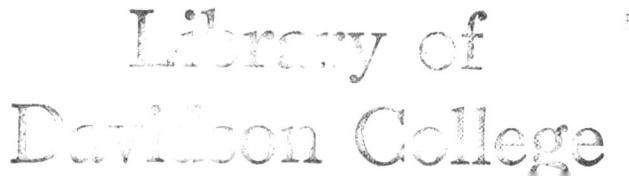

psycholinguistics.[6] It originally involved three partner disciplines — linguistics, psychology, and information theory. Information theory soon dropped out, and before long psycholinguistics became in reality a branch of experimental psychology interested in Native Speaker and trying to find in him psychological correlates of the grammatical entities and processes postulated by linguists. The question of the psychological reality of grammar and grammatical entities had been debated for years. Psycholinguistics, for some of its practitioners, became an effort by psychologists to test in the psychological laboratory certain effects that might be predicted if one took seriously the thought that people have grammars in their heads.

My view of this work, easy in retrospect, is that grammatical theories are not psychological theories. They are theories in a tradition that has developed out of the logical part of Stoic philosophy, not out of the physical part, a different tradition where studies of the *psychē* were located. Grammatical theories are theories of language, idealizations distilled from patterns of sames and differences in texts — occurrences, cooccurrences, and nonoccurrences. They are not theories of Native Speaker. This point makes it difficult to design meaningful psycholinguistic experiments and to interpret what significance if any may be read into the many results already reported in the literature. It is a fallacy to set up a grammar on standard linguistic evidence and stuff it into the head of Native Speaker as a theory of how he speaks and understands. Grammar is a theory of language, not of people.

Another effort that started in the early 1950's — one that I was associated with — was to try to find out how to translate languages by machine. Computer technology was expanding rapidly. There was a perceived need for improved international communication after a devastating war, and structural linguistics appeared to offer procedures for discovering how meaning is signalled. The best that technology and scientific linguistics had to offer would be harnassed to overcome the barriers of Babel. The difficult problems would be tackled one at a time. First the machines would have dictionaries; later they would incorporate grammars that could aid in untangling the syntax and resolving some of the ambiguities in the input text. Semantics would have to come later: little work had been done in that area by structuralists. It was hoped that the translations produced, though imperfect and inelegant, would eventually be useful.

The significance of this development for our topic is that the computer offered for the first time a complex information processing device. With this it was proposed to try to automate a linguistic activity that up to then had only been carried out by human brains. It thus became possible to think of the computer and its linguistic program as a crude model of Native Speaker. How seriously should we take the idea that our programs might be models of Native Speaker? Perhaps people accomplish such tasks in ways quite different from those programmed into the computer. If we put a grammar in the machine and think of it as a model, the question of the psychological reality of grammar comes into question. In particular, if people really do calculate with grammars when they talk and understand, what procedures are used? What is the temporal order in which the operations are carried out? How much temporary or working memory is required to keep track of grammatical constraints?

An effort to answer these questions turned up an intriguing result. The type of grammar we were using had been derived from the best work of such structuralists as Leonard Bloomfield, Charles C. Fries, Zellig Harris, Eugene Nida, and Rulon Wells. An adaptation of Noam Chomsky's phrase-structure notation was employed,[7] augmented by a simple mechanism for handling discontinuous constituents and a subscript notation for handling detailed subcategorization. This is a type of grammar that has recently come back into favor in the work of some linguists. The procedure adopted for producing sentences to order was to apply these rules in sequence from top to bottom and left to right of the syntactic tree. The words of a sentence would then be produced one at a time in the same order in which people produce them when they speak. Then in investigating the question of how much temporary memory would be needed, it was found that no more than about seven unexpanded nodes of the derivation would ever have to be held in memory at the same time.

Efforts were made to find naturally occurring sentences in text that would require more memory than this. None were found. Efforts were made to concoct sentences that would require more memory. Invariably the results were monstrosities that any informant would reject as ungrammatical, extremely awkward, or incomprehensible. Apparently no more than about seven syntactic constraints are ever active at any one time. This led to a rather detailed hypothesis about language structure that proposed a *raison d'être* for many of the observed complexities of grammar and a mechanism for how they might have come about historically (1960).

Although this work appeared to answer a number of questions, it raised some new ones. In spite of its apparent success in yielding insights, the model was admittedly inadequate: it lacked a semantic part, for example. It is a frequent occurrence in science, however, that an inadequate or incomplete theory is able to account for some of the phenomena and make accurate predictions. In this case the predictions of the hypothesis were borne out not only in the data considered in the original investigation, but also in later comparison with data not originally known to the investigator. There turned out to be a detailed fit of the theory to the known facts of the historical change of the English genitive between A.D. 900 and A.D. 1300 (Yngve 1975b). The challenge, therefore, has been to understand exactly what the grain of truth in the theory is and how to expand the theory to meet its obvious shortcomings.

In retrospect it seems clear that the grain of truth in the theory is the degree to which it approximates a model of Native Speaker. Its shortcomings are related to its heavy reliance on grammar, for people do not have grammars in their heads that they regularly use for speaking and understanding.

A third development in the struggle for a theory of Native Speaker in this era of late structuralism has been the expansion of work in ethnographic linguistics, sociolinguistics, and linguistic variation. Here one finds a healthy focus on people, how they talk, and the relation of their communicative activity to a variety of cultural and social factors. Here Native Speaker finds many friends and protectors. Unfortunately, the standard theories in linguistics have been of little help. Therefore much of the work has had to be carried out with a primary focus on data and with as little theory as possible. The inadequacy of grammatical theories for this work is understandable, once again, because a theory of language is not a theory of people.

Probably most linguists are genuinely interested in people and how they communicate. But they are stuck with the concepts and methods of Ancient Greece inherited through the normative grammatical tradition. They are ambivalent about the psychological reality of grammar, wishing that it were true but suspecting that it isn't. Noam Chomsky has raised ambivalence to a fine art by introducing a 'systematic ambiguity' into his use of the term grammar. It is not enough simply to declare that a grammatical theory has psychological reality. It must be shown on the basis of scientific evidence that it has. Chomsky has laid down a distinction between competence and performance which is simply the current reincarnation of the ancient distinction between the logical and the physical. In his hands it is used to insulate grammar from having to meet the burden of testability against evidence from Native Speaker. Under this conception modern scientific linguistics would be placed outside the realm of science. It is ironic that a theory derived from Greek epistemology becomes epistemologically unsound when pressed into service as a theoretical base for a scientific linguistics.

Under the guise of fighting the anarchy of extreme empiricism, the banner of rationalism has been raised. The ideal speaker-hearer has been enacted into law, and if Native Speaker does not conform he is indicted as a willful lawbreaker. He is denied the final voice in determining, under proper controls, the content of his own theory. The appropriate mode of government of a scientific linguistics is that of science: a government by the rule of law, not by decree; by laws that are not the edicts of rationalists trying to intuit the truth, but laws resting solidly on the customs and usages of the populace. Excellent models abound in the other natural sciences.

Some philosophers have laid down a distinction between syntax, semantics, and pragmatics. One of the most significant trends in recent years has been the move by both linguists and philosophers into the study of pragmatics. Since pragmatics studies the relation of language to its users, there is the hope that Native Speaker may finally get a theory of his own. However, pragmatics does not really study people. Instead it continues in the logical part of philosophy, not in the physical part, proposing principles and laws which, like grammar, the poor benighted Native Speaker is supposed to use as a guide if he is to aspire at all to the higher reaches of logical and linguistic perfection. Once again, as pragmatics becomes another branch of the theory of language, Native Speaker is in danger of being left without a theory, and those of us who have struggled so hard on his behalf will once again be thwarted. What is needed is not another component of the theory of language, but a reorganization of linguistics. Linguistics should move once and for all out of the logical part of philosophy into the physical and become a true natural science. Linguistics should acknowledge once and for all that its true object of study is people, the human individual and the human group, Native Speaker and his namesakes.

THE BIRTHRIGHT GRANTED

When August Schleicher wanted to make linguistics a natural science, he accepted concepts of language and grammar from tradition. He took language for the object of the new science as a matter of course. But natural sciences study natural objects. His conception that language is an organism, a sort of fourth kingdom, was ingenious: it gave the impression that linguistics was the study of a natural object. But it soon became apparent that language is not an organism with a life of its own, and serious talk of living languages was abandoned. The mystical concept lingered on, however. Saussure, although he allowed himself to speak of language as an organism, realized its mythical status: "Other sciences work with objects that are given in advance," he said, "and that can then be considered from different viewpoints; but not linguistics . . . . Far from it being the object that antedates the viewpoint, it would seem that it is the viewpoint that creates the object" (1916:23; 1966:8). Language and the other objects of grammar are not physical objects of nature. They are created by a viewpoint. That viewpoint, as we have seen, is the viewpoint of the logical part of the philosophy of Ancient Greece.

But if we take people as the object of linguistics, Schleicher's and Saussure's problem of an object for a scientific linguistics disappears, for people are certainly given in advance and they can be considered from different viewpoints.

Recall that the usual methods of the linguistics of language are the Alexandrian methods of recurrent sames and differences in text or corpus. Thus Bloomfield, one of the most careful linguistic thinkers in this century, had noted that the study of *language* could be carried out *without special assumptions* only as far as physiological and acoustic phonetics. The trouble was that speech-sounds were infinitely varying. With no two utterances being alike on this plane, the methods of recurrent sames and differences could not be applied. To carry the study of language beyond this point he had to turn to Native Speaker to make the judgments of same and different for him. But his object of study was language, not Native Speaker. Instead of using these judgments directly for deducing the linguistic properties of Native Speaker, he wanted to take them as applying to language, and this required him to make a special assumption: "Phonology," he wrote, "and, with it, all the semantic phase of language study, rests upon an assumption, the fundamental assumption of linguistics: we must assume that *in every speech-community some utterances are alike in form and meaning*" (1933:78) (original emphasis). Through the concepts of 'form and meaning' Bloomfield introduced the Stoic view of language as a relation between sound and meaning. Through the concepts of 'utterance' and 'alike' he introduced the ideas of discreteness, segmentation, and linguistic contrast. And through the concept of 'speech-community' he introduced the idea of uniformity. All by assumption. In his careful way he was simply being explicit about what had been implicit in the tradition. Native Speaker's judgments of same and different were, with this *a priori* justification, taken from him and interpreted as judgments about 'utterances' from which the structure of 'the language' was to be discovered.

If, on the other hand, we take people as the object of linguistics, the judgments can be interpreted directly as evidence about the properties of Native Speaker, not language. Being an object that is given in advance, Native Speaker does not, like language, have to be created by a special assumption that provides that point of view.

Now the goal of linguistics, according to the usual conception, is to achieve *a scientific understanding of language.* This goal is widely accepted. Let us refer to the discipline dedicated to this goal as *the linguistics of language*, using Saussure's term. This term will refer here to linguistics as it is usually conceived today, and will not necessarily imply the particular distinctions drawn by Saussure. According to the usual linguistic practice, the linguistics of language starts with data in the form of text or corpus, obtained or augmented by informant judgments; analyzes the data by the methods of sames and differences; and works out the structure of language, which is then expressed in terms of grammar in the broad sense. This usual conception of moving from data to grammar can be pictured as at *a* in figure 1.

The Struggle for a Theory of Native Speaker 45

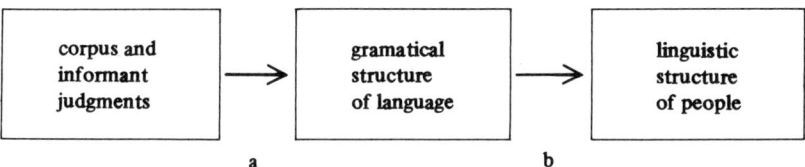

a b

Figure 1 Under the usual conception of linguistics (*a*), data in the form of corpus and informant judgments are taken from Native Speaker and used as a basis for working out the structure of language. For this Bloomfield's fundamental assumption of linguistics is required. It is then tempting (*b*) to use an assumption of the psychological reality of grammar to justify inserting grammar into the head of Native Speaker to serve as the linguistic structure of the individual or groups of individuals.

Now under this usual scheme, linguists who are interested in Native Speaker, and that includes most of us, are tempted to make the additional assumption that grammar has some psychological reality, that people have grammars in their heads which they use when they speak and understand, that grammar is an adequate representation of the linguistic structure of Native Speaker, or some approximation to it, or used in some way by a connected theory of performance. Under this view, one would move from data to grammar and then to the structure of Native Speaker. It can be pictured as at *b* in figure 1.

However, the idea that people have grammars in their heads is a mistake. Think carefully about it. They certainly have something in their heads, but it is not grammar. Note what has happened. Data that comes from Native Speaker under this scheme is not used directly in determining the structure of Native Speaker: it is taken from him and used in determining the structure of language, a mythical entity not originally present and requiring a special assumption for its introduction. Then the result, a grammar, is mistakenly placed in the head of Native Speaker on the erroneous assumption that it is psychologically real. Grammar derives not only from the data but from the traditional assumptions as well. The only reason that language and grammar appear at all in this picture is the force of the tradition inherited from the Greeks through normative grammar. It is a reflex of Schleicher's organism concept, introduced to give linguistics an object of study.

But if we take people as the object of study in linguistics, there is no need to introduce a mythical object by a special assumption, and no call for an erroneous assumption of the psychological reality of grammar. With people as the object of study, linguistics becomes a true natural science, for people are objects of nature. The only assumptions needed are the widely understood and accepted assumptions of science, such as that there is an external reality that can be studied, and that things don't happen without a cause.

Is a viable scientific linguistics possible that takes people as its object rather than language? First of all, it should be said that any such linguistics, though transformed, should account for all the real phenomena that currently concern linguists. Remember that all evidence about language derives ultimately from people. It is therefore also, and primarily, evidence about people.

What would be the goal of a linguistics that takes people as its object instead of language, and that tries to determine the linguistic structure of people, individually and collectively, directly from observations of people without a detour through language? It has been proposed that the goal of such a discipline should be *to achieve a scientific understanding of how people communicate* (Yngve 1975a,c). Such a discipline may be called *human linguistics* to distinguish it from the linguistics of language. A discipline according to this scheme can be pictured as in Figure 2.

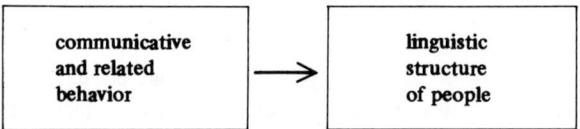

Figure 2 Under a human linguistics conception, data obtained from Native Speaker are used directly as a basis for investigating the linguistic structure of the individual and of groups of individuals. The special assumptions required for the detour through language are not now needed. Only the usual assumptions of a natural science are needed.

The data obtained from Native Speaker and used in deducing his linguistic structure under this scheme could be informant judgments, but they need not be. They could be responses in naturally occurring conversations or other communicative interactions. They need not be verbal responses: gestures and other behavior may be communicative. Furthermore, since communicative behavior 'directs, controls, and correlates human activities' the responses of Native Speaker to communicative behavior may at times be read from the associated human activity that is being coordinated.

What methods should be used in human linguistics? It is appropriate to use the methods of recurrent sames and differences that are already familiar in linguistics. However, these methods will be applied to the study of people, not language. It is worthy of remark that many other natural sciences also use methods of sames and differences.

What kind of a theoretical structure would be needed in human linguistics to take the place of grammar in the linguistics of language? This is a question that would require many chapters to answer, but I will try to provide a brief overview here.[8] First of all human linguistics is divided into two interrelated

The Struggle for a Theory of Native Speaker 47

branches, a theory of the individual and a theory of groups. Both individuals and groups are known theoretically as dynamic state systems with properties determined so as to account for the data. State theories have been employed in science for at least 300 years and by now are quite standard and well-known. Their adaptation to linguistics, however, has turned out to be neither simple nor trivial if a theoretical structure is desired that does not rest on unwarranted special assumptions and that is adequate for handling the enormous scope and quantity of detailed linguistic data. It is not possible simply to take an existing state theory and apply it blindly in linguistics, for that would circumvent important questions at the very foundations of the discipline.

In the theory of the individual we have to account for the fact that everyone is different, but that people show similarities. The sames and differences of individuals are understood theoretically in terms of properties postulated to account for the data. The methods used are similar to methods used in the other natural sciences for postulating the properties of natural objects – from electrons to elephants and from violets to volcanoes. Here Native Speaker comes into his own as a child of nature in a theory that grants him the dignity of his uniqueness, and recognizes the reality of his own properties. He can turn his back on those who would make him a private in an army of ideal speaker-hearers and then give him demerits if he does not conform.

In the theory of groups we have to understand the properties of groups, small and large, from two individuals in a conversational linkage to the largest of communities. We have to be able to understand a community in terms of the many smaller interrelated groups that make it up. But most important, we have to understand the reciprocal relations between individual and group, how to connect theories at the individual level and at the social level.

Would such a discipline be adequate for the needs of linguistics? At this point enough work has been done to say with some confidence that the answer is yes. It can adequately cover all the phenomena presently covered in the various components of grammar although it does it in a different way. It can handle more difficult phenomena, from anaphora to metaphor. It can cover linguistic variation in all its dimensions, and the phenomena of linguistic change. It is appropriate for developmental linguistics because it is really people who develop, not language.

Since the theory of the individual is automatically endowed with psychological reality it is an ideal theory to contribute to a revitalized psycholinguistics. It interfaces well with theories in cognitive psychology and other branches of psychology that study the individual.

And the theory of groups in human linguistics has a social reality that suits it for interfacing with a more adequate sociolinguistics and with other relevant theories that deal with groups of people.

How about the theory of language? Will we be able to get along without it? Probably not for a long time to come because there is so much yet to do in human linguistics. The old country will still be there, exporting its culture if not its form of government. But the new country contains a vast and exciting frontier to be explored. It will accept the hard-won knowledge from the old, and some of the know-how, while rejecting the superstitions. In principle a human linguistics discipline promises to cover everything now covered by the linguistics of language, and it promises to cover it in a more satisfactory manner, providing more adequate coverage and a better integration of disparate phenomena into a unified body of theory. Furthermore, there is some indication that the current theoretical confusions in linguistics are caused basically by the fact that the traditional assumptions of language and grammar often stand in the way of fulfilling the needs of modern scientific linguistics. The linguistics of language has often served us well. It is not infrequent in science that an inadequate or incomplete theory can account for some of the phenomena and make accurate predictions.

Human linguistics holds out the promise of meeting the century old challenge of Hermann Paul, "that of showing how the single individual is related to the community; receiving and giving; defined by the community and defining it in turn; and how the younger generation enters on the heritage of the elder" (1889:xxx). If we can do this, we will have finally granted Native Speaker his birthright, a theory of his very own.

NOTES

1. Unfortunately the original Stoic writings have not survived. The best single source is the article on Zeno in the third century A.D. bedside reader *Lives of Eminent Philosophers*, by Diogenes Laertius. See, for example, Hicks (1925). In characterizing the Stoic position I have leaned heavily on the Hicks translation, but have made a few minor improvements.
2. Not to be confused with the quite different nineteenth century doctrine of thesis, antithesis, and synthesis.
3. A reconstruction of Stoic logic can be found in Mates (1953).
4. In notes for a lecture dating to about 1830. Published in Rask (1932–33).
5. Schleicher cited *The Philosophy of History*. See any convenient edition. They all read like nonsense today. Schleicher made great contributions as a linguist. His confusions stem from an acceptance of unexamined preconceptions from older philosophical speculations.
6. For a report on early views of psycholinguists see Osgood and Sebeok (1965).
7. Transformations would not work well in this application.
8. A book on the subject is being prepared for early publication under the title *Human Linguistics: The Scientific Study of How People Communicate*. I would like to thank Eric Hamp, Paul Friedrich and James McCawley for comments on an earlier draft of this paper which have helped me to improve its precision and clarity.

REFERENCES

Bloomfield, L. (1933). *Language.* New York: Henry Holt and Company.

Fick, A. (1871). *Vergleichendes Wörterbuch der indogermanischen Sprachen.* Göttingen: Vandenhoeck & Ruprecht's Verlag.

Gardiner, A.H. (1932). *The Theory of Speech and Language.* Oxford: Oxford University Press.

Hicks, R.D. (1925). *Diogenes Laertius: Lives of Eminent Philosophers, with an English Translation.* London: William Heinemann, New York: G.P. Putnam's Sons.

Jakobson, R. (1971). 'Quest for the Essence of Language.' In *Roman Jakobson Selected Writings* 2. The Hague: Mouton.

Lehmann, W.P., ed. and trans. (1967). *A Reader in Nineteenth-Century Historical Indo-European Linguistics.* Bloomington: Indiana Univ. Press.

Malinowski, B. (1937). 'The Dilemma of Contemporary Linguistics.' *Nature* 140: 172-3.

Mates, B. (1953). *Stoic Logic.* Berkeley and Los Angeles: University of California Press.

Osgood, C.E. and T.A. Sebeok, eds. (1965). *Psycholinguistics: A Survey of Theory and Research Problems.* Bloomington: Indiana University Press.

Osthoff, H. and K. Brugmann (1878). 'Vorwort,' *Morphologische Untersuchungen auf dem Gebiete der indogermanischen Sprachen* 1. pp. iii-xx.

Paul, H. (1889). *Principles of the History of Language.* Translated from the second edition of the original by H.A. Strong. New York: Macmillan.

Rask, R. (1932-33). *Ausgewählte Abhandlungen* 2. Copenhagen: Levin & Munksgaard.

Sapir, E. (1929). 'The Status of Linguistics as a Science.' *Language* 5: 207-14.

Saussure, F. de (1916). *Course de Linguistique Générale.* Paris: Payot.

Saussure, F. de (1966). *Course in General Linguistics.* Trans. Wade Baskin, New York, Toronto, London: McGraw-Hill.

Schleicher, A. (1848). *Zur vergleichenden Sprachengeschichte* (Sprachvergleichende Untersuchungen 1). Bonn: H.B. König.

Schleicher, A. (1850). *Die Sprachen Europas in systematischer Uebersicht* (Linguistische Untersuchungen 2). Bonn: H.B. König.

Schleicher, A. (1860). *Die Deutsche Sprache.* Stuttgart: Verlag der I.G. Cotta'schen Buchhandlung.

Schleicher, A. (1861). *Compendium der vergleichenden Grammatik der indogermanischen Sprachen* 1. Weimar: Hermann Böhlau.

Schleicher, A. (1865). *Ueber die Bedeutung der Sprache für die Naturgeschichte des Menschen.* Weimar: Hermann Böhlau.

Yngve, V.H. (1960). 'A Model and an Hypothesis for Language Structure.' *Proceedings of the American Philosophical Society* 104: 444-66.

Yngve, V.H. (1975a). 'The Dilemma of Contemporary Linguistics.' In A. Makkai and V.B. Makkai, eds., *The First LACUS Forum 1974.* Columbia, South Carolina: Hornbeam Press.

Yngve, V.H. (1975b). 'Depth and the Historical Change of the English Genitive.' In the *Journal of English Linguistics* 9: 47-57.

Yngve, V.H. (1975c). 'Toward a Human Linguistics.' In R.E. Grossman *et al.*, eds., *Papers from the Parasession on Functionalism, April 17, 1975,* Chicago: Chicago Linguistic Society.

TH. T BALLMER

A Typology of Native Speakers

ABSTRACT

The task and function of **native speakers** is taken to be, in this article, to provide the *basis* for an *empirical linguistics*, connecting so to speak linguistic *theory* and linguistic *facts* as an *measuring device*. A *typology* of the **native speaker** is proposed with the aim of clarifying this imputed task of the **native speaker**. The *typology* in its full length is summarized at the end of the paper. Besides the classificatory outcome which is interesting also for its own sake there is another extremely relevant result of the typology: the **native speaker** as explicated by the typological and definitional investigations does not seem to provide a complete basis for the empirical validation for the whole range of languages and linguistic products of interest to the linguist. Various extensions of the notion of **native speaker** have to be envisaged.

THE FUNCTION OF THE NATIVE SPEAKER IN LINGUISTICS

Before starting any kind of analysis of the native speaker the question should be considered what the relevancy of the **native speaker** for theoretical and experimental linguistics is.[1] In other words, a fruitful analysis of the native speaker *presupposes* a clear conception of what the function of the **native speaker** is for linguistics.

The proposal on which the development of this article is based is the following:

(1) The **native speaker** is the pivot which relates linguistic *theory* with the *facts* of language structure and language use.

The **native speaker** thus interpreted is taken to be the *measuring device* telling the linguist what is true or false of (some) language. This view, however, cannot be more than a *first approximation*. For native speakers of a language are apt to make lots of mistakes: they may hesitate, stutter, misunderstand, forget etc. A native speaker of a language is therefore not **perfect**: making mistakes, he cannot, hence, be taken as a fully reliable source of information about language. Moreover each language allows for variants. Correspondingly there are more central and less central variants of that language. As is readily seen a native speaker is not necessarily **typical** in the sense of being rightaway a speaker of a *central* variant of the language in question. Furthermore, a native speaker is not necessarily an **expert** on the language, having explicit knowledge about the language, i.e. a working *metalinguistic* knowledge, neither is he a **representative speaker** being necessarily socially *acknowledged* as serving as an informant or an arbiter of the language.

These reflections indicate that the **native speaker** cannot fulfil the task of relating linguistic theory and facts in an unproblematic way. There seem to be serious obstacles in making the **native speaker** the central figure of empirical linguistics.

The aim of this article is therefore to characterize speakers of a language according to various dimensions in order to prepare a qualified answer to "who is the measuring device for linguists?" The typology of (native) speakers is therefore guided by the fundamental problem of establishing the basis of an empirical linguistics.

NATIVE SPEAKERS, NON-NATIVE SPEAKERS, AND NATIVE NON-SPEAKERS

In order to get more readily into a complex field let us start with some definitions. These definitions should lead to a working basis for notions relevant for our discussion such as **speaker, native speaker, language** etc. Let us begin with a definition of **native speaker**.

A very, very literal definition of a **native speaker** (which we do not really make use of in the sequel) is the following:

(2) Def_0: A NSP_0 (Native Speaker of a zeroth type) of a language L is able to *speak* L "by birth".

This means, expressed in more biological terms, that an NSP_0 knows his language L without learning it: the (chromosomal or extrachromosomal) genes determine language L uniquely. *No human being* is a native speaker in that sense. Otherwise there would not be any environmental dependency of first language learning: a Chinese child would then become a (native) *speaker* of Chinese even if grown up in a Latvian family. The language would be inherited. Accepting animal communication systems as languages, a female worker bee provides a good example of an NSP_0, however. Its language does not depend on a teacher's language. The higher the evolutionary state of a living being, the more flexible (in general) are its properties and abilities. Human beings show (probably) the highest flexibility of instrumental,

A Typology of Native Speakers

especially linguistic abilities. The capability of environmental language learning according to bio-social conditioning is one expression of evolutionary perfection.

(3) Def_1: A NSP_1 (Native Speaker of a first kind) of language L is [an organism] able "by birth" to *learn to speak* a language.

Thus, in biological terms, a NSP_1 [under normal living conditions] is able to *learn to communicate* by linguistic means. This ability is genetically determined. Every human being, as we may infer from this, is a clear case of a NSP_1.

A first typology of potential speakers of a language is then:

(4) $\neg NSP_0 \quad \wedge \quad \neg NSP_1$ (Native Nonspeakers)

$NSP_0 \quad \wedge \quad \neg NSP_1$ (Native Speakers)

$\neg NSP_0 \quad \wedge \quad NSP_1$ (Native Language Learners)

Human beings are really *native language learners* (NLL, i.e. $\neg NSP_0 \; NSP_1$).

The notion of native speaker depends essentially on the language of which the native speaker is a speaker: somebody may be a native speaker of *Haussa*. He will not then (typically) be a native speaker of *Japanese*.

Hence, a proper typology of native speakers forces us to take into account a gradation of languages: there are native speakers of extremely simple "languages" (chemical codes, anatomic codes, behavioral codes, conditioned behavioral codes) or of more complex "languages" (limb motion codes, sound codes, generative codes, creative codes[2]). Accordingly, we arrive at a typology of native "speakers" of the following kind:

(5) | Native "Speakers" | Code or Language |
|---|---|
| microbes | chemical codes |
| plants | anatomic codes |
| animals | behavioral (conditioned) codes |
| higher animals (birds and mammals) | limb motion and sound codes |
| apes | generative codes |
| man | creative codes (creative spoken language) |
| cultural man | external trace codes ("Schrift", creative written language) |
| technical man | dynamic machine codes (by means of computers as instruments; creative mechanico-formal language) |

Typology (5) can really be taken as a refinement of (4). The sequential order, in both cases, is established on the basis of (*evolutionary*) *development*: from non-speakers to speakers and, more specifically, to speakers of increasingly complex codes/languages. Later stages in the typology (typically) presuppose earlier stages.

With respect to the previous definitional and typological proposals it is now possible to give a first definition of a **native speaker**:

(6) **Def$_2$**: A **native speaker** of a language L is an organism *able to produce* adequately token expressions of L in communication and has *learned* this ability in the process of primary socialization.

This is to say that **native speaker** has *learned* his language as a first language and has not forgotten it. Because he has learned language L, a **native speaker** [of language L] is at least an NSL$_1$. The language he learned [and did not forget] is at least of the complexity of a *creative* code/language. Thus it seems, as a *result* of these rather theoretically oriented considerations, that a **native speaker** is typically a human being. He does more than generatively play with symbols: he uses symbols in order to creatively build up his cultural knowledge on the basis of a *necessary* or *random* (these notions are discussed at length in Monod 1971) evolution by more or less goal directed context changes (i.e. mutative changes and memorized selections).

DIMENSIONS OF QUALITY

For a useful notion of **native speaker** we need a typology of his qualities. An answer would be provided to the question: what is a good native speaker, good with respect to the purpose chosen, namely to provide the empirical link between linguistic theory and linguistic facts?

According to definition **Def$_2$** of a native speaker, we could maintain at first sight that every human being is a **native speaker** (of his first language).

Closer inspection shows that this is not so. Infants do not (yet) speak, very old men and similarly aphasics no longer speak, and certain social or mental defects imply inability to speak any language at all. Thus it is *not* true that *every human being* is a *native speaker*.

We may conjecture that every speaking human is a native speaker of a language. This is not true either, as results from bilingualism-studies show. The typical case is that bilinguals are not native speakers of either language. Moreover there are those people who have forgotten their native language for various reasons, e.g., because of living abroad in an environment

A Typology of Native Speakers

linguistically different from the native one. Hence the implication from *speaking human being* to **native speaker** does not hold.

Thus we may conjecture that at least most speaking members of a language L are **native speakers**. Even this weak statement is often falsified: In a country (like Germany) where the major communicative means is a *standard educated speech* (Hochsprache) the native dialects may be substituted regularly in early school by the *non-native* standard. The native dialects are more often than not forgotten.

This being so, we are amply licensed to ask whether some native speakers are better than others and what their properties are.

The falsifying cases of the statements above lead us to the following definition of a *good* **native speaker**:

(7) Def_3: A **native speaker** of a creative (spoken) language L is a human being *able to produce* adequately expressions of L in communication, who is normally socialized and who *acquired* this ability in the process of primary socialization.

A **native speaker** is old enough to know the language and not so old as to have forgotten it. He is healthy in every relevant respect, thus especially neither blind, deaf, handicapped, paralysed, nor does he lisp, stutter or have a cleft palate. He is monolingual, he lives in his birthplace, his family, especially his mother, speakes (natively) his nature language L, the place where he lives is strictly monolingual: there is no standard speech/dialect split and there are no other competing languages.

We see that according to this definition the requirements for a **native speaker** are extremely specialized. The question may arise whether for each (natural) language there exist at least some **native speakers**. We shall take up this question further below (cf. (9b)).

First, we should investigate whether there are abilities of a more general kind which a **native speaker** should have, in order to live up to the requirements (standards) of providing the empirical linguist with a reliable link between theory and facts.

Over and above having a well-functioning healthy body, exhibiting developed behavior, living in a linguistically well-established society, as we have already seen, a **native speaker** should have a working *knowledge* of his native language. This means that he must be educated enough to react adequately to the tasks and questions of the experimenting linguist/psychologist. He must understand what he has to do. He must show appropriately intelligent and adaptive behavior.

On the other hand, the **native speaker** should be sufficiently persistent as to provide reproducible data, and not to comply with the theoretical assumptions implicit in the experiment's questions. Thus the native speaker should be adaptable with respect to the overtly stated task but not with respect to implicit assumptions, in other words he should be intelligent but not too intelligent.

Besides the requirements of competence, a **native speaker** should furthermore fulfil requirements of performance. It is *not* sufficient for him to be *able* to produce adequately expressions of his native language L in the experimental situation: *to be able* in this general sense is too weak. He has to have a capability of performative perfection, i.e. of correctly producing those expressions ($\equiv$ **perfect speaker**), or at least of correcting himself with sufficient efficiency (**quasi-perfect speaker**). He should also be **consistent**, i.e. his linguistic competence should be quasi-stable. Linguistic changes should not occur during the experiment. Especially, the fact that the subject finds himself in an experimental situation should not cause him (through stress or for other reasons) to "flip out" and to produce irreproducible results.

We may ask what types of abilities of the **native speaker** are used in a linguistic experiment. The following four uses of abilities will be of interest: the **native speaker** as (1) *user* of his linguistic *intuition,* as (2) *native arguer* for or against certain positions, as (3) *user* of his *introspection,* and as (4) linguistic *theoretician.*

We shall thereby take the linguistic intuition of a **native speaker** to be his activated disposition of being able to behave as if being in a certain (linguistic) situation. A **native speaker's** *intuition* allows him — according to this view — to react linguistically appropriately, even if a situation is artificially established (e.g. by help of pictures or short texts presented by the experimenter). *Introspection* is a furthergoing ability allowing its bearer to actualize at free will and in a task-oriented way (linguistic) situations and to inspect appropriate utterances and behavior.

For a good **native speaker** the following requirements are needed with respect to linguistic experiments:

(8) native speaker	normal requirements	maximal requirements
as user of his intuition	yes	yes
as arguer	yes	yes
as user of his introspection	no	(yes)
as theoretician	no	(yes)

It is *sufficient*, as can be seen, to ask for the *normal* requirements. The experimenter has the means to direct the **native speaker's** focus of attention to the

A Typology of Native Speakers

appropriate situation. Then, however, the **native speaker**'s intuition is required of behaving appropriately with respect to that (not quite natural, but experimentally induced) situation. Introspection is not needed and may even disturb the experiment, because it opens the possibility of uncontrollable situations. The **native speaker** may *argue* conforming to the situation set up by the experimenter, but he need not — and maybe should not — make use of theoretical considerations. His judgement is then more valuable for the empirical test. A different case obtains for **native speakers** as heuristically working informants. In this case the maximal requirements of (8) may be preferred.

According to these considerations we may add to definition (7) the following clause:

(7′) The native speaker is educated enough to enter the experiment, but not so educated as to call into question its outcome.

More concretely: linguists, literary critics, writers and poets are probably not "*good*" subjects for experimental tests; nor is a person who counters the question "Can you say: lick, my son, the plate?" by saying, "I would rather forbid him to do so."

DEFICIENCIES OF THE **NATIVE SPEAKER**

The definitions and typologies of the *native speaker* presented so far render it questionable whether it is possible to base empirical linguistics on this concept of **native speaker**. For many natural languages and their dialects there may be no **native speaker** at all fulfilling the appropriate requirements. The best native speaker, so to speak, is not good enough.

The problem of founding empirical linguistics on experiments with native speakers is much more severe, however, as the following *observation* shows:

(9a) **Obs**$_1$: For many languages L of interest to the linguist there does not exist a **native speaker**.

The following list provides us with examples of this observation. These languages, while having an intrinsic interest for linguists as a subject of investigation, have no empirical bases with respect to a **native speaker**. The **native speaker** thus definitely turns out not to provide a sufficient basis for empirical linguistics.

The list is divided into two parts, namely in those cases of languages for which there are no "speakers" *at all*, and those for which there are no *native* speakers.

(9b)

language L	Remarks
1. child language	Children are "natives", but they do not yet speak the fullblown language; they "speak" a variance of the full-blown language, however.
2. Idiolects of dead persons	The (native) speaker of the idiolect in question no longer exists.
3. languages of bilinguals, multilinguals	Bilinguals are (generally) not "good" speakers of any of the languages in question.
4. dead languages, historical language states (e.g. Latin, Hittite, Middle English)	No present day speakers exist.
5. technical languages	No *native* speaker exists.
6. Standard languages (Theater speech; *Hochsprache*; elevated languages: literary and poetic languages)	No *native* speaker need exist.
7. Aphasics (through apoplexy or injury)	No *native* speaker exists.
8. ASL (American Sign Language), FSL (French Sign Language), etc.	Artificial language which may become natural and be natively learned.
9. Pidgin languages	All Pidgins are by definition languages that are not natively learned
10. Other cases: animal languages; machine/processing languages; computer/software languages, formal languages, written languages	—

The *basic question* with respect to an amendment of this situation is: is there a natural candidate to replace the **native speaker** for cases such as those referred to in (9a/b)? What is looked for is an alternative, or various alternatives for the **native speaker** of linguistically interesting variant languages. For a

A Typology of Native Speakers

most standard type of language, namely the monolingually pure (adult) present-day-language, remaining such over some generations, **native speakers** could be found, even if with some difficulty. The concept of native speaker breaks down, however, as soon as some essential language/speaker parameter is shifted: age of the "speaker" (→ child language), living status of the speaker (→ dead persons), homogeneity of language (→ multilingualism), present-day use of the language (→ dead languages), natural topic (→ technical language), social stratification (→ standard speech), health (→ aphasics), communicative medium (→ ASL), language contact (→ Pidgin), etc.

In order to overcome these difficulties we have to introduce various substitutes for the **native speaker**. For cases such as *terminological* and *standard languages* we need **experts**. **Experts** have explicit knowledge about the language uses and may even appeal to normative decisions. This is admissible in so far as terminological and standard languages are normative to a certain extent. For the linguistic products of *aphasics* and *children* there are no **expert speakers** available, however. An aphasic is not what we may want to call an expert of his language, nor is a child. Aphasics and children are **representative sources**: they are acknowledged by linguists to be *informants* of the linguistic output they produce. *Bilinguals,* though not fully endowed with the abilities of a **native speaker** are more than **representative sources**. They show a high faculty of deciding about right and wrong in the language they speak and are acknowledged by linguists to do so. Therefore they may serve as what we could call **representative arbiters**. Dead languages (or nearly dead languages such as some Indian languages for which no native speech community exists) need other sources of information. Texts, tape recordings or video-recordings computerized information in short **records**, are most helpful. But they do not, of course, *replace* a native speaker. The linguist working with such material can in certain cases get near to the abilities of a native speaker of a dead language, as a **secondary expert**: by dealing with the available **records** he may have acquired a partial competence of the language he studied.

Thus we conclude that the central and basic notion of **native speaker** splits into a series of alternative notions, if certain parameters like natural topic, social stratification get differentiated. No undivided alternative notion replacing the **native speaker** uniformly could be found. There is no simple notion covering those alternatives like: **expert speakers, representative sources, representative arbiters, records, secondary experts.**

Example (10) overleaf shows a possible way of representing the correlation between *normality* and *deviation* with respect to the two dimensions LANGUAGE PARAMETERS and MEASURING DEVICES.

We may sum up these results by saying that a thorough analysis of the notion of **native speaker** led to a dissolution of this notion properly speaking.

(10)

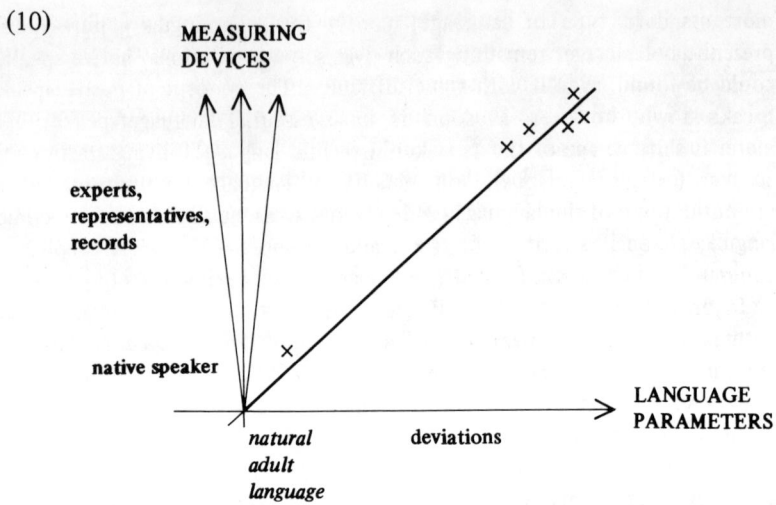

The expectation of founding empirical linguistics on the native speaker cannot be met. A series of flanking notions need to be used for this purpose. Before we summarize and connect the various aspects of the notion of **native speaker** and come to a general assessment, we shall focus on another problem with that notion: the problem of **native hearers** and the communicative relevancy of addressees for our topic.

THE NATIVE SPEAKER IN THE SPEECH SITUATION

Linguists never speak of a **native hearer**. Does this show a further defect in the conceptual framework of linguistics or is the reason simply that **speaker** is understood more comprehensively as somebody having the ability to produce *and* the ability to understand linguistic expressions? Could one say that more attention should be paid to **native hearers** than to **native speakers** on the grounds that normally everybody understands more in a language as a hearer than he is able to produce as a speaker? We may introduce the more neutral notion of a **native communicator**, perhaps. Be this as it may, there is still a problem of what abilities, produtive or receptive, render someone a **native communicator**. Are two deaf twin children having developed their own sign language **native communicators** (users) of that language? Is, in other words, one addressee sufficient to make a system of linguistic products a language? Is it even possible to waive even this much? Was *Lester Young* speaking (using) a language, when he uttered phrases in an idiom which nobody *except him* could understand? He seemed to have had recurrent

A Typology of Native Speakers

elements in his speech. Furthermore, could something be a language if not even the producer of it understands it, as is partially the case with the users of *Babel-17* in S. Delany's science fiction story *Babel-17*? Or, to give this question a more realistic touch, does an average **native communicator** understand fully what he is saying? It could very well be, considered from a more sophisticated point of view, that most utterances made are not (really) *understood* in their meaning and their consequences, because the consequences conform to the purposes of a higher order system such as biological or social evolution which is normally beyond the conscious control and attention of the individual in question.

On this basis of discussing the (native) communicator of a language who does not communicate with (fully) consciously understanding addresses, new light is shed on Wittgenstein's notion of a private language (cf. Wittgenstein, 1958). The problem is, how can a speaker be sure that he refers to the correct experience for the addressee when referring, for instance, to his own (or to the addressee's) *pain*? Is it important that there is a strict correspondence to what he means, is the language "natively" learnable in case no such (strict) correspondence exists? Are there, in other words, (parts of) languages which can be natively learned without being understood ideally, languages which do not, in all respects serve an immediate communicative purpose?

Another aspect for which addressees seem to be relevant for **native communicators** is their continuous linguistic presence. The interaction of a **native communicator** and his addressees is a necessary condition for rehearsing his linguistic abilities as a **native communicator**. However, the positive effects of rehearsing may be cancelled out by the fact that the addressees develop another variant of their dialect/language and spoil our **native communicator** in his nativeness. Thus the question arises: what continuous changes of dialectal environments are admissible to maintain the nativeness of a speaker.

The **native communicator** and his potential addressees form what is called a **language community**. In a sense this community is a social and political artefact or at least a theoretical construct. The reason is that every human being speaks his own idiolect or even idiolect*s*.

This situation poses severe problems. (1) Why and how can people communicate who all use different languages? It seems that **communicators** overcome this difficulty with the ability of approximate understanding and by having a much better *analytic* competence than a *productive* one. This bio-socially entrenched fact renders the communicative language systems operative and open for development (mutation, selection and memorizing tradition). (2) On what basis are we licensed to use the notion of a language, if there merely exist (native) **communicators** producing different idiolects? An answer to this problem can be tried on a statistical level. Politically a solution is sometimes sought on a normative level: an "academy" or a "grammar" is said to provide the norm of how to speak (and write) correctly. (3) How is it possible to empirically justify statements about idiolects? Does not the notion of an individual, subjective and erring idiolect producer conflict with the objectivistic standard of empirical approaches? Here a longer discussion is in order (cf. v. der Geest, this volume), but it should be mentioned that empiricity is intimately linked with reproducibility. If it is guaranteed that an idiolectal speaker gives use to recurrent and contextually reproducable results, free from arbitrary and voluntary interferences, no principled objection can be raised from an empirical point of view. To meet these conditions will not be an easy matter, however. Special attention must be paid to not abusing idiolect communicators in linguistic argumentation.

On the basis of what has been said here, we may safely draw a distinction between three kinds of **native speakers** or **native communicators**, and thus extend our typology:

(11) idiolect speaker (communicator)
↓
statistical speaker (communicator)
↓
normative speaker (communicator)

The order of these three types of **natives** can be argued on the grounds of presupposition relation. Idiolect speakers are presupposed for a statistical analysis, a statistical analysis, even if informal, is presupposed for establishing a norm.[3]

A TYPOLOGY OF "NATIVE SPEAKERS"

The preceding discussions led us to question intensively and from multiple points of view the soundness of the notion of **native speaker**. Summarizing, we may say that the primary purpose of providing an empirical basis to linguistics cannot be fulfilled completely by the **native speaker**. For typical and central cases of linguistic communication the **native speaker** is good enough, however, and gives us a sound starting point.

We shall therefore summarize the various typological proposals for the **native speaker** given in this paper in a comprehensive synopsis. This synopsis serves as a classification of the notion of **native speaker** properly speaking as well as of notions in the conceptual field around the **native speaker**. The comprehensive typology is divided into the following four sub-typologies: a *phylogenetic* typology, an *ontogenetic* typology, an *individual* typology and a *metatheoretic* typology. It goes without saying that there are some

A Typology of Native Speakers

overlaps and some gaps. The typology displayed cannot be more than a first proposal for charting the pathless topic concerning the linguistic measuring device **native speaker**.

(12) *A Typology of the Native Speaker*:

(12.1) *Phylogenetic Typology* [cf. (4), (5)] [4]

native non-speakers	microbes plants animals	chemical codes anatomic codes behavioral (conditioned) codes
native speakers	higher animals (birds and mammals)	limb motion and sound codes
native language learners	apes man cultural man technical man	generative codes creative codes external trace codes dynamic machine codes

(12.2) *Ontogenetic Typology*[5] (Bio-social Typology)

Property	Role
unable to speak	infant
primary language learner	child (various phases)
secondary language learner	adolescent
average user	adult
language degeneration	old person, aphasic

(12.3) *Individual Typology* [cf. (7), (8)] [6]
(The *features* of a typical Native Language Learner NLL, arranged according to their relative importance).

1. Producer (i.e. conceptualizes and articulates expressions of a creative spoken language L)
2. Analyser (i.e. hears, understands and processes expressions of a spoken language L)
3. Learning environment with respect to L: primary socialization

4. Age: living, adult (neither child nor senile person)
5. Health: operating normally (5.1. receptors o.k.: eyes, ears, brain, 5.2. effectors o.k.: brain, tongue, mouth)
6. Intelligence: medium
7. Linguistic Failures: none (7.1. phonetical: 7.1.1. sound [no lisping], 7.1.2. rhythm [no stuttering] ; 7.2. syntactic; wellformed, wellstructured; 7.3. semantic: meaningful; 7.4. pragmatic: adequate; 7.5. textual: coherent)
8. Language Competence: monolingual
9. Linguistic Environment: native language L (this implies: birth place = place of residence of NLL, of his family = working place of NLL and his family and friends)
10. Linguistic Education: NLL ≠ writer, poet, literary critic nor linguist but normal language user.
11. Performance Abilities: quasi-perfect communicator
12. Intuition: well-working
13. Introspection: not needed
14. Argumentation Abilities: well-working
15. Theoretical Abilities: not needed

(12.4) *Methodological/Linguistic Typology* [cf. (10), (11)]

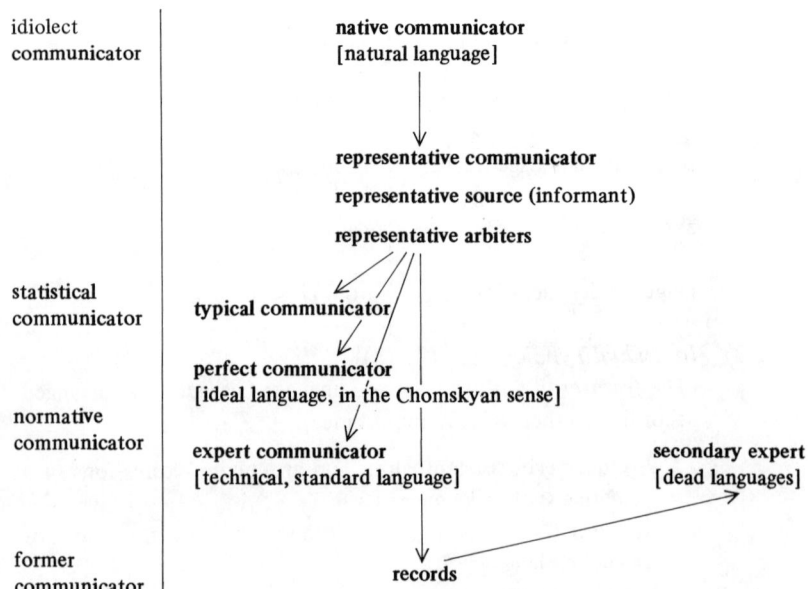

A Typology of Native Speakers 65

A final consideration got inspired by a suggestion of Florian Coulmas. Accordingly, I would like to propose a certain strategy which allows us to extend the typology of **native speakers** to a typology of **speakers (communictors)** in general. This definitely *transcends* the topic of this paper, but it shows how the analysis could be carried further. Also some light may be shed back on the types of the **native speaker**. The strategy proceeds as follows. Starting from the unordered set of English nouns designating persons, professions, characters etc., we may group those nouns together which designate people exhibiting a similar linguistic behavior. Thus we may come up with a group such as *aphasic, mute, deaf-mute*, a group like *teacher, professor, tutor, master* or another like *author, writer, belletrist, novelist* etc. After a complete listing and ordering of those nouns into groups we may arrange them into a systematic network of coherence. The result would be a *structure* exhibiting the most important **communicator** roles as expressible in *English*. In other words, those **communicator** roles are brought to prominence which the language (here English) considers most prominent by lexicalizing (I refer here to a principle which is best called *Principle of Relevance*, which says, roughly, that a language considers those matters to be relevant which are expressed in a succinct conventional way, e.g. by lexical items or even morphologically). A very tentative classification based on this *lexical analysis* would look as follows. It can be taken to be an extension of the ontogenetic typology (12.2) of the **native speaker**. In the sequence of infant (unable to speak), child, adolescent (language learners), adult (averagely able) we may insert **temporary** and **professional communicators**: (12.2'). This sequence is completed by those unable to speak through injury, illness, i.e., language degeneration: *aphasic, mute, deaf-mute, stutterer, lisper, old persons.*

See example (12.2') overleaf:

(12.2′)

temporary and **professional communicators**

	producers	non-producer	reproducers	receptors	judges	investigators
oral communication (general)	speaker sayer utterer talker chatterer	mime mimic	spokesman broadcaster mouthpiece actor tragedian/ienne comedian/ienne narrator	hearer listener addressee audience	critic reviewer commentator censurer censor surveyor referee assessor (satirist)	philologist linguist psycholinguist sociolinguist glottologist lexicographer etymologist grammarian semasiologist onomasiologist
task-oriented oral communication (professional)	preacher teacher master tutor professor instructor lecturer	manager commander guide seller	follower disciple convert	novice schoolboy schoolgirl pupil learner student		
written communication (general)	author writer		translator interpreter paraphrast exegete expositor copyist transcriber calligrapher	reader bookworm bibliophile bibliomaniac		
task-oriented written communication (professional)	poet versemaker belletrist novelist reporter journalist pressman columnist	essayist literary man dramatist biographer historian	editor editorialist			

A Typology of Native Speakers

NOTES

1. Bold face expressions in this article refer to notions of systematic character in linguistics. Thus the informal notion of *native speaker* is to be lifted, by a series of explications, onto a level of systematic relevancy, giving rise to the notions of **native speaker**.
2. I call creative codes here semantically and pragmatically interpreted (generative) symbol systems which exhibit at least mechanisms of context change, i.e., of memory, i.e., local history. This is a precondition of phylogenetic as well as ontogenetic creative development.
3. For a more thorough discussion of the methodological issues on the notion of ideolect speaker cf. especially Botha (1973) and van der Geest (1980).
4. Köhler (1917) provides enough evidence for generative conceptual capacities of apes. Modern research in teaching linguistic abilities to apes suggests simple generative capacities also on the communicative level.
5. Eventually an ontogenetic typology of this sort should include much more detailed information. Psychological and psycholinguistic research is needed along the lines initiated by Piaget/Inhelder 1972.
6. The features presented here for the typical (or prototypical) "native speaker," or in short prototype "native-speaker" are seen to provide a frame for classifying the less typical forms of communicators. The procedure to arrive at less and less natural communicators is simply to negate an increasing number of features or features of increasing importance.

REFERENCES

Botha, R.P. (1973). *The Justification of Linguistic Hypotheses*. The Hague: Mouton.
Chomsky, N. (1965). *Aspects of the Theory of Syntax*. Cambridge (Mass.): MIT Press.
Delany, S. (1966). *Babel-17*. London: Sphere Books, [1969].
van der Geest, T. (1980). "How to Become a Native Speaker." In this volume pp. 317–353.
Köhler, W. (1917). Intelligenzprüfungen an Menschenaffen. Heidelberg: Springer, [1973].
Monod, J. (1971). *Zufall und Notwendigkeit*. München und Zürich: Piper.
Piaget, J. and Inhelder, B. (1972). *Die Psychologie des Kindes*. Freiburg.
Wittgenstein, L. (1958). *Philosophische Untersuchungen*. Frankfurt: Suhrkamp, [1971].

JACOB MEY

"Right or Wrong, My Native Speaker" Estant les Régestes du Noble Souverain de l'Empirie Linguistic avec un Renvoy au Mesme Roy

ABSTRACT

Native Speakers, like royalty, are much too much made of. It is my thesis in the present paper that we should demystify the concept of Native Speaker, and stop paying him (!) the obeisances that earlier linguists thought indispensable.
Native Speakers, like other mishaps, seldom come alone. There will always be a Native Speaker that can be used to fill one's hollow facts and to plug a trivial rule gap. Far from reigning in sovereignty, Native Speaker is thus a sad and sorry figure: royalty without a realm, a relative ruler without roots in reality. We may even say that Native Speaker looks a distant relative of that other infamous linguistic refugee: Chomsky's Ideal Speaker/Hearer.
But more importantly, I argue that we do the *real* speakers and hearers of languages injustice by focusing on the Native Speaker in his splendid isolation. The need for a realistic appraisal of the Native Speaker concept includes, and must result in, a growing concern for the needs of the true native speakers: the users of language.

TROUBLE WITH KINGS

Royal Blood is a nuisance, both for its unfortunate carrier and for the subjects who have to put up with the exorbitant demands for loyalty that seem to be the hallmark of royalty. Such has been the situation for hundreds of years. With the advent of parliamentary democracy, things seemed to get a little better. The sovereign was declared untouchable (which he always had been, though in a different sense). Or, as the political philosophers put it: "The King can do no wrong." This seemingly innocent and obsequious formula meant in reality the end of royal powers. For whoever can do no wrong, pretty soon can't do anything at all. Royalty was deprived of its power, which of course had been the idea all along.
Native Speaker in the structural linguistic tradition is a King. By linguistic legislation (however implicit), he cannot do any wrong. He is the ultimate authority in linguistic matters: "The Native Speaker is always right." The

structural linguists (such as Pike 1947, or Nida 1949) held this truth to be self-evident. Native Speaker is the final criterion of matters linguistic: his verdict settles all linguistic disputes, be they about sentences, linguistic postulates, innate ideas, or what have you. Like the Kings of Old, Native Speaker can do no wrong. He is above all laws: he is the Law himself, the Rule of the realm, the referee of the linguistic ballpark. (Later on I'll say a few words on why Native Speaker is preferably a King, not a Queen).

However, as soon as we start scratching the glamorous surface, all sorts of things seem to be wrong. First of all, where does King Speaker, First and Last, come from? What is his lineage and descent? Being native, he must be born. But nobody is born a speaker: even linguists have sometimes recognized this. As such, Native Speaker is a figment of our imagination. Cf. the following quote from a paper by Steven Davis (1979): "Children are not born knowing how to speak any language, but given the proper exposure to a language at the appropriate age, they rapidly become *native speakers* [my italics] of that language." Or, with an old adage: "*Poeta nascitur*, Native Speaker *fit*." But not only is Native Speaker's birth legendary, and his birth rights fictive: King Native Speaker's power is exercised in strict accordance with the directives of his ministers, the wily, seemingly subservient linguists, who in reality wield almost Machiavellian powers. The King of the Game is subject to the Magister Ludi.

As a result, the King's identity is but an image in a mirror that the linguists hold up to themselves. Having seen his image, the King turns around and leaves, "and forgetteth what he hath seen" (cf. St. James 1:23-24), and no wonder: the image is not his own, but the linguist's. Thus, Native Speaker has been effectively dethroned by that great Egalizer of linguistics: the introspective linguist, whose "fiery face struck the speaker dumb," as popular tradition has it about another Egalizer.[1] In the final verdict, it's the linguist's own idiolect that carries the day: "Right or wrong, *my* native speaker."

NATIVE SPEAKER'S AVATARS

Despite his seemingly lofty and ethereal status, Native Speaker in fact possesses a host of quite well-defined attributes. He is a person of many faces, none of which are his own. It may be useful to list a few of these characteristic traits. Native Speaker is, among other things:
adult (or nearly so);
male (as a rule, but of course depending upon availability);
educated (at least he should know his language, even if it "only" is a dialect);
competent in linguistic matters (the "ideal informant" even anticipates the linguist's wants);

more or less sophisticated (although, of course, the glory of science remains with the linguist).

And so on.

We see that King Native Speaker looks quite familiar: he is a product of middle class culture, a true *Roi Bourgeois,* as the attributes quoted above testify. Nevertheless, identifying Native Speaker may be a harder task than expected. If we look more closely into the different features that characterize him, there seems to be no end to the ways we can have it with this Burger King. Depending on our bias, he may appear in other avatars, too, many of which seem contradictory and/or at variance with the features cited above. Let me quote a few of these, just to give you an impression.

At times, Native Speaker may appear on the scene as either a gourmet, a car buff, an imperalist warmonger, a peace freak, a women's libber (yes, indeed!), a specialist on strategic weaponry, a musicologist, a businessman, a bloodthirsty duckling-and-hippie-killing farmer, a gay, or even a simple college freshman.

Native Speaker is, furthermore, known to deliver high-grade verbiage of the absolutely vacuous kind, to have been the repetitious and boring producer of mindless old utterances of the type "John kissed Mary" (that is, if he didn't hit or kill her first). As far as Native Speaker's utterances are concerned, they have occasionally been decorated by a question mark, an asterisk or even a *Mogen David,* depending on whether his speech was characterized as doubtful, ungrammatical, or maybe even Jewish, God forbid.

If establishing Native Speaker's identity thus seems to be a pretty hopeless task, things get even worse if we try to pin down his functions in the community-at-large. Is he solely a decorative figurehead, like his royal prototype? Since his functions are so hard to define, what's wrong with them? What's wrong with Native Speaker, when he seemed to be so right? Native Speaker's problem is that, despite his multifaceted appearances, there is nothing that he *really* can do. Specifically, he cannot help us to solve any *linguistic* problems that we may have; and how could it be otherwise, for wasn't he essentially a Dumb Monarch? Besides, he has only as much power as the linguist assigns to him, which surely can't be a whole lot, or his help wouldn't be needed at all. Consider again quarrels of the my/your idiolect type. Can we solve any real problems this way? Does appealing to our own intuitions even (embodied in a Mythical Arbiter) help us settle any disputes? Clearly, the answer is 'No.' Invoking Native Speaker's authority does nothing more for us than internalize our linguistic problems, or assign them to the areas of liminality and undecidability, where Native Speakers of all ages and times move around like shadowless, imageless spectres. Wouldn't it then be better to leave them alone, like Mavilis' dead, walking on the asphodils of their pasts, trying not to remember their lives' and languages' bitterness, rather than stirring up the clear waters of their oblivion? What can a linguist offer these linguistic undeads? And what would be a correct way to commemorate their shadowy existence? How to honor them in a *Festschrift*? Why not rather weep those among ourselves, who perchance want to be silent, but have to speak? (Cf. Lorentzos Mavilis, *Lithi*).

THE IMPORTANCE OF GOING NATIVE, OR: TAKING NATIVE SPEAKER SERIOUSLY

It seems to me that what Native Speaker needs, is not more linguists hanging around him in order to make him more so called "correct sentences," or to pass judgment on the ones he already has uttered. Rather, we should take Native Speaker seriously. But how?

Suppose that we really want to take Native Speaker seriously. The first problem is then, to find him. But what does "native" *really* mean? Does it have anything to do with "being born"? Then the newborn child would be a native speaker *par excellence* ("Out of the mouth of babes . . . "). The problems of nativeness will be considered presently. Let's for the moment consider the possible adult varieties of native speech. Clearly, to have a native speaker with the Protean qualities that I enumerated above would be tantamount to give up the whole idea of a real Native Speaker. We might as well pronounce the Native King of Speech dead on arrival.

What is involved in finding a "real" native? There is a serious ethical problem here, that linguists (like other workers in the socalled humanities) until recently have not come to grips with. In old days, "native" territories were considered as natural hunting grounds for missionaries, colonialists, and scientists. The latter called the natives "informants," but they were hunting game all the same. Now, if you look in the textbooks of linguistics or anthropology, or in the various "structural sketches" of "exotic languages" that linguists and missionaries have produced over the past hundred years, there is one essential quality that constitutes the real Native Speaker's most valuable asset: he can speak the language, or as linguists say, "produce utterances." Such utterances are usually taken rather undiscriminatingly as "material," or data, for a linguistic or other analysis (remember the old saying: "all's grist to the linguist's mill"). However, we should never forget that the "utterances" in question are the expressions of some real persons' very real needs and wants, and not just something that Native Speakers naturally happen to do.

As an instance, consider the speaker as a child, the young Native Speaker. Much (or even most) of children's linguistic activity happens on the adults' premises, but without the competence and ability that are characteristic of adult language use. To use children's speech in a mere descriptive fashion (as

Right or wrong, my native speaker 73

many linguists have done, especially with their own children) is a classical case of linguistic exploitation. It deserves this name in the same way and for the same reasons that, for example, anthropological research that only aims at providing young anthropologists with the necessary Ph.D's can be characterized as oppressive and exploitative: it purports to serve Science, but serves the Scientist. As far as the Object of Science (the "informant," our Native Speaker) is concerned, his or her task is finished when the thesis is out, and apart from a line or two in the preface to the finished work, there is nothing in it for them.

As a possible illustration of an alternative approach to this problem consider again the oppressed young Native Speaker. In his or her situation, what is most important is to get a good grasp of the language in order to be able to use it (not only, but perhaps mainly) defensively. What children need is to learn to use their language so as to be able to avoid adult exploitation, linguistic or otherwise. For the adults this means to respect "their" Native Speakers: "teach your children well" (Crosby, Stills, Nash and Young).

WILL THE REAL NATIVE SPEAKER PLEASE STAND UP?

It will by now be abundantly clear, that our first impression of Native Speaker as the uncrowned King of linguistics by no means covers the true situation. Far from being an independent Sovereign, he seems to be the tributary of the Powers that Be in linguistics. Rather than a real entity, he is a shadow, not even of himself, but of the real ruler: the linguist. When Native Speaker utters, we hear His Master's Voice. This brings us to another point. I promised above to explain why I characterized our Native Speaker tentatively as a King, not a Queen, and why all references to him were unigender only. Let me give you, by way of illustration and argumentation, what we used to call a corpus of data. (Source: Bloomfield 1933: 158ff.)

John ran. John fell. John! Bill ran. Dan fell. Johnny, Billy, Danny. Poor John ran away. John hit Bill. Bill hit John. Away ran John. John? John. Boy! Mr. Smith! Watch John. The boys. The boys ran. The boys went home. John runs fast. The boys run fast. Latin *pater filium amat* 'the father loves the son'. Latin *filius patrem amat* 'the son loves the father'. *The boys are here. John is. Did John run? Will John? John's here. A policeman. The man I saw yesterday.*

So much for the examples in chapter 10, "Grammatical Forms," of Bloomfield's classical work *Language*. (I have only counted one instance of each example: the actual rate of occurrence is much higher.) Against this overwhelming masculinity, female examples are in the minority of three: and they all refer to the same case, derivation by suffix from a masculine word (type:

duke:duchess, prince:princess). So, if females are allowed into the linguistic realm at all, it's by derivation only: Adam's rib all the way up! One might, of course, object that this is all old stuff, and of course Bloomfield was an MCP, but so was everybody (!) at the time. Well, in case you think so, let me tell you about some observations that the women's group made at the recent Nordic Research Seminar on Psycholinguistics (Wullsjö, Sweden, August 1979). They found the same pattern in the reference pronouns that is displayed above: when in doubt, choose *he*, and even in cases where a *she* or *her* would be appropriate grammatically, a *he* or *him* creeps in unobtrusively. To even begin to speak of equal rights in grammatical reference still seems to be a far cry from reality (see the recent report in the *Journal of Pragmatics* by Heinämaki and Skutnabb-Kangas 1979)).

So our Burger King wasn't a King — and now she isn't even a Queen! Ground meat or chopped fish: the profits drop into the same box, while we try to stomach the results. But why is this so? Well, the "King" turned out to be his Master's shadow, his mirror image, as you remember. No wonder then, that the Native Speaker of the linguistic world is a *he*. Until there is equal opportunity and equal employment in real life, there will be no equality in the examples that (we let) Native Speakers utter. (I am discounting the "fad" effect here, for the same reason that I questioned the use of politically "in" examples elsewhere (see Haberland and Mey 1977: 7).

Who, then, is the "real" Native Speaker? Historically, the notion of the "real" as the uncontaminated, natural, ideal, original is a product of 19th century Romanticism. While Man Friday had no intelligible language, Paul and Virginie were very eloquent indeed. The scientific interest for strange and incomprehensible tongues is, however, not only a side-effect of literature: to believe so, would commit us to the worst kind of idealism. Romantic literature, as so many times before in the history of letters, serves as a compensation: while the lower classes are out there somehow killing the Indians, the Negroes, the gooks (or whatever the natives are called), the folks at home can indulge in all sorts of innocent idolizing of the mysterious, inscrutable, exciting, and thrilling life styles of the black, brown, yellow or red nations. This helps, too, to overcome the paradox that the "natives" at the same time were White Man(!)'s greatest obstacle to progress, *and* his only means to reap overseas or domestic profits by way of cheap labor.

What the Noble Savage was for Mr. Average Businessman (!), Native Speaker thus became for the linguist. Not coincidentally, the first scientific interest in American Indian languages was a by-product, so to speak, of the research work of a physicist, Franz Boas, who became North American Native Speaker's first·scientific defender, to be followed by people like E. Sapir and a host of other American and European linguists. (On this development, see the interesting observations by Haberland 1977: 56). But while the scientific

Right or wrong, my native speaker

interest in the Noble Savage, Native Speaker, certainly has helped linguists and anthropologists to long years of relative prosperity, there have been little or no beneficial side-effects for the native speakers themselves. With the demise (physical or otherwise) of the Noble Savage, the inevitable question comes up: What with Native Speaker?

NATURALLY SOCIALIZED, NATIVELY SPEAKING

So our King slept with his fathers: long live the Real Native Speaker!

There is an inherent contradiction in the terms *native* and *speaker*, as I have drawn your attention to above (in the third section). That opposition can be made more explicit by asking what is the *underlying* contrast between the terms, for which I have chosen the terms "natural" and "social". These concepts are often seen as contradicting each other. Naturalness is the opposite of convention, whereas convention is for many people what constitutes our life in society (at least on the surface). Society is thought of as imposing its laws and rules on us; in doing so it restricts our "natural" anarchistic tendencies. (The Greeks had words for this opposition: *phúsei* was what came by nature, *thései* what was arranged for by social settings).

Clearly, such an understanding of the terms "natural" and "social" must lead to an unredeemable opposition between the two. In the human sphere at least, it's not *just* Nature or *only* Society; most of the time humans are in arms against Nature just as much as they're in rebellion against Society. Which proves that humans are not natural; but then they're not exclusively social either (small surprise, indeed). Clearly, we need a more sophisticated approach to the relationship between the natural and the social, which will then be applied to our special case: the Naturally Social Speaker.

For humans, it's natural to be social. Their nature is society. Socialization is a necessary condition, even for the most solitary recluse. To put it a little paradoxically: it's more natural to be social than it's social to be natural. Now what has this to do with our Native Speaker?

As we have seen above (third section), there is nothing "born" about speakers' ability to speak. If anything, the physical event of birth is important only because it marks the beginning of a possible socialization. Socialization, however, is not an abstract event. It is a process that takes place in a concrete society. Although all humans are born to be socialized (or maybe better: to realize their social potential), there is a great difference between a working class child's and a middle class child's possibilities for socialization. Or between adults' and children's. Or between "primitive" peoples' and highly civilized and prosperous nations'. And so on.

Native Speaker becomes natural through the socialization process of his or her concrete society. This means that there are at least as many different Native Speakers. *Native Speaker*, rather than reflecting the linguist's biases, should be viewed as a reflection of the society he or she lives and has grown up in.

WHOSE NATIVE SPEAKER?

Even Hovdhaugen (1977) has remarked that the whole idea of Native Speaker being always right is questionable, as long as it's the linguists who determine to what extent the maxim is valid. Native Speaker's righteousness reflects, in many cases, a self-righteousness on the part of the linguist: "What do you mean, are you questioning my data?" One forgets that it's after all the linguist who decides what's going to happen to those data, and to what use they will be put.

I would like to bring out the extent of the linguists' muddling by asking: Whose is Native Speaker, when the chips are down? As I said in the previous section, Native Speaker is not his own Man, her own Woman, but Society's. Moreover, society is not by any means a homogeneous collection of identical individuals using the same language in identical ways. There are at least as many different kinds of native speakers as there are divisions in society. To pretend that all "men" are born equal and that this moreover is a truth which is "self-evident" (!), is just as false as assuming that all natives speak equal. The question "Whose Native Speaker?" reduces thus to the question: What class of society does Native Speaker belong to? The problems of class language (and of social dialectology as a whole) are far too complicated to deal with in the scope of this contribution. Let me refer the readers to what I have written on this subject elsewhere (Mey 1978, 1979, and 1980 (forthc.)) Rather, I will discuss another aspect of Native Speaker's alleged perfect linguistic competence by pursuing Hovdhaugens question: What *do* we allow Native Speaker to say?

My thesis is, that Native Speaker is subject to heavy censorship from the linguist's side, because, as a speaker of the language, he or she should come as close to the ideal picture of the language-user that linguists have in their heads to begin with.

This gives us one dimension of restrictions. But it's by far the least interesting one.

If we focus on the domains of linguistics (classically divided into phonology, morphology, syntax, semantics, and pragmatics), we see that Native Speaker's importance decreases as we proceed up the linguistic "hierarchy". While Native Speaker's judgment is absolutely to be relied upon in matters of phonetics, phonology, and morphology (even if he or she speaks some

Right or wrong, my native speaker 77

obscure dialect), when we get to syntax, matters become less clear. Are judgments of syntactic regularity on the part of native speakers always to be trusted? The linguist's intuition about possible constructions in other languages than his/her own may be misleading: but neither do native speakers always agree. Constructions that to one native speaker are perfectly acceptable, may seem wrong, or at least unfamiliar, to another. And when it gets to semantics, there seems to be no reason to rely on the native speaker's intuitions more than on those of somebody, who, although not a native born speaker, has acquired a reasonable mastery of the language. Actually, this "non-native" speaker may produce semantic (and sometimes even syntactic) construction, that strike one as particularly appropriate to describe a situation or characterize an object, yet are unfamiliar to a native speaker.

In this connection, there are two points I'd like to make. First, although we officially (and as linguists) subscribe to the principle of the native speakers' first-born rights, most people will be willing to tolerate deviance more readily in the realm of morphology than phonetics, of syntax than of morphology, of semantics than of syntax, and so on. The reason is that a semantical deviance can be due to many factors, among other things the wish of the (non-native) speaker to express him/herself in a deviant way; whereas in phonology, for example, a deviance will usually be considered a *non possumus*. Actually, the same holds for natives: errors of pronounciation (for example of the kind that gives one away as low-status speaker) are not voluntarily made, but rather avoided, sometimes at great cost. The poet, however, is free to play with the language and create neologisms to capture a poetic idea. As an example, consider the well-known and often quoted *a grief ago* (Dylan Thomas); or take the prose of such non-natives as Igor Stravinsky, or Vladimir Nobokov, or even Roman Jakobson. These authors, although certainly not native users of English, and clearly distinguished from natives with respect to speech, are nevertheless universally accepted and acclaimed for their contributions to their adopted languages and literatures. Or, to take another example, is a third generation New York born American of Ukrainian Jewish descent, whose speech still is very characteristic of his ethnic background, acceptable as a Native Speaker? The answer is: Yes, provided he or she satisfies certain conditions. Which brings me to my second point.

I want to suggest the following hypotheses about Native Speaker's "nativeness": Not only is being a Native Speaker, and being accepted as such, a property that has to be differentiated along *linguistic* dimensions, but also, and more importantly, nativeness is not autonomous in itself, but is related to social origin and class. Notice that this time I am not focusing so much on the speech itself (or on language use), as on the acceptance or non-acceptance of speakers by the speech community. The relations between speech itself and social class, with all their consequences, will not be discussed here. What

Figure 1   The importance of being a Native Speaker or: Speech's Labour Lost.

My thanks to Henrik Otterstrøm, Birkerød, Denmark and to the editors of *Solidaritet* for their permission to reprint the above drawing.

Right or wrong, my native speaker

Translation of text in Figure 1:

(At the Employment Office):
"Sorry, but we can't give you a job before you have learnt Danish"
(So she starts learning . . .)

(Language Learning Situation)
Scraps and bits of Danish conversation of the type
"John and Mary look at a hat"
plus Danish "tongue-breakers"

(At the Factory)
(She has landed a job)
(Different kinds of Mechanical and Human Noise, type Kerdunk, Plunk, Clank, Whizz plus the exclamatory force of the foreman's speech acts!!!)

(Source: *Solidaritet* nr. 4. Sept., 1979)

I'm talking about is something different: what kind of tolerance do people have towards non-native forms of speech?

Using an Orwellian slogan, one would say that maybe all speakers of a language are native, but some are more native than others. Or, conversely, all foreign users of a language are non-native speakers, but some are decidedly less native than others.

Let me take an example. According to the Danish newspaper *Land og Folk* (11th August 1979), Turkish woman workers in Denmark were going to have to prove sufficient command of Danish in order to receive unemployment benefits. The somewhat specious reasoning behind this was something like the following: if you don't speak the language well enough, then you can't be said to be really looking for a job, or to "be available to the labor market," as the official expression has it.

There is, of course, no doubt that insufficient command of the language of the host country can be a serious obstacle to finding and holding down a job. What I want to stress here, however, is that this principle is applied very selectively. At the bottom of the ladder are the unskilled workers, whose labor is dispensable in times of economic crises. At the other end of the hierarchy one has super-qualified personnel, who in many cases don't even have to bother to acquire the host country's idiom. Especially in cases where these officials represent the foreign capital interests that have the real say in matters pertaining to the Danish economy, the demands for (native) command of the host language are replaced by an almost servile attitude towards the foreign speaker. His or her language becomes the preferred idiom even in cases where the native born Danes would handle themselves and their affairs far better if they insisted on using their native languages, and either leave the translating to an interpreter, or force the non-native to "go native"! But even "going native" is a flexible concept. The visiting head of state has only to utter a few phrases in the applicable native tongue, and is immediately showered with compliments. Underpaid female workers cannot even retain their lousy jobs if they can't pass a language test. We don't tolerate a foreign accent in a Pakistani guest worker, but whoever thought of firing Henry Kissinger, for his heavily German-influenced brand of American English? The late King of Norway, Haakon VII, spoke "King's Danish" until the day of his death. And the president of Unilver's Danish daughter company, Dansk Unilever A/S, is a Norwegian, but who cares about Reidar Due in police circles?

It's all the more strange that native language skills should become a matter of survival precisely there where they, after all, are least important. Think, for example, of the small amount of speech interaction that is factually possible in most of the work situations where such labor is employed (the assembly line, to take a particularly striking example, (see Fig. 1)). Which would indicate that there is no direct correlation between the "use" and the "usefulness" of language. Non-native use or even no use at all of the host language is tolerable only in those cases, where the user has high social status, irrespective of the factual conditions of language use: the latter can and will always be accommodated to suit the persons with power in society. Thus our conclusion is that the degree of nativeness of a speaker is to a great extent a function of his or her social status, more precisely of the power that derives from her or his social class.

To mess up my original image, we have now not only divested Native Speaker of his regalia and blown the whistle on his scientific pretentions; we have in fact reduced him to a bare skeleton.

The following sections can serve as an epitaph on his sorrowful demise.

SO WHAT?

So Native Speaker is caught with his pants down. Whose is the shame and where do we go from here?

First of all, we have to remember that naked facts and Naked Subjects tend to go together. The protagonist of Science who proclaims that his quest is for facts, naked facts, and nothing but the facts, is to blame for the embarrassment that Native Speaker, much against his or her will, has been exposed to. The blame for Native Speaker's sorry plight has to be laid at the linguist's door who has proclaimed a unilateral interest in "pure research" and "just the facts." For what does a "naked fact" in "pure science" really stand for?

Science is the study of intelligible relations within a particular field of knowledge. However, fields *as such* are mere abstractions, in particular in the humanities. To study a field of human activity such as language use without taking the user into account is indeed tantamount, not only to removing all the speaker's clothes, but to dress him down to the bare bones. The Naked Subject, the Nude Skeleton of Linguistics has replaced the Native Speaker. And the linguists themselves suffer from what C. Wright Mills has called a "methodological inhibition:" which means that you cannot see social facts and their relations because of the way you go about finding and stating those facts, i.e., because of your sociological method. (Some would call it a bias rather than a method). When Method (or "Grand Theory", as Wright Mills calls it elsewhere) starts to determine what facts you can find and what facts you have to "keep out" of your scientific eyesight, then truly we have to do with a case of the tail wagging the dog, the tool killing the worker (Wright Mills 1973:57; cf. also Mey 1979:13).

Thus the idea of the Native Speaker as commonly established in much of contemporary linguistics has as its necessary methodological correlate the specialist doing the kind of "pure research" that I referred to above, rather than "establishing an intelligible field of study" (Wright Mills 1973:57). Native Speaker, in his dressed-down appearance, is very much different from the Noble Savage he historically relates to. However, the blame is not his: Native Speaker as the Naked Subject is a true offspring of the primitive psychologism that is characteristic for Native Science. (Remember that *naive* and *native*, despite their etymological identity, denote quite different qualities).

But back to the first question: What happens next? Do we, does Native Speaker, have anywhere to go to hide our/her/his nakedness?

RIGHT OR WRONG, WHOSE NATIVE SPEAKER?

So far, this article has depicted all the things that are wrong with Native Speaker. Isn't it about time that we find something nice to say? What's right with Native Speaker, or better, how can we make it right with him/her?

First of all, we have to do something about Native Speaker's identity. To call in a notion such as "androgynous" in order to cover the discriminatory distinction of the sexes in linguistics presents certain drawbacks. Rekdal & Skutnabb-Kangas (1977), who introduced the term in linguistics, intended it to be a cover concept ("either-or/both-and"). However, the very use of a unitary term in the case of discrimination by distinction ("he" for "(he and/or) she"), may give us the illusion of an identity that is just as false as the discriminatory distinction that the authors seek to avoid. Native

Speaker is not a "both-and" being, something which is easily implied by the use of a term such as "androgynous": Native Speaker should be a "he" or a "she," but is mostly a "he," also in real life. Now I'm not saying that the authors meant this when they suggested the term; but only that their use of a "uni-term" description may lead us into errors of the same kind that they explicitly denounce. Where things are lawless or undefined, the stronger definition carries the day, and the law is in the hands of the gunmen. (!)

Second, to defend Native Speaker against the linguistic usurpation and exploitation described above, we would create a positive climate where the term may be used without all the drawbacks and negative connotations that we have discussed above. How to do this?

It should be made clear from the beginning that Native Speaker comes in two sexes, different ages, and conflicting social classes. Native Speaker should be treated as a human, not as a figment of some linguist's imagination. With regard to sex, I have already stated what I consider are the dangers involved in the use of uni-terms. Similarly, with regard to age and class, we should ask ourselves where we are at ourselves, and why we would like Native Speaker to look like one of us, rather than like one of the "others." Do equal rights for all speakers mean less privileges for us? Does acceptance of varying speech norms threaten our own linguistic security? Would we like everybody to speak like the "better classes" (in the same vein that school children in Denmark are taught what their teachers think is "Oxford English" – i.e., ideally whatever is defined as "the speech of educated classes in Southern England," or the upper class "received" speech of the public schools). Why shouldn't we rather concretize our Native Speaker image as one of a person in need of linguistic assistance, somebody who might profit from contact with linguists, rather than one whose linguistic competence (for whatever it's worth) may be converted to the cash values of linguists' scientific production and professional prestige? There's a lot that's *really* wrong with native speakers (and non-native as well) in many countries of the world. Linguists could make a contribution towards the betterment of these wrongs if they stopped quarreling about whose native speaker is right. Rather, let's think about the things that are really wrong with Native Speaker, and try to make them right for him and her. We could, for instance, replace the completely academic concept of "correctness of utterances" by the pragmatic one of "knowing one's way around in one's language," i.e., understanding the conditions and limitations of one's own and others' linguistic competence in producing and understanding language. Let's get rid of royalty and come down to reality. Kick out the decrepit Burger King from Native Speaker country, and let the speaking workers of all nations unite!

RENVOY AU ROY

Right on then, linguists
Let's follow our King
T. Native Speaker
Fortune will bring

Science's for ever
Linguistics is good
But whose are your data
Whose is the food?

N. Speaker, you're human
Famish you can
Slave in society
Woman or man

Linguists have always
Clung to your tracks
It's about time we
got down to the facts

How many ways of
Saying the same
Correctness was never
The name of the game

Speak to be spoken
Hear to be heard
Where speakers gather
Society's third

Right on then, linguists
Get this fact clear:
Our Native Speaker
No longer is here

All Native Speakers
All the King's men (!)
Cannot put the linguists
Back in Paradise again.

NOTE

1. The allusion is to the popular ballad about Oliver Cromwell, who egalized away another dumb king. (see Trevelyan 1964: 429).

REFERENCES

Bloomfield, L. (1933). *Language*. New York, NY: Holt, Rinehart & Winston.
Crosby, D. et al. (1972). 'Teach your children well.' *Four Way Street*. Atlantic 60003 (MC).
Davis, S.: 1979. 'Speech Acts, Competence, and Performance.' *Journal of Pragmatics* 3(5).
Haberland, H. (1977). 'Defizit und Differenz als linguistische und soziale Kategorien.' *Linguistische Berichte* 49:54-62.
Haberland, H. & J. Mey (1977). 'Linguistics and Pragmatics.' *Journal of Pragmatics* 1: 1-12.
Heinämäki, O. & T. Skutnabb-Kangas (1979). 'Sex roles in scientific discourse.' *Journal of Pragmatics* 3(6).
Hovdhaugen, E. (1977). 'Om det a være lingvist.' In Rekdal, O. & T. Skutnabb-Kangas, eds.
Mey, J. (1978). 'Marxism and Linguistics.' *Journal of Pragmatics* 2: 81-93.
Mey, J. (1979). 'Introduction.' In Mey, J., ed., 1979.
Mey, J. ed., (1979). *Pragmalinguistics: Theory and Practice*. The Hague: Mouton Publishers. (Janua Linguarum, Series Maior 85 – volume 1 in the Rasmus Rask Studies in Pragmatic Linguistics).
Mey, J. (1980). (forthc.) *Whose Language?* The Hague: Mouton (in preparation).
Nida, E. (1949). *Morphology*. Ann Arbor, MI: University of Michigan Press.
Pike, K. (1947). *Phonemics: A Technique of Reducing Languages to Writing*. Ann Arbor, MI: University of Michigan Press.
Rekdal, O. & T. Skutnabb-Kangas (1977). 'Om androgyn (bade-och/varken-eller) lingvistikk.' In Rekdal, O. & T. Skutnabb-Kangas, eds., 1977.
Rekdal, O. & T. Skutnabb-Kangas, eds., (1977). *Vardagsskrift til Jan och Jens*. Uppsala. (Box 513, S-751 20).
Trevelyan, G. M. (1964). *History of England*. London: Longman.
Wright Mills, C. (1973). *The Sociological Imagination*. Oxford: Oxford University Press. [1959]

KENNETH L. PIKE

Wherein Lies 'Talked-About' Reality?

ABSTRACT

From ancient times philosophers and scientists have wondered about the relation of unity, identity, change, and reality. From Heraclitus to Einstein and Polanyi the problem recurs. In this paper, we give our suggested "tagmemic" answer to it: Man cannot know the 'thing-in-itself'; No data known to us are observer-neutral. The native speaker adds his emic component as he organizes by self and society, his universe of discourse. The linguist is just a native speaker in a different universe of discourse. Purpose is part of what exists and has to be retrieved from native speaker (including linguist) by his speaking and acting. For this reason, I have felt more akin to the modern physicist than to the recently popular logical linguist.

In my view, reality-as-knowable-by-man lies not in abstraction-from-man but in person-in-relation-to-item. Man cannot know a certain thing without having some kind of relation, direct or indirect, to that thing. If he has interest in it sufficient to lead him to talk about it, and if he has (or can obtain) information about it, or experience with it, sufficient to allow him to talk about it, some relationship with that item has been established before – or while – he talks about it. That relationship either affects or becomes a component of that ability-knowledge. The precise amount of information prerequisite to such talk by a person about an item is not under discussion here. He may begin in a minimal way, with no more than a name for it, or an unlabelled allusion to it obtained from someone else.

This view denies that a theistic scholar can know or talk about the 'thing-in-itself' apart from some relation to man or to God, but does not deny that things exist within such a relationship. And the materialistic scholar with a prior commitment to a nontheistic view of the universe can believe (relative to that prior commitment) in the presence of items or situations unknown to any man – whether now in a remote desert, or earlier before man was evolved by principles inherent in nonconscious energy. Both the theist and the nontheist hold to some kind of unexplainable beginning of our currently observable world. Although I hold a theistic view, it does not, so far as I know, affect those phases of the empirical argument under discussion here.

But I urge, further, that any naïve 'native speaker' is as much a person who is an *observer* of items, and a *talker-about* items, as the scholar. To treat the native speaker as *merely* an object, merely something not affecting the reported data of which-he-is-a-part is to miss a component of reality at its heart, i.e. — for the rest of this paper — as knowable by man. The data observed and reported *about* the action of the native speaker, or reported about the *reports* from a native speaker about his actions, are deeply affected and related to the nature, experiences, purposes, and beliefs of that speaker. That is, no data known are observer-neutral, And — I maintain here — to pretend that one can abstract one's report away from such observer-relation is to distort reality as it can be (and must be) known by a scholar, or talked about by him. Abstraction totally away from all observers (including the native speaker and including actions of inference or imagination by them) and claiming for that abstraction an ultimate reality would be a distortion of the reality of person-in-relation-to-item being implicitly studied (even when denied) by an analyst.

The analyst, however, is himself also a person (I am glad to affirm about myself and colleagues who may disagree with me!) and, therefore, also affects the data which he is talking about. He in part structures the data as he selects or organizes perceived, or deduced, or imagined features of it. The analyst is, in fact, a native speaker. (Has he by chance managed to cease to be one in his own eyes, in many activities?) He has in an exaggerated form some of the characteristics of the nonscholar; but he has no potential or action, in principle, whose type is not found in the bush (though his testing procedures may be refined, his hypotheses more explicit at times, and his postulates more coherent on the lower levels of his hierarchy of beliefs). As native speakers, academic or otherwise, we may any of us choose to talk about abstraction. This, I thoroughly approve of, provided we find it interesting or useful for our own observer-determined purposes, and provided that we treat such abstractions as useful constructs without claiming for them (or for rules or features, or taxonomies) the nature of ultimate reality denuded of all personal observer component, like the smile of the Cheshire cat.

There are several approaches through which one may attempt to illustrate (not to 'prove') the presence of an observer affect on data which he is talking about. The first affects a determination of what the native observer will report as 'same' for purposes of normal action in his daily life. Must a river have water, in order to be a river? If so, it would follow that into the same river "we both step and do not step" — as Heraclitus affirmed centuries ago (in Patrick 1889:104); and the specific water molecules would be different each time, because "other waters are flowing" (94) (and if the water were not folowing one would hardly be stepping into a river proper). *Identity within change* was seen to be a problem when talking about the continuity or

'Talked-about' Reality

recognizability of any unit way back there. It is perhaps even more so now that we know more about the details of the minute wearing away of surface atoms on an item — say a table — which is being used, or weathered; or differences in the retina image when the table is viewed from different angles and distances.

This problem shows up in an exchange between the philosopher Samuel and the physicist Einstein (in a book by Samuel, 1952, which includes a letter by Einstein commenting on Samuel's work.) Einstein (158) says: "The most elementary concept in everyday thought, belonging to the sphere of the 'real,' is the concept of continually existing objects, like the table in my room. The table as such, however, is not given to me, but merely a complex of sensations is given to which I attribute the name and concept 'table.'" The naming is important, since "only those form the material of science which allow of univocal expression," leading from "the data of consciousness to 'reality'" by way of such "conscious or unconscious intellectual construction." As a sample, the attribution of name and concept to the complex of sensations comprising the table "is a speculative method, based on intuition" and it "is of the greatest importance" to see that such a table concept is, "like all other concepts," "of a speculative-constructive kind" comparable to "those concepts in physics which claim to describe reality." Thus he can reject the illusion that daily experience is real but that physics has concepts which are merely ideas; and therefore he has "a paradox, namely that reality, as we know it, is exclusively composed of 'fancies'" (158-9), but in which the justification for the concepts of physics is (159) "that these concepts and relations stand in a relation of 'correspondence' with sensations;" and justification of our choice of concepts "lies exclusively in our success."

Einstein's comment is in response to Samuel's disagreement with some phases of philosophy (3) which invented "elaborate systems of fictional abstractions" such as "'qualities,' 'principles,' 'essences,' 'categories,'" or "'chance,' 'destiny,'" which were given as "causes of all the phenomena of matter and of mind" and of "fortunes of men and of nations." Samuel feels (4) that now physics has been "tending to revert" to approaches which have been discarded by philosophy for three hundred years. He rejects (39) Bohr's claim that we are not after disclosing 'the real essence' of phenomena, but 'relations between the manifold aspects of our experience;' and Samuel insists, rather, that "our ultimate goal" must remain "the essential nature of the phenomena themselves." And so he differentiates (40) between various mental concepts which can never in themselves be the cause of physical events (e.g. "Chance, Statistical laws, Spacetime, or any other fictional abstraction"), and (6) an event, which "is any kind of happening — the movement of an electron or of a star . . . a thought in a mind" since "any and every phenomenon may be analyzed into events." In this framework, Samuel feels

(6-7) that the idea of a Chippendale chair is real not only in that it exists as a reality in the mind, but that it also embodies something in the universe that existed — and without which the universe would have been different. He wants to keep these two orders of reality clearly distinct, lest we end up not with physics, but (6) with the "grin of the Cheshire cat in *Alice in Wonderland*."

But beyond Heraclitus and Einstein, what can the rest of us add? Since physicist and philosopher so forcefully treat with *naming* and the *verbalization* of concepts about reality, should not the linguist enter the discussion between them, discussing from his own specialized viewpoint something of the nature of naming? Allow me to do so — as an English native speaker, of course. Even here the nativeness of the speaker is by no means irrelevant. Einstein says (157) of his letter: "I felt not able to formulate this in English but did it in German." If reality-as-perceived has no deep relation to reality-as-talked-about, why should native language be relevant? If perception, talking, and knowledge are at a deep metaphysical level unrelated, why should nativeness be so important to an apparently competent (!) bilingual?

A quarter of a century ago I coined the terms 'emic' and 'etic' (Pike 1954, Chapter 2; 1967 second edition) for discussing cultural problems (including linguistic) related to these. In the process of moving from a known (native) culture (including but not restricted to one's native language) to one unknown to the analyst, the analyst inevitably is startled. Various items or components of events (spoken or acted) which seem so clearly distinct to him are by-passed by the native actor as irrelevant. These events seem either to be below the level of conscious notice by the native actor (the native speaker) or — if he does observe them in some way before or after training — they are not likely to affect his routine behavior. That is, the native actor responds to a set of situations or items or events as if somehow they were identical, in spite of obvious differences perceived by the analyst. The differences do not make a difference, normally, to the native as he behaves in his normal cultural setting. In such an instance, the differences are etic, but the identity is emic. (The linguist will know, of course, that the term 'etic' is taken from the end of the word 'phonetic' but 'emic' from 'phonemic' — but that need not affect our nonlinguistic reader seriously here.) Once one learns to act within the constraints of the emic distinctions of a culture, he is prepared to take part in the behavior of that culture as a foreign insider — i.e., as one who gets along with crucial matters, although with obvious minor variations. If, in addition, he learns to control all the etic variants of the culture (difficult to do, once adolescence is past) he becomes a native insider — he has 'lost his accent' in speech or behavior.

Thus, to behave properly (emically) about tables and chairs, he must be able to know (most of the time at least) whether he is dealing with a table or

'Talked-about' Reality

a chair, lest he sit at the wrong time on a table, or put food at the wrong time on a chair — and lest he be unable to recognize as *off-norm* an acceptable time for sitting on a table or putting food on a chair. In buying chairs, he must be able to distinguish Chippendale from other types (in certain subcontexts and for certain purposes) under penalty of being unacceptable to some subculture involved or in a discussion about his own household furnishings, or being able to live within his bank account.

Purpose, acceptability, relation to others and to cause and effect, therefore, are tied into emic features of human perception within a culture and with the universe. Our more recent treatment (Pike and Pike: 1977, Chapter 12) of language in context of behavior (and we find ourselves unable to discuss language satisfactorily without such including context) brings purpose directly into linguistic description of the referential hierarchy of language — an aspect of language behavior which reflects directly upon particular human acts, items, or perceptions. Therefore, we can be sympathetic to Einstein's insistence (see above) on the success of the use of abstractions — as making them correspond eventually to the way the universe behaves — as in some sense relevant to the reality of those abstractions. Purpose, as a crucial ingredient of some phases of human action finds its analogue in the relevance of a concept in its leading to the successful prediction of the results of an experiment.

Now I would like to quote briefly three other authors who have touched on a topic related to this one, either by discussing reality in relation to the observer, or by discussing the problem of identity within difference:

Bridgman, for example, ties meaning to operationalism — which applies both to native speaker and to the analyst himself: "The concept of table and cloud and star is successful in dealing with certain aspects of my experience; hence they 'exist.' In short, this is the operational meaning of existence" (1936:51). Before I was myself specifically talking about etics and emics, he was faced with its enormous problems from a different point of view. Concerning identification of a thing or event, he said: "It seems to me that the existence of this property of 'sameness' acquires its plausibility in terms only of a feeling for an underlying 'reality,' which seems to me almost metaphysical in character, and to which I can see no way of giving sufficient operational sharpness" (79); since there are "unanalyzable intuitively recognizable elementary happenings" (75). And my utilization of the term universe of discourse, or observer standpoint seems to be related to his 'frame,' with identification of an item requiring two observers, with 'transformation' of their 'coordinates' across their frames: "Each observer determines in his framework the coordinates of a succession of physical happenings, and then the transformation of coordinates is accomplished by correlating the coordinates obtained by the two observers for what they agree are the *same* happenings" (77); but this points him to difficulties, since "If quantum theory is right, the ultimate elementary act of observation must be the reception of perception of a single photon, a process which by its essential nature cannot be participated in by two observers" (84, and cf. 86). He feels that "we will be increasingly driven in this direction in the future by the emphasis of wave mechanics on the observer as a necessary part of any physical system" (13); and "The role of the observer cannot be adequately understood without an appreciation of the way he must think, although it must be admitted that wave mechanics is still a long way from any treatment of this aspect of the observer" (13). But it is precisely here, it has long seemed to me, that physics and linguistics merge: linguistics is involved — or should be — in specifying some of the characteristics of the observer, in relation to his language; and Bridgman includes language and communication as crucial to the whole: "the two frames which they describe in the same language" (80).

Yet my aim here — to bring both analyst and native speaker as both integrated into analysis and description — is still a dream for him: "If we are ever successful in including the observer as part of the system" (122).

Polanyi, physicist turned philosopher, on the other hand, rejects "the scourge of physicalism" ([1959] 1969:46); and says "My analysis of machines and living beings entails the rejection of Ernest Nagel's claim to describe machines and living beings in non-teleological terms. Nothing is a machine unless it serves a useful purpose, and living organs and functions are organs and functions only to the extent to which they sustain life. A theory of knowledge based on tacit knowing does not require that we purify science of references to mind or to the finalistic structure of living beings" (157), covering, thus, inventors of machines, analysis of machines, and native reaction to their use. As for the problem of sameness and difference, Polanyi says that "Plato was the first to be troubled by the fact that *in applying our conception of a class of things, we keep identifying objects that are different from each other in every particular*. If every man is clearly distinguishable from another and we yet recognize each of them as a man, what kind of man is this, as which all these men are recognized?" ([1962] 1969:165). But he adds that "The difficulty is not eliminated by specifying the characteristic features of man, since in doing so we must again repeatedly use one name for instances of a feature that are different in every particular" (166); and "we are assuming here that our integrative powers can resolve the apparent contradiction involved in taking an aggregate of objects which differ in every particular to be nevertheless identical in some other way" (167).

The logician Langer seems rather to find such problems non-existent to her approach: "*Things* are easy to identify; two beings named 'John,' when actually present, are not likely to be treated erroneously as one person (like

'Talked-about' Reality

the two heroes called 'the King' in Gilbert and Sullivan's *Gondoliers*), because it is apparent to every one that there is *this* John and *that* John" ([1937] 1953:56).

It is in part this treatment by logicians of identities as almost self-evident, that – perhaps – makes me feel much more kinship philosophically with physicists than with logicians or mathematicians. And this in turn explains in part the sharp disjunction of my treatment of language as a component of behavior ([1954], 1955, 1960] 1967^2) with many current treatments of grammar which are heavily influenced by logic or mathematics as embracing or comprising abstract sets of rules or abstract relationships (cf. Harris 1952, Chomsky 1957, Lamb 1968, Šaumjan 1971).

A major revolution is needed to get the discipline to a sharper focus on the concreteness of reality, with its included components of native-observer's emic structuring of his experience of the world, and to the analyst-observer's re-structuring of that native experience for symbolic presentation to us in a manner emically analyzed, i.e., isomorphic (ideally) to that native experience, or etically analyzed, i.e., in part non-isomorphic to that experience.

REFERENCES

Bridgman, P.W. (1936). *The Nature of Physical Theory.* New York: Dover Publications.
Chomsky, N. (1957). *Syntactic Structures.* The Hague: Mouton.
Harris, Z.S. (1951). *Methods in Structural Linguistics.* Chicago: University of Chicago Press.
Lamb, S.M. (1968). *Outline of Stratificational Grammar.* Berkeley: University of California Press.
Langer, S. (1953). *An Introduction to Symbolic Logic.* New York: Dover Publications.
Patrick, G.T.W. (1889). *The Fragments of the Work of Heraclitus of Ephesus on Nature.* Baltimore: N. Murray.
Pike, K.L. ([first edition 1954, 1955, 1960] 1967). *Language in Relation to a Unified Theory of the Structure of Human Behavior,* second edition. The Hauge: Mouton.
Pike, K.L., and E.G. Pike (1977). *Grammatical Analysis.* Dallas: Summer Institute of Linguistics.
Polanyi, M. (1969). *Knowing and Being: Essays by Michael Polanyi,* ed. by M. Grene. Chicago: University of Chicago Press.
Samuel, H.L. (1952). *Essay in Physics (with a letter from Dr. Albert Einstein).* New York: Harcourt, Brace. (Quotations used by permission of Curtis Brown Ltd.)
Šaumjan, S.K. ([1965] 1971). *Principles of Structural Linguistics.* The Hague: Mouton.

ASA KASHER

Minimal Speakers, Necessary Speech Acts

ABSTRACT

A person's pragmatic competence is not his full-fledged repertoire of speech acts. It is much less than that and it is much more than that. The present paper is a defence of these claims, resulting in some general observations on the nature of the native speaker of language.

Mastering a natural language means becoming proficient in the use of its expressions under appropriate circumstances.
   Being proficient in the use of sentences of a natural language under appropriate contexts of utterance involves having mastered rules which govern the activity of using those sentences under those circumstances. Different kinds of speech act are characterized in terms of different systems of such governing rules.
   Mastering a natural language seems, then, to involve mastering different systems of rules, each system governing speech acts of a certain kind.
   This seemingly straightforward observation is not as innocuous as it looks. Actually, it harbours an important blur which should be disposed of.
   Consider some of Austin's examples of explicit performatives.[1] When a person says 'I name this ship the *Queen Elizabeth*,' while smashing an appropriate bottle against the stern, he, or rather she, is indulging in naming a ship. "The uttering of the words is, indeed, usually a, or even *the*, leading incident in the performance of the act . . . , the performance of which is also the object of the utterance . . . "[2] However, "it is always necessary that the *circumstances* in which the words are uttered should be in some way, or ways, *appropriate* . . ."[3] Thus, the rules governing speech acts of ship naming specify which sentence serves under which circumstances as the leading vehicle of a ship naming. According to one of these rules, a person cannot name a ship by uttering 'I name a ship *etc.*,' if she or he is not the person appointed to name the ship.
   Could a person get mastry of current English without being aware of such essential rules of ship naming, rules which govern the use of certain English sentences?

Similarly, is a person's knowledge of English incomplete in some sense in case he is willing to utter sentences such as 'I bet you sixpence it will not rain tomorrow' without knowing that "for a bet to have been made, it is generally necessary for the offer of the bet to have been accepted by a taker"?[4]

If a person cannot gain mastery of a natural language without acquiring knowledge of the essential rules of ship naming, betting and bequeathing, then such rules should be taken to be rules of the language, or rules the existence of which is prior, in one sense or another, to the existence of any rule of language. Since there is no reason to consider the institutions of ship naming or betting as more fundamental than language, we conclude that if a person cannot gain mastery of a natural language without acquiring knowledge of the essential rules of ship naming or betting, then such rules are part of the language.

However, ship naming and betting, bequeathing and marrying are all on a par with Chess playing. One may gain perfect knowledge of a natural language without knowing how to name a ship or how to marry, to exactly the same extent that one may master a natural language without knowing how to play Chess using the appropriate expression of the language for marking a check or a checkmate.

Put differently, if you know that the word 'go' is a name of a game played between two players who alternately place black and white stones on a checkered board, but you think that the board has 20, rather than 19, vertical lines and the same number of horizontal lines, then your knowledge of the game and not the knowledge of your language is the one which is incomplete. Similarly, if you know that the uttering of the sentence 'I name this ship *etc*.' is part of a rule governed action of naming a ship, but you know nothing about having to smash an appropriate bottle against the stem of the ship when uttering that sentence, then your knowledge of the prevalent ship naming regulations is clearly imperfect, but this reflects nothing upon your linguistic competence.

Notice, however, that such an argument, though easily applied to the cases of ship naming and betting, bequeathing and marrying, acquitting and introducing, is not applicable to some important kinds of speech act. If you don't know that a speech act of asserting that some state of affairs obtains requires at least a belief on your part that that state of affairs obtains, then you are prone to linguistic error of the type examplified by Moore's paradox: 'Brutus stabbed Caesar but I do not believe that Brutus stabbed Caesar.'[5]

Thus, the claim that mastering a natural language is mastering different systems of rules, each governing speech acts of a certain kind, is indefinite in an important way. If this claim is understood as referring to all kinds of speech act, including, for example, convicting and praying, as well as advising and promising, asking and asserting, then it is simply wrong, as has been

Minimal Speakers

shown in our previous argument. If, however, the claim is meant to refer to only some kinds of speech act, then the problem arises of how to draw the limit between those kinds of speech act to which that claim refers and those to which it does not refer. This is the problem of *pragmatic demarcation of language*.[6]

A solution of this problem would be directly related to the problem of drawing a defensible distinction between analytic and synthetic statements. Not only is the problem of pragmatic demarcation of language a pragmatic counterpart of the problem of semantic demarcation of it, but also, as I have shown elsewhere,[7] a solution of the first will provide us with a solution to the latter. Presently, I would like to put forward general strategies which might result in a better understanding of Language, if not in solving those demarcation problems.

A pragmatic demarcation of language will take the form of, or induce, a distinction between kinds of speech act which belong to language and other kinds of speech acts. *A minimal speaker* of a natural language is a person who has mastered just those systems of rules which govern those kinds of speech act which belong to language. We shall dub the latter '*necessary speech acts*.' Thus, the pragmatic repertoire of different types of speech act at the disposal of a minimal speaker consists of just the necessary speech acts.

Notice that at the present state the concepts of *minimal speakers* and *necessary speech acts* are related to language in general. At a different stage it would be possible to consider minimal speakers of a certain language as well as necessary speech acts of that language.

Consider, first, what may be called '*the fundamental method*' of showing a kind of speech act to be necessary. The fundamental method takes the form of an argument to the effect that if any kind of speech act is necessary, then kind A of speech act is also necessary. Hence, if mastering a natural language requires having mastered any kind of speech act, it also requires having mastered kind A of speech act.

The fundamental method can be used to show the fundamental role played in Language by Assertion. To see that the fundamental method applies to Assertion, we may use the following line of argument:[8]

Any kind of speech act is governed by rules which specify "mental conditions," such as desires, intentions, preferences, reasons, etc. Using a broad sense of the term 'thought,'[9] we may safely say that any kind of speech act involves a speaker who entertains thoughts. But, as Davidson has shown, having a thought, in that broad sense of the word, requires that there be a background of beliefs.[10] Consequently, any kind of speech act involves a speaker who entertains beliefs.

Beliefs are related to truth. If I believe of a bank-note that it is a forgery, then indeed I hold it true that the bank-note is a forgery. This seems to be an innocent truism, but actually it bears some important consequences. If truth is a matter of evidence and justification, then beliefs should rest on evidence or require justification of another appropriate type. I have evidence concerning that bank-note, because of which I believe that it is forged; I am generally justified in relying on my perception of the colour of objects in front of me unless there is a reason to cast doubt on the appropriateness of the conditions of vision, and that is why I am justified in holding it true that the book I am now looking at is of a yellow colour.[11]

Now, by showing that beliefs require justification, in which evidence may play a significant role, one has shown that beliefs are results of acts of judgment. Even when a belief seems to have sprung into one's mind, such as in the case of perceptual beliefs, a related judgment is discernible. To deny that would be on a par with denying the existence of a judgment on the part of a Chess master who immediately responds to his opponent's move. Quick or short cut judgments are judgments all right.

What, then, is a judgment? Frege put it as follows: "When we inwardly recognize that a thought is true, we are making a judgement: when we communicate this recognition, we are making an assertion,"[12] but we follow Dummett in being opposed to this view of the relations between judgments and assertions: "judgment, rather, is the interiorization of the external act of assertion. The reason for viewing the two this way round is that a conventional act can be described, without circularity, as the expression of a mental state or act only if there exist non-conventional ways of expressing it. Most judgments, however, it would be senseless to ascribe to someone who had not a language capable of expressing them, because there is no 'natural' behavior which, taken by itself, is enough to express those judgments."[13]

Adopting Dummett's argument, we conclude the outline of our case for the necessity of assertion: Assertion is prior to judgment, judgment is prior to belief, belief is prior to any thought, which, in turn, is involved in any kind of speech act. Assertion is, therefore, prior to any other kind of speech act.[14]

Notice that the argument we have just outlined is stronger than what we have called 'the fundamental method' as applied to Assertion. Whereas the latter would require an argument showing that Assertion is necessary if any kind of speech act is such, the former argument shows that the institute of Assertion is present in a language whenever any other kind of speech act is present in it.

Assuming that Assertion has been established as necessary, one may try to extend our knowledge of what minimal speakers can do by using what may be called *'relative methods'*. Let us consider, for example, the case of questions, i.e., speech acts of asking.

Minimal Speakers

R.G. Collingwood made quite a few interesting remarks about the role of questions in our intellectual life. In his autobiography[15] he argued that knowledge is a process in which first a question and then an answer play the major roles. To know, then, is to gain an answer to a question. In the logic that Collingwood developed in order to sustain his theory of knowledge, propositions exist only as answers to questions and a proposition is true only if it is a right answer to a given question.[16] These ideas are further developed by Collingwood in his *An Essay on Metaphysics*,[17] where questions are claimed to rest on presuppositions without which the former would not arise. Such presuppositions are either relative, considered as answers to earlier questions, or "ultimate," i.e., not stemming from any inquiry, and thus, being neither true nor false.

If Collingwood was right in arguing that whenever Assertion is a kind of speech act present in a natural language so is Question, then his arguments may be taken to show that minimal speakers can both ask and assert.

It is interesting to notice that Collingwood's idea is present in earlier writings. First, in his own *Philosophical Method* he claims that "every affirmative judgement no doubt contains some negative elements . . . Any judgement predicates a concept, and whenever we affirm one specific concept we deny the other specifications of the same genus. 'The book which I am looking for is green;' here, what is denied is that the book is blue, brown, or any other specific colour . . . if you want to be clear as to what you are asserting, be clear as to what you are denying . . ."[18]

Compare Collingwood's words to what had been written some forty years earlier but published only much later:

A judgement is often preceded by questions. A mathematician will formulate a theorem to himself before he can prove it. A physicist will accept a law as an hypothesis in order to test it by experience. We grasp the content of a truth before we recognize it as true, but we grasp not only this; we grasp the opposite as well. In asking a question we are poised between opposite sentences. Although it is usually only one side that is expressed when we speak, the other is still always implied; . . . now whatever can thus be posed in a question, we wish to call a content of possible judgement. Therefore the content of any truth is 'a content of possible judgement,' but so too is the opposite content. This opposition or conflict is such that we automatically reject one limb as false when we accept the other as true, and conversely. The rejection of the one and the acceptance of the other are one and the same.

These observations were indeed made by Frege and published in his posthumous writings.[19]

Even if one does not adopt Collingwood's view about the priority of questions over assertions, another relative method may be tried for showing that if minimal speakers can assert they can also pose questions.

Consider two minimal speakers who are aware of each other. Each of them is aware of his own ability to assert, which he often does in the presence of the other, who is also aware of his ability to assert and who also often does it in the presence of the former minimal speaker. Moreover, speech acts of assertion performed by one of these speakers are rightly interpreted by the other minimal speaker as such. We assume, then, that minimal speakers have the mutual knowledge that minimal speakers can assert.[20]

Granting that minimal speakers *qua* persons are purposive and resourceful, it would be only natural to believe that minimal speakers, who know that each of them can and does assert, will try to use each the assertive powers of the others. Minimal speakers will try to elicit assertions of their fellow minimal speakers.

A minimal speaker will be interested, not in his fellow's merely engaging himself in asserting, but in the latter's making an assertion of a certain type, appropriately related to certain objects, states, processes or whatever the former minimal speaker is interested in at the moment. Thus, attempts to elicit assertion should vary to the same extent that assertions differ from each other. Since there are no natural, non-linguistic ways of conveying the differences between assertions, there could not be natural, non-linguistic ways of trying to elicit all different assertions. This is why attempts to elicit assertion in a natural language should be performed within the same language. If a question is an attempt to elicit assertion or judgment,[21] then clearly questions are of a linguistic nature. Hence, minimal speakers will have in their language not only assertions but also questions.[22]

Thus far we have tried to show that minimal speakers are, in a sense, less equipped than ordinary speakers of natural language. Although asserting and asking are necessary, assuming the above outlined arguments to be forceful enough, some other speech acts do not belong to necessary kinds. Not everything an ordinary speaker of a natural language can do with words, a minimal speaker can do as well.

However, a minimal speaker is more than a restricted repertoire of speech acts. Underlying any linguistic proficiency on the pragmatic level are some general features of the human mental equipment. I would like to mention a few examples.

Linguistic activity is ideally rational. An ideal speaker opts for a linguistic action which, to the best of his belief, attains his purpose at the moment most effectively and at least cost, *ceteris paribus*. Such a principle of rationality provides grounds for accepting Grice's conversational maxims as explanatory principles of meaning and understanding.[23] But rationality principles are not confined to language. On the contrary, they apply to language as well as to any other human sphere of purposive activity. I have

Minimal Speakers

shown elsewhere that principles analogous to the well-known conversational maxims function similarly in art.[24] Minimal speakers are rational persons.

Speakers' rational activity in the sphere of language is performed by following rules. Systems of such rules share an important logical property of being constitutive. Thus, for example, rules of assertion do not regulate a given sphere of expression but rather introduce a form of expressive activity. A kind of speech act logically depends on the system of rules which governs speech acts of it.[25]

Again, that interesting and important property of natural language is not a feature which characterizes it. The distinction between language and every other sphere of human activity does not rest on the distinction between constitutive and non-constitutive systems of rules. Major domains of human activity, much more important than the garden variety example of games, involve acts governed by constitutive systems of rules. Such are, for example, the spheres of morality, religion and art.[26] It would carry us beyond the scope of the present paper to show that an innate feature of the human mind is involved in many of the human spheres of activity involving constitutive systems of rules, but let me put forward my conviction that minimal speakers are innately equipped with the capacity of acting within and creating new constitutive systems of rules.

In conclusion I would like to mention a further line of inquiry. When we reach a stage of much more advanced understanding of the properties of minimal speakers, we might be able to provide better understanding of the extent to which human beings are necessarily social, if not a new proof that they are of such nature.[27]

NOTES

1. Austin (1962; 1976: p.5ff).
2. *Ibid.*, p. 8.
3. *Ibid.*
4. *Ibid.*, p. 9.
5. See Moore (1942: pp. 540-543).
6. I have used these terms and discussed that problem in Kasher (1978).
7. *Ibid.*
8. The following is just an outline of the argument. A fuller account will have to consider many philosophical points which I ignore in the sequel.
9. I follow here Davidson's use of the term in his (1975).
10. *Ibid.*, p. 9ff. See also Vickers (1976: ch. 0).
11. Dummett's view of truth is here adopted. See Dummett (1978: pp. 1-24). I have found Williams (1973: pp. 136-151) of some use here.
12. Frege (1969; 1979: p. 139). See also pp. 2, 251, and Bell (1979).
13. Dummett (1973: pp. 362-363).

14. Priority is here meant, indeed, in a logical sense, rather than in any temporal sense. We do not suggest any evolutionary consequence of the present observation.
15. Collingwood (1939: ch. 5).
16. The problems of relating assertions to questions have not been ignored by logicians. See, for example, Harrah (1963: pp. 25-30), Harrah (1969) and Manor (forthcoming). I have benefited much from discussing Ruth Manor's papers on questions with her. In her forthcoming paper she defines assertions in terms of questions and answers.
17. Collingwood (1940).
18. Collingwood (1933: pp. 106-109).
19. Frege (1969; 1979: pp. 7-8). See also Belnap and Steel (1976: p. 17f).
20. See footnote 8.
21. Since a person may pose a question to himself, questions should not be restricted to assertion eliciting.
22. Arguments concerning the necessity of other speech acts will be discussed in Kasher (1980b).
23. See Grice (1975). Kasher (1976) shows how to derive Grice's conversational maxims from suitable rationality principles.
24. Kasher (1980a).
25. Although some of the ordinary analyses of constitutivity are not fully adequate I do not see reason for dropping that concept, *pace*, for example, Warnock (1971: p. 37ff).
26. Concerning morality, see N. Kasher (1979), which includes a new, useful criterion of constitutivity. Concerning religions which are of a constitutive nature, see Kasher (1977). On the constitutive nature of art one can learn from Dickie (1976), though he does not describe it as such.
27. Langford (1978) is of interest in the present context.

REFERENCES

Austin, J.L. (1962). *How to do things with words.* Oxford: Oxford University Press. Second edition, J.O. Urmson and Marina Sbisa, eds., Oxford: Oxford University Press [1976].
Bell, David (1979). *Frege's theory of Judgement.* Oxford: Clarendon Press.
Belnap, N.D. and T.B. Steel (1976). *The logic of questions and answers.* New Haven: Yale University Press.
Collingwood, R.G. (1933). *An essay on philosophical method.* Oxford: Clarendon Press.
Collingwood, R.G. (1939). *Autobiography.* Oxford: Oxford University Press.
Collingwood, R.G. (1940). *An Essay on metaphysics.* Oxford: Oxford University Press.
Davidson, D. (1975). 'Thought and talk,' In *Mind and Language,* edited by S. Guttenplan, Oxford: Clarendon Press, pp. 7-23.
Dickie, G. (1974). *Art and the aesthetic.* Ithaca: Cornell University Press.
Dummett, M. (1973). *Frege, Philosophy of language.* London: Duckworth.
Dummett, M. (1978). *Truth and other enigmas.* London: Duckworth.
Frege, G. (1969). *Posthumous writings.* English edition, Oxford: Blackwell [1979].
Grice, H.P. (1975). 'Logic and conversation,' In *The logic of grammar,* Dickenson, Encino and Belmont, California, pp. 64-75.
Harrah, D. (1963). *Communication: A logical model,* Cambridge: MIT Press.
Harrah, D. (1969). 'Erotetic logistics,' In *The logical way of doing things,* edited by K. Lambert, New Haven: Yale University Press, pp. 3-21.

Kasher, A. (1976). 'Conversational maxims and rationality.' In *Language in focus; Foundations, methods and systems*, edited by A. Kasher, Reidel, Dordrecht, pp. 197-216.
Kasher, A. (1977). 'Language and religion.' In *Language and religion*, edited by M. Halamish and A. Kasher, Tel-Aviv: University Publishing Projects.
Kasher, A. (1978). 'On pragmatic demarcation of language.' *Theoretical Linguistics* 5: 251-260.
Kasher, A. (1980a). 'Language and art,' *Qav* 1.
Kasher, A. (1980b). 'Ingredients of speech acts,' *forthcoming*.
Kasher, Naomi (1979). 'Deontology and Kant,' *Revue Internationale de Philosophie* 126: 551-558.
Langford, Glenn (1978). 'Persons as necessarily social,' *Journal for the theory of social behaviour* 8: 263-283.
Manor, Ruth (forthcoming) 'Answers and other reactions,' mimeo.
Moore, G.E. (1942). 'Reply to my critics,' In *The philosophy of G.E. Moore*, edited by P.A. Schilpp, Illinois: Open Court, La Salle, pp. 533-687n.
Vickers, J.M. (1976). *Belief and probability*, Dordrecht: Reidel.
Warnock, G.J. (1971). *The object of morality*, London: Methuen.
Williams, B. (1973). *Problems of the self*, Cambridge: Cambridge University Press.

PART TWO

Methodology

H. SCHNELLE

Introspection and the Description of Language Use

ABSTRACT

Methodological as well as systematic considerations make it desirable to include careful introspection among the evidential sources leading to description and explanation. The reasons given against introspection are conclusive only with regard to superficial use of introspection, but not with regard to careful introspection such as is exemplified by some types of phenomenological introspection. Indeed, introspection has given us valuable insights: The development of rule systems and computational principles such as Turing machines based on introspective evidence of the conscious process of computation. This analysis has to be supplemented by evidence from physiology and introspection on processes requiring less consciousness. The result of both analyses is that the processes under discussion may well be rendered by a double-layer operative system described in the article. In any case, rule systems (such as rewrite systems) are procedurally inadequate systems for language description, since they involve use of descriptive means derived from the analysis of processes under conscious control, whereas processing syntax and semantics is in general not of this type.

INTRODUCTION

At least for the last fifty years, linguists seem to have agreed that linguistics can do without introspection. Influential philosophers argue that philosophy should learn this lesson. They recommend that one should not succumb to the temptation of "a dream world of introspection" (Quine, 1974, p.34) or, even worse, to a world of ideas. They deplore the fact that "perversely, there persists an old and stubborn tendency . . . : to appeal to the ideas when theorizing about words." (*ibid*, p.35). Instead, in their opinion, languages should be presented as wholly public phenomena. It is assumed that some kind of structural analysis may lead to a theory presenting the regularities shown by the sets of expressions underlying the observed or observable sets of utterances. Though admitting that, taken in isolation, the grammatical structures and meanings assigned to expressions or utterances are not observational, one maintains that the assignments are nevertheless justified by the whole body of observations. Syntax (including morphology and phonology) and semantics can be considered to be theories defining the structures and meanings. Moreover, it is assumed that not only the sets of linguistic expressions are thus determined in their organization, but that language use in general is governed by the system expressed by grammatical and semantic theories.

All of this looks very appealing indeed: Linguistics as a science that merely applies rigorously the methods that have proven useful in other sciences describing and explaining the facts of our world.

However, this account of linguistics leaves another area of research strictly outside the realm of linguistic analysis, namely, the description of those internal mechanisms enabling the organisms to master the linguistic regularities stated by the theory. Concerning this problem area some linguists would agree with Quine when he writes: "To look deep into the subject's head would be inappropriate, even if feasible, for we want to keep clear of his idiosyncratic neural routings or private history of habit formation. We are after his socially inculcated linguistic usage . . . " (Quine, 1960, p.31). They would furthermore agree with his argument that, even where language refers to events internal to the organism, language use can be learned and analyzed on the basis of public stimuli.

For the man who has learned his language lesson some of the stimuli evocative of 'Ouch' may be publicly visible blows and slashes, while others are hidden from the public eye in the depths of the bowels. Society, acting solely on overt manifestations, has been able to train the individual to say the socially proper thing in response even to socially undetectable stimulations. (Quine, 1960, p. 5).

But there are other linguists who may wonder whether all of this should be accepted without argument. Is it true that society acts solely on overt manifestations? Or isn't it fairly safe to assume that every individual proceeds on the assumption that others are like him internally at least in essential respects. This assumption may be based on the external appearance of the others, but it bears on his internal structure and the character of internal events. Genetic determination and internal sensations may play a role. To start with the latter: Do we not all assume that everyone else experiences a stomach ache just as we do, to take but one example? If this is true, people, if faced with a crying baby, may well act on the assumption that it has a stomach ache. Certainty that the baby does indeed suffer from a stomach ache is not required; high probability of the assumption is sufficient. Introspection is a basis for certain inferences about possible states in other organisms.

It may well be that philosophers want to block the path to the nebulous world of ideas as early as possible, but it is rather doubtful that this attempt corresponds to people's practice. Moreover, is it true that neural routings are idiosyncratic? Neurophysiology proceeds rather on the assumption that at

Introspection

least certain general patterns and configurations are not idiosyncratic at all. No, the behaviorist's position is not as well established as is often assumed.

Attempts "to look deep into the subject's head" – to take up Quine's words – may still be worthwhile and justified, even important. Therefore some linguists believe that it is not only the task of linguists to define the sets of regular expressions of languages and assign structures and meanings to these expressions, but that in addition their description should contribute to the description of the internal structure and the internal processes of the organism which enable it to have command of these expressions.

To many linguists the easiest way to comply with this requirement is to impute to the organism the competence for the structures described by the theory. This involves ascribing the structures determined by the theory, (e.g. constituent and transformational structures, meanings, speech acts etc. correlated with expressions) to the organism; the organism "has" these structures in the sense of being competent for them, i.e., of having some psychological mechanism in whose application the structures introduced by linguistic reasoning[1] play some role. Imputing a competence in this way does not specify, however, the character of the psychological mechanism. The relation between linguistic structures and psychological mechanisms is still referred to a secondary discussion about the relation of competence and performance. I do not think that this distinction is useful in the present context. I have two arguments for this: the first is a practical one, the second, theoretical.

Two years ago I had a colloquium with colleagues from other disciplines who were also working on language. The psycholinguist argued that we should meet in analysis and descriptions of language of a psychologically concrete type and give up the distinction between a more or less formal description of competence and a description of performance to be left to the psychologist. I argued from the point of view of division of labor: We should first know what the regularities of languages are – this is the task of the linguist and the analytical philosopher – and then find out in a second step how these regularities are brought about by the organism, granting that, in this second step, we would need to cooperate with other disciplines.

I have changed my mind in the meantime. Since we would have to take into account the concrete processes anyway, we might as well take an interest in them right away. This does not yet decide the question of whether we should distinguish between competence and performance but it may provide a basis for the discussion of what the distinction really *is*.

Let us now turn to the theoretical argument. If our problem is recursive, we have to conceive of it as constructive, hence procedural, or at least as constructively defined. Hence, in any event, we need a mechanism to enumerate the structures or assignments we want to determine. It is well-known from the general theory of recursive devices that there are quite a number of procedurally different, though formally equivalent devices. Why not select the appropriate one by criteria based on internal procedures of the organism having command of the structures defined?

Let me assume now that you grant the conclusion, at least for the sake of further argumentation. We are then concerned with "looking deep into the subject's head." It is important to be quite clear as to what to look for. Consider the position of the logical reconstructivist who might say that, in his description, he renders his own internal processes in the more rational moments of his life. Such a person would look for evidences of the structures, intuitions of speech acts, and the like.

In my opinion, this is, however, not the direction of research which is the most fruitful one to take, because even in our most rational moments many features are used without being consciously focused on. It is thus difficult to get a really clear picture of them. One should rather look for the general internal structure and processing features in the organisms which determine the general form of procedural grammar as an alternative to the structure oriented universal grammar. Indeed, we should be ready to change, if necessary, our well established methods of recursive description and translate our results into other formats for grammar, semantics and pragmatics formats, i.e., appropriate as a meeting ground for the various disciplines engaged in the description of languages and language use.

Obviously, there are two analytical ways "to look into a subject's head" that are concerned with *the internal structure and processing in the organisms*. The first is brain physiology, the second introspection. Neurophysiology of the brain is considered to be theory-laden, yet there is some inclination among linguists to take its results into account.

There is less inclination to accept introspection except, perhaps, for judgments as to the similarity of expressions, the acceptability of expressions, or the use of expressions. Elimination of introspection is, however, neither justified nor fruitful. Introspection, if carefully applied, should be given its share.

This is the thesis which I want to defend in this article, in trying to refute the arguments for the exclusion of introspection and in discussing some positive results.

I shall try to show that phenomenological analyses and constructive physicalistic and physiological analyses of structures underlying linguistic behavior as well as structural analyses may put their analytical results in the same model. In other words, they may well cooperate. Since, however, there is still a strong feeling in philosophical and linguistic circles against introspection and, perhaps, phenomenological analysis, I will argue from the phenomenological view of *the model perspective*.

Let me summarize the gist of my argument for phenomenological introspection in six points:

Introspection　　　　　　　　　　　　　　　　　　　　　　　　　　　　　　109

1. The arguments of behaviorism and structuralism against introspection are not conclusive. On the contrary, some of the most important results of scientific reasoning of our century has been derived on the basis of introspection, namely:

2. Careful introspection has contributed to the analyses of the human computing processes which resulted in the system of rules developed by Turing and Post and used by Chomsky to formulate grammars.

3. However, the simple transfering of the rule systems thus derived to unconscious processes such as syntax processing is inappropriate and has led to misunderstandings. Instead, careful introspection should also be given its share in an adequate description of language use, in conjunction with other experimental and conceptual methods.

4. Introspection can be used to eliminate certain proposals of grammatical description as possible candidates on procedural accounts and can provide indications about the form of possible candidates.

5. Introspection can provide indications about the character of an appropriate conceptual basis for semantics, in particular concerning the notion of time and related notions.

6. Though I am not yet sure about the results concerning the role of images and imagination in the process of linguistic understanding, research in this field seems to be promising.

In order to explain my position, I shall first discuss the arguments against introspection advanced by those behaviorists and generativists who make claims about the internal structure of human beings.[2] In connection with this discussion, I shall treat the first two of the arguments just mentioned. In the third section I will briefly discuss introspective evidence for the structure of the descriptive system that matches cybernetic descriptions of the human brains.

The fruitfulness of this kind of description for the analysis of the conceptual basis for semantics has been presented elsewhere[3] and will be further shown in research in progress.

The arguments of the present article will be further supported by the analysis of phenomenological research on the one hand and of Wittgenstein's ideas on time on the other hand.[4]

BEHAVIORISTIC AND GENERATIVISTIC ARGUMENTS AGAINST INTROSPECTION

I shall first discuss whether the arguments advanced by behaviorism or generativism for the exclusion of introspection as guided by careful phenomenological analysis are sound.

During the past twenty or thirty years, W.V. Quine has made a heroic attempt to give a clear outline of the behavioristic explanation of the interaction of observation and conceptual scheme in disposing of the conditions of our surrounding. His problem is the following: How can we describe the ways "whereby the human animal can have projected . . . science from the sensory information that could reach him according to his science" (Quine, 1974, p. 2) by making use of scientific methods and theory alone. In handling this problem, Quine finds it necessary to discuss in particular how the human animal could have projected the *conceptual scheme of ordinary language* as a basis of science. He thinks that behavioristic epistemology is in line with the scientific analysis of the world in general, whereas introspection and old sense data or modern *Gestalt* epistemology is not (Quine, 1974, § 1).

In starting to execute his program, he freely uses terms such as "perception," "perceptual similarity," "induction," "expectation," "memory traces," "salience," "traces as images." Reflecting on this, he confesses that "the mentalistic idiom is at the tip of one's tongue," even of his own (ibid, p.31). But, more liberally than in earlier days, he concedes that "mentalism . . . has its uses as a stimulant. Like other stimulants it should be used with caution." But he continues: "Mental entities are unobjectionable if conceived as hypothetical physical mechanisms and posited with a view strictly to the systematizing of physical phenomena." (*ibid*, p. 31/2).

Very well! Let us imagine a scientist devising an automaton in terms of one of the versions of automata theory in order to explain linguistic behavior. Does he follow Quine's advice or not? There is certainly a sense of the word mechanism, in which the scientist devises a mechanism in describing an automaton. But is it a physical mechanism? It becomes one only by interpreting − or rather: implementing − the procedural descriptions through the appropriate wiring of a network or the programming of a wired mechanism.

But is the term "physical" really necessary in Quine's advice? Couldn't we just say that mental entities are unobjectionable if conceived as hypothetical processes or process structures and posited with a view strictly to the systematizing of phenomena? With this formulation we leave it undecided whether the process structures will be instantiated by physical mechanisms or by introspectively verified experiential processes or both.

In taking this neutral position, we shall have to judge behavioristic and physicalistic approaches by their structural content rather than emphasis on

Introspection 111

the physicalistic credo. A first occasion for critical examination presents itself in the discussion of peripheric information, the cornerstone of behaviorism. Quine is forced to grant a distinction between stimulation of receptors of an organism and awareness of that same stimulation. The former is characterized by Quine as reception, the latter as perception. But, or so it is claimed, "perception also, for all its mentalistic overtones, is accessible to behavioral criteria. It shows itself in the conditioning of responses." Quine immediately proceeds to illustrate:

Thus suppose we provide an animal with a screen to look at and a lever to press. He finds that the pressed lever brings a pellet of food when the screen shows a circular stripe, and that it brings a shock when the screen shows merely four spots spaced in a semicircular arc. Now we present him with those same four spots, arranged as before, but supplemented with three more to suggest the complementary semicircle. If the animal presses the lever, he may be said to have perceived the circular Gestalt rather than the component spots. (Quine, 1974, p. 4).

What is the basis for describing perception in such a way? If I put myself in the animal's place, I would not say that I perceived a circular *Gestalt* but simply that I tried to do something that seemed best to avoid another shock. It is the behavioristic *analyst* (!) who classifies my reaction as having seen a *Gestalt*. But *I* do not see any reason justifying his statement. Indeed, in cases where it does not matter scientifically, i.e. in cases where our only aim is to determine outward behavior (as in many experiments with animals or even with aphasics, little children, and other organisms we experience as dissimilar to ourselves), we may accept the result. But we should not obscure what we did by interpreting our results to suit our philosophical purpose. Either we should stick to the interpretation that we, the analysts (!), classified the results as being best suited to our descriptive purpose, or we can impute something like perception to the animal. But in the latter case we have to admit that the basis of this imputation is our own perception which we are aware of in a specific sense. No, Quine did not show in his remark that awareness and introspection can be eliminated in the strong sense from the discussion of perceiving and learning. In this sense, it may well be that the "perverse persistence" of some people to appeal to introspection when theorizing about words, so much deplored by Quine, is unavoidable if the analyst does not want to study an artefact instead of a fact.

Let us now turn to the generativists. Though Chomsky and the generative grammarians do not share the behaviorist epistemology — quite the contrary — they do not relate their explanations empirically to the experiences of particular people — except to judgments about the acceptability of sentences. Their explanations are instead determined by structure conditions, such as basic assumptions concerning transformational generative grammars, which are claimed to be related to genetics and biology but not directly to some internal experience.

Let us follow some of Chomsky's arguments: "Imagine a scientist, henceforth S, who is unencumbered by the ideological baggage that forms part of our intellectual tradition and is thus prepared to study humans as organisms in the natural world" (Chomsky, 1976a, p.282). Quite in line with this proposal, he elsewhere applauds (Chomsky, 1976b, p.2) Lenneberg's intention "to see the study of language assimilated to the natural sciences." "So viewed, linguistics is the abstract study of certain mechanisms, their growth and maturation. We may impute existence to the postulated structures at the initial, intermediate and steady states in just the same sense as we impute existence to a program that we believe to be somehow represented in a computer." (*ibid*, p.3). It is obvious, then, that, on this point, the difference between Chomsky and Quine is nil; the gist of their quarrel lies elswhere.

In this context, Chomsky takes up the question of the 'psychological reality' of the linguists constructions. He is not quite clear about the fact that the attacks come from at least two different directions. From one direction comes the claim that psychological tests may provide for a higher degree of 'psychological reality' than ordinary linguistic considerations about judgments concerning sentences. Here Chomsky has a relatively easy time. "I take it," he writes, "that the question at issue is whether it is legitimate to 'impute existence' to the 'apparatus,' the properties of which are characterized by particular grammars or by universal grammar" (*ibid*, p.4). In discussing this question it turns out that we simply have evidential support of some kind or other and adding more evidential support does not make the claims more real but at most better founded theories. This is correct.

The situation is different, I think, with respect to attacks from the other direction. Here, attacks are related to the question of "whether the cognitive structures S [the scientist] is attributing to the organism constitute some kind of belief or knowledge" (Chomsky, 1976a, p.302). Chomsky states the problem as follows: "To know a language, . . . I am assuming, is to be in a certain mental state, which persists as a relatively steady component of transitory mental states. What kind of mental state? I assume further that to be in such a mental state is to have a certain mental structure . . . " (Chomsky, forthcoming Ch. II). Up to this point I would agree completely. But, continuing the sentence, Chomsky becomes more specific and problematic, in my opinion, when he speaks of "[mental structure] consisting of a system of rules and principles being a finite representation of these structures." He says that the scientist S, describing the mental state of a subject," . . . might refer to the postulated cognitive structure as a 'system of beliefs,' and to the postulated finite representation [of the cognitive structure] as his subject's 'axiomatization' of his system of beliefs. The axiomatization and many

Introspection 113

beliefs that are implied by it will be unconscious, no doubt, and inaccessible to introspection" (*ibid*, pp. 302/3). This is important in the present context. More specifically, Chomsky writes: "What is 'known' [in the sense of conscious 'knowledge of'] will be rather ill-defined and, perhaps, a scattered and chaotic subpart of the coherent and important systems and structures [attributed]" (*ibid*, p. 304). I would agree that the particular beliefs are ill-defined if considered in isolation and that an axiomatization is not accessible to introspection.

But the negative result about the role of introspection is partially due to the way Chomsky states the problem. Even if we accept the system of rules and principles used in the theory of generative grammars as a method of axiomatization[5] one must nevertheless acknowledge that a system of rules is only one possible version of a recursive definition. There are a number of other versions of such a definition which are equivalent in their analytic power, such as Turing-machines, recursive functions and growing automata networks.[6] Therefore, the decision to adopt one of the systems should be motivated by descriptively relevant features. This has been done by Chomsky, in a sense, in making clear that constituent structures and transformations of constituent structures seem to be most easily related to rule systems. But I think I have shown that constituent structures can be related as easily, or perhaps even with greater perspicuity to growing automata networks.[7]

Moreover, in addition to the various alternatives among kinds of recursive definitions, we have additional openness indicated by the well-known result of the general theory of automata that a given task (input-output condition) can be realized by procedurally quite different systems, even if the systems are restricted to the same kind of recursive definition. In order to decide among the alternatives one would have to look again for additional descriptively relevant features about language processing.

In view of the available evidence, Chomsky made the wrong decisions. My argument is mainly based on introspective evidence. It is in three parts. First, I shall argue for introspection in matters of the linguistic understanding process in general and of syntactic processing in particular. Secondly, I shall show that rule systems as adopted by Chomsky are introspectively based on the analysis of *conscious* processes of computation, whereas syntactic processing and ordinary semantic processing are not of this type. Thirdly, I shall show that the network processing systems which I call "one-layer operative systems" could provide for syntactic processing.

In addition to this argument which is mainly confined to syntax, I shall go on to the discussion of more general phenomenological evidence leading to the concept of a system consisting of two interacting subsystems. In a final section I shall discuss the structure of such a system.

THE ROLE OF INTROSPECTION

Let us state the problem again. Imagine that a particular task is given, such as the definition of a class or classes of expressions one for each syntactic category, or of an assignment of structures to expressions. We assume that the classes or assignments are recursively enumerable. It is well-known that various methods of recursive description can be used for this purpose. They are equivalent, if judged only with respect to the given task. But if, in addition to the task itself, there is evidence about the kind and structure of the procedures actually followed by the organism in solving the task, we may well take this evidence into account.

As already indicated, neurophysiology may give us some indication, to the effect that brain processes involved in these tasks are parallel processes of firing neurons determined by the properties of the neurons and the connections — the wirings — between the neurons. Taking this into account, we could be led to using operative networks formally corresponding to such neural networks for a description of the processes solving the given tasks, instead of rule systems for whose reality we have no neurophysiological evidence.

But nothing can prevent us from using the other way of looking inside our own heads, namely introspection. Indeed, we really should use this source. Simply neglecting this possibility would lead each of us into a problem which I state as my personal problem, though it may well apply to everybody else. The problem is the following: At least some of the statements of syntax and semantics are claimed to apply to *my* use of *my* language — besides other people's uses of the language. Let us assume that there is an essential difference between what is imputed to me and what I experience. It seems obvious to me that the statements about my use of my language should also explain to me what is going on inside myself, if it is claimed that it is just this what they describe. Either the statements should match my experience or they should explain the difference, otherwise I would not be satisfied. If everybody else were satisfied with the explanation of my use of language, but I myself cannot find a correlation between what is claimed and what I experience, I would consider this methodologically odd.

One may perhaps argue that it is advisable not to care too much about one's own experience in trying to set up explanations of general application. If, for example, we are interested in the shape of the noses of human beings, it is not necessary that my ordinary experience of my own nose matches directly with this description.

Very well! But am I not justified, in spite of this, to ask for an explanation of the fact that I do not ordinarily see my own nose as having this general shape?

The analogy with the nose is not directly applicable to linguistics. In the case of the nose I *see* that other people's noses comply with the general description and that I can see my own nose under special circumstances, such as seeing myself in a mirror, as being of the same general shape.

In linguistics, this is not so. Reflecting on a number of statements of syntax and semantics, I came to the conclusion that I cannot find a simple correlation with my ordinary use. First doubts came already in considering the arguments concerning my command of linguistic structures. The problem became unavoidable, however, in the case of the analysis of tense and time that can be found in linguistic and logical analyses of language.

I came to the conclusion that I cannot find any correlation with my ordinary linguistic usage and I suspect that, perhaps, other people have been merely *persuaded* to believe the explanations given so far; though by closer introspection, they might come to scepticism corresponding to mine. Consequently, I hold that, since we do not *see* syntactic or semantic structure as obviously as we see other people's noses, there is no way to avoid the conclusion that everybody who has command of some language described by linguists is challenged by the description to judge the legitimacy of claims with respect to his own experience.

I admit that these judgments must be undertaken with appropriate care. There are dangers involved in introspection, no doubt. Furthermore, there are indications as to where results of introspection may be fruitfully obtained and where not. It seems relatively clear to me and is supported by many arguments advanced against introspection such as the argument against what is called "the museum myth,"[8] that introspective evidence about the meanings or structures of particular words and sentences is unrealiable, diffuse, and sometimes biased. The attack against the mind conceived as consisting of a collection of mental images, one for each linguistic expression, and accessible and analyzable by introspection, was justified. On the other hand, Chomsky was quite right in arguing that this does not exclude setting up descriptive units, such as structures, conditions on paraphrasing etc., such that command of such structures can be imputed to speakers or hearers. But, if any such information on structures and meanings of particular linguistic units can be obtained, it is only possible on the basis of structural considerations such as those applied by generative grammarians and the structuralists in general. But whether such methods are accepted or rejected, it is generally agreed that in this area introspection is not helpful, but misleading.

The case for introspection seems to be quite different, I think, with respect to global and procedural evidence concerning the form of grammars (including semantics) as well as certain basic elements of conceptualization, such as space and time, that are central to semantics. Furthermore, it is possible that the nature and role of images in the process of linguistic understanding can be further clarified by careful introspective analysis. In short, introspection bears mainly upon grammatical processes and the role of basic conceptualization and imagination in semantics.

It is clear that careful introspection is not easy and should follow guide lines that show how to avoid pitfalls. I think that such guide lines may be obtained from the studies of phenomenological research which provide a wealth of case studies.

To be sure, I do not believe the claims of phenomenological analysts that by using their methods we might find rock bottom for epistemology, i.e., that phenomenology constitutes a kind of first philosophy. But I see no reasons why the methods proposed and developed in certain branches of psychology should not be applied. In particular, it seems quite clear to me that the personal problem mentioned above can be answered by applying these methods.

The plea for introspection outlined above seems to present a challenge to modern linguistics which has tried to avoid an account of speakers' internal experiences. It will turn out, however, that a systematic analysis along these lines may nevertheless lead to a peaceful cooperation between "mechanistic" and "phenomenalistic" approaches. Let me briefly indicate how this can be understood.

From a mechanistic point of view it is well recognized that very different mechanisms may explain the same behavior. We are therefore free to look for additional criteria that may select from the classes of mechanisms with equivalent behavior. Such criteria may well be derived from introspection, why not? Starting, on the other hand, from introspection, we notice that our stream of experience shows certain global characteristics and regularities, and it seems quite satisfactory to make use of the descriptive means of mechanisms to explain these regularities. After all, it was already Spinoza, followed by Leibniz, who spoke of an *automaton spirituale*.[9]

THE INTROSPECTIVE ANALYSIS OF COMPUTING

Chomsky adopted the rule systems of Post, which are similar to those of Turing, to his ways of describing grammars. At the time Chomsky adopted them, there was a certain agreement to emphasize the formal equivalence between various methods of recursive definitions. This was only possible by neglecting their procedural aspects. The situation was quite different at the time these systems were invented. Turing and Post took some pains, then, to show that the processes followed by a human computer are indeed rendered by the systems of rules proposed. This could only be shown by reference to introspection.

Introspection 117

In his first article Turing asks "What are the possible processes which can be carried out in computing a number?" (Turing, 1936, p. 135). He admits that "all arguments which can be given are bound to be, fundamentally, appeals to intuition . . . " (*ibid*). He starts with the following description:

Computing is normally done by writing certain symbols on paper[10] . . . I assume, then, that the computation is carried out on one-dimensional paper . . . The behavior of the computer at any moment is determined by the symbols he is observing, and his 'state of mind' at that moment . . . Let us imagine the operations performed by the computer to be split up into 'simple operations' which are so elementary that it is not easy to imagine them further devided . . . The most general single operation must therefore be taken to be one of the following:

(A) A possible change (a) of symbol together with a possible change of state of mind.

(B) A possible change (b) of observed squares, together with a possible change of state of mind . . .
(Turing, 1936, p. 135-137).

The computing process as such is described as a sequence of application of single operations (rules) involving states of mind. Similarly for Post in his description of the computing process that appeared in the same year:

We have in mind a *general problem* consisting of a class of *specific problems*. A solution to the general problem will then be one which furnishes an answer to each specific problem.
 In the following formulation of such a solution two concepts are involved: that of a *symbol space* in which the work leading from problem to answer is to be carried out, and a fixed unalterable *set of directions* which will both direct operations in the symbol space and determine the order in which those directions are applied. (Post 1936, p. 289).

In 1950 Turing wrote:

The reader must accept it as a fact that digital computers can be constructed and have been constructed, according to the principles we have described and that they can in fact mimic the actions of a human computer very closely. . . . If one wants to make a machine mimic the behavior of the human computer in some complex operation one has to ask him how it is done, and then translate the answer into the form of an instruction table. (Turing, 1950, p. 2103).

True, it has been shown by Turing and others that their description of what is computable is equivalent to the abstract characterization of the class of recursively enumerable functions. Thus, their result can also be taken by its abstract content without taking into account the original intention to mimic the human process of computation.
 Chomsky has always insisted that the content of the rule system of a

grammar should be taken in this abstract sense. He even pretends that he cannot understand how somebody could take it in its non-abstract sense as a simulation of what is going on in a human brain.

That this has created a lot of confusion had to be expected, if one takes into account which considerations rules have been derived from, namely from *introspection of the process of computation* controlled by careful attention on the part of the computing person. The attention is directed towards a correct application of the rules; in this way the person obeys the rule.

Nowadays, it is very obvious that the application of the rules does not mimic what is going on in a speaking or understanding person. Understanding is not a sequential application of rules. How do we know? By introspection, obviously!

Chomsky tries to solve the ensuing problem by drawing a sharp distinction between competence and performance. Not that there are no rules of performance, but the rules for competence and performance are different and – this is very important – the descriptive status of the rules is different: For Chomsky the *sequence of application* of rules and the *sequences* of auxiliary symbols they are operating at – one symbol at a time – does not have any descriptive status, i.e., they do not represent anything. The reader should not interpret these features of the rule systems. Why? Because their interpretation would lead to false conceptions about what is going on in the processing of syntax and semantics.

But if we could obtain some idea about the kind of processing going on, shouldn't we use it in an attempt to construct a process that *has* some features that might perhaps mimic what is in fact going on. And we know that a large class of alternatives to rule systems is available that might perhaps match this idea. In any case, one negative result is quite clear – and it is strange that Chomsky always evades the arguments to this effect – that a generative grammar is not a possible candidate for a mimicry of internal processes. To derive positive insight is much more difficult, I agree, but I do not see any sound argument that could prevent us from trying to clarify the introspective basis of this problem just as the fathers of the explication of computing processes did with the problem of consciously controlled computation.

To sum up: I agree with Chomsky that "to know a language ... is to be in a certain mental state, which persists as a relatively steady component of transitory mental states. ... to be in such a state is to have a certain mental structure ..." (Chomsky, forthcoming, Ch. II). But in view of the different descriptive means of describing such a structure, we should look for further evidence on the basis of which we could select an appropriate system. Chomsky's decision to confine description to rules and linear auxiliar representations (strings of auxiliary symbols) is not justified and has the drawback that we

Introspection 119

have to state explicitly that certain procedural and representational means should not be given an interpretation.

I shall now discuss the structure of alternative proposals which may be derived on an introspective basis.

PHENOMENOLOGY AND CYBERNETICS − THE INTERACTION OF TWO SUBSYSTEMS

A discussion of some primitive results of phenomenological analysis which I shall present elsewhere[11] leads us to the following structural assumptions: We have a field of experiential data undergoing permanent modification (the stream of experience) determined by immanent conditions of structuring, on the one hand, and we have a center of awareness that may be directed toward particular elements in the field of experiential data (the stream of experience). The elements in that field may be considered as indices of objects − starting from these indices, awareness is turned to one or the other aspect of the objects under consideration. The term object is to be taken in the wide sense including, for example, events. Among the aspects of the objects we may also include the linguistic expressions that can be used to refer to the objects or to present the objects (or events).

The conditions determining the movement of attention toward a new datum are structural factors in the experiential field such as salience on the one hand and a selection among the salient data in the experiential field on the other. This selection may be determined by the horizon of the object under consideration or more generally, by a *theme* under consideration. But, as already mentioned, after the attention has been directed toward some new datum, this datum is immediately "classed" as a determination of some object, i.e., as one determination in a system of systems of possible determination.

It turns out, then, that perception is, according to phenomenological analysis, an interaction of two operative subsystems: the operational system constituting the stream of experience and the awareness system (presented as the activity of ego). In considering closely the procedural aspects of the two subsystems and of their interaction one discovers that the former has analogies with an operative network, such as that considered in network-theory of automata[12] or in neurophysiological descriptions of the brain.[13] The second system is usually considered to be the core of conscious operation.

This double layered system closely resembles the account given by the neurophysiologist Eccles among others. Eccles is led to postulate a particular interaction between brain and consciousness which he seems to consider to be of a non-material kind. But such a conclusion is not necessary. We may well analyze the structure of the second layer also, following the results of

Turing's introspections. We are, thus, led to describe this layer as a program-controlled automaton, such as a Turing machine, since the program-controlled automaton has been developed, as already shown in the course of an analysis of those internal processes strictly under the control of awareness. The Turing scheme is one of the possible schemes rendering the essentials of conscious operation (conscious in the highest degree of conscious awareness). On the other hand, an operative network with its multitude of parallel streams of information seems to be related to processes having lesser degrees of consciousness or awareness.

This leads naturally to the question whether we could or should not use the language of the general theory of automata and programming as a system of cybernetic metaphors appropriate to capture and formulate certain results of phenomenological experience.

Obviously, one might ask whether it is worthwhile or advisable to substitute the original phrasings of Husserl or other phenomenological analysts by cybernetic metaphor. Note that the essential aspects of phenomenological analysis are not phrased in a language with ordinary interpretation. This is to be expected; since the facts of phenomenological analysis can only be detected on the basis of a *particular reflection* about what is going on in perception, there are no ordinary terms with ordinary interpretation directly giving the results of this reflection. Use of metaphor is therefore unavoidable in attempting to explicate what is going on. In this situation it is quite doubtful whether metaphor taken from ordinary language has priority over metaphor taken from other fields. If the metaphor from the other field is richer in its explanatory power and precision, then it may well be preferable to ordinary language metaphor, which is always in danger of suggesting shallow familiarity.

Since, on the other hand, cybernetic metaphor taken in ontological and epistemological neutrality has a venerable tradition – as already indicated above (see reference to Spinoza and Leibniz, p. 116) – its rigorous application is worth the effort.

Let us therefore pursue the analogy between the results of phenomenological analysis on the one hand and cybernetic metaphor – or automata and programming theory, to be more specific – on the other. In reflecting further on our first impression we come to the idea that the results of phenomenological analysis perhaps point to some interesting variant of a Turing machine, namely a Turing machine with an active tape. Instead of being simply a store, the tape itself constitutes a process: an operative network instead of a store. The "reading" of the "tape" is not only determined by the control automaton of the Turing machine – as in ordinary Turing machines – together with the inscriptions on the program tape but also partially by the patterns presented by the permanently changing data of the "tape."

Introspection 121

Instead of this type of a double-face system we may also replace the Turing head and control by a rewrite-system determining the manipulation of some field of symbol-configurations but such that this field itself has the faculty of changing.

Considered strictly from a formal point of view, the system is no different from a system of two Turing machines working simultaneously on the same tape. The difference derives a procedural aspect. One system operating in parallel and not controlled by a center of control (determined by a program or a system of rules) but by the appropriate wiring only.

This model of an operative two-level model has recently come under attack by the neuropsychologist J.W. Brown (see J.W. Brown, 1976). He points to the fact that in psychoanalytic formulations "the emphasis is usually on a two-level system with complex mechanisms of interaction postulated between levels." He joins in a critique already advanced by D. Rapaport who wrote:

We have no reason to assume theoretically that these (Cs,subCs) are the only two kinds of consciousness possible. Observation and experience, on the one hand, suggest that there is a group of such states of consciousness ranging between the hallucinatory consciousness characteristic of the dream and waking consciousness . . . (D. Rapaport, 1961).

J.W. Brown argues for taking consciousness to be a cognitive form of certain types of internal processes. The character of this kind of consciousness changes with the phylogenetic and ontogenetic development of the structures having that cognitive form. He points to experiments with language where the tested person is unaware of the acts he executes (if awareness is taken in the strict sense) but would still be considered as doing something consciously. This obviously goes in the same direction as Chomsky's argument that we should not feel obliged to take the term "knowledge of language" in the strict sense.

Now, we may well agree with Chomsky and Brown that there are degrees of operative control shown by organisms with a brain which are not easily accessible to introspection. But I am convinced that these controlled processes show some features, such as parallelism of operation, that are not characteristic of the processes where awareness in the strict sense is involved. Therefore, these processes should not be presented, as Chomsky does, by processes that obviously show the features of controlled operation under focussed awareness, namely symbol manipulating mechanisms.

In doing this one may be led to erroneous conclusions as was Chomsky. In earlier days, Chomsky argued for generative competence of speakers of ordinary language by pointing out that the well-formedness of complicated sentences might be *difficult* to judge by native speakers but, if given pencil and paper, they might easily find out. This argument assumes a coherence between automatized processing as in ordinary language understanding and conscious processing as in controlled pencil-and-paper operation. But introspectively they are quite different. It is true that consciously controlled operations might be automatized if often applied, but the very fact that it takes some time points to the fact that other ways of processing are built up. The generative character of syntax cannot be backed up by such arguments. As I have shown earlier[14] it is much easier to clarify what generativity means in a model of information flow for syntax. As to Brown's arguments, they do not show that a level of consciously controlled operation in the strict sense does not exist, but only that the other level of subconscious operations is in itself not simple but complex and amenable to layering into levels according to *degrees* of consciousness.

It thus turns out that the concept of a Turing machine with an active tape or — in other words — of a two-layer operative system can be justified. The two systems are coupled at those operative positions whose activations either cause the functioning of the unconscious layer of the operative system or attract the attention of the control head of the conscious system. It is obvious then that *a position in our two layer operative system is a point whose activation* — and in some cases also its non-activation — *may attract attention,* i.e., *a position is a possible awareness focus* in terms of introspective evidence. It is merely a focus in the sense that, having attracted awareness, it does not automatically convey the complete information connected to the focus. On the contrary, the awareness has to investigate the information related to the focus of awareness in order to uncover the "content" of the focus. As in structural analysis, the "meaning" of an element (point) is the relation it has to other elements.

In considering the procedural properties of the basic layer of the operational description we are led to the formal system presented in the next section.

OPERATIVE NETWORKS

Formally, an operative network may be characterized as a topological space together with two sets of possible valuations over the points of this space, the first defining the momentary local states of the space, the second the local operative properties of the space.

Introspective reports about the diversity and complexity of internal processes are sometimes rendered by the metaphor of a sea with a multitude of twinklings whose changes seem to follow some complex regularities, though the nature of these regularities cannot be grasped directly. The concept of an

Introspection 123

operative network meets this admittedly poor description.

On the other hand, procedural networks such as those proposed for the descriptions of nerve networks and their functioning can be shown to be special cases of the concept of operative networks. The demonstration is as follows:

An operative network can be defined as a quadruple

$$O = (P, Q, V, D)$$

where P is a set of points of the "space" of the operative network, Q is a topology over P, V is a set of values assignable to the elements of P. D is the essential part in the present context. It assigns to each element x of P a sensitivity law D_x determining the change of the valuation at x depending on the values of the topological neighbors of x. More precisely: For every value of x and every subsequent value of x — i.e., for every value switch at x — there is a sensitivity condition comprising all neighboring configurations which may cause the switch.

In the case where the topology over P is determined by giving for each x (ϵP) a finite number of immediate neighbors, D can be defined as follows:

Let V^n be the set of n-tuples over V,^{1} V^n its power set, $V \times ^2 V^n$ the set of pairs of members from V with subsets of the sets of n-tuples and F, the set of possible sensitivity laws b

$$F = \underset{i}{U} V^{(V \times ^3 V^n)}$$

such that the first argument and the value differ for each F.

Then, D is a mapping defined in P with values in the power set of F satisfying the following constraint. A position x (ϵP) having n neighbors can only be assigned (a set of) n+1 place functions (ϵF).

If D_x is a function assigned to x and $y = D_x(u,v)$ where y, uϵV, y$\neq$u and v ϵ π V^n then we shall say that (u, v) is the valuation change or value switch at x caused by each member from v. D_x can also be conceived of as giving for each possible value switch at x the neighboring value configurations that may occur as a cause for that value switch.

Now, modular nerve nets as described in cybernetics[15] are special cases of operative networks. The set P can be identified with the set of formal neurons. Q is a mapping of P into the power set over P, assigning to each P the set of its immediate neighbors. V is the binary set $\{0,1\}$, where 1 can be interpreted as the firing state and 0 as the non-firing state of a formal neuron. A position (formal neuron) can react to a configuration of neighboring firing and non-firing neurons by the change (value switch) (O,1), i.e., by changing from non-firing to firing. We shall stipulate that the change (1,0) "comes by itself," i.e., is "caused" by the class of all possible neighboring configurations. Therefore, the value 1 is not stable. On the other hand, the value O — i.e., non-firing — is a stable state of the neuron; it persists as long as certain neighboring configurations are not present.

In consequence, a sensitivity law for a position having n immediate neighbors consists of a pair whose second member is 1 — the value of the function — and whose first member is a pair consisting of O and a set of n-tuples over {O,1} , each n-tuple in the set giving a configuration causing the neuron to fire, i.e., to switch from state O to state 1. Since the value of the function and the first member of the argument pair is fixed by definition, it suffices to determine the neighboring configurations causing a switch. For ordinary modular nets, these configurations can be calculated globally on the basis of an n-tuple of input weights (rational numbers) and a threshold t as follows:

The switch O → 1 (firing) occurs if and only if the following condition holds:

$$\sum_{i=1}^{n} w_i x_i \geqslant t$$

In many networks the situation is further simplified by allowing the w_i only to take values in $\{-1,+1\}$, '−1' meaning inhibitory and '+1' excitatory synapses.

Analyzing modular networks as operative systems which can be supported introspectively as well as physiologically — at least in principle — provides for a framework into which introspective impressions of parallel experiences as well as physiological experiences can be represented. It is merely the interpretations — or perhaps partial interpretations — that differ in both cases. The demonstration gives a rough indication of my proposal that physiological research and psychological introspection may cooperate in terms of the same framework of description.

In view of the psychological interpretation, operative networks of the type described above will be supplemented by a centrally controlled Turing-type — or program-controlled — automaton which can operate on certain data at positions of the operative network just as the operative network can. This seems to be quite clear from a psychological point of view. From a physiological point of view the nature of such a system is much less clear. There are, however, influential scientists, such as Eccles[16] who argue for such a system cooperating with the modular system neurophysiology assigns to brains.

NOTES

1. Linguistic reasoning based on structural comparison of linguistic facts, i.e., the structural (linguistic) method (in the broad sense).
2. I would agree that my discussion would be irrelevant for those linguists who do not make any claims as to the psychological or physiological relevance of their statements or theories.
3. See Schnelle (1980 a).
4. See Schnelle (1980 b), Schnelle (1980 c).
5. This has been challenged by H.H. Lieb, 1974/76. But we shall accept Chomsky's position in this article.
6. See e.g. Burks, 1963.
7. See Schnelle, 1964.
8. See Chomsky (forthcoming) Ch. I, p. 10 for a recent discussion.
9. See Schnelle, 1970, 1971a, 1971b.
10. Later (Turing, 1950, p. 2102) adds: 'Insofar as the human computer does the calculations in his head a part of the store will correspond to his memory.'
11. See Schnelle (1980 b).
12. See e.g. Burks, 1963.
13. See e.g. Eccles in Popper-Eccles, 1977, Chapt. E1 for a brief introduction.
14. See Schnelle, 1964.
15. E.g. Arbib, 1964.
16. See Popper, Eccles, 1977.

REFERENCES

Arbib, M. (1964). *Brains, Machines and Mathematics.* New York: McGraw Hill.
Braffort, P. and Hirschberg, D.; eds. (1963). *Computer, Programming and Formal Systems.* Amsterdam: North Holland.
Brown, J.W. (1976). 'Consciousness and Pathology of Language.' Chapt. 4 in R.W. Rieber, ed.
Burks, A.W. (1963). 'Programming and the Theory of Automata.' In Braffort, P., Hirschberg, D., eds., [1963].
Chomsky, N. (1976a). 'Problems and Mysteries in the Study of Human Languages.' In Kasher, A. [1976].
Chomsky, N. (1976b). 'On the Biological Basis of Language Capacities.' Chapt. 1, in Rieber, R.W., ed. [1976].
Chomsky, N. (forthcoming). Rules and Representations.
Davis, M., ed. (1965). *The Undecidable.* New York: Raven Press.
Kasher, A., ed. (1976). *Language in Focus: Foundations, Methods and Systems.* Dordrecht: Reidel.
Lieb, H.H. (1974/76). 'Grammars as Theories: The Case for Axiomatic Grammar.' *Theoretical Linguistics* 1: 39-115; *Theoretical Linguistics* 3: 1-98.

Newman, J.R., ed. (1960). *The World of Mathematics*, Vol. 4. London: G. Allen and Unwin.
Popper, K.R., and Eccles, J.C. (1977). *The Self and its Brain*. Berlin-New York-London: Springer.
Post, E.L. (1936). *Finite Combinatory Processes, Formulation I.* Cited from pp 288ff, in Davis [1965].
Quine, W.V. (1960). *Word and Object*. Cambridge, Mass.: MIT Press.
Quine, W.V. (1974). *The Roots of Reference*. La Salle, Ill.: Open Court.
Rapaport, D. (1961). 'Consciousness.' In *Problems of Consciousness*, Trans. Sec. Conf., New York: Josiah Macy Foundation.
Rieber, R.W. (1976). *The Neuropsychology of Language*. New York: Plenum Press.
Schnelle, H. (1964). 'Programmieren linguistischer Automaten. 'In K. Steinbuch, S.W. Wagner, eds., *Neuere Ergebnisse der Kybernetik*. München: Oldenbourg.
Schnelle, H. (1970). 'Linguistics and Automata-Theory.' In B. Visentini, ed., *Linguaggi nella società e nella tecnica*. Milano: Edizioni di Comunità.
Schnelle, H. (1971a). 'Geistesgeschichtliche Grundlagen der Kybernetik.' *Humanismus und Technik* (Berlin) 14/3, 29–37.
Schnelle, H. (1971b), 'Automat, Automatentheorie, Stichworte.' In J. Ritter, ed. *Historisches Wörterbuch der Philosophie 1*.
Schnelle, H. (1980a). 'Pre-tense.' In C. Rohrer, ed., *Time, Tense and Quantifiers*. Tübingen: Niemeyer, 329–354.
Schnelle, H. (1980b), 'Phenomenological analysis of language and its application to time and tense.' In H. Parret et al., eds., *Possibilities and Limitations of Pragmatics*. Amsterdam: Benjamins.
Schnelle, H. (1980c). 'Wittgenstein on time and tense and the linguistic turn.' In R. Haller, ed., *Language, Logic and Philosophy*. Wien: Hölder-Pichler-Tempsky.
Turing, A.M. (1936). 'On computable numbers, with an application to the Entscheidungsproblem.' Cited from reprint in: M. Davis (1965).
Turing, A.M. (1950). 'Can a machine think?' Cited from reprint in: J.R. Newman (1960).

ESA ITKONEN

The Concept of Linguistic Intuition

ABSTRACT

It is argued in this paper that the current distrust of linguistic intuition is based on the fact that the modern philosophy of science has been unable to develop an adequate concept of intuitional science. Yet intuitional sciences do exist, and some steps are taken here towards characterizing them. Justifying the use of linguistic intuition does not mean denying the legitimacy of observation of and/or experimentation upon linguistic behavior. Rather, these different ways of gaining knowledge about language ought to be put into systematic relation with each other.

PRELIMINARY REMARK

The characteristic property of a native speaker of a language L, which distinguishes him from those unfamiliar with L, is his intuitive knowledge of L. Therefore it seems befitting to discuss the concept of linguistic intuition in a Festschrift for the Native Speaker. My remarks have to a large extent the purpose of elucidating a line of thinking that has been put forward in Itkonen (1974), (1975a), (1976a), (1977), (1978a), and (1980). The references will mainly be to Itkonen (1978a), henceforth to be abbreviated as *GTM*.

THE CONCEPTS OF INTUITION, INTROSPECTION, AND OBSERVATION

A cognitive act must be distinguished from its object. A cognitive act is necessarily subjective, its object may be intersubjective. A cognitive act cannot be defined without reference to its object. In the present context I shall deal only with three cognitive acts, namely intuition, introspection, and observation (cf. *GTM*, Sect.5.2).

Observation pertains to things and events existing in the intersubjective spatiotemporal reality, which means that it is directly mediated by one of the five senses. One can touch an observable thing, and one can see or hear an observable event. Observation always contains more or less theoretical elements. One can touch an archbishop in spite of the fact that 'archbishop' is not, in any sense, a concept of 'pure observation'.

Introspection pertains to subjective sensations caused mainly, but not exclusively, by spatiotemporal things and events. In other words, the object of introspection does not exist in an intersubjective reality, although it has (mainly) been caused by something that does exist in such a reality.

Intuition pertains to concepts or rules existing in an intersubjective normative reality. (I would characterize as secondary uses of intuition those cases where intuition, coinciding with observation, pertains to spatiotemporal entities exemplifying concepts or rules.) The entities of the normative reality are not spatiotemporal, which means that they are not observable. Concepts and rules can be neither touched nor seen nor heard. Nor is it possible to reduce concepts or rules to something that can be observed (cf. *GTM*, Ch. 7.0). It is also impossible to eliminate concepts and rules by reducing intuitions-*cum*-objects-of-intuitions to mere intuitions (cf. *GTM*, pp.134-35, esp. n.73). Although one cannot help postulating the irreducible existence of concepts and rules, their ontology is often felt to constitute a difficult problem (cf. *GTM*, Sect.5.1).

Intuition shares some properties with memory and others with self-awareness. The objects both of intuition and of memory are intersubjective and not present to the senses. (I omit here the cases of one's memories of past introspections.) The objects of both intuition and of self-awareness are unobservable in principle; for instance, when I become aware of observing something, I do not, and could not, observe my act of observing.

The 'intuition/introspection/observation' trichotomy as presented above may seem somewhat crude. But it can be refined *ad libitum*; and it is certainly preferable to the current practice in linguistic literature where no attempt is made to keep these three concepts separate. I wish to emphasize that the use of an undifferentiated concept of 'experience' (*'Erfahrung'*) serves no useful purpose. Everything from physics to mysticism is based on, or related to, experience. The use of a concept like 'intersubjectively controlled experience' is only slightly more useful because it contains both observation and intuition (cf. 6th section – Philosophy, Logic, and Autonomous Linguistics as examples of Intuitional Sciences).

INTUITION AND OBSERVATION IN LINGUISTICS

Intuition pertains to norms while observation pertains to space and time. Applied to linguistics, this means that intuition pertains to rules of language, or to criteria by which linguistic behavior, i.e. either speech or evaluation

Linguistic Intuition 129

of speech, is judged to be correct or incorrect. Autonomous linguistics in the sense of grammatical analysis, i.e. as comprising the spectrum from phonology to pragmatics, is based on intuition, while sociolinguistics and psycholinguistics are based on observation/experimentation. Linguistic variation (in geographical or social space or in time) constitutes the point at which intuition alone is no longer sufficient, or at which autonomous linguistics shades off into non-autonomous linguistics (cf. *GTM*, Sect.5.4). In Itkonen (1980) I have shown in some detail, by analyzing the actual descriptive practice of socio- and psycholinguists, that observational/experimental sciences like socio- and psycholinguistics necessarily *presuppose* an intuitional science like autonomous linguistics. The concepts of autonomous linguistics and of socio- and psycholinguistics coincide in the concept of (linguistic) *rationality* (cf. Itkonen *forthcoming*). Rational linguistic behaviour is analyzed on the basis of an intuition pertaining to *norms* of rationality. Here as elsewhere, knowledge of norms presupposes observation of actual behavior, but cannot be reduced to it. This is just one particular instance of the well-known gap between 'ought' and 'is'.

TWO TYPES OF FALSE CONSCIOUSNESS CONCERNING THE USE OF LINGUISTIC INTUITION

There are two principal ways in which the use of linguistic intuition can be, and has been, misunderstood. First, intuition is recognized as intuition, but it is used where it should not be used. The standard example of this type of misunderstanding is the Chomskyan 'mentalism,' which, starting from one set of intuitional data, makes hypotheses about psychological mechanisms and tests these against another set of intuitional data, instead of subjecting them to observational/experimental tests (cf. *GTM*, pp. 82-85).

Second, intuition is used where it should be used, but it is mistaken for observation. In other words, people who analyze their own intuitive knowledge of correct sentences or speech acts claim to be observing events in space and time. The standard example of this type of misunderstanding is the Bloomfieldian 'empiricism,' which recommended the analysis of a corpus of utterances, but in fact analyzed self-invented sample sentences. Even today this misunderstanding continues to be extremely common (cf. Itkonen 1980, Sect. I A).

For the sake of completeness I mention still another possible source of confusion. It is sometimes claimed that "intuitions are observations." If this slogan is taken literally, it is just as nonsensical as the sentence "men are women." It can, however, also be taken to mean that in the intuitional sciences intuitions play the same role as observations do in the observational sciences; but then the slogan expresses a trivial tautology.

THE REASON FOR THE SECOND TYPE OF FALSE CONSCIOUSNESS

It is a historical fact that sociolinguistics and psycholinguistics have grown out of autonomous linguistics. In this case, as in many others, the temporal primacy of X vis-à-vis Y coincides with its logical primacy. It is easy to understand, and in a sense inevitable, that sociolinguists have taken their methodological orientation from sociology, and psycholinguists from psychology. By contrast, practitioners of autonomous linguistics have, almost without exception, taken their methodological orientation from physics. This surprising fact can be explained by two historical reasons.

First, the Anglo-American philosophy of science during this century has been almost exclusively dominated by (neo-) positivism, which claims that the observational/experimental methods of physics must be applicable to all sciences (cf. *GTM*, Chaps. 1.0 and 3.0). Second, and as a corollary of what precedes, the philosophy of such intuitional sciences as logic and philosophy (of science) has remained almost nonexistent. In other words, philosophers have been fond of analyzing such concepts as 'virtue' or 'scientific explanation,' but they have given almost no (meta-) analysis of what it is that they are doing, i.e. what are their data and what, precisely, are the methods they apply to these data. The difficulty of applying one's analytical tools to one's own philosophical activity is illustrated, e.g., by Stegmüller's (1970, pp.15-19) contention that the scientific progress is inseparably connected with the transition from qualitative via comparative to quantitative concepts. But Stegmüller's claim cannot hold true of his *own* science (which happens to be the philosophy of science), because he uses a huge number of qualitative distinctions, e.g. that between the set $\{x\}$ and its member x, which cannot be transformed into quantitative continua. The same lack of methodological self-understanding is generally characteristic of the work in formal logic as well.

The internal connection between the two preceding points can be succinctly expressed by quoting Habermas (1968, p.9): "Lack of self-reflection *is* positivism."

Autonomous linguistics rests on the use of intuition, and therefore its methodology is a particular case of the general methodology of the intuitional sciences. As we just saw, however, no such methodology has as yet been explicitly formulated. Therefore the practitioners of autonomous linguistics, in order not to lose their methodological self-respect, have been forced to accept the methodology of the observational/experimental sciences, which culminates in the methodology of physics. But this requires that although they in fact use intuition, they must deny doing so. From this the curious situation results that people who do nothing but analyze their own intuitive knowledge of self-invented sentences or of imaginary speech acts claim to be

Linguistic Intuition 131

investigating informant behavior according to the strictest canons of experimental science. "In this context the linguists' capacity for self-contradiction seems almost unlimited," as I put it in Itkonen (1980).

The acceptance of the methodology of physics is customarily justified by the claim that autonomous linguistics and physics are similar to each other. Now it is perfectly evident that all sciences *qua* sciences have something in common, for instance the simultaneous striving after generality and specificity as well as the falsifiability of proposed descriptions or theories. Therefore it is true that autonomous linguistics and physics are 'similar'. However, it is also true that two things are not similar *tout court*, but rather in some definite respect and as compared to something else. In other words, if we are to speak of two things as similar, we must put them into a proper perspective. As regards autonomous linguistics and physics, the proper perspective is provided by such intuitional sciences as philosophy (of science) and logic. When we take these sciences into consideration, we notice that autonomous linguistics is much more similar to them than to physics, indeed that autonomous linguistics is *different* from physics.

PHILOSOPHY (OF SCIENCE), LOGIC, AND AUTONOMOUS LINGUISTICS AS EXAMPLES OF INTUITIONAL SCIENCES

I have shown in some detail that the methodologically central concepts of generalization, explanation, prediction, and testability are the same in autonomous linguistics on the one hand and in philosophy (cf. *GTM*, Ch. 11.0) and logic (cf. Itkonen 1975b and *GTM*, Ch. 10.0) on the other. For my conceptions of philosophy and of logic I am indebted, respectively, to Pap's (1958) analysis of the intuitional foundations of analytic philosophy and to the constructivist approach of the so-called 'Erlangen school' (cf. *GTM*, Sect.2.6), which are important exceptions to the above-mentioned lack of methodological self-understanding in philosophy and logic.

It must be emphasized that *intersubjective testability* is an essential characteristic not only of observational/experimental sciences, but also of intuitional sciences. Intuitive knowledge of concepts and rules is a type of *agent's knowledge*, i.e. of knowledge about what it is correct or incorrect to *do* (cf. *GTM*, Sect.8.1). Rules, and hence knowledge of rules, can only exist in a community, where one person's knowledge of rules and, consequently, his rule-governed behavior are constantly controlled by other persons' corresponding knowledge and behavior (cf. *GTM*, Sects.4.2.5 and 6.4). This type of *social control* is the basis for the intersubjective testability as it occurs in the intuitional sciences; but the methodologically crucial point is that the resulting concept of testability cannot be reduced to, or reinterpreted in terms of, observational/experimental testability as it occurs, say, in physics.

Linguists have been disturbed by the existence of unreliable and conflicting linguistic intuitions, but this should be no cause for alarm, because the same phenomenon occurs in other intuitional sciences too (cf. *GTM*, p.286). Moreover, their *descriptive* research interest enables linguists to resort to observation of and/or experimentation upon actual linguistic behavior as soon as intuition proves insufficient or unreliable. This course of action is generally not open to philosophers or logicians because of the *prescriptive* nature of their research interest. The reference to the use of observation/experimentation shows that I am emphatically *not* trying to restrict linguistics to autonomous linguistics. On the contrary, I maintain that autonomous linguistics must be transcended, and in Itkonen (1977) and (1980) I have analyzed in some detail the relation of autonomous linguistics to such forms of non-autonomous linguistics as socio- and psycholinguistics. However, I do claim that autonomous linguistics remains a distinct and logically necessary component of any possible type of linguistics.

POPPER'S MISCLASSIFICATION OF THE SCIENCES

An adequate understanding of linguistic intuition is hindered by the fact that the modern philosophy of science possesses no adequate concept of intuitional science (cf. 5th section — The Reason for the Second Type of False Consciousness). Popper (1963a) represents the prevailing opinion. He divides (p.197) theories into the following three groups: (a) logical and mathematical, (b) empirical and scientific, (c) philosophical or metaphysical. This trichotomy is seriously misleading, because it misrepresents the status both of logical and of philosophical theories. (I shall say here nothing about theories of pure mathematics.)

First, Popper claims (p.195 and 197) that a logical theory can be falsified only by proving that it is inconsistent. But this is not true. I have shown that, for instance, a system of deontic logic is falsified by showing either that formally valid formulae generated by it are intuitively invalid or that formally invalid formulae not generated by it are intuitively valid (cf. Itkonen 1975b and *GTM*, Sect.10.2).

Second, Popper claims (pp.193-94) that philosophical theories cannot be falsified at all. As examples of philosophical theories he mentions (universal) determinism and epistemological irrationalism, but these examples are far from representative. Philosophical theories of a more standard type are definitely falsifiable. In fact, Popper displays here the same lack of self-reflection which was seen in Sect.5 to be characteristic of Stegmüller. When,

Linguistic Intuition 133

for instance, Popper (1963b) criticizes Carnap's solution of the demarcation problem, he obviously means to say that Carnap's theory is *false* and his own is *true*; if this is so, then he has falsified Carnap's theory; but this is certainly a philosophical theory; therefore philosophical theories *can*, contrary to what Popper set out to prove, be falsified. I have indeed shown that, for example, theories of ethics can be falsified in a perfectly straightforward way (cf. *GTM*, Sect.11.1; also p.314, n.6).

In sum, instead of Popper's misclassification we get the following trichotomy (still omitting the case of pure mathematics): (a) intuitional theories, (b) observational theories, (c) metaphysical 'theories'.

THREE DIFFERENT MEANINGS OF 'EMPIRICAL'

In recent years there has been some controversy, at least in part initiated by Itkonen (1974), about whether or not linguistics, or more precisely autonomous linguistics, is an empirical science (for documentation and discussion, cf. Itkonen 1976b). To a large extent, this discussion has been vitiated by the fact that most discussants have refused to give any definition of 'empirical'. To bring some order into this particular chaos, I shall present here three distinctions and bring out, in accordance with them, three meanings of 'empirical' which seem the most important ones to me.

(a) empirical$_1$ vs. nonempirical$_1$ = science vs. non-science or 'metaphysics'
(b) empirical$_2$ vs. nonempirical$_2$ = observational/experimental (empirical$_1$) science vs. intuitional (empirical$_1$) science
(c) empirical$_3$ vs. nonempirical$_3$ = synthetic vs. analytic sentences of an (empirical$_2$) theory

'Empirical$_1$' is defined as 'testable in principle'. Accordingly, e.g., physics, autonomous linguistics, ethics, and deontic logic are empirical$_1$, whereas epistemological irrationalism, theology, and poetry are nonempirical$_1$. Chomsky (1978) and Botha (1979, Sect.5.4.1), for instance, explicitly accept this definition of 'empirical'. This is inconsistent, however, because they clearly indicate that they would consider ethics and deontic logic as nonempirical.

'Empirical$_2$' is defined as 'testable in principle on the basis of particular spatiotemporal occurrences.' Accordingly, physics is empirical$_2$, whereas autonomous linguistics, ethics, and deontic logic are nonempirical$_2$. This is the definition of 'empirical' which I have always used (cf. *GTM*, Sect.1.1). The reason why autonomous linguistics turns out to be nonempirical$_2$ is, briefly, the *normative* character of its data. A sentence describing a well-established norm (or rule) can be falsified neither by an action conforming to the norm nor by an action violating it, which means that the sentence cannot be falsified by particular spatio-temporal occurrences. This brief characterization is open to several objections which are answered in detail in *GTM*, Sect.6.1.

'Empirical$_3$' is defined as 'synthetic' or 'nondefinitional'. The 'empirical$_3$ / nonempirical$_3$' distinction is meant to bring out the fact that the sentences of an empirical$_2$ theory may be divided into syntehtic or nondefinitional ones and analytic or definitional ones. It is a well-known fact that, depending on one's point of view, one and the same sentence, say, Newton's first axiom of motion, may appear either as a definition or as a synthetic sentence (cf. Nagel 1961, pp.181–82). Therefore the application of 'empirical$_3$' is context-dependent in a way that the application of 'empirical$_1$' or 'empirical$_2$' is not. (Personally I think that a nonempirical$_2$ theory too contains empirical$_3$ elements, which means that I am committed to the existence of synthetic *a priori*. For simplicity, I shall not discuss this question here.)

Following Lakatos (1970), Botha (1978, Sect.7.2) calls the methodological usefulness of testability, especially falsifiability, into question, on the ground that scientists do not in fact take falsification as seriously as in Popper's opinion they should. This argument might seem to undermine, *inter alia*, my distinction between empirical$_2$ hypotheses and nonempirical$_2$ rule-sentences (or norm-sentences). That is, it might be said that even if the rule-sentences are spatio-temporally unfalsifiable, the same is to some extent true of empirical hypotheses. But then the term 'empirical$_2$' would lose the meaning it was given by the definition.

Lakatos' argument has, however, no impact on my definition of 'empirical$_2$'. This can be shown in two steps. First, falsification of theories must not be confused with their apparent falsification. The history of science shows that even when a theory has been contradicted by (spatiotemporal) evidence, it is rational to suspend the judgment for some time, since the evidence may turn out to have been faulty in one way or another. But if the evidence is faultless, then the theory has been genuinely falsified. I define an empirical (i.e. empirical$_2$) theory as one which can be genuinely falsified by particular spatiotemporal occurrences. Second, (genuine) falsification of theories must not be confused with their rejection. Even when a theory is genuinely falsified by (spatiotemporal) evidence, it is rational not to reject it until a better theory has been invented. But this fact in no way undermines the methodological significance of falsification.

MISUNDERSTANDING THE NATURE OF LINGUISTIC INTUITION: THREE EXAMPLES

In my previous writings I have often criticized the position of transformational grammar vis-à-vis the concept of linguistic intuition. In order not to repeat myself, I shall consider here three recent publications of a largely non-transformational orientation.

Kasher & Lappin (1977). The authors set out to prove that "to a large extent, analyses of the methodology of science which have focused on the physical sciences can also be applied to linguistics" (p.65). In practice they discuss only similarities, and not differences, between physics and (autonomous) linguistics. We have seen on pp. 130 f. above that this procedure gives a definitely one-sided picture of linguistics. Besides, some of the similarities turn out to be fictitious. Kasher and Lappin define intuition as "internal inspection" (p.74) or "introspection" (p.75). They do not mean to say, however, that intuition is different from observation. On the contrary, intuition and observation are equally "personal" (i.e. subjective); in fact, intuitions *are* observations (p.75). What is obviously wrong with this kind of reasoning is the fact that the undeniable difference between the *objects* of intuition and observation entirely disappears from view. Similarly, I do not think that it is correct to characterize observations and intuitions as "empirical data" for physics and linguistics, respectively (p.73 and 75). It is more accurate to say that events (as observed) and sentences or speech acts (as intuited) are the data for physics and autonomous linguistics, respectively. This formulation clearly brings out that we cannot indefinitely postpone discussing the *ontological status* of the objects of (linguistic, logical, or philosophical) intuition.

In my view Kasher and Lappin are right to reject the Popperian conception that there are no sentences whose truth-value is known with absolute certainty. They do this by relativizing the concept of certainty to definite contexts: in a common sense context it is not rational to doubt something that may be doubted as a matter of course in a scientific context (pp.68-72). However, I would be willing to go even farther. It seems quite clear to me that there are a huge number of sentences, namely sentences describing rules of language, whose truth-values are known context-independently with absolute certainty. Although Kasher and Lappin claim (p.75) that intuitive knowledge of language can always be doubted, I just cannot see in what kind of context one could doubt the truth of, e.g., *"Two* means a number, and not an animal, whereas *cat* means an animal, and not a number." Or, if the truth of this sentence can be doubted, so can the truth of each and every true (sic!) arithmetical sentence, beginning with "Two and two makes four." Again, this brief characterization is open to several objections; these are answered in *GTM*, Sects.5.3 and 6.1-2.

Cooper (*1978*). Cooper accepts the positivistic philosophy of science (p.51). He considers the human mind as a black box and proposes to use the standard methods of experimentation to make hypotheses about what is inside the box (pp.27-29). He concentrates on the linguistic component of the mind and intends to offer an empirical theory of logical pragmatics (p.1). The experiments are to be performed on rational speakers of English; they take the form of a 'What-Do-You-Know' game, in which questions about the validity of inferences are put to, and answers given by, the ideal speaker-hearer.

Cooper's view of what kind of research he is conducting rests on a complete misunderstanding. The nature of this misunderstanding becomes evident, e.g., in the passage where he claims (p.87) that "empirical tests have shown belief in the [premises] to be accompanied invariably by belief in the [conclusion] among rational speakers of English." Cooper nowhere provides an independent criterion of rationality. On the contrary, from what he says elsewhere (e.g. p.73), it is clear that if someone fails the test, i.e. if he fails to recognize the principles of formal logic (even where these are in fact quite difficult to understand), he is not a rational speaker of English.

Cooper succumbs here to the positivistic fallacy whose pervasive influence on contemporary theoretical linguistics I have analyzed in several of my writings. To be sure, he cannot help realizing that what he is doing does not at least *look* like observation/experimentation as carried out in physics. To explain away this discrepancy between 'logico-linguistics' and physics, he resorts to two standard arguments.

First, he claims (p.89) that the paradigmatic situation of grammar-writing is the one in which the grammarian, aided by informants, is writing the grammar of a language unknown to him; it is only an accidental fact that he, Cooper, happens to describe a language which he knows perfectly, and thus acts, in fact, as his own informant. Always when I encounter this argument, offered by linguists who have never worked with informants or described an unfamiliar language, I am amazed that people can bring themselves to make that which never happens a rule and that which always happens an exception. I do not deny, of course, that linguists sometimes describe languages which they know less than perfectly. I myself have described Merovingian Latin (cf. Itkonen 1978b), which, because of the nature of the existing texts, no one knows perfectly. But this is precisely why I know that describing an unfamiliar language (e.g. Merovingian Latin) is *different* from describing a familiar language (for me, Finnish). Linguists who have never described unfamiliar languages can only suspect the existence of this difference.

Second, Cooper claims (pp.68-69) that the normatively binding rules of speaking and, in particular, of inferring, are 'idealizations' in precisely the same sense as the idealizations used in physics; but he does not even try to

Linguistic Intuition 137

show what, precisely, this alleged analogy consists in. On the basis of such an inexact use of terms like 'idealization' or 'theoretical concept' it is possible to prove anything, for instance that physics and ethics are entirely similar (cf. *GTM*, Sect.7.2).

It is good to point out that there is no reason why the 'What-Do-You-Know' game could not be used as a genuinely experimental device. But then it is certain that the results of the corresponding experiments would exhibit the same kind of variation as is commonly found in experimental studies on the psychology of logic (cf. Osherson 1975).

Finally, Cooper's black-box methodology is entirely superfluous because he, even before starting to play the 'What-Do-You-Know' game with himself, knows quite precisely what will be inside the box: he will place in it all standard principles of formal logic, and a player who fails to play the game in accordance with these principles is shrugged off as irrational. This conclusion is not affected by the fact that in his case study on 'if – then' (pp. 158–211) Cooper genuinely tries to go beyond standard formal logic and to establish something approximating 'natural logic'. What he is doing is still to analyze his own intuitive knowledge of valid inferring in English. For a further discussion of Cooper's logico-linguistics, cf. Itkonen (1979).

Finke (1979). Finke concentrates on the question of empiricalness of (autonomous) linguistics, but his entire undertaking is vitiated by the fact that he keeps confusing the value-laden definition of 'empirical$_1$' with the value-free definition of 'empirical$_2$'. He begins (p.2) by asking whether or not linguistics is empirical, and he emphasizes that this is a "rational" and "genuine" question. But later (pp.96–97) it turns out that this is after all a pseudo-question, because it *must* be answered affirmatively. Those who answer it negatively do not possess an "even half-way realistic conception of empirical science." Moreover, their attitude is *morally wrong*, as is evident from the fact that they, in opposing the prevailing opinion, display an "incredible disdain of the judgment and experience of many linguists."

Now, confusing value-laden with value-free definitions is serious enough; but two remarks may be added concerning the way that Finke uses a reference to the majority opinion as part of a scientific argument. First, the majority of linguists use the term 'empirical' without taking the trouble to define it, so it is difficult to know what they mean by saying that (autonomous) linguistics is empirical. If I may make a guess, I would assume they are claiming that (autonomous) linguistics is empirical$_1$. No one would dispute this claim. Secondly, let us assume, for the sake of argument, that what the majority of linguists mean to say is that (autonomous) linguistics is empirical$_2$. Does it follow, as Finke seems to think, that they are right? In my opinion the answer is 'No'. There is a difference between science and politics. A political question, e.g. the election of a president, can be decided by a majority vote. But it is not true, in general, that scientific questions can be decided in the same way.

The confusion between 'empirical$_1$' and 'empirical$_2$' recurs elsewhere under a somewhat different guise. On the one hand, Finke makes (pp.30-31) an absolute distinction between logical and empirical theories, which means that he must have the concept of empiricalness$_2$ in his mind. On the other hand, he openly admits (p.58) that empiricalness is a *value*, which means that this time he must have the concept of empiricalness$_1$ in his mind. His entire discussion is permeated by the same ambiguity.

Finke realizes that empiricalness (which is now, again, veering towards empiricalness$_2$) is intimately connected with observation of space and time; at the same time he maintains (p.59) that the customary distinction between intuition and observation is "insufficient." Now, if a distinction is insufficient, or crude, it should be refined, but not eliminated (cf. 2nd Section – The Concepts of Intuition, Introspection, and Observation). This is, however, precisely what Finke does to the 'intuition/observation' distinction. He claims, essentially, that our linguistic knowledge is *ultimately* related, in one way or another, to the spatiotemporal reality perceptible by one of the five senses; and therefore (autonomous) linguistics is empirical (pp.66-67 and 97-99). This argument, which was already encountered in connection with my discussion of Cooper, proves nothing; or, at most, it might be taken as proving the empiricalness$_1$ of (autonomous) linguistics (although I doubt it). It is easy to show that such nonempirical$_2$ concepts such as 'virtue,' 'scientific explanation,' or 'valid inference' are related to people's actual behavior, and hence to space and time, in precisely the same way as are the concepts of 'correct sentence' and 'correct speech act' (cf. *GTM*, Sect.7.2).

In Finke's opinion (p.97) linguistic knowledge cannot be certain because the existence of languages is contingent. This argument does not prove what it is meant to prove, because the rules of chess, for instance, can be known with absolute certainty in spite of the fact that the existence of the game of chess is contingent. The standard response to this is to drop the contingency argument, but to insist that rules of language are not comparable to rules of chess. This view sounds plausible, but can in fact be shown to be wrong from the methodological point of view (cf. *GTM*, Sect.6.1). Besides, there are more direct ways of finding out whether or not we can know anything about our own language with certainty (cf. discussion of Kasher and Lappin).

CONCLUDING REMARK

The nature of linguistic intuition, which I have been discussing so far, implicitly defines its scope and limits. The scope of (the justifiable use of) intuition is certainty, and the limits of intuition are the limits of certainty. Two main types of phenomena lie beyond these limits. First, my linguistic intuition does not tell me what linguistic phenomena occur in space and time. For instance, I know Standard Finnish, but I do not know how often the speakers of Standard Finnish use, say, relative clauses as compared to complement clauses. In order to know these things, I must start observing and counting. Secondly, my linguistic intuition operates only at the level of my (self-) consciousness and does not tell me what psycholinguistic processes go on under this level. Nor does mere observing and counting tell me what psycholinguistic processes are going on in other people. In order to know these things, I must resort to the hypothetico-inductive methodology of the experimental sciences.

REFERENCES

Botha, R.P. (1978). 'Protecting General-Linguistic Hypotheses from Refutation.' In *Stellenbosch Papers in Linguistics* 1: 1-31.
Botha, R.P. (1979). 'Methodological Bases of a Progressive Mentalism.' In *Stellenbosch Papers in Linguistics* 3.
Chomsky, N. (1978). 'A Theory of Core Grammar.' *Glot* 1: 7-26.
Cooper, W.S. (1978). *Foundations of logico-linguistics.* Dordrecht : Reidel.
Finke, P. (1979). *Grundlagen einer Linguistischen Theorie.* Braunschweig: Vieweg.
Habermas, J. (1968). *Erkenntnis und Interesse.* Frankfurt a/M: Suhrkamp.
Itkonen, E. (1974). *Linguistics and Metascience.* Studia Philosophica Turkuensia II. Kokemäki: Risteen Kirjapaino.
Itkonen, E. (1975a). 'Transformational Grammar and the Philosophy of Science.' In E.F.K. Koerner, ed., *The Transformational-Generative Paradigm and Modern Linguistic Theory.* Amsterdam: John Benjamins, 1975, pp. 381-445.
Itkonen, E. (1975b). 'Concerning the Relationship between Linguistics and Logic.' Indiana Univ. Linguistics Club.
Itkonen, E. (1976a). 'Was für eine Wissenschaft ist die Linguistik eigentlich?.' In D. Wunderlich, ed., *Wissenschaftstheorie der Linguistik.* Frankfurt a/M: Athenäum, 1976, pp. 56-76.
Itkonen, E. (1976b). 'Linguistics and Empiricalness: Answers to Criticisms.' *Publications of the General Linguistics Department of the University of Helsinki* 4.
Itkonen, E. (1977). 'The Relation between Grammar and Sociolinguistics.' *Forum Linguisticum* 1: 238-54.
Itkonen, E. (1978a). *Grammatical Theory and Metascience.* Amsterdam: John Benjamins.
Itkonen, E. (1978b). 'The Significance of Merovingian Latin to Linguistic Theory.' In *Four Linguistic Studies on Classical Languages, Publications of the General Linguistics Department of the University of Helsinki* 5: 9-64.
Itkonen, E. (1979). 'Does Combining the Computer Analogy with Logical Semantics Produce a Theory of Pragmatics?' In *Papers from a Conference of General Linguistics, Seili 29.-30.9. 1979, Publications of the Linguistic Association of Finland.*

Itkonen, E. (1980). 'Qualitative vs. Quantitative Analysis in Linguistics.' In T.A. Perry, ed., *Evidence and Argumentation in Linguistics.* Berlin: Walter de Gruyter, 1980.

Itkonen, E. *(forthcoming).* 'Rationality as an Explanatory Principle in Linguistics.' In H. Geckeler *et al.*, eds., *Festschrift für Eugenio Coseriu*, Tübingen: Gunter Narr.

Kasher, A., and S. Lappin (1977). *Philosophical Linguistics.* Kronberg: Scriptor-Verlag.

Lakatos, I. (1970). 'Falsification and the Methodology of Scientific Research Programmes.' In I. Lakatos and A. Musgrave, eds., *Criticism and the Growth of Knowledge.* Cambridge Univ. Press: Cambridge 1970, pp. 91–196.

Nagel, E. (1961). *The Structure of Science.* New York: Harcourt, Brace & World.

Osherson, D. (1975). *Logical Abilities in Children, vol. 3: Reasoning in Adolescence: Deductive Inference.* Hillsdale: Lawrence Erlbaum Associates.

Pap, A. (1958). *Semantics and Necessary Truth.* New Haven: Yale Univ. Press.

Popper, K. (1963a). 'On the Status of Science and Metaphysics.' In K. Popper, *Conjectures and Refutations.* London: Routledge & Kegan Paul, 1963, pp. 184–200.

Popper, K. (1963b). 'The Demarcation between Science and Metaphysics.' *Ibid.*, pp. 253–92.

Stegmüller, W. (1970). *Probleme und Resultate der Wissenschafts-theorie und Analytischen Philosophie, vol. 2: Theorie und Erfahrung,* Berlin: Springer-Verlag.

JON D. RINGEN

Quine on Introspection in Linguistics*

ABSTRACT

W.V. Quine questions whether the linguistic intuition of native speakers provides evidence relevant to assessing the descriptive adequacy of transformational generative grammars. In this paper Quine's reasons for scepticism are presented and assessed. It is argued that Quine fails to establish that linguists' appeals to speaker intuition must lead in a circle, but that Quine succeeds in posing a very real challenge, namely to specify and justify ways of objectively checking which intuitive meta-linguistic judgments speakers actually make.

Transformational generative linguists assert that data concerning the linguistic intuition of native speakers is essential for the evaluation of transformational generative grammars and theories of language.[1] These data include the intuitive meta-linguistic judgments of speakers and they are allegedly gathered by the method of introspection – by querying an informant concerning his judgments about expression tokens presented by a linguist.[2]

W.V. Quine argues that transformationalists' use of the method of introspection leads them in "an oddly warped circle."[3] Quine questions whether any warrant can be had for concluding that the method of introspection gives evidence relevant to assessing the descriptive adequacy of transformational generative grammars.[4] Quine's reasons for scepticism are extremely instructive. If pursued to their source, they reveal that at issue is whether it is more reasonable to pursue a mentalistic or a behavioristic research program in linguistics and the psychology of language. Because this is so, Quine ultimately fails to establish the circularity of linguistic argumentation involving introspectional data. Indeed, in his zeal to vindicate behaviorism, Quine is in danger of falling into circularity himself. Nevertheless, Quine's call for clarification of criteria is one which deserves the serious attention of those linguists who (as mentalists) aim to identify grammars which specify constituent structures of sentences which are psychologically real.[5] Quine's challenge is to specify how data consisting of intuitive meta-linguistic judgments are to be objectively checked. Unless this challenge is answered, mentalistic linguists are in the embarassing position of being crucially dependent on data whose reliability they cannot teach their students how to check.

Quine's conception of the method of introspection can be characterized as follows:

1. The linguist presents an informant with an expression token (T_i) and a query (Q_i) which has the form:
   O_i: This (i.e., T_i) is P_i? (Where P_i is a meta-linguistic term.)
2. The informant responds either by assenting, or dissenting or with bewilderment.

1. and 2. constitute what Quine calls the method of introspection.[6][7][8] It is not clear whether Quine objects in principle to the use of this method. He does object, however, to the conclusions that many linguists seem to think data provided by the method allow them to draw.

Quine is critical of Noam Chomsky's "obscure doctrine that natives tacitly prefer one system of grammar to another that is extensionally equivalent to it." Quine's problem is this:

... suppose a language for which we have two extensionally equivalent recursive systems of grammar: two extensionally equivalent definitions of a well-formed string. According to one of these systems, the immediate constituents of a certain sentence are AB and C: according to another they are A and BC. This enigmatic doctrine says that one of these analyses is right and the other wrong, by tacit consensus of the native speakers. How do we find out which is right?[9]

Quine would raise similar questions concerning two extensionally equivalent grammars, each of which struck a different separation between those well-formed strings which are grammatical but not meaningful, those which are meaningful but not grammatical, and those which are both grammatical and meaningful. The general problem which Quine presents is to specify the conditions under which one rather than the other of a pair of the allegedly incompatible consequences of two extensionally equivalent grammars is correct. Quine argues that the method of introspection which Chomsky has identified as being indispensable can be of no use in determining that only one of two such grammars is right and he suggests that questions concerning what constitute the immediate constituents of a sentence or whether a given sentence is grammatical but not meaningful are not questions of fact at all but rather questions about what set of rules is most convenient for accomplishing the linguist's task of giving a recursive specification of the well-formed strings/significant phonetic sequences of a given natural language.[10]

Chomsky, of course, is at odds with Quine. He recommends a search for descriptively adequate grammars. Chomsky attributes to speakers an intuitive sense of the distinction between meaningfulness and grammaticality,[11] as well as an intuitive sense of what constitutes the constituent structure of

Quine on Introspection 143

sentences.¹² He holds that the issue concerning which, if either, of two extensionally equivalent grammars is correct is a question concerning which of the grammars best corresponds with the tacit grammatical knowledge which speakers acquire in the course of learning their language.¹³ Hence, where Quine sees a question of convenience Chomsky sees a question of fact.

Chomsky has recommended use of the method of introspection to determine which, if any, of the incompatible implications of alternative grammatical hypotheses are correct. Quine discusses this recommendation in some detail:

... ask the natives ... in their language, whether the real constituents of ABC are AB and C. Does this pose an embarassing question of translation? Well, then let the native language be English. The essential question remains; we do not really understand our own English question. We are looking for a criterion of what to count as the real and proper grammar, as over against an extensionally equivalent counterfeit. We are looking, in the specific case, for a test of what to count as the real or proper constituents of ABC as against counterfeit constituents. And now the test suggested is that we ask the native the very question we do not understand ourselves: the very question for which we ourselves are seeking a test. We are moving in an oddly warped circle.¹⁴

To my knowledge, Quine has nowhere provided a more explicit characterization of what he takes the oddly warped circle to be. Nevertheless, Quine's thought experiment concerning radical translation provides a basis for inferences concerning the characteristics Quine has in mind.¹⁵ These characteristics emerge most clearly against a background consisting of reasons mentalistically inclined linguists *should* give for viewing the method of introspection to be relevant to the task of evaluating the descriptive adequacy of alternative extensionally equivalent transformational generative grammars.¹⁶

Guided by common sense, a mentalistically inclined linguist should argue strongly that the informant's response to a linguist's query is *relevant* to the question of what constituent structure (or other meta-linguistic property) an expression token actually exhibits.¹⁷ On the mentalist's view, linguistic fact is constituted by the tacit grammatical knowledge of competent speakers. Informant *judgments* constitute a reflection of linguistic fact. They can be taken to constitute an application of the informant's grammatical knowledge to the specific expression tokens presented by the linguist. Under appropriate conditions, the informant's *responses* (assent, dissent, self-report, or bewilderment) give evidence concerning what the informant's meta-linguistic judgments are, but it is the informant's meta-linguistic judgments that it is important to identify. (On the mentalist view, informant response can be evidence of linguistic fact only insofar as it is evidence of tacit grammatical knowledge.) Thus, given the mentalist view, if the method of introspection is to yield data relevant to the confirmation or disconfirmation of alternative extensionally equivalent grammars it must provide warrant for attributing to the informant a meta-linguistic judgment which either matches or contradicts the judgments predicted by the grammar.

To illustrate, recall Quine's hypothetical example. On the mentalist view, at most one of the grammars could represent the informant's tacit grammatical knowledge. The mentalist rationale for employing the method of introspection requires that the method provide the linguist with grounds for concluding that the informant judged the constituent structure to be AB and C, A and BC, or neither. Quine argues that the method of introspection could not provide the linguist warrant for attributing to the informant any one of these judgments rather than the other. Quine is sceptical about whether any satisfactorily theory independent data could provide grounds for ascribing the kind of judgments needed by mentalists to assess the relative merits of alternative extensionally equivalent grammars.

The crucial step in Quine's argument can now be identified. Common sense dictates that an informant's assent to a query (e.g., This [a specific expression token T_i] is P_i? [where P_i is a meta-linguistic term]) would give the linguist warrant for ascribing to the informant a judgment described in the terminology of the query (e.g., that T_i is P_j.) only if the informant and the linguist understood/interpreted the query in the same way. This could be called the requirement of mutual understanding.[18] Quine's arguments for the indeterminacy of radical translation imply that the linguist could have no evidence that the requirement of mutual understanding was met which could be obtained independently of the evidence (concerning meta-linguistic judgment) which the method of introspection was meant to provide.

On Quine's view, the linguist's warrant for concluding that on a given occasion the requirement of mutual understanding is met can consist only of evidence that the *stimulus meaning* of the linguist's query is the same for both the linguist and the informant.[19] This constraint is a consequence of the conditions imposed by Quine on radical translation. Reflection on the implications of this constraint brings Quine's "oddly warped circle" into full view.

Evidence for sameness of stimulus meaning would be evidence that under a given set of stimulus conditions the query in question would prompt the same response (e.g., assent or dissent) from both the linguist and the informant. But, if the linguist can have evidence of this, then querying the informant serves no purpose. If the linguist does not have evidence of this, any conclusion that the informant has judged the query true or false is completely unwarranted. This is Quine's "oddly warped circle."[20] If linguists' use of the method of introspection leads them in this circle, they must reject their belief that the method can provide the linguist with data which confirms that one of a set of alternative extensionally equivalent grammars is descriptively adequate. The anatomy of Quine's argument deserves close study. Quine explicitly allows that his method of introspection (i.e. the method of query and assent) provides the linguist with some legitimate data. He asserts that the method provides part of the evidence necessary for identifying the speech dispositions of informants.[21] For Quine, hypotheses about the speech dispositions of informants are the basis for any recursive specification of the well-formed/significant strings in a language. These are simply the infinite number of strings of theoretically unlimited length which, by hypothesis, speakers of the language would use and respond to without excessive bewilderment. In this way, a recursive specification of the significant/well-formed strings in the language is required to be consistent with the speech dispositions of informants. These dispositions determine the extension of any adequate grammar.[22] Quine's argument, however, does put limits on the kinds of data which the method of introspection can be expected to supply. It is crucial to be clear on just how severe these limits are. Quine's argument has been reconstructed here as an attempt to show that the method of introspection can be of no use in choosing between two grammars which, in Quine's sense, have essentially the same extension. However, Quine's argument has considerably wider implications than that. If sound, Quine's argument establishes that most ascriptions of intentionality are essentially indeterminate as well.

An organism's behavior can be described in intentional terms (e.g. as action) only on the assumption that the behaving organism itself puts an *interpretation* on the behavior so described. In this sense, a hand movement can be described as the *act* of opening the book *Word and Object* only if the person whose hand is moving interprets his behavior in that way. Similarly, an emitted sound can, in this sense, be correctly described as the assertion "I am trying to understand Quine" only if the sound is on that occasion interpreted by the speaker in that way. Normally, we hold that the weightiest evidence we can have concerning what an actor's interpretation of his action is is evidence that the verbal description of his actions that we would give is a description which the actor would accept (if he understood the description in the same way we do and was being honest with us and with himself.) But, problems arise here that parallel those involved with the ascription of judgments. An agent's assent to an action description constitutes evidence that his action has been correctly described only if the description is understood in the same way by the agent and his questioner. That is, the mutual understanding condition must be met. But the only evidence that Quine allows for this is evidence of sameness of stimulus meaning of the query. On a given occasion, evidence for or against sameness of stimulus meaning would be identical with the only evidence available concerning whether a given utterance correctly described the action. Quine's "oddly warped circle" emerges again. It seems clear that it would emerge for any ascription of intentionality whatsoever.[23] Quine's argument not only rules out meta-linguistic judgments as data, it entails the indeterminacy of most ascriptions of intentionality as well.[24] We need to consider the implications of this argument for linguistic methodology.

At most, Quine has established that the method of introspection will provide mentalists with legitimate evidence for deciding between alternative observationally adequate grammars only if the linguist can have some theory independent grounds other than evidence of sameness of stimulus meaning for concluding that the mutual understanding condition was met. But, Quine's argument shows that no such evidence can be had only on the assumption that evidence concerning non-intentional behavioral dispositions is the only relevant theory independent evidence available. But, this is a central thesis of the kind of behaviorism which mentalistic linguists do and must explicitly reject.[25] If Quine's argument against introspective methods in linguistics depends on this assumption, then Quine's argument moves him in a viciously warped circle. He is assuming that sentences expressing an informant's interpretation/understanding of sounds and behavior cannot be used to make factual assertions unless one can operationally specify in non-intentional terms the states of affairs whose presence is necessary or sufficient for correctly saying that an informant understood a specific expression token in a specified way.[26] This, however, is an assumption that any mentalist would contest. Mentalists would maintain that the assertions they make about speaker's tacit grammatical knowledge are only indirectly testable if at all by non-intentional behavioral data.[27] In addition, mentalists would almost certainly allow that the truth of the datum statements they require the method of introspection to provide (i.e., statements about an informant's meta-linguistic judgments) almost certainly depends on assumptions concerning the informant's understanding of queries as well as many other assumptions (e.g., concerning the informant's intentions and his beliefs about the world.) But, mentalists would certainly maintain that nothing said by Quine establishes that a theory independent test of these assumptions is impossible. The mentalist's response here is unassailable.[28]

This, of course, is not the end of the matter. Mentalists have so far only issued promissory notes concerning criteria for checking the veracity of their grammatical hypotheses in general and of statements concerning the meta-linguistic judgments of informants in particular. Few linguists even take seriously the problem of identifying theory independent (even if intentionally described) tests of claims that specific theoretically relevant meta-linguistic judgments were made.[29] Quine has not shown that such tests are impossible, but he has raised the question of what such tests might be. He has shown that part of the difficulty in finding such tests is to identify tests

Quine on Introspection 147

of the informant's understanding of the linguist's queries which do not depend on the assumption that the hypothesis under test is true and which consist of evidence other than that used to determine what the informant's meta-linguistic judgments are. Mentalists avoid addressing this problem on pain of simply not having any reliable checks on data concerning what an informant's judgments are. This leaves the reliability of what mentalists claim as indispensable data in serious doubt.[30, 31]

NOTES

* A shorter version of this paper was read at the Sixth International Congress of Logic, Methodology and Philosophy of Science, Hannover, Federal Republic of Germany, August 22-29, 1979. The writing of this paper was supported by an Indiana University Summer Faculty Fellowship and Grant SOC 75-13423 from the National Science Foundation. I would like to thank E. LePore for helpful comments on an earlier draft of this paper.
1. See Chomsky (1964, 64-67, 79-81; 1965, 8, 18-27) or virtually any textbook inspired by Chomsky's work, e.g., Bach (1974), Baker (1978) and Fodor, Bever, and Garrett (1974).
2. For discussion see Botha (1973, 173-256), Chomsky (1961, 223-227; 1964, 19-81; 1965, 193-194) and Ringen (1977a,b).
3. Quine (1970, 392-393).
4. Chomsky (1965, 24) characterizes descriptive adequacy as follows:

A grammar can be regarded as a theory of a language; it is descriptively adequate to the extent that it correctly describes the intrinsic competence of the idealized native speaker. The structural descriptions assigned to sentences by the grammar, the distinctions that it makes between well-formed and deviant, and so on, must for descriptive adequacy, correspond to the linguistic intuition of the native speaker (whether or not he may be immediately aware of this) in a substantial and significant class of crucial cases.

Descriptive adequacy is contrasted by Chomsky with observational adequacy which is achieved by a grammar if it "presents the observed primary data [corpus data] correctly." (Chomsky 1964, 62). For further discussion see Chomsky 1964, 62-91; 1965, 30-37.
5. See footnote 4. This also is the view endorsed in Fodor and Garrett (1966) and in Fodor, Bever, and Garrett (1974, 21).
6. See Quine (1960, 29ff; 1970, 389).
7. No doubt most contemporary linguists would accept this characterization as being correct as far as it goes. Unfortunately, contemporary linguists have had remarkably little to say about how querying an informant should be conceived. Books on field methods (e.g., Samarin 1967) give some hints as do Botha (1973), Carden (1976), Chomsky (1964; 1965), Greenbaum and Quirk (1970), and Labov (1972a,b; 1975). Much of the discussion by theoretical linguists suggests that the method of introspection involves eliciting from the informant self-reports concerning what their meta-linguistic judgments are. This gives two models of the method of introspection:

(1) eliciting assent or dissent to queries (Quine's method of query and assent) and (2) eliciting self-reports of meta-linguistic judgments. (For discussion of the method designated (2) see Ringen (1977a,b).) Quine would raise identical questions about both versions of the method of introspection. I will argue that the constraints imposed by Quine's criticisms are constraints which cannot be accepted without rejecting any claim to be doing mentalistic linguistics.

8. The method of query and assent is one way of checking speakers' responses to utterances and hence, in Quine's view, essential to determining what speech dispositions a speaker has. See Quine (1953, 1960, 1969). Also see the discussion on pages 6 and 7 above. Quine's queries typically would not involve meta-linguistic terms.

9. Quine (1970, 391-392). For Quine, two grammars are extensionally equivalent if and only if they generate exactly the same set of terminal strings. Chomsky would call the grammars in such a pair observationally equivalent (see footnote 4 above) or equivalent in weak generative capacity (see Chomsky 1965, 60). Quine (1970, 391-392) hints at a readiness to be convinced that "there is, indeed, an unarticulated system of grammatical rules which is somehow implicit in the native mind in a way that an extensionally equivalent system is not." But, he asserts, "For me such a conviction would depend in part on a clarification of criteria," and Quine adduces reasons for concluding that the method of introspection cannot provide the needed clarification. Examining these reasons will reveal what is really at stake.

10. Quine (1953, 1970).
11. Chomsky (1957, 15).
12. Chomsky (1965, 24).
13. See Chomsky (1965, 21-27) and footnotes 1 and 4 above.
14. Quine (1970, 392). More realistic examples of the sort Quine has in mind are discussed in Chomsky (1965, 22-24) and Akmajian and Wasow (1975).
15. Quine's most detailed discussion of radical translation is found in Quine (1960, 26-80). Discussions of the bearing of this thought experiment on the topic of this paper can be found in Root (1976; 1977), LePore (1977), and Rosenberg (1967).
16. I have examined these reasons in some detail in Ringen (1977a,b).
17. See Ringen (1977b) and Itkonen (1978) for discussion of the relevance of intuitive judgments for testing grammars.
18. A similar point could be made about self-reports. For discussion see Ringen (1977a, b). In addition, a more general version of the requirement could be formulated for *any* use of responses to queries as evidence of judgments. This requirement would simply be that the linguist must know how the informant understands the query. Notice that meeting this condition is only a necessary condition on the defensibility of linguists' ascriptions of meta-linguistic judgments to informants. Meeting the condition does not guarantee the correctness of judgment ascriptions consistent with it.
19. For discussion of the notion of stimulus meaning see Quine (1960; 1970).
20. This reconstruction of Quine's "oddly warped circle" is set out with exceptional clarity in Root (1976).
21. See Quine (1969, 97) and footnote 8 above.
22. For discussion of this point see Quine (1960, 1970, 1974, 1975a,b).
23. Indeed, insofar as assenting or dissenting is intentional, Quine's method of query and assent cannot depend on describing the informant as engaging in either of these. Quine cannot consistently maintain that a given movement or sound is interpreted by the organism emitting them as either assent or dissent. At best, Quine can

Quine on Introspection 149

opt for consistently using the term assent and dissent to identify certain patterns of movement or sound. Presumeably, one of the sources of the indeterminacy of radical translation is that linguists could adopt alternative conventions concerning what they would count as assent, dissent, or bewilderment.

24. Quine (1974, 329) accepts this consequence. He asserts:

> Of course, I seconded Brentano, at one point in my own writing, on the irreducibility of intentional discourse to proper scientific discourse. But I took an attitude unlike Brentano's. He thought the irreducibility showed we needed a science of intention; I thought it so much the worse for intentions. (See also Quine 1960, 220-222.)

25. Thus, Chomsky (1964, 52) asserts:

> The common characterization of language as a set of "verbal habits" or as a "complex of present dispositions to verbal behavior, in which speakers of the same language have perforce come to resemble one another" (Quine 1960, 27) is totally inadequate. Knowledge of one's language is not reflected directly in linguistic habits and dispositions, and it is clear that speakers of the same language or dialect may differ enormously in dispositions to verbal response, depending on personality, beliefs, and countless other extra-linguistic factors.

For a useful discussion of the differences between behaviorist and mentalist views of the relation between data and theory see Fodor (1968, 49-90).

26. Quine defends this assumption in Quine (1960).
27. See for example Chomsky (1964, 62-63; 1965, 18-27), Fodor (1968; 1974), and Fodor, Bever, and Garrett (1974).
28. Even Quine (1951) has argued that hypotheses are not testable either directly or in isolation.
29. Chomsky (1965, 20-21) takes a very relaxed view of this problem:

> ... at a given stage of investigation, one whose concern is for insight and understanding (rather than objectivity as a goal in itself) must ask whether or to what extent a wider range and more exact description of phenomena is relevant to solving the problems that he faces. In linguistics, it seems to me that sharpening of the data by more objective tests is a matter of small importance for the problems at hand. One who disagrees with this estimate of the problem situation in linguistics can justify his belief in the current importance of more objective operational tests by showing how they can lead to new and deeper understanding of linguistic structure. Perhaps the day will come when the kinds of data that we now can obtain in abundance will be insufficient to resolve deeper questions concerning the structure of language. However, many questions that can realistically and significantly be formulated today do not demand evidence of a kind that is unavailable or unattainable without significant improvements in objectivity of experimental technique.

This provides one illustration of the similarity between Chomsky's views on the assessment of scientific research programs and the views developed in Lakatos (1970).

30. Compare the quote in footnote 29 above with the discussions in Botha (1973),

Carden (1976), and Labov (1972a,b; 1975). These writers give reason to believe that the current "problem situation" in linguistics is such that the future progress of the mentalistic research program for linguistics and psychology of language depends in large measure on determining what relevant checks on introspectional linguistic data could possibly be. Donald Davidson (1973, 1974, 1976) has made an interesting start in identifying the specific obstacles that must be overcome if attempts to specify the required checks are to succeed.

31. It would seem that any serious assessment of the epistemic status of mentalistic claims to knowledge about language can proceed only after progress has been made in specifying how the veracity of introspective datum statements in linguistics can be legitimately checked. For some remarks on this topic see Ringen (1975, 1978).

REFERENCES

Akmajian, A. and T. Wasow (1975). "The constituent structure of VP and AUX and the position of the verb *be*." *Linguistic Analysis* 1: 205-245.
Bach, E. (1974). *Syntactic Theory*. New York: Holt, Rinehart, and Winston.
Baker, C. (1978). *Introduction to Generative Transformational Syntax*. Englewood Cliffs: Prentice-Hall.
Botha, R. P. (1973). *The Justification of Linguistic Hypotheses*. The Hague: Mouton.
Carden, G. (1976). *English Quantifiers: Logical Structure and Linguistic Variation*. New York: Academic Press.
Chomsky, N. (1957). *Syntactic Structures*. The Hague: Mouton.
– (1961). "Some methodological remarks on generative grammar." *Word* 17: 219-239.
– (1964). "Current issues in linguistic theory." In Fodor and Katz (1964), pp. 119-136.
– (1965). *Aspects of the Theory of Syntax*. Cambridge: The M.I.T. Press.
Davidson, D. (1973). "Radical interpretation." *Dialectica* 27: 313-328.
– (1974). "Belief and the basis of meaning." *Synthese* 27: 309-323.
– (1976). "Hempel on explaining action." *Erkenntnis* 10: 239-253.
Fodor, J. (1968). *Psychological Explanation*. New York: Random House.
– (1974). *The Language of Thought*. New York: Thomas Y. Crowell.
– and J. Katz (1964). *The Structure of Language*. Englewood Cliffs: Prentice-Hall.
– and M. Garrett (1966). "Some reflections of competence and performance." J. Lyons and R. Wales, eds., *Psycholinguistic Papers*. Edinburgh: Edinburgh University Press, pp. 135-182.
– T. Bever and M. Garrett (1974). *The Psychology of Language*. New York: McGraw-Hill.
French, P., T. Uchling Jr. and H. Wettenstein, eds., (1975). *Studies in the Philosophy of Language*. Morris: The University of Minnesota Press.
Greenbaum, S. and R. Quirk (1970). *Elicitation Experiments in English: Studies in Use and Attitude*. Coral Gables, Florida: University of Miami Press.
Guttenplan, S., ed., (1975). *Mind and Language*. Oxford: Clarendon Press.
Hook, S., ed., (1969). *Language and Philosophy*. New York: New York University.
Itkonen, E. (1978). *Grammatical Theory and Metascience*. Amsterdam: John Benjamins.
Labov, W. (1972a). *Sociolinguistic Patterns*. Philadelphia: University of Pennyslvania Press.
– (1972b). "Some principles of linguistic methodology." *Language in Society* 1: 97-120.

Quine on Introspection 151

Labov, W. (1975). "Empirical foundations of linguistic theory." In R. Austerlitz, ed., *The Scope of American Linguistics*. Lisse: The Peter de Ridder Press, pp. 77-133.

Lakatos, I. (1970). "Falsification and the methodology of scientific research programmes." In I. Lakatos and A. Musgrave, eds., *Criticism and the Growth of Knowledge*. New York: Cambridge University Press, pp. 91-196.

LePore, E. (1977). "Reply to Professor Root." *Philosophical Studies*.

Quine, W. (1951). "Two dogmas of empiricism." In Quine (1963), pp. 20-46.

— (1953). "The problem of meaning in linguistics." In Quine (1963). pp. 47-64.

— (1960). *Word and Object*. Cambridge: The M.I.T. Press.

— (1963). *From a Logical Point of View*. 2nd ed. rev., New York: Harper and Row.

— (1969). "Linguistics and philosophy." In Hook (1969), pp. 95-98.

— (1970). "Methodological reflections on current linguistic theory." *Synthese* 21: 386-398.

— (1974). "Comment on Donald Davidson." *Synthese* 27: 325-329.

— (1975a). "The nature of natural knowledge." In Guttenplan (1975), 67-82.

— (1975b). "Mind and verbal disposition." In Guttenplan (1975), pp. 83-96.

Ringen, J. (1975). "Linguistic facts: A study of the empirical scientific status of transformational generative grammars." In D. Cohen and J. Wirth, eds., *Testing Linguistic Hypotheses*. New York: John Wiley, pp. 1-41.

— (1977a). "On evaluating data concerning linguistic intuition." In F. Eckman, ed., *Current Themes in Linguistics*. New York: John Wiley, pp. 145-160.

— (1977b). "Linguistic data: Intuition and grammar testing." Paper discussed at the Roundtable Session on Linguistics as an Empirical Science, Twelfth International Congress of Linguists, Vienna, Austria.

— (1978). "Knowledge *about* language." Paper presented at the Fourth Annual Minnesota Conference on Language and Linguistics, Minneapolis, Minnesota.

Root, M. (1976). "Speaker intuitions." *Philosophical Studies* 29: 221-233.

— (1977). "Quine's thought experiment." In French, Uehling, and Wettstein (1977), pp. 225-239.

Rosenberg, J. (1967). "Synonymy and the epistemology of linguistics." *Inquiry* 10: 405-420.

Samarin, W. (1967). *Field Linguistics*. New York: Holt, Rinehart, and Winston.

KONRAD EHLICH

Native Speaker's Heritage. On Philology of "Dead" Languages*

ABSTRACT

Native speakers leave behind traces of their linguistic activities. Philology analyses them, trying to reestablish the languages of those relics. Philology and linguistics share a common subject, language, but they also differ in various respects. In my paper, I discuss some of the relationships between them (section 1.). Relevant parts of the similarities and differences can be described by reference to the specific use they make of various types of Native Speakers and of their activities. First, I discuss some relations of linguists and native speakers (section 2.), then I point out the philologist's dilemma (section 3.). In order to find out about the differences between linguists and native speakers, I describe those types of researchers exhibiting these differences most obviously: the linguistic fieldworker and the type of native speaker he works with (section 4.), the introspectionist and the hidden native speaker he refers to (section 4.2.), the philologist of "dead" languages and his work with situationally detached texts (section 5.). The philologist's work combines the main theoretical figures characterizing the fieldworker's as well as the intuitionist's work. It is described by means of the category of "hermeneutic circle" (section 6.). A discussion of philological research strategy leads to four questions concerning the entirety of activities of linguists beyond those parts which are accounted for in the respective theory of science and methodology (section 7.).

1. LINGUISTICS AND PHILOLOGY[1]

Linguistics is a newcomer in the scientific world. Its rapid development has made us forget that the scientific occupation with language has a long history. Its name is philology — a scientific discipline which nowadays stands somewhat puzzled before the new science of linguistics — progeny now grown up and gone independent. Linguistics, on the other hand, does not seem to remember any of its predecessors.

In fact, both branches of the study of language — though sharing a common object — seem to work along different lines without taking much cognizance of each other. Apparently, they treat their common subject in very different ways.

The relation of linguistics and philology was much closer when it was understood that occupation with language means occupation with texts. The discovery of *spoken* language and its acceptance as a legitimate object of scientific analysis marks one of the most decisive theoretical and practical turning points in the history of language-science. "Modern" linguistics is basically synchronous linguistics. Much of modern linguistic methodology is designed for tackling tasks which spring up with that sort of object and that sort of analysis.

2. LINGUISTS AND NATIVE SPEAKERS

In as much as linguistics turned towards the analysis of spoken language and actual speech events, "Native Speaker" became one of its head figures. There are two main types of "Native Speaker" which are the most prominent ones for the linguist's everyday activity. *One* is the native who speaks a language which is *unknown* to the linguist. The linguist's aim is to establish a description of the native's language and in order to do that he tries to get the native to collaborate with him. This is the classical type of native speaker. He started his career somewhere "in the field." Whenever the linguist (anthropologist, ethnologist, etc.) happened to arrive in a district with a hitherto unknown language there were one or several candidates who could enter into the role of "Native Speaker." This type of native speaker bridges the gap to an alien world, to a world unknown to the linguist. He opens the doors to the linguist's destination, the treasuries of unknown languages and cultures. It is mainly in the context of anthropology and ethnology that this first type of native speaker finds his employment or, better, his exploitation.

The *second* type of native speaker is less known. He differs from the first one to a great extent, being a native speaker in disguise. He is the linguist himself, acting as producer and proliferator of the "data" of his work. His mother tongue is, at the same time, the language under investigation. It is the language, or "dialect" or even "idiolect" of the linguist which stands as an example for all the fundamental capacities and competences that are in play when people talk. The linguist is his own native speaker — the more so whenever a claim on grammaticality or acceptability of a sentence, of a self-produced datum, is challenged or counterclaimed by someone else. Then, it is the native-speaker-linguist who draws all his knowledge about the object of inquiry from his own language, since, in the last instance, it is his own idiolect that matters, that is considered as the object of analysis.

The two types of native speakers deserve to be distinguished by different names. Let us call the first one the *"native native speaker (NNS),"* the second the *"linguist native speaker (LNS)."*

Linguists who work with data provided by NNS are *empirical linguists.*

Native Speaker's Heritage

Linguists relying on data provided by LNS are called intuitionists or introspectionists. Of course, the different approaches of empirical and of introspective linguistics are not simply identical with the difference between NNSs and LNSs. But the least we can say is that there is a strong tendency of them to cooccur with the two types of native speakers.

Both types of native speaker provide their interviewer with the best possible information about his subject, and they enable him to expand his knowledge in a systematic way according to its actual state and according to the procedural prerequisites which the linguist has decided to follow on methodological grounds. Thus, both, NNS and LNS, contribute to solve the linguist's professional problems.

3. THE PHILOLOGIST'S DILEMMA

None of these helpful collaborators, neither NNS nor LNS, stands ready to support the philologist's work. Whereas the linguist finds himself in a position such that he can rely on the native speaker's information, provided that he takes care of well-established strategies of inquiry, the philologist is confronted with a different situation. Its peculiar characteristics are most obvious in the case of data from hitherto unknown languages. He finds himself face to face not with a speaker of any language but with written documents about which the only thing he knows with certainty is that they are linguistic entities.

By identifying them as linguistic entities, the philologist knows that they are comprehensible. His dilemma is hence the gap between (potential) comprehensibility and (actual) comprehension, and his task is to bridge this gap. In order to do that the philologist has to re-construct the language of the data at hand. For the philologist the achievement of this task is not generally an aim in itself, but rather a resort for understanding the contents of the data written in the language in question. Thus, philology is a *subsidiary* scientific discipline.

4.1. Field Workers and Native Native Speakers: Entering a Foreign World

The gap between comprehensibility and comprehension so characteristic of the philologist's work seems not unlike the situation encountered by the linguistic field worker. What, then, is the difference between the conditions of their respective work?

The field worker enters the field, i.e., the life situation of the native speakers. He intrudes upon their actual speech situation. In so doing, he tries to integrate into the native speakers' world — however spellbound he may be at first because of the unknown language of his new environment. The integration into the native speakers' world, if it is at all successful, brings about fundamental identifications between the native speakers and the linguist. Their common world is a common domain of inter-action. It enables them to achieve mutual understanding, by reinstantiating the qualification for language as a means and medium of communication.

A major consequence of this common world for both, native speakers and field worker, however restricted it may be in the beginning, is the constitution of a common *"origo"* in Bühler's (1934) sense. It has two essential consequences. First, it enables the field worker, to acquire a knowledge of an elementary subset of linguistic entities, namely of *deictic expressions*, and to make use of them for the expansion of his linguistic knowledge; deictic expressions, though small in number, are of outstanding importance for all linguistic activity.

Second, the common "origo" enables the field worker to make use of a complex combination of two procedures: *pointing at* and *identifying* things, persons, and so on, and hence learning their names. The common *origo* as a domain which constitutes a common sensual approach to the world for the native speakers and the field worker and to enact a common practice provides the linguist with the opportunity to *observe* the *use* of language of native speakers in everyday life, and to enhance his knowledge by asking for *names* of entities and activities at which he can point. The linguistic means for doing so is the so-called "ostensive definition," a combination of a *deictic* procedure and an act of *naming*.

The linguistic interest of the field worker in his interaction with the native speaker leads towards a set of sophisticated methods for optimizing the acquisition procedures of knowledge about linguistic structures of unfamiliar languages. Moreover, these methods lead to the compilation of guide books of practical field work such as those by Samarin (1967) or Healey (1975) thus making available the experiences of many linguists as a useful tool for further application.

Now, what are the main features of the linguist's work with NNS, as regarded from the point of view of action theory? To my mind, its most outstanding characteristic can best be described in terms of the notions of 'alien' and 'de-alienation'. The linguist who enters any "field" and lets himself get involved in linguistic activity with the native speakers comes to the field as a stranger – and the language which is the regular means of communication there is itself strange to him. That means, the linguist has the status of an alien (cf. Schütz (1944)). This, of course, is a serious obstacle to carrying out linguistic as well as other activities within the host community. Nevertheless, this obstacle is only a relative one, the real obstacle being that the language is alien to him. All of his efforts aim at transforming the *alien* language into a *familiar* one. He wants to become well-informed on the language's structures, and he wants to become well-acquainted with its use. He improves his knowledge about the unknown language by using the native speakers' elicited and spontaneous utterances for collecting data and information as best he can. The efficiency of his work, to a large extent, depends upon the opportunities of eliciting data and making inquiries about them. The process of transforming the alien, unknown language into a familiar one I would like to call *'de-alienation'* of the language for the linguist.

As the linguist obtains his information by means of a combined methodology based on his sharing the native speakers' world he learns about his subject not only in a purely theoretical way. Quite the contrary is the case. His inquiries of the native speakers are part of intruding into the foreign world and of "appropriating" its language to himself. (In many cases, this very process results in a partial expropriation, and hence destruction, of the native speakers' culture who loose their own traditions and who are overwhelmed by another culture which tends to absorb them; cf. Kummer, this volume).

By this process, however, the linguist is not only introduced into a *new language*, but also into a *new practice*; thus, the activities of the field worker in cooperation with, and/or outsmarting of, the native speaker are a *practical approach* towards his language. In learning the language, the linguist learns about the native speakers' world: he realizes language as a *"Lebensform"* ("form of life," Wittgenstein[2]). As regards the language under consideration by the researcher, the process of de-alienation is a controlled and systematic adoption of a form of life, an adoption which is carried out in a practical way.

4.2. Introspection

Let us take a look now at the introspective linguist's activity. The object of his introspection is his own language, or, to be more exact, the knowledge of his language. His theoretical reflection is carried out by permanent recourse to his linguistic intuitions. All the data he needs he finds in his own linguistic knowledge. Thus, the introspectionist relies on himself for linguistic evidence: he is his own native speaker. This fact is to be accounted for with the term of the 'linguist native speaker (LNS)'.

As is well known, the linguist who uses his own intuitions as data for his theory refers to his own *competence* as the ultimate basis for his linguistic judgments. However, the notion of 'competence' is not without problems. It is a practical abbreviation which lets aside a lot of general issues which are of fundamental theoretical importance for linguistic analysis. 'Competence' tends to individualize and to reify language. The functional qualities of language as a means towards a variety of ends, and its ultimate character as a "form of life" tend to become neglected by an approach which is centered on the concept of intra-psychic competence.

Nevertheless, the intuitionist's view is one of great importance for doing linguistics. What exactly is the theoretical figure the introspective linguist executes when "looking into himself"? His competence is a "mechanism" enabling him to use his own language effectively. He is familiar with the language in his mind — on a practical basis. He is able to speak his language. Whereas the field worker who contacts the native speaker enters an alien world and tries to systematically transform it into a familiar one, the introspective linguist is part of a world which is completely familiar to him, knowing his language. But his knowledge is of a practical kind, it is a knowledge which he makes use of in every day life. Unlike "normal" speakers of his language, however, the linguist is not content that his competence functions all right in actual speech situations, he wants to know how it works. This means that, in order to become aware of what he does when he is speaking, he looks at the language familiar to him in practice from a point of view which has little or nothing to do with his actual practice. This figure is the exact opposite of that of the field worker. When analyzing his own intuitions, the introspective linguist treats as distant and strange something which is quite familiar to him: His procedure is an *alienation* (in the sense of *Verfremdung* (Brecht)). In making his every day linguistic practice the object of investigation he turns it into something alien. The structures of his object can only become visible if the process of alienation is successful.

5. DIFFERENCES AND PARALLELS BETWEEN FIELD WORKERS, INTROSPECTIONISTS AND PHILOLOGISTS: DETACHED TEXTS AS LINGUISTIC OBJECTS AND THE CONSEQUENCES FOR LINGUISTIC WORK

Quite different from the situation of the field linguist who works with native speakers is the situation of the philologist. As was pointed out above, the philologist has no native speaker to talk with. He finds himself in an *isolated, solitary position*. The only linguistic connection to any native speaker he comes across are *relics* of the native speaker's linguistic activities. These relics are called *texts*. Texts are native speaker's heritage. What, then, are texts? Of course, there are hundreds of "definitions" of 'text'. Only few of them take into account the relationship of text and linguistic activity. However, it is from this angle that those characteristics of text can be seen most clearly which bring about structural determinations for the philologist's analyses.

Texts differ characteristically from speech acts. Speech acts have a speaker and a hearer who share a common situation, namely the speech (or speech act) situation. This fundamental characteristic is missing with texts (cf.

Native Speaker's Heritage

Ehlich 1979, § 6.). They are spoken (or written) at a specific time t_i. The hearer or reader of the speech act uttered at t_i is typically *not* copresent in the speech situation. Rather, the adressee exists at another time, t_j, $i<j$ (and in many cases at another place.) Whereas technical means have provided possibilities for bridging the spacial distance, there is no *direct* means of overcoming the time lag. Thus, mankind has invented procedures of tradition, which are supposed to bring about a solution for these difficulties. In order to make 'tradition' possible, the propositional and illocutionary qualities of a speech act have to be transferred to a time different from that of its utterance. It is at this point that texts are needed, and have been invented. Thus, texts are means of transmitting previous speech acts to later adressees. That means that the speech situation is in itself *distended*. Speaker and hearer do not share a common time nor a common place which could enable them to share a common "*origo*." On the contrary, texts are means serving to overcome the limitations of the individual, temporarily fixed speech situation, and of the narrow lines which are determined by its *origo*.

Thus, the "speech situation" is one for the speaker and another one for the hearer and the latter is removed from the former. Nevertheless, the transmission of the speech act is oriented towards an addressee. But the distention of the speech situation can cause unprovided results of transmission: the text can reach hearers/readers other than those it was aimed at, if, for example, it is transmitted along unintended lines, or it can be preserved much longer than had been planned at the time of production.

The latter circumstances constitute the normal situation into which the philologist enters: his data are texts which were never *addressed* to him but which have been *transmitted* to him. The philologist is a secondary hearer/reader of texts which were handed over to him by chance. We may say, then, that the philologist is a *contingent hearer/reader* of a text, the term 'contingent' being taken in its exact philosophical sense.

I have said before that the philologist's situation is, paradoxically spoken, a gap. From what was said above, it has become obvious that this gap is a result of a number of specific qualities of the linguistic means for transmitting speech acts in distended speech situations, namely in texts. Texts tend to dissociate from the transmitting process for which they had been invented, and to develop a "life of their own." Let us call texts of this sort *detached texts*. Detached texts are the genuine material for the philologist's contingent reading activity. The detachment of the texts dissociates them from all of those speech situation factors which warrant their actual understanding. Thus, detached texts are texts the understanding of which has been *virtualized*: there is comprehensibility but no actual comprehension. Again, we have come back to the philologist's dilemma.

His task, now, is to reestablish an understanding of the detached texts. In order to do so, he reconstructs their language. But there is no speech situation with its normal stock of persons who speak the language, of a common place, time, pointable surroundings, etc. The philologist has nothing but one little segment of the whole, distended speech situation: the text in its supposed comprehensibility. His task is therefore quite different from that of the field worker: the field worker enters NNS' world — the text has entered the philologist's world. It demands to be read and to be understood. The philologist, within his normal, every-day environment, his actual form of life, has to follow the text's appeal. His task is to establish a foreign, alien world within his own world. In other words: his task is not to accomplish a de-alienation, but his work leads to an *alienation* which is brought about by the text's introducing of an alien world into that of its actual reader. The alienation again is more one of *"Verfremdung"* than of *"Entfremdung."*

The philologist is bound to reconstruct a foreign world. The medium of reconstruction is the *philologist's mind*. The gap between (virtual) comprehensibility and (actual) understanding can be bridged within the philologist's head. He has to integrate into his mind a new part of world-knowledge, a part hitherto unknown to him but becoming increasingly detailed as he learns more about the language of the text.

Knowledge about the language of the texts can not be acquired by recourse to NNS. The solitary philologist depends on his own faculties and capacities. His mind has to re-establish the linguistic knowledge of a language which — in the worst case — is "dead," and no NNS can help him. By re-establishing the knowledge of the foreign language that language itself finds a new linguistic potential. It can be understood again (and might even be re-used, as is the case, for example, with languages like Ivrit).

The field worker has a practical contact to the language he studies, and, by means of the common *origo* and the visibility of the speech situation, he learns the new language not only as an abstract language but as a "form of life." (section 4.1.). The philologist can do nothing of that sort; on the contrary, he has to integrate the foreign world into his own mind. In a way, the result of his activity is an *imagination*, a mental representation of a language in his mind. There is no practice at all. The practice has passed away with native speaker's death, and the philologist is his heir. Moreover: his "succession" is by no means a legitimate entailment; it is in some way indirect, beyond the devisor's intent.

Re-establishing linguistic knowledge on a dead language brings about a *post-native state* for the philologist as speaker of the previously dead, bequeathed and handed-down language. Let us next consider the question of what this position of the philologist is like in terms of the two types of native speaker we find in linguistics, NNS and LNS. This question reveals a surprising answer: as has been stated above, there is no NNS. But we find

Native Speaker's Heritage 161

the philologist in a position that is parallel to that of the 'linguist native speaker (LNS)'. The philologist develops a kind of linguistic knowledge of which he makes use by introspection. Since there is no native speaker NNS, he himself is the only one who can really "speak" the language, i.e., who develops a concrete, individualized competence in that language, a competence comprising all of the elements that make a language. This secondary competence of the philologist is open to introspection, and introspection is the main way how the philologist comes to systematic results on the structures of his subject. Thus, we find him on the side of the introspective linguist. The philologist is his own LNS. The close relationship to intuitionist linguistics seems to set him apart from empirical linguistics which relies on NNS.

But the philologist's proximity to the intuitionist linguist does not include all of his linguistic characteristics. Though he is the only speaker of the language he analyses, he has developed his competence in a different way from that of the 'linguist native speaker'. LNS learned the language in the normal course of primary language acquisition. In that, LNS is a real native speaker of the language which he analyses. The philologist, on the other hand, learned the language in another way. In order to make it available for linguistic analysis, he had to employ a number of complicated methods enabeling him to become a LNS. The ordinary course of language acquisition in childhood comes to an end when the language is adopted in such a way that the speaker can use it for every conceivable purpose as part of his everyday life. In other words: the process of language acquisition is completed once the learner has acquired the "form of life."

The philologist will never arrive at this state – simply because there is no such "form of life" any more. Thus, he has to find extrinsic criteria which tell him when his linguistic competence in the object language is sufficient. In order to fulfil this need, he has to develop a methodology to disclose the structures of the native speaker's heritage. Thus, the philologist, too, "travels" to a foreign domain. His travels, however, do not take him to a foreign land but to a time different from his own life time. Intruding a foreign domain and getting involved within it makes his endeavor parallel to that of the field worker. His methodology is an archeological, and radicalized, counterpart of the field worker's approach to his field. The methods which can be used for breaking the code of the texts at hand have to be much more sophisticated in order to make accessible the foreign world of native speakers who are not available for inquiry or direct questioning. The philologist's position is similar to the field worker's but he has to put up with considerable difficulties working under quite intricate conditions. How can these complications be mastered? In order to answer this question, we have to gather up the results on the philologist's activities we have found out so far.

6. PHILOLOGICAL METHODOLOGY: THE HERMENEUTIC CIRCLE

So far, we have arrived at a twofold result: (a) We have seen that the philologist is necessitated to put himself into a position which is similar to that of the 'linguist native speaker'. (b) In order to achieve this position he applies (in a radicalized fashion) field methods which are normally used to elicit the native native speaker's linguistic knowledge and to occasion his utterances. These methods are adapted to the detached texts, that is a corpus of random utterances not having been produced for the use of the linguist's inquisitive purposes. The methodological demands are fulfilled in such a way that the philologist uses quasi field methods, methods for questioning a NNS — but the role of this NNS is played by himself as the only person who has at his disposal the linguistic knowledge of the foreign language, who has revived the "dead" language by becoming a 'linguist native speaker (LNS)'.

Thus, the philologist *combines the two alternative approaches to the study of language* discussed above. On the basis of this re-unification of NNS and LNS and of field worker and introspectionist can he fulfil his task.

The positions of field-like methods and of intuitionist approaches to the knowledge about his object language incorporated in his mind mark *two poles* of the philologist's activity. Of course, he cannot occupy both of them at a time. That means that the philologist's work is a *process* in the course of which he moves from one position to the other. He starts with reconstructing and building up a competence of the foreign language, which, in the first place, is rather incomplete and rough. In doing so, he has to run through the two positions of a field-like methodology and of a rudimentary intuition about the language represented in the texts. By increasing his own competence of the "dead" language he can support his empirical approach with increasingly pertinent and accurate structural material. On the other hand, the empirical approach contributes to the elaboration of his competence of the language. This continuous movement between the two poles of the philologist's work is characteristic of his linguistic activity.

The procedure of the field worker has been described as a *de-alienation* by means of the acquisition of the "form of life" of NNS. The structure of the intuitionist linguist's procedure is that of a methodologically controlled *alienation* of his own tacit linguistic knowledge, the knowledge that constitutes his competence. This knowledge is raised to the level of conscious awareness by means of self-report in the course of which the linguist treats himself as LNS.

Now, considering the philologist's work in the light of these two theoretical movements, we find him involved in a process of *continous alternation between de-alienation and alienation* which, as a whole, constitutes his analytic activity.

Native Speaker's Heritage 163

This alternating movement has been described in the classical theory of philological work, namely hermeneutics.[3] The elementary figure of the hermeneutic process is known as the *'hermeneutic circle'*. The hermeneutic circle is a movement between a previous set of notions on the text and a continous alternation of these notions by confronting them with the text itself. This process is a process of alienation (critique of pre-established notions) and de-alienation (construction of a better understanding of the text). The movement from comprehensibility or understandability of the text to its comprehension and understanding is the movement of building up a linguistic knowledge which, for purpose of analysis, can be approached by introspection, and of changing previous stages of this knowledge by re-confronting it with the texts to which the knowledge refers.

To sum up: the hermeneutic structure of the philologist's work comprises a methodological complexity of two approaches which have been separated into two different linguistic methodologies, an empirical, field method, and an introspective intuitionist method. They are based on two types of native speakers — the 'native native speaker' and the 'linguist native speaker'. The procedures of contact of the linguist with NNS and LNS, respectively, have different results, and the corresponding methodological dichotomies, characterizing the state of the linguistic art, are equally different. Philology, and the philology of "dead" languages in particular, exhibits a combination of the different approaches. Owing to the specific structure of the philologist's task, this combination is a *conditio sine qua non* of his work. He has to compensate the lack of 'native native speakers', with some random relics of their linguistic activities. These relics are texts which generally are detached from the context of use for which they were originally written. The philologist re-establishes the language under investigation by making himself a potential 'linguist native speaker' — by means of a methodology which is similar to that of the empirical linguist who has direct access to the 'native native speaker'.

While combining parts of the methodology of both, introspective linguistics and linguistic field work, philology also differs in some respects from both of them. Unlike the field linguist who enters the world of the 'native native speaker,' the philologist has to build up knowledge about an alien world by means of archeological reconstruction which will never put him into a position of real-life participation in the foreign world. On the other hand, the philologist, though largely and necessarily applying intuitionist concepts in his work, can never fully rely on his own competence, as the 'linguist native speaker' can. The philologist is always open to new empirical evidence from the texts which may urge him to change his competence in a systematic way.

7. FOUR OPEN QUESTIONS

In the foregoing, I have discussed linguistic methodologies along the lines followed in linguistic methodological discourse itself. The combination of empirical and intuitionist methodology in philology gives rise to a number of questions of a more general methodological outlook which might lead beyond the dichotomies of those methods. They are concerned with the actual conditions and the actual progress of linguistic work and with the limitations brought about by these methodologies. I can not enter into the discussion of these problems in the context of the present paper, but, to conclude, I want to state four of them in a hypothetical way.

(i) Could it be that empirical linguistics is involved in the hermeneutic circle in a way similar to that of philology if one regards the actual practice of field work?

(ii) The "corpus" of data in distributionalist linguistics in various respects plays a role similar to that of the detached texts in philology. Does the distributionalist, then, construe a research situation which is merely an artificial analogy of that of the philologist, without that being necessary since the distributionalist does have access to NNs?

(iii) Could the philological method of combining empirical and introspective procedures serve as the basis of a critique of isolated intuitionism which reduces the 'linguist native speaker's' language to a "private language" (in Wittgenstein's sense)?[4]

(iv) Could a critical and comparative investigation of the philological method on the one hand and the linguistic methodologies on the other lead to methodological reflection of linguistic practice and thus reconquer the common grounds of the various forms of language-related sciences?

NOTES

* I thank the editor for the inestimable support of a 'near native speaker' he gave me in order to make my Anglo-German paper readable for the original 'linguist native speaker' who, without doubt, nowadays by and large is a speaker of English.
1. cf. Anttila (1973).
2. The relevant texts are quoted and discussed in Zabeeh (1971), § I/3; s. esp. pp. 346 s.; cf. Hunter (1971).
3. cf. Gadamer (1975), and see also Itkonen, this volume.

4. cf. Klemke (1971) § 9.-13.15.

REFERENCES

Anttila, R. (1973). 'Linguistik und Philologie.' In Bartsch, R. & Vennemann, Th., eds., *Linguistik und Nachbarwissenschaften*. Kronberg: Scriptor.
Bühler, K. (1934). *Sprachtheorie*. NP 1965. Stuttgart: Gustav Fischer.
Ehlich, K. (1979). *Verwendungen der Deixis beim sprachlichen Handeln*. Frankfurt, Bern, Las Vegas: Peter Lang.
Gadamer, H.-G. (1975). *Wahrheit und Methode*. 4th print. Tübingen: Mohr.
Healey, A. (1975). *Language Learner's Field Guide*. Ukarumpa (Papua New Guinea): Summer Institute of Linguistics.
Hunter, J.F.M. (1971). "Forms of Life" in Wittgenstein's *Philosophical Investigations*. In: Klemke, E.D., ed., *Essays on Wittgenstein*, § 14.
Itkonen, E. (1980). 'The Concept of Linguistic Intuition.' In this volume.
Klemke, E.D., ed. (1971). *Essays on Wittgenstein*. Urbana, Chicago, London: University of Illinois Press.
Kummer, W. (1980). 'Malinche, Patron-Saint of Informants?' In this volume.
Samarin, W.J. (1967). *Field Linguistics*. New York: Holt, Rinehart and Winston.
Schütz, A. (1944). 'The Stranger.' In *The American Journal of Sociology* 49 (6): 499-507.
Wittgenstein, L. (1953). *Philosophische Untersuchungen* (Philosophical Investigations), ed. by G.E.M. Anscombe and R. Rees. Oxford: Blackwell.
Zabeeh, F. (1971). 'On Language Games and Forms of Life.' In Klemke, E.D., ed., *Essays on Wittgenstein*, § 16.

PART THREE

Field Work: Techniques and Ethics

EUGENE A. NIDA

Informants or Colleagues?

ABSTRACT

Informants, the unsung heroes of so much linguistic research, can and should make a much greater contribution if only their latent capacities are adequately developed through sufficient informal training by collaborating linguists. Furthermore, the joint efforts of informants and linguists can result in far more relevant insights on a much more profound level of linguistic inquiry, particularly in the areas of discourse structure, sociolinguistic usage, and semantics. Moreover, such collaboration can make possible long-term programs of continuing research, with accompanying personal enrichment derived from shared intellectual goals and concerns.

The unsung heroes of linguistic endeavors are undoubtedly the countless native speakers who have served as informants to linguists working largely in Third-World languages. There are probably no more patient people in the world than these native speakers who have often been subjected to some of the strangest and sometimes stupidest types of interrogation. One Ph.D. candidate rushed up to her professor and insisted that she simply could not get her informant to be consistent in repeating minimal pairs, even though she had had him repeat two words continuously for forty-five minutes — no wonder! On another occasion a budding linguist insisted on asking a Kiowa Indian whether his language had "minimal pairs," to which the informant replied, "No, but we do have small apples." On another occasion a young linguist expressed severe disappointment with an informant, since there was no correspondence between the terms for 'horse,' 'back,' and 'riding' and the composite expression 'to go horse-back-riding.'

Some informants prove to be extremely competent and well informed. In fact, on one occasion I was demonstrating to a group of students some of the techniques of elicitation by using a simple paradigm in one of the Indian languages in Oklahoma. After obtaining four forms of a transitive verb with the pronominal elements 'I,' 'you' (sg.), 'he,' and 'we,' the informant mentioned, "In the next form you will find a velar glottalized stop." It is too bad that all informants cannot be trained in linguistics — and perhaps that is what we as linguists really should do, namely, make colleagues out of informants.

One can and must expect some difficulties in working with native speakers, and some of the difficulties can scarcely be anticipated. On one occasion Charles Hockett invited me to join him in working with a Potawatomie speaker in Wisconsin. She was a fascinating person with a rich wealth of native lore, but her pronunciation of fortis and lenis consonants became periodically difficult because of a large wad of chewing tobacco which she required as part of her compensation for informant work. The only thing to do was to rush through the easier forms of a paradigm while the saliva gathered, and then go back immediately to the complex forms as soon as the informant had spit into her handy tomato-can spittoon.

Some of the most brilliant informants I have ever worked with were some Bushman natives in Tsumkwe, Namibia. The clarity of their pronunciation, their capacity to detect my difficulties in identifying the numerous clicks, their sensitivity to the complex tonal contrasts of their K'ung dialect, their enormously rich vocabulary, and their unusual ability to analyze subtle syntactic distinctions rivaled anything I have ever experienced in the more than 150 languages in which I have had the opportunity to work with informants. I could not help but feel that here were men who could make a really important contribution to our understanding of language structure if only they had the opportunity for training.

In general, informants have a far greater potential than many linguists realize. Too often such informants are restricted to responding to elicitation of forms without context. As a result the forms may vary from day to day. More than one person has complained to me that an informant will provide one answer on one day and the very next day will insist upon something quite different in response to the same elicitation. This was of course fully understandable, for the elicitations had no controlling context. In fact, on one occasion a young linguist elicited various forms of the verb 'to cook,' but on the following day an entirely different set of forms was given in response to the linguist's same questions. Actually, the language had a number of verbs for 'cook,' for example, 'to roast meat,' 'to boil vegetable matter,' 'to roast grain,' 'to bake bread,' and 'to broil fish.' In eliciting forms one should always begin with the framework of a text and on the basis of such a context elaborate the various structures so as to determine both the paradigmatic and the syntagmatic relations.

Some of the difficulties which linguists encounter with informants are due to the attempt of native speakers to be of genuine help. In one instance, an informant realized that the linguist was progressing very slowly in learning the language, and so the informant adjusted his dictation of narratives to the linguist's level of comprehension. As a result the sentences in the texts averaged between two and three words, and the linguist was convinced that he had discovered a language with a unique syntax of short sentences.

Informants or Colleagues?

In another instance, a linguist chose to make up utterances on the basis of presumed models and then to check them out with an informant by asking, "Can I say so-and-so?" To which the informant invariably replied that it was possible. Finally, however, the linguist became suspicious and asked what such expressions meant, and the informant replied, "Nothing!" And then went on to explain that the linguist often said things which meant nothing.

Though it would be excellent if informants could be trained to be linguists, this is largely an impracticable goal, but there are certain types of training which can easily be undertaken and which can pay rich dividends, both for the linguist and for the informant.

In the first place, if an informant is illiterate, he should be instructed in how to write his own language. The very problems involved in his learning to use an orthography can be particularly instructive for the linguist, since this is one of the most important ways of determining some of the crucial differences between phonemes, graphemes, and morphophonemes. If the language has only been recently reduced to writing, some of the 'mistakes' made by the informant will be particularly useful in determining if some changes in the orthography should be introduced. If the orthography is a traditional one, the 'mistakes' can reveal a great deal about the tendency to preserve the graphic unity of morphemes despite phonological and morphological conditioning. Since most traditional alphabets are largely morphophonemic, the informant's difficulties in mastering the system will be highly revealing.

If the informant knows how to write, he should be encouraged to write down legends, myths, folktales, and personal accounts. At first, an informant's texts are likely to be painfully simple and short, but he can be taught something about elaborating episodes and relating a series of episodes into a story.

Once a person has learned to write with a fair degree of acceptability, he or she should then be taught how to manipulate language for different audiences, for example, for children, adolescents, and adults. As an informant learns how to use different registers, he becomes conscious of syntactic and semantic elements which he previously used but which he had never thought about or analyzed.

Some linguists have strongly objected to recommendations for training informants since such instruction would seem to be a serious waste of time and energy, but this is far from being the case. In the first place, an informant who can write his language well is a rich source of text data. Furthermore, in the process of learning how to write for different audiences and on different levels of complexity, he can acquire a capacity for insights which a linguist is rarely able to match. All of this presupposes, of course, that the linguist is concerned with learning more about the language than is usually necessary for a PhD. dissertation. But it is clearly this deeper knowledge of language which is so essential if real linguistic progress is to be made.

Linguistics is at a point where future studies in discourse structure, semantics, and locutionary acts must be studied on a far more sophisticated level than has usually been the case in the past. Moreover, it is not enough to elaborate theories about language merely on the basis of intuitive insights into one's own mother tongue. We need a far richer store of linguistic data from a far wider range of language families. It is especially at this point that a trained informant can provide essential data.

Informants need not be professional linguists in order to make important contributions to knowledge, but their training should not stop with instructions on how to write down texts. The informant's insights into the structures of his language are crucial, but balanced judgment cannot be obtained unless an informant has at least some exposure to the science of linguistics and to the structures of other languages. It is usually impractical for an informant to enroll as a student in a linguistics program. But a linguist can often encourage and help an informant to become familiar with the basic aspects of linguistic theory, and it is frequently possible to make arrangements for an informant to learn two or three other languages.

Such a course of training presupposes a linguist's contact with a language and an informant over a period of a number of years. This is basically what must be done if important advances are to be made in the analysis of the semantic structures of language and the semiotic systems of a culture. Ultimately publications resulting from this type of research and collaboration can be a matter of joint authorship.

Such a collaborative arrangement between linguist and informant is admittedly an ideal one, but in view of the strategic importance of such a team approach to basic linguistic research, one inevitably asks why this has not been the practice in the past. There are obviously a number of reasons why such a program has not been followed. In the first place, grants for linguistic research in exotic languages are often restricted to no more than one year. As a result, field work is inevitably superficial, in fact, so superficial that one often gets a false impression about the languages in question, for in the descriptions of structures there are no opposing analogies, no contradictory data, no unresolved problems, no fuzzy sets, no messy categories, and few if any anomalies. Unfortunately, there is too great a tendency to be highly selective in describing language structures. We like our results to be neat and tidy, symmetrical and balanced, holistic and without disturbing exceptions. But language structures are often unsystematic, and as Sapir used to say, "All languages leak."

Another reason for lack of continued study and analysis of a Third-World language is that after completing a Ph.D. program linguists often engage in quite different types of linguistic work, and interest in continuing field work

Informants or Colleagues?

is pushed aside by more immediate and pressing concerns. Furthermore, there is a tendency for linguists to want to explore a number of different languages superficially rather than to concentrate on one. This provides important insights and certainly enriches one's view of language, but it does not result in the type of study which seems to be increasingly so essential for really significant progress in our science.

Perhaps mention must also be made of the human tendency to "use people," and therefore of the desire to get out of an informant as much as one can for the amount of money and time invested. Short-term advantages almost always seem to outweigh long-term commitments, and to commit oneself to a language and to the training of an informant involves a long-term program.

On the other hand, if an informant has been adequately trained, it is possible to continue a long-term commitment to a language despite other work and responsibilities, since the linguist and the informant can then act as colleagues and through the years invaluable data can continually be gathered and analyzed.

Quite apart from the advantages of greatly improved interpersonal relations, more effective use of time and energy, and increased opportunities for more extensive research, collaboration between a linguist and a trained informant can result in significantly more satisfactory results. This is not merely a matter of two heads being better than one, but of collaboration between two persons with complementary skills and knowledge. But an informant must be trained to the point where he understands the why's of a linguist's inquiries and is able to intelligently object to a linguist's proposals and initial analyses.

Unfortunately, there is too often a tendency for informants to respond to elicitation on the basis of what they believe a linguist wants to hear. And it is not easy to convince people that they should correct or criticize one who is paying them a salary. There is, of course, some protection against error in using several informants, and there may be advantages in forming a team of several native speakers. But one intelligent informant who is adequately trained may be enough, especially if he is given instruction in field techniques and can himself become involved in obtaining supplementary language data from other speakers.

First-rate analytical study of a language usually requires the combination of a linguist and a native speaker. This is usually the only guarantee that the data will not be unduly influenced by the pressures of frames and patterns. Even when a linguist is working on his own mother tongue it would be important to check items constantly with a trained informant. Having written a dissertation on English syntax, for which I used myself as principal source for English usage, I realize how very easy it is to be unintentionally influenced by one's own theory of language. Too often we find only what we are looking for. But when there can be a team approach to linguistic research, the results are likely to be much more satisfactory, especially in those instances in which the linguist provides the theoretical framework and the informant the hard data.

WERNER KUMMER

Malinche, Patron-Saint of Informants?

ABSTRACT

Using as examples the function of Malinche in the Spanish conquista of Mexico, the function of the informant Dayuma in the pacification of the Aucas in Ecuador, the missionary linguistics of German protestant missionaries in the area of the Dschaggas in Tansania and the fictive account of the pacification of the Ibos in Chinua Achebe's "Things fall apart," the social context of work with "native speakers" during the period of European colonial expansion is explored. In a critique of existing work in the history of linguistics it is proposed to expand the field of this history to a treatment of the social functions of linguistic work in third-world countries since the time of European expansion and to discuss new functions of linguistic work in a time of decolonization and the building of independent states in the former colonies.

INTRODUCTION

If one examines the relationship in which native speaker and linguist confront one another from a historical point of view, then one recognizes that these relationships were always embedded in the respective context of the relationships between both societies to which both parties belonged. This relationship was, from the age of discovery onwards (during which time the circle of languages with which the Europeans came into contact freely widened), mostly that of colonial expansion. In this process the representatives of the linguistic role, either as missionaries, researchers, colonial officials, traders or settlers took part or they profited by it, either as anthropologists, ethnologists, social scientists or, in rare cases, as linguists. In the same way the representative role of informants functioned in the relationship, not only as deliverers of speech data, but also as 'collaborators' of the colonizers, be it as missionaries, agents furthering the cultural assimilation, translators, representatives of the colonial power in lower governmental positions or colonial intelligentsia. In many instances, it was the informants who became the new leading class among the colonized people and tribes and who, under the patronage of the colonizing countries, re-structured the economic and social framework to the extent that it fitted into the colonial context.

While the social sciences, i.e., sociology, anthropology, have been concerning themselves with the problem of 'de-colonisation' for a long time,[1] the more reflecting members of the missionary churches are also discussing their colonial past,[2] whereas the official theory of linguistics and its historical analysis does not deal with the embedding of linguistics in the context of colonial expansion, although the biggest linguistic institute 'The Summer Institute of Linguistics' (SIL) which delivers linguistic data in the framework of its militant missionary policies, has, in recent years, been under sharp attack.[3] The criticisms of SIL's activities was mostly offered by cultural-relativist anthropologists and development-sociologists and were not received seriously among linguists and were generalized, so that except for apologetic literature on its own behalf by SIL, hardly a linguistic echo was heard.[4] The apologia of the SIL is right to the extent that the work criticized, a combination of linguistics and missionary work, is not a speciality of this institution in particular, but is based on the entire as yet unresearched inheritance of linguistics in Third World countries. It would be necessary to examine the whole history of the expansion of geographical dimensions of the linguistic sciences within the framework of European colonial expansion, in order to move away from the suppression of the colonial past in linguistics or from the selective accusation of such institutions as SIL, towards a re-definition of the role of linguistic activity in developing countries. One main hindrance of such reflection and of such a re-definition is the rigid reference of the theory of linguistic history. The history of linguistics to date, has been so much concerned with historical analysis of methods, that not once did the growth of knowledge about world languages enter into its field, let alone a reflection of the embedding of one society into another through such growth. Only in those philologies from specific areas (African, Oriental and American Studies) which, in the 19th Century, became separated from the general science of linguistics, is the beginning of the development of critical theories visible, in order to come to a close understanding of the linguistic problems of each region.

It would be wrong to write a history of this colonization process of linguistic entrenchment through the work of 'native-speakers' with a retrospective Utopian view as starting-point, accusingly stating that European colonial expansionism should never have happened, and in doing so, overlook the many aspects of the work which has become fruitful in the process of de-colonization and the rebuilding of new countries. The contemporary work of linguistics in Third World countries is linked up to traditions, which were begun by European or American missionary societies or by former colonial governments. It is of importance that those aspects of linguistic work useful for the autonomous economic and cultural development of the new states are filtered out from these traditions and that those aspects are eliminated which support the process of colonial or neo-colonial penetration or which are based on the demands of cultural or religious missionary work founded on European traditions. Thus the main emphasis will ideally be placed on the development of the field of activity of the linguist who sets about the task of emphasising the language problems of the Third World on the basis of the findings of theoretical linguistics — a goal worth aiming for. But he must have practical objectives which fall within the framework of the autonomous development policies of the new independent states and thereby can undertake tasks which arise from the positive traditions of linguistic work in developing countries.

In this article it is not possible to give more than a few suggestions which may help in solving the far-reaching task of critical analysis of the embedding of linguistic work in the mechanisms of colonial expansion and which may lead to a re-definition of the linguist's task in developing countries. Thus the main emphasis is on the analysis of specific cases of the colonial and neo-colonial embedding of linguistic activities; such a study, based on certain cases, results from the difficulty of compiling a coherent picture (even if merely for selected regions) from the scattered sources on the history of Catholic or Protestant missionary societies or from the reports of the language policies of the different colonial powers and from the few historical-linguistic studies about this problem. The search for reference material presents a special problem in view of the fact that linguistic work, as well as being done in conjunction with Catholic missions, also falls within the framework of colonial government, but is treated as a sub-category of the total work. Detailed descriptions are only presented in the writings of individual reports concerning actual work done in missionary stations or in small administrational units, whereas in the entire history of missionary or colonial activities, only a summary account of linguistic work is given, if any. Particularly this exclusion of sources for small units in the framework of European expansion demands that a detailed study be carried out in the archives of missionary societies and colonial government departments which has not been possible for me up to this time. Such a study, despite its problems, would be worthwhile, as this work, termed 'research in the field' was directly concerned in the past with the population of small villages or regions and not work in the administrative departments for whole regions or countries, and would retain this character today and in the future. The study of actual work in small units has, therefore, not only historical interest, but also contributes to the building of a concept of development aid which takes as its starting-point not abstract development models for an entire country, but takes as a basis the needs and problems of single units of population, such as villages or regions.

CASE 1

As a first example of the linguistic problems arising from this embedding process through the cooperation of informants within the mechanism of colonial conquest is the story of Doña Marina, who is referred to as the proverbial representative of the 'collaborator' who worked hand in hand with the conquering power in Latin America.[5] When Hernan Cortéz advanced from Yucatan to Tabasco, in the Maya-speaking region, the man Jeronimo de Aguilar, who had been ship-wrecked on the island of Cozumel, served him as translator. The Maya-speaking region ended in the Coatzacoalcos area and Cortéz entered a region where Nahuatl, the official language of the Aztec kingdom was spoken. Jeronimo de Aguilar did not know this language. After initial wars with the Tabasco tribes the Indians submitted to the Conquistadors and as a tribute presented Cortéz with, amongst other things, twenty women, one of whom was Malinche, who after baptism received the name of Doña Marina. She was the daughter of a Caziken from the Coatzacoalcos region. After the death of her father and the re-marriage of her mother, she was handed over to relations and was sold as a slave, so that her claims to any inheritance would be annuled. Malinche was bilingual in Maya and Nahuatl, so that Jeronimo de Aguilar could pass on Cortéz's instructions to her in Maya and she could then translate into Nahuatl:

> Doña Marina could speak the language of Coatzacoalcos, which is the official language of Mexico and was able to speak the language of Tabasco, just as Jeronimo de Aguilar could speak the language of Yucatan and Tabasco, which is the same language; they got on well together and Aguilar translated everything into Spanish for Cortéz which was a great help to our 'Conquista'. Thus, many things resulted from this which, praise the Lord, were favourable to us. I wished to explain that because we would not have understood the Mexican language without Doña Marina (Castillo 1976:62).

Malinche worked closely with the conquering Spaniards; Cortéz had her married to an officer, but used her as an important adviser in all questions concerning the 'Conquista'. In the conquest of the Aztec kingdom she proved herself useful not only as a translator, but also as spy and leader of negotiations with high Aztec officials. After her return to her native land she took over the government in Tabasco as successful representative of the Spanish interests and helped in the adaptation of the tribes of the region to the European interests and steered through a modification of the prevailing culture under the military protection of the Spaniards. Malinche's fate illustrates some important functions of 'native speakers' within the context of colonization: initially the informant acts as a bridge between the conqueror and the society to be subjugated; this function is carried out by means of that individual's bilingualness, which makes the unknown language accessible through transferring it into a language known to the conqueror. More important, however, is the informant's changing-sides, thus making known the cultural and social structure of the group to be colonized to the invaders. This function is mostly left in the background in linguistic theories of the informants' work, although it is the dominant function for the conqueror in every colonial context, to which the function as translator is only secondary. The transition to the conqueror's culture usually results from the presence of anomalies in the Indian's own culture, although it is this aspect that has branded Malinche with the sign of the archetypal traitor in the eyes of the Latin American Indians. In Malinch's case, her collaboration with the Spaniards allows her to promote her rights of inheritance, in other cases the conquerors exploit the contradictions amongst the tribes, to win allies. In any case the individual or group on the edge of or outside their own society is predestined to be active as informant for the conquering group.

Malinche has a promoter function vis-à-vis her own society, in as much as she implements not only the mechanisms of colonial domination, but also the culture of the conquering Spaniards, because she herself is incorporated in and representative of this dominant culture. She can take over this function because through her transferrence of allegiance to the other side, she, as representative for her tribe, has established a bridge to the dominant society, in as much as she submits to their dominance and yet, at the same time, identifies with it and accepts the norms imposed by the conquerors and passes them on to her tribe. As mistress of Cortéz, Malinche embodies in model fashion this form of 'identification with the aggressor' through which the partial acceptance of colonization results. As promotor she comes under the protective wing of the conqueror from the position on the edge of her own society into an independent ruling-position, worthy of emulation, and thus becomes a bearer of the responsibility for the cultural changes imposed by colonialism.

CASE 2

An example to show that this embedding of linguistic activities of informants in the context of colonialization does not only belong to the past is illustrated by the story of the Auca woman Dayuma, whose story is on the whole similar to the role played by Malinche.[6] When in the Thirties oil was discovered in the Auca territory in the Amazonas region, Ecuador, the Dutch Shell Company tried to set up bore-sites in a region using Mera as base. The Aucas attacked this base and although the Ecuador government ordered military intervention, they did not succeed in pacifying the Auca tribe. When the SIL, in the Fifties, carrying out field-work within the framework of their missionary activity as 'Wycliffe Bible Translators,' concluded a treaty with the Ecuador government, which gave them permission to study the Indian groups of the country, the linguist/missionary Rachel Saint, whose brother had been killed on a missionary expedition amongst the Aucas, made the acquaintance of the Auca girl Dayuma, who had fled from her tribe and was working on a hacienda on the edge of Auca territory. Rachel Saint learnt the language of the Aucas from Dayuma and drew up a rough outline grammar. Dayuma was converted to a form of Fundamentalist Protestantism, that which the Wycliffe Bible Translators represent and, for public-relations purposes was flown to the U.S.A. where, on behalf of the SIL, she took part in a talk-show with Rachel Saint. On tour through the United States, where Dayuma, amongst other things, professed her Christianity at a huge Billy Graham meeting, she learnt the wonders of 'the American way of life.' On her return to the Amazonas region, Dayuma served the SIL as a bridge to make contact with the Aucas. She was flown by SIL helicopters over Auca villages and relayed to the people by loudspeaker that the Foreigners were peaceful and that they wanted to exchange Auca goods for those from their 'civilized' countries. The Aucas came to the places arranged for such exchange purposes and thanks to the language knowledge of Rachel Saint, the missionaries were able to carry out direct trade with the people. As a result of the convincing power of the American goods exchanged, Dayuma was allowed to return to her tribe and was able to convert a portion of its members to Christianity. Within the baptised group she adopted a position as leader, which altered the policies of the tribe: it split into two groups — one under Dayuma which adopted a new production and cultural form and the other which held on to its traditional social form as 'Savage Aucas.' Dayuma's new policy meant the return of the oil companies, whose representatives were brought to the region by SIL's jungle air-service and introduced into tribal society. A pilot of SIL explains the service offered by the missionaries for the benefit of the oil-companies:

At the end of the Forties the Shell Oil Company lost many workers as a result of Auca spears. Shell Oil decided to leave Ecuador for different reasons. Then, suddenly, since the discovery of vast oil reserves in the tropical forests of the east, 21 companies with a labour-force of 1500 men are working there. As soon as they advance, we fly ahead and explain to those Aucas, who are in their path, that the companies are coming. We convince the Aucas that they should get out of the way. This is all done with the help of Auca Christians spreading the news by loudspeakers attached to the planes. If the Indians move out of the area we inform the oil-companies. As a result of this close cooperation by radio and telephone through our office in Quito, no human life has been lost up till now, thanks be to God (Arbeitskreis ILV 1979:95).

As the oil trusts bought up Auca land from the Ecuador government, a reservation for the Aucas was established in 1969. Due to the limited size of

Malinche, Patron-Saint of Informants? 181

the reservation, the Aucas were forced to change their economy from that of a hunter-cultivator one to a solely planter-economy in the form of individual ownership of small parcels of land. The resettlement in the reservation, against which mainly the non-Christian Auca groups resisted, was carried out by the SIL under Dayuma's direction. SIL itself was promised two big land regions from former Auca territory by the State. Here, they set up the mission stations of Limoncocha and Tigueno, from where further missionary work and economic consolidation were possible. At the end of the Sixties, a polio epidemic all but wiped out the people of the Auca reservation and during the Seventies malaria and other sicknesses increased in the new, strange environment, to such an extent that the birth rate dropped drastically. By this time, Dayuma, with SIL backing, had taken control of the pacified tribe.

In comparison to the story of Malinche, Dayuma's involvement has become more complicated in several respects. The colonizers no longer assume the role of conquerors by military means, economic exploiters or destroyers of culture. The task of colonization is now divided among oil trusts, the Ecuador government and missionaries. This distribution of roles amongst soldiers, government officials, entrepreneurs, traders, missionaries, ethnologists and linguists typifies colonial development in its advanced form and contrasts with the simple conquest by 'conquistadors', who with the help of troops fulfilled all these functions in one. Although, to the colonized society, the connection is made clear between missionary consolidation and the establishment of trade relations on the one hand and the external or internal colonization through administration and military force on the other. It is possible that naive missionaries, linguists and ethnographers or traders do not subjectively experience this context, yet the different characteristic moulds prove to be parts of a unified process of colonial penetration which leads to the subjugation and cultural and economic re-structuring of the colonized group. Which of the fractions within the colonizing 'society' gains the right to 'open the doors' into a particular region depends on many factors. While the military and the administration institutions following in its wake frequently lay down the beginnings of colonization in easily accessible areas, in regions of strong resistance or unfavourable geographical conditions it is missionaries, researchers or traders who frequently opened the way to colonization.

CASE 3

A good example to show the connection between missionary and trade cooperation in a region which was, to an extent, followed by European settlement and as a result by colonial power, were the plans of David Livingstone at the end of his travels from Luanda to Quilimane in Mozambique. On his journey all the tribes of this region gave him protection, above all the Makololo, who hoped, by doing so, that he would create more trade with the Portugese colonies resulting in higher prices for their ivory and other goods than those obtainable in Cape Colony. Livingstone's missionary activities were not taken seriously by the tribes but were accepted due to the role he would play in creating trading routes by which they could obtain the highly-prized European goods and rifles. He was granted delegations of warriors who transported and protected his belongings in the hope that they might later use the tracks discovered by him for their own trade caravans. Livingstone, however, hoped to set up more trade relations for these countries as a first step towards a colony for European settlers:

> The routes into the interior should be free for all; instead of a handful of miserable forts which can scarcely call an acre of land their own, proper colonies must be established. If, instead of the military colonies, we had civilian ones with emigrants with wives, ploughs and seeds and instead of military detachments with trumpets and drums could see such groups of settlers entering, then we might hope that East Africa's luck would return (Livingstone 1939:484).

As an accompanying step the natives should be encouraged to produce their own cash crops, particularly cotton for the English market and missionaries should guarantee the necessary cultural change required for such a development:

> All are, indeed, in favour of carrying out trade, but have never been given any indication on the matter as to which raw materials they should grow which are useful to trade. Their land is suitable for the growing of cotton and I dare to hope that if one were to bring them better seed than their own native seed and encouraged them to such cultivation, while assuring them of a market for their goods, we would, as a result of such endeavours, assure the heathens of a more effective and lasting benefit (*ibid*. 491).

In the case of Dayuma, the function of the mission and the trader functions are seen as inseparably linked. Here, transition to the new culture and values — above all to Christianity — is achieved through the power of conviction in the materialistic culture of the 'American way of life' in which she can participate if she identifies with the aggressors from the tribe's point of view. Commensurate with the notion of the distribution of activity between the colonizers it is of no consequence that she is unaware of the fact that she, by siding with the SIL opens the doors for the oil-companies and the Ecuador government. Thus, she has a bridging function not only for the SIL, but also for the other fractions and accepts this function as her attitude to the tribal reservations shows. *Vis-à-vis* her own tribe, Dayuma, like Malinche, has a

Malinche, Patron-Saint of Informants? 183

promoter-function; she serves as a model for a cultural change of direction under the protective patronage of the colonizing society and takes over the leading position in the 'pacified' tribe. Her authority is based, on the one hand, on the power of conviction of the American goods, on the other hand on the military and burocratic potential of the state of Ecuador, which stands behind the SIL and the oil-companies.

CASE 4

While the history of Auca pacification serves as an example illustrating the 'door-opening' function of a missionary society, the following example of the establishment of a Protestant-Lutheran mission amongst the Dschaggas of the Kilimanjaro region illustrates the case where linguistic work in the context of missionary work follows in the footsteps of colonial expansion. On July 25th, 1893 an agreement was signed between Great Britain and Germany ceding the Kilimanjaro region to Germany. Thus, the territory of the Dschaggas, who lived as a tribe sub-divided into many varied dialectal groups in the highlands around Kilimanjaro, passed into the hands of German government administration represented by a military post in Aruscha. Amongst the Dschaggas, missionaries from the English Christian Missionary Society had been active since 1885 on invitation of the chief, Rindi; they now had to give way to the German Protestant Mission. Meli, Rindi's successor, used the withdrawal of the English missionaries to shake off the sovereignty of the foreign colonialists and burnt the mission down. As he was unwilling to recognize German overlordship and also opposed the establishment of a German mission, German troops had to be sent into action against the Dschaggas. The Dschaggas joined forces with groups from the Masai tribe and tried to drive the German troops and missionaries out of Moschi and the surrounding mission stations. On November 18th, 1896, as the missionaries, under the protection of 30 Askaris, set about founding a new mission station, they were attacked during the night by the combined force of Dschaggas and Masai; two missionaries were killed. In a punitive expedition the German colonial military force was combined and several of the Dschagga chiefs, including Meli, were hanged. Under the protection of the military, some missions were hurriedly built. Those chiefs put in power by the German authorities cooperated *nolens volens* with the missionaries and gave them land on which to build their missions:

The savage Aruscha tribesmen had undertaken the attack in order to prevent the whites once and for all from entering Meru lands. The Maro tribe had been more or less swept along by events. Now, however, the German military forces' post in Aruscha held the tribes in check. This enabled the renewed suppression of the Meru through the mission. When Krause and Fickert undertook an expedition, the chief Menawara was most obliging towards them. He turned out, in fact, to be highly deceitful. Krause's accusation of wilful mistreatment of his underlings sent him to the gallows. His successor was Sambeke. Even servants now became readily available. For the site of the mission station, they chose to found it not where the murder had taken place, which was feared by the people and had therefore become desolate, but Nkoaranga in Bembe, not far from the chief's abode. In May 1902, Krause conducted the first Sunday service in Kiro. The first small chapel was inaugurated on June 22nd (Fleisch 1936:273).

Wherever resistance by the Dschaggas or Massai occurred against the establishment of missions the missionaries put themselves under the protection of German military power:

That the leader of the military post, Freiherr von Reitzenstein, received the missionaries in friendly fashion was not without influence on the conduct of Chief Sabaia. Immediately a school was started and two more followed in the tribes of Chief Ndasekoi and Saroni (*ibid.* 274).

Conversely, for the chiefs who allowed stations to be built in their territory, the missionaries came to be seen as defenders against the military power:

(Chief Schangali) came under suspicion of having conspired with the Masai. Müller (a missionary) intervened on his behalf to First-Lieutenant Merker, Johannes' successor. As a result he was set free and together with Müller was received triumphantly by his own people. But the worry arising from the false accusation and Johannes' departure, in whom he placed great trust, made Schangali decide to abdicate (*ibid*. 275).

While the missionaries clearly identified with the German colonial power, they adopted rather an *ad-hoc* course in their policies towards the advancing colonists who were taking the best land from the Dschaggas and Masai, a policy between collaboration and representation of the Dschaggas' interests, whereas in the fundamental principles they stood clearly on the side of the colonists. Thus, they defended not only the forcible eviction practised by the settler, but also the tax on huts which was to provide workers for the new plantations as well as compulsory labour for 90 days a year and child labour on the plantations which led finally to the result that the Dshaggas should be persuaded away from their traditional form of subsistence production and be steered towards the production of cash crops:

The Dshaggas as independent farmers are not willing to undertake work on European plantations. To raise the hut-tax requires only a short working-time or child-labour. As a result there is a shortage of workers on the numerous established plantations. In 1909 there are plantations which are worked almost exclusively by children. The planters therefore desire compulsory labour. When it eventually comes, it is merely a fact that every native has to be able to show 3 work-cards each with 30 days a year marked on them. The missionaries were not able to ignore this fact! The spread of child labour kept the children from schooling and brought with it health and moral dangers. Therefore, one reacted, if not against every form of child labour, then at least against the unregulated kind, in the same way as one does not actually reject compulsory labour, but only that form which makes peasants out of independent small farmers (*ibid.* 281).

The Dschaggas frequently reacted against the encroachments of the settlers and the unjust methods of compulsory labour and turned to the missionaries who took up such complaints in a very diplomatic fashion:

In the individual case the missionary, who understood the tribal language and stayed longer than the frequently-changing officials, was, naturally, often called in as mediator. The Council advised a policy of caution, but did not, however want to hinder the missionaries in the execution of their duties. Only once did a conflict arise and thereby led to the replacement of a missionary. Bleicken considered it his task to help the natives – culturally and socially. He tried to further the cultivation of wheat and encouraged flour-production, but he also got involved in colonial politics, particularly in all kinds of settler disputes. The Council warned about his inept dealings and about too strong an involvement in cultural affairs, which might hinder him in his actual missionary work (*ibid.* 281).

On the whole, the missionaries represented all the interests which the Colonial Office in Berlin represented and allowed itself an independent line only in settlement matters unrelated to the major policy line which were contrary to the interests of the mission itself:

The Council and the missionaries were obviously keen to perpetuate loyalty to and independence of the colonial authorities on an equal basis. It seems that good relations between them and Berlin were maintained. On the other hand, the mere founding of missions in the colonies was an object of extreme distaste – increasing to the level of sayings 'Missions, malaria, black swamp fever and locusts are the enemies of the settlers (*ibid.* 281).

The anger of the settlers towards the mission is mainly explained by the fact that from 1900 onwards many converted Dschaggas began to found coffee-plantations in competition with them and the missionaries gave them support in this enterprise.

The attitude of the missionaries towards the Dschagga society was ambivalent. In the economic sphere they were striving towards a dissolution of the collective economy and towards the establishment of private 'parcelled' ownership of land, while in the cultural sphere they replaced the old tribal and extended-family ties by Christian communal forms. At the same time, within the framework of their policy towards 'native-orientated' hierarchical structures, they supported the traditional tribal ties which had been loosened by wage-labour on the plantations and by the introduction of a money economy:

One saw in those Dschagga orders something worthwhile, which, in one's own people, had been lost in the dissolution into one amorphous mass (*ibid*. 303).

By the dissolution of the economic foundations for such ties through the introduction of private minor capitalist forms of economy, they were, however, achieving rather a further dissolution of the thought and behaviour patterns which accompanied these ties, by reference to the Protestant Ethic on individuality:

Yet the counterpoise to that attitude, which clearly recognizes the 'chosen' status of Christians called forth from the sin of natural liaisons was, in fact, not lacking. Its danger is, out of piety, out of the perhaps necessary superficial dissolution of such ties in the individual case, to make a law for all members of the community and to proceed with a false sense of individuality and lack of historical foundation. It is good, therefore, if both attitudes complement each other and thus maintain the balance of tension (*ibid*. 303).

The most important point, which for the missionaries was a contradiction in their contemplation of the culture of tribal organisation was the question of polygamy and the ceremonies of male and female circumcision, rituals carried out in initiation rites on attaining adulthood. Although the missionaries realized the economic function of polygamy in the traditional society, they demanded the choice of one woman to the exclusion of all others from male tribesmen in order that members should be accepted into a Christian community. This rigid demand for monogamy created great resistance and limited the spheres of interest of the mission. They proceeded with firm church discipline particularly against the customs of Masai society where extra-marital sexual intercourse was permitted both prior to and after marriage, according to long-established tradition. Pupils at the mission schools who followed these traditional rites were severely punished and excluded from the activities there. Circumcision rites, which regulated the important division of the traditional society into age-groups, were forbidden completely by the missionaries or were replaced by Christian ceremonies. The missionaries had little success in their fight against these handed-down traditions. One part of the tribe remained outside the Christian community and continued to practice their own economy and traditional way of life. The other half, though converted to Christianity, continued to carry out such practices in secret or developed their own syncretist forms of religion which replaced those of traditional society. Only a small proportion practised Christianity according to the discipline of the church. This group had a superior economic position as a result of the support from the mission and acted as promoters for the newly-colonized society. The main functions were those in the mission schools where they were trained as assistant teachers and were paid by the missionaries. They also served as a model for the cultural change in the outlying villages. They imitated the life-style of their masters and won the leadership of their subordinates in the tribe, all under the protection of the mission, colonial military forces and administrative authority. They were also the informants for the linguistic work carried out by the missionaries who learned the various Dschagga dialects from them. In the mission schools a regional variety of standardized Dschagga was spoken in class; in the larger centres of population a form of Swahili was used as lingua franca. The Bible was translated into the school-varieties of Dschagga as was necessary everyday church literature. In 1909, the missionary Raum wrote the first Dschagga grammar. The future assistant teachers were a source of income for their fathers because they received a small wage for the work that they undertook in the mission schools with which their parents could pay a part of the hut-tax. It is true, however, that in the raising of this labour-force for the partially very extensive agricultural and craft enterprises, the missionaries were in direct competition with the plantation owners, who ran their business using child-labour. With the returns from their undertakings the missionaries financed not only their schools, but also the wages and pension funds for their personnel, who, however, were partly paid directly from Germany by the mother church.

Because the assistant teachers were, from early on, educated as an avantgarde of the new colonial culture, during the rest of their lives they remained under church control. They were a potential for a colonial intelligentsia who could inform on any trace of resistance to the mission and thereby to the colonial power, while they also served a promoter-function in the cultural re-organization of the tribe. As long as they did not modify their function through links with tribal resistance movements, they were a troop of Malinches for the conquering German colonial power.

CASE 5

In the examples mentioned so far, the process of colonial penetration was reconstructed from the documents of the colonizing by Conquistadors, missionaries or colonial administrators, the necessity of such a procedure is explained by the fact that scarcely any documents exist which reflect the process seen through the eyes of the colonized people. In most colonized regions it was only possible after the de-colonization to write or to reflect on the history from the colonized group's point of view. The next example is given by such a literary model; it is the story of the missionary and colonizing process amongst the Ibo tribe from Umuofia described in Chinua Achebe's novel "Things fall Apart." Compared to the sources of the missions and the historical accounts of colonial administration the literary model has the advantage that it is written from the viewpoint of the colonized people in a non-neutral way and generalizes many individual experiences. In a summarized fashion, the story shows the history of the village Abame's variant of the cooperation between mission and colonial power. One day an albino arrives in the village on a bicycle, that is an albino from the villagers' point of view — in fact, a white missionary. The elders question the village oracle who has heard of such albinos and predicts that they will conquer and destroy the village. As a result the villagers kill the missionary and tie his bicycle to their sacred tree. After some time, albinos with some blacks appear, see the bicycle hanging there and disappear again. Some time later, the whole village is attacked and razed to the ground by black soldiers under the command of white men. All the villagers except for a few are killed. In Umuofia the colonial conquest goes ahead less dramatically. A white missionary, Mr Brown, appears with some converted Christian Ibos from another region who act as translator and promoter for him. The people from Umuofia who know the story of Abame allow him to enter the village unhindered. He builds a mission-house and church near the village with the help of his followers. He soon is followed by a trader who exchanges western goods for palm-oil and other village products. After the mission is able to win over only outsiders from the tribe and convert them, it begins to gain more followers as a direct result of this trade. Soon after the missionary and the trader, a District Commissioner appears on the scene in Umuofia and he, with the help of his bailiff, locks up the natives who pursue the customs being opposed by the mission:

But apart from the church the white men had also brought a government. They had built a court where the District Commissioner judged cases in ignorance. He had court messengers who brought men for him to trial. Many of these messengers came from Umuru on the bank of the Great River, where the white men first came many years before and where they had built the center of their religion and trade and government. These court messengers were greatly hated in Umuofia because they were foreigners and also arrogant and high-handed. They were called kotma, and because of their ash-coloured shorts they earned the additional name of Ashy Buttocks. They guarded the prison, which was full of men who had offended the white man's law! Some of these prisoners had thrown away their twins and some had molested the Christians. They were beaten in the prison by the kotma and made to work every morning clearing the government compound and fetching wood for the white Commissioner and the court messengers (Achebe 1958:58).

After his establishment in Umuofia, Mr Brown sends only African assistant missionaries to the surrounding villages, as, for example, Mr Kiaga to Mbanta. The village assembly grants him a parcel of land in a forbidden section of the forest as a place for his church, in the expectation that the gods will destroy him. As nothing evil happens to him, he wins over his first followers, including Nwoye, the son of the hero of the novel, Okonkwo, who goes over to

Malinche, Patron-Saint of Informants? 189

the Christians because of his resistance to his father and to the old social order. Nwoye has the role of Malinche in the novel; after he has been questioned and beaten by his father Okonkwo because of his change of allegiance, he decides to become an assistant-teacher for the mission himself:

> Nwoye went back to the church and told Mr Kiaga that he had decided to go to Umuofia, where the white missionary had set up a school to teach young Christians to read and write. Mr Kiaga's joy was very great. 'Blessed is he who forsakes his father and mother for my sake,' he intoned. 'Those that hear my words are my father and my mother' (ibid. 138f).

Mr Kiaga explains that all the gods of the Ibos are only wooden figures and the god of the white men alone exists. The inhabitants of Mbanta leave him and his growing community in peace because the converts are clan comrades, against whom no war may be waged:

> There was no question of killing the missionary here, for Mr Kiaga, despite his madness, was quite harmless. As for his converts, no one could kill them without having to flee from the clan, for in spite of their worthlessness they still belonged to the clan (ibid. 142).

The first conflicts between the groups converted to Christianity and the traditional society of Mbanta break out when an especially devout convert kills a python, the sacred creature of the Ibos. As a result, the village cuts off the Christians from the clan and denies them access to the water-holes and food-stores. The blockade is only lifted after the miscreant dies. In Umuofia too, a delicate balance is just maintained between the traditional society and Mr Brown's Christian group, particularly after the palm-oil trade has brought money to the town and the mission-school educates 'cadres' for the new administration functions of the tribe:

> And so Mr Brown built a school and a little hospital in Umuofia. He went from family to family begging people to send their children to school. But at first they only sent their slaves or sometimes their lazy children. Mr Brown begged and argued and prophesied. He said that the leaders of the land in the future would be men and women who had learned to read and write. If Umuofia failed to send her children to the school, strangers would come from other places to rule them. They could already see that happening in the Native Court, where the D.C. was surrounded by strangers who spoke his tongue. Most of these strangers came from the distant town of Umuru on the bank of the Great River where the white man first went. In the end Mr Brown's arguments began to have an effect. More people came to learn in his school, and he encouraged them with gifts of singlets and towels. They were not all young, these people who came to learn. Some of them were thirty years old or more. They worked on their farms in the morning and went to school in the afternoon. And it was not long before the people began to say that the white man's medicine was quick in working. Mr Brown's school produced quick results. A few months in it were enough to make one a court messenger

or even a court clerk. Those who stayed longer became teachers; and from Umuofia labourers went forth into the Lord's vineyard. New churches were established in the surrounding villages and a few schools with them. From the very beginning religion and education went hand in hand. Mr Brown's mission grew from strength to strength and because of its link with the new administration it earned a new social prestige (*ibid.* 163f).

It is unimportant to trace the exact course of the further conflicts which are speeded up by the change of missionary from Mr Brown to Mr Smith who acts less diplomatically, for already at this juncture the end of the former society is pre-destined. As Okonkwo realizes, the transition of the Christian classes to the new wielders of power, defined in the triple constellation missionary, District Officer and trader, is the decisive factor in the colonial break-through, which, at the same time, means the end of the old tribal way of life:

The white man says that our customs are bad. How do you think we can fight when our own brothers have turned against us? The white man is very clever. He came quietly and peacably with his religion. We were amused at his foolishness and allowed him to stay. Now he has won our brothers, and our clan can no longer act like one. He has put a knife on the things that held us together and we have fallen apart (*ibid.* 160).

The model of the colonisation of Umuofia shows the significance of the function of collaborators in a classically distinct light, during the period of the split between traditional society and colonization. The mission which establishes a bridge between the traditional society against a background of military menace, indoctrinates the Malinches in its schools, who are important in the de-structuring of the traditional society and set up new power institutions under the protective overall patronage of the colonial power. For the tribe, the struggle against them is hindered by the fact that, for a long time, through the old orders, they are considered holy members of the clan; when it comes to the decisive confrontation the colonial power is already strengthened to such an extent, that it is only logical that it leads to pacification in the interests of the colonists and thereby to the ultimate implementation of the colonial structure. The link between the missionary and his Christian-convert informants, who, for him, perform a bridging function to colonial society and later a promoter-function of the new order, is the essential core of this process in the culmination of colonialism.

DISCUSSION

The examples analyzed should make the reader sensitive to the problems of colonial and neo-colonial linguistic activities through 'native-speakers' in the

Malinche, Patron-Saint of Informants? 191

past and present, so that the social content of such work is recognized and the function of linguistic work in a de-colonized world may be re-defined. In the standard works on research in the field such as Samarin's *Field Linguistics* or Kibrik's *Methodology of Field Investigations in Linguistics,* the social embedding of work with informants is only seen under the technological aspect of possible obstacles to an adequate appraisal of the language structure; the relationship between linguists and informants as a central form of the interested influences of one society on another which has a long strongly-tainted colonial history, is hardly given consideration. The danger arises, therefore, that either behind the curtain of a purely scientific study, the old patterns of the indoctrination of a class of Malinches as a 'back-door' for the interests of the ruling society may be practised further or that naive linguists, unknowingly, achieve a colonizing effect through their work with 'nativespeakers.' Their one-time informants frequently become a connection to the society to which the linguist belongs and they imitate ways of life which they have learnt from their working-together, even when he has long returned to his native country from his field-expedition. It would be useless to demand that linguistic work in regions of the Third World should leave behind no effects, but it is necessary, on the other hand, to ask which effects would serve the autonomous development of the region best. The decision about this lies mainly in the hands of the inhabitants of the regions themselves, in many cases not necessarily in government departments, but it is also possible, quite independent of detailed studies in a region, to illustrate the field of activity of the linguist in a developing country in order to guarantee an appropriate professional education. As preliminary work for such a definition, the analysis of such linguistic functions up to now would have to be undertaken in much more detailed fashion than has been the case so far. As an example for the present state of linguistic reflection about its own history only one monograph about the linguistic activities of missionaries, Victor E. Hanzeli's *Missionary Linguistics in New France,* which examines the work of Catholic, particularly Jesuit, missionaries in the French Province of Quebec and neighbouring regions, can here be cited. The reader learns much about the missionaries' difficulties in learning the Algonquian and Iroquois languages of the region, especially Huron, but the whole social context in which the linguistic work of the missionaries proceeds, remains concealed. The objectives of the mission are only outlined in the form of a trivializing presentation of the missionaries as the struggle against the kingdom of Satan and the linguistic studies are brought into this context alone:

Still the language studies of the missionaries were essentially utilitarian and subordinated to their preoccupation with spreading the Gospel. Missionary activities were conceived in the Ignatian spirit as military campaigns conducted against the Devil and his tools in the world, and the native languages were 'armes necessaires à la guerre' (Hanzeli 1969: 45).

The missionaries appear in Henzeli's portrayal as men of God, who are tortured and killed for inexplicable reasons by the ungrateful savages, especially by the blood-thirsty Iroquois:

> Jogues also profited from the armistice and moved back into the Iroquois country again, but the Mohawks, though they had agreed to his coming to them, suddenly reneged on their agreement and killed him. The death of Jogues was the first but by no means the last and cruellest execution in the series of killings which stained the missionary records of New France. In the war of extermination fought to bitterly by the Iroquois against the Hurons in 1648–1649 many Jesuits stayed with their flock and were killed in their midst, earning the crown of martyrdom (*ibid.* 22).

What is left out is the fact that the French in Quebec Province establish a widespread fur-trade, particularly in beaver-pelts, with the Algonquin and Iroquois tribes and that in connection with this, trade routes were set up deep into the interior of the country and the Jesuits served the function as advance outposts along them. Left unmentioned too, is the trade rivalry between the English and French, which led to bloody wars between tribes allied to them or linked to them through the trading network. The French missionaries served in this competition as agents of their province and educated in the tribes entrusted to missionary care, groups of Indian converts who represented French interests. From Hanzeli's ill-considered, unreflected, historical linguistic description it is impossible to re-construct the actual deep-rooted social activities of the Catholic missionaries. Although his book offers some progress compared with the usual purely theoretical historical-linguistic descriptions, because it places the linguistic work of the missionaries in a colonial region in the forefront of research, it fails in the task of exemplifying the social functions of this work in the framework of European colonial history. It is the recognition of these functions alone which can guarantee that linguistic work in developing countries does not contribute to the education of groups of Malinches – a fifth column for the penetration of neo-colonial society as Gerardo Reichel-Dolmatoff formulates in his essay "El Misionero y las Culturas Indigenas":

> A contemporary idea in education is the grooming of natives to fulfil leading roles. But if we are honest: Who was thinking at the time that maybe an Indian should decide the fate of his tribe? From the outset, given the *a priori* dominant position of our society, they will only be a fifth column, a useful instrument in the acceleration of the destruction-process of their own culture (Jaulin 1976: 298).

If linguistics wishes to make a contribution to the development of the Third World, it must cease to make Malinches out of the 'native-speakers' with whom it works.

NOTES

1. For Anthropology and Ethnology a good introduction to the consideration of the problems associated with their role in the framework of European colonial expansion are offered by: Gérard Leclerc: "Anthropologie und Kolonialismus," Rodolfo Stavenhagen: "Classes, Colonialismo y Aculturación" and the reports from the First Barbados Conference, "La Situación des Indigena en América del Sur." For Sociology a good general survey is given by: Rodolfo Stavenhagen: "Cómo descolonizar las ciencias sociales?"
2. Alternative models for the work of the church in developing countries were discussed specifically in the light of the methods of Paolo Freire, see Freire 1975.
3. A lengthy documentation of the social context of the work of the 'Summer Institute of Linguists' is given in 'Die frohe Botschaft unserer Zivilisation' Reihe 'pogrom.'
4. For a subjective definition of the work of the SIL see: "Wycliff Bibelübersetzer – Selbstdarstellung," Burbach-Holzhausen.
5. A more detailed report of the story of Malinche is in Bernal Diaz del Castillo's "Historia de la Conquista de Nueva Espana."
6. A detailed account of the history of Dayuma is to be found in the chapter 'Ecuador' in the report "Die frohe Botschaft unserer Zivilisation." Available literature is also cited.

REFERENCES

Achebe, Chinua (1958). *Things fall apart*, African Writer Series. London: Heinemann.
Arbeitskreis ILV (1979). *Die frohe Botschaft unserer Zivilisation. Evangelikale Indianermission in Lateinamerika*, pogrom: Wien: Göttingen.
Castillo, Bernal Diaz del (1976). *Historia de la Conquista de Nueva Espana*. Editorial Porrúa.
Fleisch, Paul (1936). *Hundert Jahre lutherische Mission*. Leipzig: Verlag der Evangelisch-Lutherischen Mission.
Freire, Paolo (1975). *La situación del Indigena del América del Sur*. Tierra Nueva: Biblioteca Cientifica.
Hanzeli, Victor E. (1969). *Missionary Linguistics in New France*. The Hague: Mouton.
Jaulin, Robert, ed. (1976). *El Ethnocidio a Través de las Américas*.
Kibrik, A. (1977). *Methodology of Field-Investigations in Linguistics*. The Hague: Mouton.
Kotey, Paul F.A., Haig Der-Houssikian, eds. (1976). *Language and Linguistic Problems in Africa*. Columbia: Hornbeam Press.
Leclerc, Gérard (1976). *Anthropologie und Kolonialismus*. Frankfurt, Berlin, Wien: Ullstein.
Livingstone, David (1939). Afrika. *Die erste Durchquerung des schwarzen Erdteils*. Bern/Stuttgart.
Reichel-Dolmatoff, Gerardo (1976). 'El Misionero y las Culturas Indigenas.' In Jaulin, ed. 1976, pp. 290 ff.
Stavenhagen, Rodolfo (1977a). 'Clases, Colonialismo y Aculturación.' In *Las Clases Sociales en Mexico*. Editorial Nuestro Tiempo.
Stavenhagen, Rodolfo (1977b). 'Como descolonizar las ciencias sociales.' In *Sociologia y Subdesarrollo*. Editorial Nuestro Tiempo.
Warneck, Gustav (1905). *Abriß einer Geschichte der protestantischen Missionen*. Berlin.

HARTMUT HABERLAND

A *Minimum Morale* on how not to Listen to the Native Speaker

ABSTRACT

This chapter is about objectivity in science. It indicates a tradition of Western science (which is called the Columbus paradigm) and records some of the cases where native speakers *have* spoken.

LET IT BLEED

When Christopher Columbus came to the island of Guanahaní on Thursday, October 11, 1492, he met for the first time natives of what for the Europeans was the New World. In his logbook, he wrote,

Ils n'ont pas des armes, et ils ne savent pas ce que c'est; car je leur fis voir des épées, et telle était leur ignorance qu'ils les saisissaient par le tranchant, en se coupant les doigts. (Columbus 1961, p. 44).[1]

This incident could be one of the first accounted-for attempts to collect data of the kind Cicourel calls "obtrusively obtained" (1974, p. 1564). Columbus appears here as a pre-anthropologist. Since he cannot understand what the natives say, he cannot collect his data by simply asking. But it is important for him − for obvious reasons − to know whether the natives have any knowledge of weapons. So he has to apply a behavioral test, which the natives gladly perform, impressed by the

bonnets de couleur et quelques colliers de verre qu'ils mettaient à leur cou, ainsi que d'autres petits objets de peu de valeur (1961, p. 44).

They take Columbus' sword in their hands and cut their fingers. The visiting anthropologist can pin down a piece of evidence which indicates the ease of conquering those islands for the Spanish crown. Such a conquest, as Columbus points out, will be worth its while: not only because of the islands' beauty and wealth, but also in order to win new subjects to the Spanish king:

On doit pouvoir en faire des hommes de peine excellents, et ils ont l'esprit éveillé, car je vois qu'ils répètent tout de suite ce que je leur dis. Je pense donc qu'il sera facile de les convertir, d'autant plus qu'il me semble comprendre qu'ils n'avaient aucune croyance particulaire. (1961, p. 45).

How did the history of linguistics go ever since? Have the linguists-anthropologists, visiting or just dropping by with a switched-on tape recorder, ever *listened* to a native speaker? Or have they just written down how she[2] reacted when provided with a well-forged stimulus?

According to Tom Lehrer, "If people can't communicate, the very least they can do is to shut up." And the consequence for any linguist who happens to be a moralist would be to ask his or her colleagues to stop eavesdropping. Anything said by the Native Speaker can be used against her — if not by the linguist, by at least anybody who has paid for, or just happens to read, the linguist's research results.

If we see the whole issue as a methodological problem, the point is clear: The Native Speaker's consciousness about her own language is of a kind which often makes her statements of little interest to the linguist. Germans will gladly tell you that their language has long consonants (like in *kommen* 'to come'), Greeks that <η> represents a long [i:], and Danes that *tigge* 'to beg' and *tikke* 'to tick' are not homonyms at all. Labov's Martha's Vineyard study provides a good example of people who know that they sound different, but are unable to tell the linguist why (Labov 1963, p. 298). But you, as a linguist, know better. Therefore, you don't want to listen to them. You want the truth. So you trap them using a test. You cannot ask a person, "What's the level of abstraction you are able to work at?" Instead, you ask, "Where do you buy chewing gum?" And the answer is, "At Tony's." The Native Speaker has probably tried to be helpful, but what you write down is, "subject not able to distinguish levels of abstraction," and you are ready to correlate this finding with the speaker's social class (and/or race).

Viewed from the vantage-point of the annals of our science, this development of "objective methods" turns out to be a historical necessity. Other relevant milestones in that development are: the growth of American ethnology out of the U.S. Geological Surveys[3] and the birth of American structuralism out of Neopositivist methodology. This again, should cause no hard feelings. When Powell, the first director of the Bureau of American Ethnology, redeemed philology out of "the hands of metaphysicians" (quoted in Darnell, 1969, p.47), he perhaps even did its objects a good turn. But on the other hand, the objects themselves of the science (which are called subjects in the surveys) have reacted against being used this way. Anjum (1978, p.283f.)

A Minimum Morale 197

quotes Pakistani workers in Norway who express their sentiments concerning immigrant researchers: "I do not like to meet any research person. They sell my feelings." "They come and ask questions and nothing changes." "They come and meet us nicely, we treat them friendly and then we become friends. After friendship, an inquiry starts. They ask about things they already know." "They do not want to listen to what I want to say." "They are just Norwegians." "They don't trust us." "I always cheat them, because they cheat us." There is also the anonymous Mexican peasant quoted by Jäcklein, who said to the visiting anthropologist, "Como to no trabajo, no sabe" (1975, p.227) — since you don't work, you don't know. And we have an account of what the natives could have told Columbus if he had been able to listen. Sixty years after Columbus, a Spanish monk, Fray Bernardino de Sahagún, compiled the General History of the Things of New Spain (*Historia universal de las coses de Nueva España*), a book written in Aztec by the survivors of the Spanish conquest of Mexico, which gives an account of everything that could be known and said in this language. Their description of Gods, people, animals, birds, stars and flowers is of extreme beauty and full of pain, and even the mere lists of words summing up the parts of the body in the Tenth book of the *History* read like a story about how real people are able to move, feel, and sense if they are not caught in somebody's trap.[4]

But, as I indicated before, there is no particular sense in moralizing. We all behave like ethnologists in everyday life (except, perhaps, on some of those rare occasions when we are in love). We defend ourselves against other people and try to avoid being 1. at their mercy and 2. to raise our level of awareness above what they are willing to tell us by words and deeds. We have learned not to display full information about what we want, feel, and think, since this information could change their wants, feelings and thoughts in a direction other than we want. This is part of our social character, and this social character has been produced through a long history. Columbus arrival in Guanahani is part of this history in the same way as there is a line from Descartes' *clare et distincte* to the use of defoliants by the US troops in the Vietnam war. It is the history of our civilisation which came into being through a long struggle against the brute forces of nature and the endeavor to enhance the productive forces of our society. Our social character has been formed according to the needs of survival: physical, emotional, and professional survival, that is. There is no particular reason why we should be different as anthropologists, linguists, or whatever we are, from the way we are as ordinary people. Our history has been the same, and there will be no way out of this history unless we change its context. Until then, the least we can do is to abandon some of our objectivity. Which means that we have to learn from objective science (which is science in the Columbus paradigm) and to put it to use wherever the objects of science start to be subjects again. And if we have learned our lesson, then we know that this is not just a matter of free will and of deliberate decision which side we want to be on. It is not a matter of good or bad morals, and it is not a matter of "openness towards the Other" (who, after all, is a fellow human being), either. It is just a question of whether our scientific activities make *sense*.

NOTES

1. Even a short text like this one represents a longer discourse. I would like to thank Uta Quasthoff, Gerhard Voigt, Tove Skutnabb-Kangas, Inger Mey, Tamar Bermann, Jacob Mey and Andreas Gutzwiller for taking turns. Andreas Gutzwiller has also suggested an alternative title for this paper, " 'The facts, Madam, the facts' — Sergeant Friday meets the Native Speaker." The reference to Columbus' logbook I owe to an article by Joachim Moebus published in the journal *Das Argument* (1973). Quotes from the *Historia universal* . . . struck me for the first time in a German translation in the periodical *Kursbuch* in 1965. The story about Tony is told in Schatzmann and Strauss (1955).
2. I am fully aware of the fact that almost half of all native speakers are male. But referring to them as *he* would blur the fact that the rest of them is female. Therefore, I will at least preliminarily stick to *she*.
3. This story is worth to be told once more (all references are to Darnell 1969). John Wesley Powell, the first director of the Bureau of American Ethnology, was a geologist, but he had a vivid interest in the languages of the North American aborigines. When he organized the last of the four big Geological Surveys of the U.S. in the 19th century, he was the first to extend the scope of the surveys to include the study of "the influence of the land on its inhabitants" (1969), p.24). Previous surveys had considered Indians as a hindrance to the acquisition of geological information. But Powell was not only interested in the languages spoken in the areas where he was doing geological research (1969, p.29), he also published linguistic and ethnographic records of the American aborigines as memoirs of the Geological Survey for a number of years (1969, p.31). It was only years later that anthropology (and, later, linguistics) became professional sciences in their own right.
4. I quote from the first paragraph of the twenty-seventh chapter of the tenth book of the *Historia universal* . . . The tenth book is entitled "The people," the twenty-seventh chapter tells "of the intestines, and of all the internal organs, and of all the external organs, and of the joints pertaining to men and pertaining to women" (Anderson and Dibble (eds.), 1950 ff., Pt. XI, p.95). Its first paragraph "telleth of the body, of the skin of men and women." In English translation, part of it reads as follows:

> **Flesh.** Fleshiness, clay, earth, our clay, foundation, our foundation, that which is our foundation, flesh of the head, flesh of the face, flesh of the lips, flesh of the neck, flesh of the chest, flesh of our hip, flesh of the thigh, flesh of the knee, flesh of our knee, flesh of the calf of the leg, flesh of the ankle, flesh of the sole of the foot, flesh of the navel, flesh of one's navel, flesh of the palm of the hand, flesh of the toe, flesh of the finger, chili-red, bloody, fatty, fatty, greasy, having serous

A Minimum Morale

fluids, having pus, thick, extensive, flabby, tissue-like, tubular, blue-green, green, blotched, blue, moist, dry, festered, gangrenous, full of blood, greasy, firm, swollen, oily, it grows, it develops, it evolves, it grows big, it enlarges, it becomes grease-stained, it becomes chili-red, it becomes pale, it becomes blue-green, it becomes firm, it becomes tender, it becomes lean, it becomes very lean, it bursts open, it heals, it becomes fat, it swells, it festers, it becomes damaged, it sickens, it becomes sick, it becomes tired, it is ripped, it is cut, it is pierced, it is split, it stretches, it becomes loose, it is resilient, it becomes hot, it becomes glowing hot, it becomes cold, it becomes cold.

REFERENCES

Adorno, Theodor W. (1951). *Minima moralia. Reflexionen aus dem beschädigten Leben.* Frankfurt/M: Suhrkamp.
Anderson, Arthur J.O. and Charles E. Dibble, eds. (1950ff). *Fray Berhardino de Sahagún: General History of the Things of New Spain (Codex florentinus).* The School of American Research, Santa Fé, New Mexico and The University of Utah. Monographs of the School of American Research, Number 14, Parts II–XIII.
Anjum, Saeed (1978). 'What foreign workers think about . . .' In Norbert Dittmar, Hartmut Haberland, Tove Skutnabb-Kangas and Ulf Teleman eds., *Papers from the first Scandinavian-German symposium on the language of immigrant workers and their children, Roskilde 19-23 March 1978.* Roskilde University Center (ROLIG-papir 12), pp. 283–284.
Cicourel, Aaron (1974). 'Ethnomethodology.' In Thomas A. Sebeok *et al.*, eds., *Current Trends in linguistics 12,* The Hague: Mouton, 1974, pp. 1562–1605.
[Columbus]: (1961). *Œuvres de Christophe Colomb, présentées, traduites de l'Espagnol et annotées* par Alexandre Cioranescu, Paris: Gallimard.
Darnell, Regna (1969). *The development of American anthropology 1879-1920: from the Bureau of American Ethnology to Franz Boas.* Ph.D. dissertation, University of Pennsylvania. Ann Arbor, Michigan: Xerox University Microfilms.
Jäcklein, K.J. (1975). 'Sentences by Mexican Indian peasants.' *The Journal of Peasant Studies* 2: 226–228.
Labov, William (1963). 'The social motivation of a sound change.' *Word* 19: 273–309.
Moebus, Joachim (1973). 'Bestimmung des Wilden und Entwicklung des Verwertungsstandpunkts bei Kolumbus.' *Das Argument* 79: 273–307.
Schatzmann, Leonard and Anselm Strauss (1955). 'Social class and modes of communication.' *American Journal of Sociology* 60: 329–338.

PART FOUR

Grammar: The Structure of Inquiry

BENNISON GRAY

Parallel Structure and "The Failure of Modern Linguistics"

ABSTRACT

Alisjahbana's 1965 critique of "the failure of modern linguistics in the face of linguistic problems of the twentieth century," although too heretical to gain a professional hearing, still understates the magnitude of the failure — a failure to acknowledge counter-examples in English as well as in Malay. The return of linguistic orthodoxy to standardized data — the replacing of native informants by The Native Speaker — has mitigated some serious problems in the field. However, what still remains is the fact that even the most widely used and taught languages are not formally consistent. Because linguistic formalism assumes such consistency, it has failed even to adequately describe such a highly standardized language as English. An example of an important but still inadeqately described feature is the distinction between separable (multi-assertion) and unitary (single-assertion) parallel structure. There are no consistent formal distinctions between the two differences of meaning. Some of the inconsistency is attributable to lack of standardization, but some of it is the result of inconsistent standardization. The Native Speaker can be a fairly reliable guide to idiomatic usage in a standardized language, but he is no help in providing an explanation of it.

In 1965, S. Takdir Alisjahbana analyzed what he called "the failure of modern linguistics in the face of linguistic problems of the twentieth century." Notwithstanding the rise in recent years of specialized satellite fields like language planning, his critique of formalist "sign linguistics" remains valid. However, in emphasizing the need for a prescriptive rather than descriptive linguistics, he somewhat confuses the issue by seeming to imply that standardized Western languages, as a result of long traditions of writing and compulsory education, are already adequately described. Yet formalist linguistic theory continues to be an impediment to the description of already standardized as well as still unstandardized languages.

An example of an important but still inadequately described feature of standardized language is the distinction between separable (multi-assertion) and unitary (single-assertion) parallel structure. There are no consistent formal distinctions between the two differences of meaning. Some of the inconsistency is attributable to lack of standardization, but some of it is the result of inconsistent standardization. The Native Speaker can be a fairly reliable guide to idiomatic usage in a standardized language, but he is no help in providing a consistent explanation of this usage. What needs to be determined in judging the significance of The Native Speaker is whether the failure of modern linguistics is in any way attributable to The Native Speaker's increasing importance in the field.

In his critique, Alisjahbana did not provide any theoretical answers, but he did contribute more than most of his fellow linguists to asking the relevant questions. As a result, he was perhaps the first linguist to publicly acknowledge the helplessness of modern linguistics to deal with the vast linguistic problems of the postwar world. In his inaugural lecture as Professor of Malay Studies at the University of Malaya, he charged that, under the influence of the sociological formalism of Durkheim and Simmel, linguists have completely dissociated their discipline from the linguistic needs of society. There is more to this charge than might meet the eye of a Western linguist who assumes that Alisjahbana is concerned only with the problem of standardizing the languages of emerging nations such as Malaysia and Indonesia. His challenge has not been taken up by Western linguists, and indeed the work itself is rarely even referred to. Fifteen years after the publication of the lecture, it is worth reexamining his charge with an eye to ascertaining if the situation has changed since 1965. Whether one agrees or disagrees with this charge of failure, the issue is of fundamental importance for the field and ought therefore to be debated. If the charge is wrong, the demonstration that it is will strengthen and clarify linguistics. If it is right, then analysis of the criticism is necessary for correcting the failure. The contention of the present article is that the charge is correct and that the implications of it are more serious and far-reaching than were actually stated.

Of course, one of the factors that makes Alisjahbana's viewpoint of interest is that he does speak from a position occupied by very few modern linguists — that of a life-time concern with the immense and unavoidable problems of language standardization. (See for example Alisjahbana 1976). At a time when linguistic theory is almost completely dominated by a belief that The Native Speaker has, or has potentially, the entire social system of his language innately programmed in his brain as both a physical and metaphysical fact, a special value inheres in those few linguists who are willing to fill the thankless role of devil's advocate. Of added interest is that the critique in "The Failure of Modern Linguistics" is carried out with no reference either to transformational-generative theory or to its originator. Yet the charge leveled against pre-Chomskyan formalists is no less applicable to the later generation. In view of the revolutionary claims of Chomskyan linguistics, it is valuable to be reminded of how little this revolution touched basic axioms and postulates.

Parallel Structure and Modern Linguistics 205

Alisjahbana contends that linguistics has failed to be a discipline with significant practical dimensions because language is taken to be a formal, abstract, atomistic phenomenon. The task that linguists set for themselves is to discover precise and consistent structural relationships that transcend all individual and local variation — to establish, in the words of Louis Hjelmslev, "an algebra of language" (1961, p.79). Alisjahbana touches briefly on various theoretical approaches to this goal (e.g. those of Saussure, Bloomfield, Jakobson, Hjelmslev) and finds them to be pretty much of a piece. They are all ultimately attempts to reduce meaning to phonology:

> But despite its extreme sophistication, or, as I would almost say esoteric character, this sign linguistics . . . has attracted a host of scholars and students. It is clear that the attraction of the phonological description and analysis of language lies in the simplicity of its methods and procedure; in describing the phonemic system of a language one does not need a thorough knowledge of the investigated language . . . . (p.7).

There are two levels to Alisjahbana's position. The first and more specific one is that 'sign linguistics' is not just of no help to those who must develop new national languages out of preexisting "linguistic chaos." It is a serious impediment:

> . . . while structural linguistics attempts to describe the phonological and morphological structure of a given language or dialect as natural social facts with its uniformity and "lawfulness," which are easily accessible to every investigator, the linguist in the developing countries faces and recognizes the problem that the uniformity and "lawfulness" are seldom clearly discernible, that the languages manifest themselves more or less as linguistic chaos. (p.9).

In regard to this level, it could be claimed that, in the fifteen years since Alisjahbana made his criticism, *linguists* have faced up to the problems of language planning in the developing countries. Yet, though it is true that a considerable amount of work has been done since then in comparison with the previous almost total neglect (see Rubin et al. 1977 for a summary), this work remains on the periphery of *linguistics*.

The recognition of relative "chaos" that language planning requires has not been followed by any compromise in the formalism that characterizes linguistic theory. Such theory continues to claim that developed languages, at least, are autonomous formal systems, and it continues to deny the evidence to the contrary (see Gray 1976, 1977b, in press a). It is still true, as Alisjahbana complained, that "development and planning do not belong to the vocabulary of this modern sign linguistics" and that linguists consider that "work directed toward an application, or towards the technical development and large scale use of a new idea, is unscholarly" (pp. 8-9). The work of Alisjahbana, Joshua Fishman, et al. has begun to make the new field of language planning respectable, but it has not had any effect on linguistic theory. Indeed, the only effect it could have is to subvert it.

Whatever linguistic engineering may be, it is neither the discovery nor the creation of autonomous formal systems. Indeed, the theoretical implications of linguistic engineering are disturbing. It begins to look as if each new area of practical problems requires the establishment of a new field, because linguistics per se cannot encompass them with formalist reductionist sign linguistics and no other kind of theory is acceptable to a would-be science. It may well be that recently established fields like language planning, TESL (teaching English as a second language), sociolinguistics, pragmatics, etc. are not indications of an expanding linguistics but of a field in disintegration. Worth noting in passing is the establishment in 1977 of the American Association of Applied Linguistics, the primary purpose of which seems to be to dissociate itself from linguistic theory and theorists. Membership can not be had for the asking but must be applied for on the basis of specific credentials and demonstrated interest in practical problems. There is a fear, and a legitimate one, that as long as linguistics retains its theoretical commitment it will be more likely to deny practical problems or to rationalize them away as insoluble than to seek solutions to them. The would-be science of linguistics looks on languages as data, not as problems. The two conceptions are ultimately incompatible.

At this specific level, that of the failure of linguistics in the face of the language problems of countries like Indonesia and Malaysia, Alisjahbana emphasizes that modern European vernaculars can not be taken as the model of raw linguistic data, because they have been subject since the Renaissance to deliberate and successful efforts at standardization. He criticizes Bloomfield's willingness to base his description and analysis of Tagalog on the information provided by just one informant. Certainly there is an important difference between getting the English language from a native English informant and getting the Tagalog language from a native Tagalog informant. The English informant is likely to represent widespread usage; Bloomfield's Tagalog informant represented no more than the local usage of his native tongue. The Native Speaker has been a central figure in linguistics longer than the Chomskyan linguist has, but only with the new orthodoxy has he risen from the ranks of informant to the role of linguist.

However, on the more general level of the failure of modern linguistic theory — its self-imposed confinement within formalism — the difference between standardized English and unstandardized Tagalog, Malay, Algonquin, etc. is only a matter of degree. If the essence of linguistic phenomena is taken to be sound, then it is possible to claim that natural, unconscious factors determine the consistent features of a formal system. It is for this reason that modern linguistics is committed to the position that writing is not language:

Parallel Structure and Modern Linguistics 207

. . . modern linguistics is too much preoccupied with the spoken language. When Bloomfield says that "Writing is not language, but merely a way of recording language by means of visible marks," he formulates of course the popular notion of written language. (p.12)

On the other hand, if it is admitted that written language is also language and that education for the purpose of advancing literacy is inevitably a standardizing process both of speech and writing, then what has been the case with English is only a more advanced form of what is now taking place with the languages of new Asian and African nations. Languages with fully developed written traditions in countries with free compulsory education are increasingly common in the world. But as Alisjahbana emphasizes, such languages ill accord with the preoccupations of modern linguists:

. . . modern linguistics has shown too little interest in the role of language in education, the most important socialization or enculturation process of our age, so that its influence on the shaping of the language of the school, is very limited. I am of the opinion that a serious preoccupation with the standard language of the school will certainly cure modern linguistics from its present anarchistic tendencies and its preoccupation with the spoken word. (p.14).

To a greater or less degree, *all* languages have undergone some standardization. Yet, because of the inevitability of change, none ever reaches a point where it is fully standardized. Consequently, there is no pure linguistic data. All languages are 'contaminated' by prescriptions about what, in the face of variation and inconsistency, ought to be the usage. American anthropological linguists were misled by the restricted nature of their contact with Amerindian native informants into omitting to take into account the diversity that would inevitably have emerged in a more extensive sampling. Similarly, English-speaking transformationalists have been misled by their use of themselves as native speakers into overlooking the diversity of usage that exists among the speakers of an unstandardized language. English is the fruit of centuries of conscious and deliberate prescription. Such prescription may often have been misguided and certainly has not succeeded in eliminating all inconsistencies. But it has made the task of the formal linguist much easier. It has made possible a basic reliance on The Native Speaker, and thereby has greatly reduced that central scientific concern — the acquiring of empirical data.

Alisjahbana is referring to the new nations of Asia and Africa when he says, "What they need is not *descriptive,* but *prescriptive* linguistics" (p.15). However, the logic of his position makes it applicable also to the study of European languages. This is not to say that the primary task of linguists is to prescribe but only that they need the means for recognizing and discussing the significant areas in all languages where form and system break down. All too often what does not fit the theory has in fact not even been described. This tended to be so in pre-transformational structuralism, and it is the rule now. The Native Speaker, now that he is a transformational-generative linguist, sees to it that nothing inconsistent with Chomsky's postulated principles even qualifies as data. From the Chomsky and Halle series, Studies in Language, comes this unabashed statement:

> Thus, if such principles are true, they are not merely contingently true in the way inductive extrapolations from empirical regularities are. Rather, they are necessarily true because, in principle, they cannot meet with counter-examples. Counter-examples cannot appear in linguistic experience because they would not count as linguistic experience. (Katz 1966: 281).

What has been the characteristic task of linguistics is to demonstrate by hook or crook that, appearances notwithstanding, languages are consistent formal systems. When one attempt fails, it is not given up until another explanation can be substituted for it. Thus Chomskyan linguistics started with the assumption that the intuition of The Native Speaker is in and of itself the reflection not only of widespread usage but also of a consistent formal system. Subsequently came the admission that on the level of "surface structure" inconsistencies and ambiguities do occur but are absent from the "deep structure." Finally, there has been the admission that "deep structure" itself must be abandoned and replaced by evidence located in "nonsuperficial aspects of surface structure" (Chomsky 1976, p.84) as interpreted by such devices as "Goldsmith's principle of recoverability of semantic relations" (1976, pp.115-16; see also Gray 1977c).

An advantage of the proposed new field of pragmatics as an alternative to linguistics is that the study of relationships between signs and users has no vested interest in the "leave your language alone" approach. Indeed, I would go so far as to claim that the basic justification for pragmatics is precisely that it definitely implies a dialectical relationship between signs and their users and thus an absence of pure data. The distinction between linguistic description and linguistic prescription is in part the result of past prescription. On the one hand, language is a dialectical phenomena because it is pedagogical: what is taught one way can and sometimes will be taught another way. But on the other hand, language is pedagogical because it is dialectical: what has no necessary definitive form can only attain a useful level of standardization by being prescribed and inculcated in the young.

The traditional "schoolmarm" predilection for attempting to inculcate uniformities and distinctions that are conspicuously inconsistent with sociolinguistic reality has not always been based on solid linguistic knowledge. But whether one approves or disapproves of schoolmarm prescriptivism (see Hall 1950 for representative disapproval), it is and always has been a conspicuous part of linguistic reality. Now, with the growing awareness of the failure of modern linguistics, we are beginning to hear sophisticated theoretical justifications for *not* leaving your language alone. E.D. Hirsch, for example, may not realize how much he is following in the footsteps of Alisjahbana, but his recent exposition of "an authentic ideology of literacy" is very much to our point. He argues that "the inherent and necessary direction of mass literacy is towards the dominance of the standard languages of the world" (Hirsch 1977, pp. 7-8). He recognizes that "written speech," has been so far "normalized" by grammarians, editors, teachers as "a consciously contrived and widely promulgated national written language" that it is essentially "transdialectal" and thus "belongs to no group or place in particular" (p.44).

The chief current candidate for world language status provides a good test case for the extent of linguistic consistency. If we find formal inconsistencies at the heart of an already highly standardized language, the case for linguistic formalism will surely have to be reevaluated.

English spelling has been standardized with some conspicuous inconsistencies — as linguists freely admit. This can be dismissed as mere writing. But English grammar has also been standardized with some conspicuous inconsistencies. This is rarely discussed, because to do so would be to undermine the belief in languages as autonomous formal systems. Whether the grammatical inconsistencies in the two kinds of parallel structure, discussed below, are of more or less practical seriousness compared to the 2000 different ways of spelling the 40 phonemes of English is not our primary concern. The primary concern is rather to emphasize that, along with restrictive and non-restrictive modification (see Gray 1978), separable and unitary parallel poses a serious threat to linguistic formalism. As a result, this important feature of English has not even been adequately described. The question of possible pedagogical *prescription* can not be dealt with until relatively unbiased *description* has been undertaken — albeit that what needs describing is in part the result of past prescription.

This is not to deny that the present article is motivated in part by pedagogical concerns. However, Alisjahbana seems to imply with his call for a prescriptive linguistics that descriptive linguistics is already well in hand. If an eminent linguist with an unquestioned commitment to pedagogy does indeed think this, there is little to be wondered at in people outside the profession assuming that the manifest ills of language pedagogy are not the result of inadequate knowledge on the part of the experts. A case in point is the recent well-documented study by Frank E. Armbruster, *Our Children's Crippled Future: How American Education Has Failed.* On the central problem of linguistic pedagogy, Armbruster contends that "back to the basics" requires no more than a deliberate choice and that success will be assured because the fundamentals of English grammar have long since been known. Furthermore, he supposes this knowledge to be pedagogically accessible in traditional sentence diagraming (p.208). Sympathetic as one might well be to the call for a more rigorous approach to primary and secondary education in literacy, it is easy to demonstrate that English grammar is still awaiting a clear, concise, consistent description. And while this would surely include a practical system of sentence diagraming, there is certainly no consensus now that such exists.

Armbruster is evidently referring to the Reed-Kellogg system, which was in fairly widespread use in American schools in the early part of the twentieth century. (See Gleason 1965, pp.142-51, for a useful summary.) This system had many virtues, but it also had some serious deficiencies that helped to bring about its eventual abandonment. The system of diagraming developed in Gray 1977a, despite some superficial resemblances to the Reed-Kellogg system, is not an attempt to revive it but an attempt to start again from scratch. To cite two fundamental differences that are not simply matters of different iconic conventions but that reflect a more accurate linguistic description, the diagrams in Gray 1977a carefully distinguish between restrictive and non-restrictive modification and between separable and unitary parallel.

The general failure of modern linguistics is the inability and/or unwillingness to recognize that on the one hand linguistic data always occurs in relation to conscious norms of consistency but on the other hand always includes actual inconsistencies as well as actual consistencies. Sometimes these inconsistencies can be explained by lack of standardization, but sometimes the inconsistencies are consistent: they are the result of standardization. Such cases are an embarrassment to anthropological and transformational formalism alike. Alisjahbana points out this failure in regard to relatively unstandardized languages. In the present article, I wish to point out a basic grammatical inconsistency that is a conspicuous part of an extensively standardized language — parallel structure in English.

The standard kind of parallel structure is a means of making multiple separable assertions. Less common, but by no means rare, is unitary parallel structure, which has the form of an ordinary parallel but is semantically inseparable. The distinction between individual assertions is, transformation theory notwithstanding, of crucial importance. There can be no "thread of discourse" (Grimes 1975) except as there are units of discourse strung in one way or another on the thread. Rhetoric, or discourse grammar, can not exist in any practical sense unless we can with a fair degree of agreement recognize and analyze minimum independent or potentially independent statements. My own long march that ended at the fundamental distinction between the two kinds of parallel structure and modification (Gray 1977a) began not with linguistic theory but with schoolmarm concerns. Parallel structure is not just one of various formal anomalies that could be discussed here; it is a central concern of any linguistic theory that aspires to include sustained discourse.

Parallel Structure and Modern Linguistics

Modern linguistic theory has had little practical relevance to the classroom, but classroom problems are likely to have serious implications for future linguistic theory. Schoolmarm concerns are not just a matter of the *who* and *whom* sort. They include the need for principles for teaching students how to distinguish what is asserted from what is only referred to. But at present, none of the major linguistic theories has formulated such principles.

The problem for formalist theories is that there is no consistent difference of form between a parallel structure that contains multiple assertions and a parallel structure that is a single assertion. Not only is subject-verb agreement of no help here, it is a positive hindrance. In the examples of parallel structure given below, there is some correlation between multiple-assertion parallels with plural inflections and between single-assertion parallels with singular inflections. However, this correlation exists in but a minority of examples. One cannot rely on agreement here, but neither can one completely ignore it. Sometimes the meaning is different depending on the singular or the plural form. Sometimes only one meaning and form is idiomatically possible. Sometimes the same meaning can appear indifferently in a singular or in a plural form. The only unequivocal statement we can make about these examples is that there is a precise semantic difference between those that are separable parallels (diagramed with straight lines) and those that are unitary (diagramed with braces). The Native Speaker is our authority for the meanings extracted from the following, and he is also our authority for what constitute the various idiomatic usages of subject-verb agreement. The inconsistencies are not his fault, but they do exemplify his failure as a linguistic theorist.

In six of these sixteen examples we recognize separable parallelism because each sentence is the semantic composite of the same two separate sentences. Sometimes adding the two sentences together requires a change in the singular/plural form of the verb for the sake of agreement:

Rose is a teetotaler.
+Fred is a teetotaler.
Rose and Fred are teetotalers.

Rose drinks lemonade.
+Fred drinks lemonade.
Rose and Fred drink lemonade.

Poor circulation is a cause of phlebitis.
+Lack of exercise is a cause of phlebitis.
Poor circulation and lack of exercise are causes of phlebitis.

{ Rose and Fred } are inseparable.

{ Rose and Fred } are teetotalers.

{ Rose and Fred } are a dull couple.

{ Rose and Fred } drink lemonade.

{ Beer and lemonade } is a shandy.

I bought the < oil and vinegar > at Safeway.

I mix the { oil and vinegar } first.

He was born in { Iowa or Idaho }.

Parallel Structure and Modern Linguistics 213

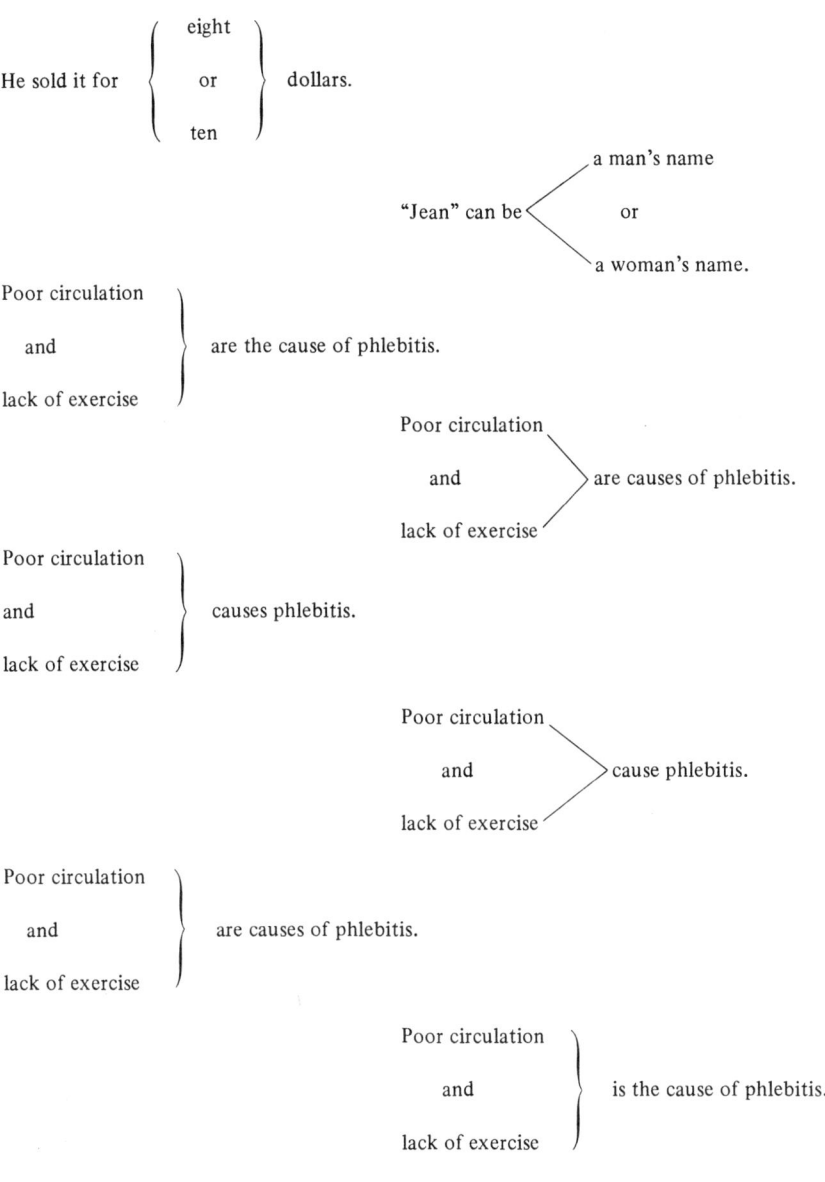

Poor circulation causes phlebitis.
+Lack of exercise causes phlebitis.
Poor circulation and lack of exercise cause phlebitis.

Sometimes adding the two sentences together requires no change of inflection:

I bought the oil at Safeway.
+I bought the vinegar at Safeway.
I bought the oil and vinegar at Safeway.

"Jean" can be a man's name.
+"Jean" can be a woman's name.
"Jean" can be a man's name or a woman's name.

The same is true of the ten examples of unitary parallel. Most of them manifest plural inflections; however, the plurality in the inflections does not correlate with a plurality of assertions, as it does for most separable parallels. It seems quite reasonable that when two things constitute a unit as far as the assertion is concerned, then a plural inflection ought to give way to a singular inflection. Thus, beer mixed with lemonade constitutes a shandy: a shandy *is* beer and lemonade. Beer is not a shandy. Lemonade is not a shandy. Only the two taken together constitute the unit that is labeled "shandy." Similarly, when poor circulation and lack of exercise taken together are said to constitute *the* one and only cause of phlebitis, we are not at all surprised to find that "Poor circulation and lack of exercise *is* the cause of phlebitis." This is quite idiomatic in English, but unfortunately it is just as idiomatic to say that "Poor circulation and lack of exercise *are* the cause of phlebitis." And for further confusion, we find that two people being inseparable and constituting a dull couple can not idiomatically be expressed with the singular *is*. There is no question that Rose in and of herself cannot be inseparable, nor that Fred in and of himself cannot be a dull couple. 'Inseparable' and 'couple' are concepts whose basic meaning requires multiple subjects. It is semantically legitimate but formally illegitimate to say:

*Rose and Fred is inseparable.
*Rose and Fred is a dull couple.

What are unquestionably grammatical errors here cause no problems of interpretation. Similarly, we can erroneously use singular forms in some separable parallels and cause no problems of interpretation:

*Rose and Fred is teetotalers.
*Rose and Fred drinks lemonade.

Parallel Structure and Modern Linguistics 215

Irrespective of the inflectional form of the verb, the very nature of drinking and teetotaling preclude the possibility of unitary parallel. The concept dictates the interpretation of the sentence.

So it is with mixing – whether the ingredients are those of salad dressing, concrete, or a dance – mixing exists only as there are two or more separate things meeting and mingling. I can say that "I mixed the oil and pigment," or I can say that "I mixed the paint." Both are single-assertion sentences. "To mix paint" means to integrate different ingredients whether or not these ingredients are specified by a unitary parallel. But if the ingredients are specified, then a unitary interpretation is as much required as it is for people being inseparable and being couples.

There remain, however, some concepts that can reasonably be interpreted either as unitary or separable. In these cases the use of inflections plays a crucial role in semantic analysis. For example, there may be various causes of phlebitis. Poor circulation is one cause; lack of exercise is one cause; there may be others. To speak of multiple causes is in English most commonly to use *cause* as the plural verb in the separable parallel:

Poor circulation and lack of exercise cause phlebitis.

In these examples the difference between singular and plural verbs has been crucial, but sometimes what is crucial for determining unitary parallel is the presence of a definite article indicating exclusiveness. In such cases the verb may be either singular or plural:

Poor circulation and lack of exercise are the causes of phlebitis.
Poor circulation and lack of exercise is the cause of phlebitis.

There is a difference of meaning here, but whether there are two (only) causes or one (only) cause makes no difference as to unitary vs. separable parallel. For the first sentence it is wrong to say (separably) that "Poor circulation is *the* cause of phlebitis." And it is wrong to say that "Poor circulation is *a* cause of phlebitis" and "Lack of exercise is *a* cause of phlebitis" add up to these two causes being *the* causes. Similarly for the second sentence it is wrong to say that "Poor circulation is *a* cause of phlebitis" and "Lack of exercise is *a* cause of phlebitis" add up to these two being *the* cause of phlebitis. In both of the above examples the use of the definite article is a semantic bar to separable parallelism.

To top off this banquet of insignificant inflectional variation, we note that it is quite idiomatic to refer to *the* unitary cause with the plural *are* as well as with the singular *is*:

Poor circulation and lack of exercise are the cause of phlebitis.

The one variation that is not idiomatic is the singular *is* with the plural *causes*, although no semantic ambiguity is likely to arise thereby:

*Poor circulation and lack of exercise is the causes of phlebitis.

Our final examples of the same forms with different kinds of meanings focuses on the ubiquitous conjunction *or*. In the unitary parallel "He sold it for eight or ten dollars" there was just one thing sold, and it brought just one price. There are not two assertions here: that he sold it for eight dollars and that he sold it for ten dollars. This use of *or* is the means of stating an approximation. It refers to estimates that set upper and lower limits. This sentence is the same sort of sentence as "He sold it for about nine dollars." *Or* can indicate an approximation (as in the unitary selling sentence); it can indicate a linking of two separable assertions (as in "Jean can be a man's name or a woman's name."); it can indicate one or the other but not both (as in "He was born in Iowa or Idaho"). The same parallel form with the same conjunction can have three distinctly different kinds of meaning. We have to know, for instance, that a person cannot be born in two different places and that Iowa and Idaho are not the sort of things (like units of money) that can provide the limits of an approximation.

Thus, while we began with the attempt to demonstrate that the same kind of parallel form can have two different kinds of meaning, we find ourselves concluding that we understated the case a bit. Not only are unitary parallels significantly different from separable parallels, there are significant semantic differences among unitary parallels. There is more to unitary parallel than two things constituting the two parts of an indivisible whole. Iowa and Idaho, for example, are mutually exclusive designations of a birthplace, which is hardly the same as calling them two parts of an indivisible whole.

Of course, there are limits to semantic interpretation just as there are to formal interpretation. And when neither set of principles is consistent, we are not surprised to find problems of ambiguity. The sentence "Rose and Fred are married" is likely to be interpreted as referring to a particular marriage, but it can also refer to a condition that can be predicated of many people. It would be quite over-straining to interpret "Ralph, Fred, Jack, and Harold are married" referring to a particular marriage. It would even be a bit forced (although times are changing) to interpret "Ralph and Fred are married" as referring to a particular marriage. Much more likely is the interpretation that Ralph and Fred (of the men in my office) have wives. This sentence is a way of distinguishing some men in the group as having wives from other men in the group who do not have wives. However, in "Rose and Fred are married"

Parallel Structure and Modern Linguistics 217

we can mean either that Rose and Fred are married to each other, or we can mean that Rose and Fred (of the people in my office) have spouses, although they are not each other's spouse. This distinguishes the single people in my office from the married ones. The married ones may be married to each other, or they may be married to people not in the office. Neither the form of the sentence nor the meaning of the words can give an unequivocal answer. This distinction between separable and unitary meaning is still the central concern, but in this case not only is the form of no help, the subject matter is of no help either. If "Rose and Fred are married" refers to two different marriages, then "Rose is married" plus "Fred is married" add up to a separable parallel. But if "Rose and Fred are married" refers to a single marriage, then it is a unitary parallel.

It is probably true that the linking of a male and a female name raises the presumption for many assertions of a unitary parallel. Thus, we can reasonably interpret "Rose and Fred raise turkeys" as meaning that Rose and Fred are doing this together. (But then we can just as reasonably conclude that "Ralph and Fred raise turkeys" means that it is a joint venture.) What is almost as reasonable, however, is that we are distinguishing those who raise turkeys from those who do not. Of the neighboring farms, only two have gone into turkeys; the rest have stayed with chickens. We would not think that "Rose Nelson and Fred Smith raise turkeys" requires the interpretation of a joint venture. Perhaps it seems more likely that two different males (Ralph Nelson and Fred Smith) have engaged in a joint turkey venture than that a male and a female have. But at this point there is much more guesswork than grammatical interpretation. As they stand, though probably not in context, these sentences are ambiguous in ways that our earlier examples of unitary and separable parallels are not. It is those unequivocal unitary constructions that make the case for the same form having different kinds of meaning.

Our discovery of formal inconsistency in parallel constructions amply demonstrates the contention that what does not fit the theory does not even get described. The seriousness of this problem is unconsciously emphasized by a major recent attempt to escape the current theoretical impasse in linguistics by making a new empirical start. The makers of the *Lingua* Descriptive Studies Questionnaire emphasize that "most descriptions of languages or parts of languages . . . are structured in terms of one of the current theories of language and thereby often do not answer the questions which would be posed by linguists of a different theoretical persuasion" (*Lingua* 1977, p.5). In this era of Kuhnian philosophy of science, the old-fashioned notion that description and theory are two different things and that the latter must grow out of the former if circularity is to be avoided is something of a minority position. In the *Lingua* questionnaire this position is phrased in a judiciously general way not so likely to offend the current dominant school of linguistics. Yet its opposition to the attempt of this school to merge data and theory in a self-contained formal system is clear enough: "while presentation of data and theorizing about data are never completely divorceable from each other, the emphasis of the present series is definitely on accurate and orderly presentation of data as a prerequisite to theoretical discussion" (p.6).

Why, then, since the present article is in agreement with this, is it not presented within the framework of the *Lingua* questionnaire? The answer is clear enough: the questionnaire, detailed as it is, has no relevance at all to the distinction between separable and unitary parallel. And what is more, it is nearly as irrelevant to restrictive and non-restrictive modification.

Among the hundreds of questions, there is only one for the restrictive/non-restrictive distinction (1.1.2.3.2): "Is there a distinction between restrictive and non-restrictive clauses?" The fact that many non-restrictive modifiers are not clauses but phrases or single words is quite ignored. (See Gray 1978). But at least the distinction between assertional (non-restrictive modification) and non-assertional (restrictive modification) is implied by this reference.

However, in regard to parallel structure, the questionnaire does not even imply the existence of the assertional/non-assertional distinction, let alone provide a precise category for describing it. Of course the compilers of the questionnaire (Bernard Comrie and Norval Smith) make no claim to having achieved exhaustive coverage this early in what is as admirable a project as it is formidable a task. Yet those who think that Alisjahbana's challenge is still waiting to be taken up, are tempted to see more theoretical bias in the questionnaire than first meets the eye. On the one hand, the *Lingua* questionnaire is motivated by a respect for systematically compiled data in the traditional rigorous scientific sense. But on the other hand, it is motivated by "the increasing interest in the study of universals of language" (p.5). Of course all science is the search for greater and greater generality: ad hoc descriptions are of minor scientific significance. Yet it may well prove to be the case that linguistic universals, if they exist at all, are the result of semantic distinctions as much as of formal distinctions. If, as seems to be the case, there is no ultimate consistency between form and meaning, descriptions of languages in terms only, or almost entirely, of atomistic forms will be seriously limited. There seems to be no inherent reason why the study of language must aspire to be as non-semantic as possible, why universals in science must be indiscriminately reductionist. But so ingrained is this axiom in linguistics that as candid and forthrightly pre-theoretical a framework for research as the *Lingua* questionnaire does not even raise the point but simply lays out the categories of a formalist sign linguistics.

Without wishing to levitate to the level of theory before establishing a

Parallel Structure and Modern Linguistics 219

solid descriptive foundation, I would like to suggest that there are alternative ways of sketching a relatively neutral descriptive framework. One such alternative is that employed in my forthcoming *Introduction to Semantic Grammar: An Outline of English*. In brief, there is Inflection (the grammar of words), Position (the grammar of phrases), and Composition (the grammar of assertions). Whatever the limitations of this claim for an exhaustive outline, it does at least recognize that inter-assertional relationships are just as much a matter of grammar as they are of rhetoric. What could be more central to grammar than distinguishing between individual assertions and multiple assertions integrated into complex sentences? That this distinguishing is so rarely undertaken in linguistic analysis represents *a* failure, if not *the* failure, of modern linguistics.

Is it fair to conclude that this failure is attributable to the increasing importance of The Native Speaker in modern linguistics? Probably not. The Native Speaker may even be the harbinger of a new linguistics that better accords with the problems that are so conspicuous to Alisjahbana.

Speaking bluntly, we could say that The Native Speaker is no more than a front man for whatever school is dominant. Speaking judiciously, we could say that The Native Speaker becomes increasingly important as linguistics finds its data in the most standardized languages. Of course the present orthodoxy does not admit that standardization, prescription, and pedagogy are basic sources of its data. But by focusing on English and The Native Speaker rather than on Tagalog and the native informant, Chomskyan linguistics does differ from Bloomfieldian linguistics. Speaking as judiciously and positively as possible, non-doctrinaire linguists could claim that the increasing importance of The Native Speaker is the light at the end of the tunnel. This light is unlikely ever to allow us to see a consistent, formal system. But it could allow us to distinguish the patterns of language from the counter-examples.

The failure of modern linguistics, the very heart of the intellectual fraud that has corrupted the field, is the dogma, made explicit by Katz, that "Counter-examples cannot appear in linguistic experience because they would not count as linguistic experience." The consequences of this dogma are both anti-scientific and anti-social. They are anti-scientific because the true nature of language can never be discerned as long as the linguist is entitled to exclude from his data all use of language that does not fit his theory. They are anti-social because the dogma denies the need for conscious and deliberate standardization, which alone makes possible the extension of communication by which societies are united.

REFERENCES

Alisjahbana, S.T. (1965). *The Failure of Modern Linguistics in the Face of Linguistic Problems of the Twentieth Century.* Kuala Lumpur: Univ. of Malaya.
Alisjahbana, S.T. (1976). *Language Planning for Modernization: The Case of Indonesian and Malaysian.* The Hague: Mouton.
Armbruster, F.E., with P. Bracken (1977). *Our Children's Cripped Future: How American Education has Failed.* New York: Quadrangle/The New York Times.
Chomsky, N. (1976). *Reflections on Language.* London: Temple Smith.
Gleason, H.A., Jr. (1965). *Linguistics and English Grammar.* New York: Holt, Rinehart and Winston.
Gray, B. (1976). "The Principle of Language," *Language Sciences* 43: 1–4.
Gray, B. (1977a). *The Grammatical Foundations of Rhetoric: Discourse Analysis.* The Hague: Mouton.
Gray, B. (1977b). 'Is Linguistics a Superstructure? The Case of Ukranian and Black English.' In R. Di Pietro & E. Blansitt, eds., *The Third LACUS Forum 1976.* Columbia, S.C.: Hornbeam, pp. 207–16.
Gray, B. (1977c). 'Now You See It – Now You Don't: Chomsky's *Reflections.*' *Forum Linguisticum* 2: 65–74.
Gray, B. (1978). 'The Fallacy of Size in Syntactic Analysis.' In *Lingua* 46: 101–13.
Gray, B. (In press a). 'Facing up to Language Mixture.' In *Orbis.*
Gray, B. (In press b). *Introduction to Semantic Grammar: An Outline of English.*
Grimes, J.E. (1975). *The Thread of Discourse.* The Hague: Mouton.
Hall, R.A., Jr. (1950). *Leave Your Language Alone!* Ithaca, N.Y.: Linguistica.
Hirsch, E.D., Jr. (1977). *The Philosophy of Composition.* Chicago: Univ. Press.
Hjelmslev, L. (1961). *Prolegomena to a Theory of Language.* Trans. F.J. Whitfield. Madison: Univ. of Wisconsin Press.
Katz, J.J. (1966). *The Philosophy of Language.* New York: Harper.
Lingua Descriptive Studies Questionnaire: 1977, *Lingua* 42: 1–72.
Rubin, J., B.H. Jernudd, J. Das Gupta, J. Fishman, and C.A. Ferguson, eds. (1977). *Language Planning Processes.* The Hague: Mouton.

JOHN HINDS

The Interpretation of Ungrammatical Utterances*

ABSTRACT

This paper advances the position that ungrammatical utterances in specific contexts may offer insight into speaker motivations and intended meanings. To set the stage for this, four separate analyses of Japanese are examined, and it is shown that there is a distinction which should be drawn between grammaticality judgments made "in the laboratory" and actual language use. Then, an actual conversation is analyzed. In this conversation, one speaker marks a noun phrase with an incorrect postpositional case marker. This ungrammaticality is shown to be an attempt on the speaker's part to disguise his role in campus cheating, the current topic of conversation.

INTRODUCTION

My topic concerns the interpretation of ungrammatical utterances which are unintentionally produced by native speakers of a language. In order to set the stage for this discussion, however, I wish to discuss first one aspect of current linguistic methodology that I believe is in error – the construction of grammars based on sentences judged in isolation by necessarily biased investigators. Throughout the course of my exposition I trust that the relationship between these topics will become clear, and moreover, that I will offer a positive suggestion for overcoming investigator bias.

In 1957, many linguists heralded Chomsky's proclamation that:

The fundamental aim in the linguistic analysis of a language L is to separate the *grammatical* sequences which are the sentences of L from the *ungrammatical* sequences which are not sentences of L and to study the structure of the grammatical sequences. The grammar of L will thus be a device that generates all of the grammatical sequences of L and none of the ungrammatical ones. (Chomsky 1957:13).

This position, as is well known and documented, triggered an amazing amount of research designed to specify the grammatical utterances of a language and to preclude ungrammatical utterances. The problem was that, in order to differentiate grammatical utterances from ungrammatical utterances, there had to be some way of obtaining information about the native speaker's linguistic competence. Chomsky (1965:18) states:

Clearly, the actual data of linguistic performance will provide much evidence for determining the correctness of hypotheses about underlying linguistic structure, along with introspective reports (by the native speaker, or the linguist who has learned the language).

What happened, of course, due in part to Chomsky's (1965:19f.) clear statements that operational tests "must meet the empirical condition of conforming, in a mass of crucial and clear cases, to the linguistic intuition of the native speaker . . . ," and that the "problem for the grammarian is to construct a description and, where possible, an explanation for the enormous mass of unquestionable data concerning the linguistic intuition of the native speaker (often himself) . . ." was that recourse to the "actual data of linguistic performance" was lost, and the sole means of data gathering became introspection. This exclusive reliance on intuitions for linguistic data is the precursor to a game played frequently at linguistic conferences and meetings, and in response to criticisms of published papers. We can call the game, "In *my* dialect." The rules are straightforward. Whenever the acceptability or grammaticality judgment of an example sentence is challenged by a member of the audience, the analyst responds with a phrase like, "Well, in *my* dialect that sentence is good/bad." Despite Chomsky's (1965:21) claim that the tacit knowledge a native speaker has may not be immediately available to the user of the language, we work with the assumption that investigators have some recourse to their own intuitions, while others are not able to see inside the investigator's heads. Thus, we are forced to accept the claim that a certain judgment is sound, the consequence of rejecting the investigator's 'intuition' being that we declare the investigator a fraud.

Labov (1978:349ff.) offers an excellent discussion of problems involved with this game, although his terminology differs from mine. Differences in grammaticality judgments, he reports, plague most papers in the generative framework. The way out of embarrassing confrontations with co-workers, of course, is to invoke the game. Labov (1978:350) states:

the author usually cites *my dialect* or *most dialects* without further discussion. The reader assumes in the first case that someone has disagreed with the author; in the second case he has asked several friends and most of them agree with him.

Linguists are allowed recourse to this game because they by and large rely only on intuitions to guide them in their search for grammatical and acceptable utterances. But why should we believe that a linguist has the capacity to tap intuitions without distortion? Carl Sagan (1973:42) has suggested that investigators in other fields are not above reproach. In the initial stages of a discussion on the possibilities of extraterrestrial life, Sagan recounts an item of historical interest:

For example, there is a famous book published about 1912 by Lawrence J. Henderson, called *The Fitness of the Environment,* in which Henderson concludes that life necessarily must be based on carbon and water, and have its higher forms metabolizing free oxygen. I personally find this conclusion suspect, if only because Lawrence Henderson was made of carbon and water and metabolized free oxygen. Henderson had a vested interest. Can we make some sort of objective judgment free from chauvinism, independent of our prejudices?

Spencer (1973) has shown that naive speakers of a language have different intuitions on the acceptability of sentences than do linguists, and we might well ask whether the linguist or the layman is more apt to have a vested interest in intuitions being compatible with proposed linguistic analyses. There is no need to talk of academic dishonesty, but of self-deception, a phenomenon well enough known in psychological research to require 'doubleblind' testing.

Labov (1978:351) sums up the situation which confronts a linguist whose major data source comes from intuitions, usually his own.

Given the unlimited character of syntactic contributions, how does one make a systematic search of the evidence? There are undoubtedly unconscious factors which lead investigators to find examples which support their own arguments and not to find counter-examples.

I believe Labov (1978) has made a strong case against the reliance on intuitions to construct a theory of grammar, and I wish to offer one more perspective to this discussion. In recent years, three studies of interest have appeared in the psychological journals. These are Bates, Kintsch, and Masling (1978), Keenan, MacWhinney, and Mayhew (1977), and Kintsch and Bates (1977). Each of these studies has shown that memory for surface structures is considerably more robust in natural environments than it is in laboratory settings. This will not come as a surprise to any who have suffered through psychological tests for credit in their undergraduate days. Typical laboratory tests are removed from reality, and processes other than those used in normal everyday interactions are brought to bear in any task which must be performed. I submit that a similar problem exists with those linguists who attempt to assign grammaticality judgments out of context. The intuitions we have for utterances in citation form are different from the feel we have for utterances in natural environments.

Four pieces of evidence from recent studies in Japanese syntax are provided. I am confident that similar results can be found for generative studies of any language.

RULES

Particle Deletion

First, Kuno (1978:254) states with respect to the postpositional particles which provide information on grammatical relations, that

> *ga* deletion (i.e. the deletion of the 'subject' marking particle) does not take place in adjectival clauses:
>
> (1) (a) taroo ga kita koto
>   the fact that Taro came
>
>   (b) *taroo (#) kita koto

Kuno elsewhere (1973) claims that the thematic particle *wa* cannot occur in subordinate clauses. Thus, for Kuno, (1c) would also be ungrammatical.

(1) (c) *taroo wa kita koto

Kuno further claims that only the particle *wa*, and never the subject particle *ga*, can be deleted. All of this is highly internally consistent, yet it is not consistent with actual language use.

I have no quarrel with Kuno's grammaticality judgment of (1b) in isolation, that is, in the laboratory. There is a high degree of agreement with his judgment among native speakers of Japanese. There is also a high degree of agreement among native speakers of Japanese that grammaticality judgments for the paradigm listed in (2) parallel those of the structurally equivalent (1).

(2) (a) watasitati ga hikkosanakya ikenai koto
    the fact that we have to move

    (b) *watasitati (#) hikkosanakya ikenai koto

However, once we leave the laboratory, we find that utterances like those in (2b) do occur, and that they are considered perfectly acceptable in context. The relevant utterance is italicized in (3K-7).

(3) A-1. de::, soko de sukosi osieta koto ga aru.
        Uh, and I taught there a while.

    W-2. ara hoNto? dono gurai?
         Oh really? For how long?

K-3. ha?
Huh?

W-4. dono gurai, kikaN?
How long, in terms of time?

K-5. a, tyotto, moo ty-hoN no tyotto.
Uh, a little, a little mo-just a little.

W-6. hoNtoo, haa.
Really, oh.

K-7. moo ne, osigoto moratte kara, *sugu watasitati hikkosanakya ikenai koto ni natta* kara, sonoo, tuzukerarenakute, tyotto zaNneN datta.
Yeah, well, after I got some work, *we had to move right away*, so, uh, I couldn't continue on, and that was a shame.

Intransitive Potential Sentences

The second area concerns recent discussions of intransitive potential sentences. Potential sentences are formed in Japanese by inserting a potential morpheme into the verb. The form of this morpheme differs depending on the verb class. In simplified terms, *-ru* stem verbals require the potential morpheme *-rare-* while *-u* stem verbals require the morpheme *-e-*. These are illustrated in (4).

(4) (a) *-ru* STEM VERBALS
taberu 'eat' → *taberareru* 'can eat'
yameru 'quit' → *yamerareru* 'can quit'

(b) *-u* STEM VERBALS
hanasu 'talk' → *hanaseru* 'can talk'
hataraku 'work' → *hatarakeru* 'can work'

Case marking may alternate in potential constructions as well. For transitive verbals, the subject marker may change from *ga* to *ni* if the object marker changes from *o* to *ga*. (5) illustrates this; particles are italicized.

(5) (a) taroo *ga* sakana *o* tabeta.
Taro   fish   ate
Taro ate some fish.

(b) taroo *ni* sakana *ga* taberareta.
    Taro   fish   could eat
    Taro was able to eat some fish.

Because the change of subject marker from *ga* to *ni* depends on the change of the object marker from *o* to *ga*, it has been claimed (Kuno 1973, Kuroda 1978, Shibatani 1977, Tonoike 1975-6) that the change of the subject marker from *ga* to *ni* cannot occur with intransitive verbals. (6) is typical of the paradigm adduced to support this claim.

(6) (a) isikawa ga hataraku.
         Ishikawa   works
         Ishikawa works.

    (b) isikawa ga hatarakeru.
         Ishikawa   can work
         Ishikawa is able to work.

    (c) *isikawa ni hatarakeru.
         Ishikawa   can work

Once again, laboratory tested intuitions support this view. However, Nagatomo (1978) has demonstrated that sentences such as (6c) occur with regularity in natural environments. The relevant sections are italicized in (7A-3).

(7) A-1. watasitati tyuugakusei wa natuyasumi ni hataraityaa ikenai no ka sira.
         Can't we junior high school students work during the summer vacation?

    B-2. N, soo rasii yo. seNsei ni kiita kedo dame da tte sa. demo ne, tonari no kurasu no isikawa ne, natuyasumi ni baito site kane tameru tte itte ru yo.
         No, I guess not. I asked the teacher, but he said no. But, you know, Ishikawa in the next classroom says he'll work part-time and save money during the summer vacation.

    A-3. soo? sore wa okasii wa. *isikawa saN ni* hatarakete *watasitati ni* hatarakenai naN te hukoohei da wa.
         Is that right? That's strange. It's unfair that *Ishikawa* can work and *we* can't.

Nagatomo claims that the relevant factor is whether there is an implied or expressed contrast involving the NP *ni*. If there is, the sentence is judged grammatical; if there is not, as is usually the case in the laboratory, the sentence is ruled ungrammatical.

Scrambling

The third area is discussed in Tamori (1977), and this involves a transformational process known as SCRAMBLING (see Muraki 1974). Tamori claims that scrambling cannot apply if postpositional particles are deleted. He presents a laboratory demonstration of this.

(8) (a) taroo ga hanako o ai sita.
    (b) taroo (#) hanako (#) ai sita.
    (c) hanako o taroo ga ai sita.
    (d) *hanako (#) taroo (#) ai sita.

Each of these sentences is meant to be interpreted as meaning 'Taro loves Hanako.' (8a) is a sentence in its most pristine form with neutral word order and all particles specified. (8b) shows that both particles may be deleted, while (8c) shows that with the particles present the noun phrases may be scrambled. (8d) purports to show that particle deletion and scrambling cannot both occur, or mistakes in interpretation will arise: that is, (8d) can only be interpreted as meaning 'Hanako loves Taro.'

Once again, a walk outside of the laboratory into the streets finds that there is often other information available for speakers to correctly interpret sentences in which scrambling and particle deletion have both applied. In (9), another sentence is presented. The verbal *suki da* 'like' is used and this verbal regularly marks its object with the particle *ga*. In this example the negative form of *suki da, suki zya nai*, is used.

(9) (a) atasi *ga* soo iu no *ga* amari suki zya nai no.
       I   that kind   very   don't like emphasis
    I don't like that kind of thing very much you know.

(9b) and (9c) show that either particle deletion or scrambling may also apply to this sentence.

(9) (b) atasi (#) soo iu no (#) amari suki zya nai no.
    (c) soo iu no *ga* atasi *ga* amari suki zya nai no.

The sentence in (10), with relevant sections italicized, shows that both transformations can actually occur in the same sentence under natural conditions. W has been discussing things she does not like about Americans.

(10) W-1. . . . atasi no itte ru no wa sugoku, naN te iu ka na, ii hoo no taido no toki.
. . . what I'm talking about is, what should I say, their behavior when things are going well.

H-2. haa.
Oh.

W-3. yosugiru wake, amerikaziN, hoNto yori mo.
They're too good, Americans, better than reality.

H-4. NN, aa, soo ka.
Hm, oh, I see.

W-5. N, soo iu no ga ki ni natta, sugoku, naN te iu ka na,
Mm, that kind of thing got to me, really, what should I say,

H-6. NN, kotyoo suru tte iu no ka sira ne.
Hm, I guess you could say they exaggerate.

W-7. NN, naNka, subete naN demo biyuutihuru da si, subete huantasutikku da si, *soo iu no (#) atasi (#) amari suki zya nai no.*
Yeah, you know, everything, no matter what, is beautiful, everything is fantastic, *that king of thing I don't like very much.*

The reason the particles may be deleted in conjunction with scrambling is discussed in detail in Hinds (1979). Simply put, grammatical relations may be expressed in Japanese by one of three means: postpositional particles, word order, or case frame 'markers' (see also Minsky 1975). Neither of the first two of these is called into play in (10W-7), but since the subject of *suki da* 'like' is a sentient being (i.e. *atasi* 'I') and the object is an abstract concept (i.e. *soo iu no* 'that kind of thing'), there can be no confusion of which grammatical role each noun phrase is playing.

'Afterthoughts'

The fourth area concerns the 'afterthought' construction, and it is discussed in Kuno (1979). Despite the fact that Kuno has elsewhere (1973) claimed that Japanese is a 'strict SOV language,' he now recognizes that in conversational environments many elements may follow the verb. He states that these elements are 'afterthoughts' (see Hinds 1979 for an alternative analysis). Specifically he (1979:62) claims that

Elements that would change the interpretation of the first part of the sentence cannot appear postverbally.

He offers the following constructed examples.

(11) (a) boku nihoN saNdo   sika itta koto ga nai.
       I   Japan to three times only went fact not
       I have been to Japan only three times.

(b) *boku nihoN ni itta koto ga nai, saNdo sika.

His (1979:63) explanation for this is:

(11a) shows that *sika* 'only' requires that a negative follow it; thus, the (sic) more accurate translation of *sika* would be 'any more than'. (11b) is ungrammatical because the first part of the sentence (up to the verb) states that the speaker has never been to Japan, while the subsequent addition of *saNdo sika* 'only three times' forces a complete switch in interpretation.

However, Hinds (1976:119) had some years earlier offered the following data, based on unrecorded but actually observed utterances.

(12) A-1. yaru?
        Do you (drink)?

     B-2. yaranai, *biiru sika.*
        I don't, *except for beer.*

Here, despite Kuno's intuitions to the contrary, a noun phrase plus *sika* may be placed after the verbal as a qualifying statement. The difficulty with Kuno's position is that it does not recognize the variety of functions that shifts in word order may have in intereactional situations (see again Hinds 1979 for details).

UNGRAMMATICAL UTTERANCES AND CONVERSATIONAL INTERACTION

In addition to problems which arise because some linguists rely solely on intuitions to formulate their data, a more serious problem exists. By ruling out of the grammar, and out of consideration, those utterances which are judged ungrammatical, the analyst loses access to some very subtle and powerful means the native speaker has to manipulate language, and conversational interactants. I report one such device, the interpretation of ungrammatical utterances to understand what speakers intend despite what they say. I suggest that comparable data may be found in conversational interactions in any language.

At the outset of this discussion I wish to point out that I am not claiming native speakers consciously distort a grammatical utterance in order to achieve this effect.

I present first some data, with the appropriate section italicized. Following that I discuss aspects of the conversational interaction, and then elucidate the interpretation of ungrammatical utterances in the understanding of information the speaker is not necessarily interested in conveying.

(13) H-1. uN, dakara, kaNniNgu ni tuite wa ne, iroiro-
Yeah, well, about cheating, there are lots of-

H-2. ore ima made itido mo yatta koto nakatta keredomo ne,
Up 'til that point I had never cheated, but,

H-3. kono mae no sikeN de ne, anoo, *tonari no gotoo ni sa, koo tira tto miro tte iu wake de yokosita N da yo.*
During the last exam, *from Goto who was sitting next to me, uh, said look, and then passed me his test paper.*

H-4. ore ga kurusiNde ru no mite sa,
He saw that I was suffering,

H-5. sore de, kono mae minakattara okorareta no de, koNdo mita wake da.
So, since I didn't look the last time and he got mad at me, this time I looked.

This section of conversation is taken from a longer tape recorded discussion of cheating. An analysis of the structural properties and the interpretation of the elliptical sentences in this section of conversation may be found in Hinds (1979).

This section comprises a conversational narrative. As such it consists of a *setting* and an *episode*. In (13H-1), the topic, or theme of the narrative, 'cheating' (*kaNniNgu*), is introduced. Notice that (13H-1) is truncated, or unfinished. This type of utterance often occurs at the initiation of a new topic of conversation (see Hinds in progress, Schegloff 1979), and it indicates that the entire episode has not yet been completely planned (Beattie 1979). In (13H-2), H establishes that he will be the main protagonist by specifically making reference to himself (*ore* 'I'), and that the story will in all probability concern his first experience with cheating. Prior statements by H have indicated that he feels people are trapped into cheating (*kaNzeN ni, soko de, ryoosiN o usinatte, zuruzuru to doronuma ni haitte iku yoo na ki ga suru N da kedo* 'you lose your conscience, and feel like you're being dragged into the swamp (i.e. you're getting wicked)').

Background knowledge then prepares the addressee for a narrative about how H had been 'trapped' into cheating. (13H-3) begins the episode. Because of the hesitation (*anoo*), it is obvious that H is not sure *how* to tell his story, although he is probably clear on *what* he wants to tell. He has already, in (13H-2), indicated that this is a story about himself. Yet, a major point of the story is that he received aid from a colleague, Goto, and in fact, that he was forced into cheating by Goto (see (13H-5)). The problem for H is to balance the saliency of the two major characters, himself and Goto, and to shift the blame for cheating from himself to Goto.

We are now in a position to examine (13H-3), to delineate its ungrammatical nature, and to determine what this ungrammaticality signals. I recognize (see Hinds 1979 and references there) that the verbal is the item of central importance in a clause. Associated with each verbal is a case frame which specifies, for Japanese, both the appropriate postpositional particle and a contextual definition of relevant properties of the individual noun phrases required by that verbal. (14), (15), and (16) illustrate this format by providing appropriate case frames for the three verbals in (13): *miru* 'look at;' *iu* 'say;' and *yokosu* 'pass over (to the speaker)'.

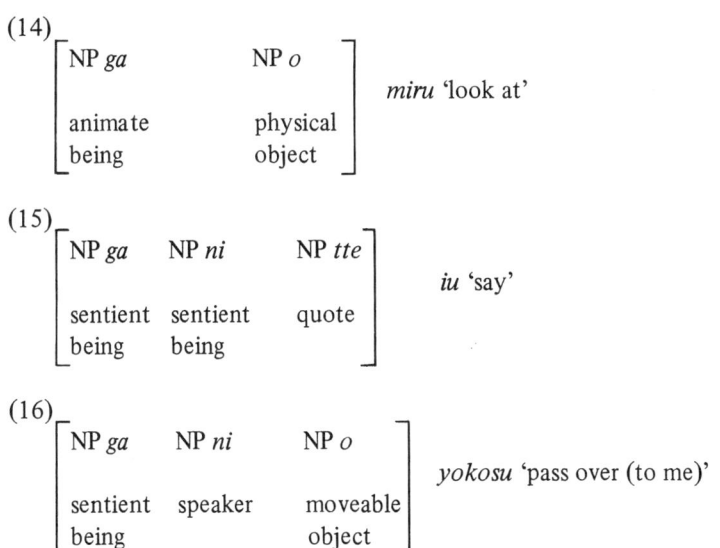

The noun phrase marked by *ga* (often referred to as the 'subject') for *miru* 'look at' must be an animate being, a category which includes animals as well as humans. The 'subject' for *iu* 'say' and *yokosu* 'pass over (to me),' on the other hand, must be a sentient being, a category restricted under normal circumstances to purposeful human beings. Because of other required relationships, NP *ga* for *yokosu* cannot refer to the speaker, although NP *ga* can refer to the speaker for either *miru* or *iu*.

The noun phrase marked by *o* for *miru* is a physical object, or anything which may be seen. Once again, borderlines may be difficult to draw, since expressions like *sora o miro* 'look at the sky' are perfectly natural. The noun phrase marked by *o* for *yokosu* refers to a subset of all physical objects; it must be something which is moveable with respect to its 'subject'. The noun phrase marked by *ni* for *yokosu* refers exclusively to the speaker, or to someone intimately associated with the speaker; while the noun phrase marked by *ni* for *iu* is any sentient being, including the speaker. The noun phrase marked by *tte* for *iu* is generally a sentence, although following McCawley's semi-facetious 'camel-belch principle' we realize that anything can be reported if it involves noise, and if it is replicable by the speaker.

The ungrammaticality of (13H-3) stems from the phrase *gotoo ni sa* 'from/to Goto'. What appears to have happened is that H began his utterance without knowing precisely how he wanted to phrase his thoughts. Because he is telling a story about himself, it is expected that the most salient character is *ore* 'I,' and that *ore* will enter into a 'chain of ellipsis' (see Hinds 1979), an indication that *ore* comprises at least part of the conversational topic. At the time H uttered *tonari no gotoo ni sa,* he probably expected to finish the utterance in some way similar to (17).

(17) (tonari no gotoo ni sa,) nanika sikeN no kotae o osiete moratta N da yo.
(From Goto, who was sitting next to me) I received the answers.

The consequences of this potential completion run counter to H's desire to project himself as an unwilling victim of circumstances. In this proposed completion, the compound verbal *osiete moratta* 'had someone teach' is used. A characteristic of the 'gerund + *morau*' verbal construction is that the 'subject' (NP *ga*) has requested that the action be done for him. An appropriate case frame is provided in (18). In (19) a case frame for *osiete kureru* 'someone teaches me' is provided for contrast.

(18) $\begin{bmatrix} \text{NP } ga & \text{NP } ni & \text{NP } o \\ \text{recipient} & \text{informant} & \text{infor-} \\ \text{of infor-} & & \text{mation} \\ \text{mation} & & \end{bmatrix}$ *osiete morau* 'have someone teach'

(19) $\begin{bmatrix} \text{NP } ga & \text{NP } ni & \text{NP } o \\ \text{informant} & \text{speaker/} & \text{infor-} \\ & \text{recipient} & \text{mation} \end{bmatrix}$ *osiete kureru* '(someone) teaches me'

Notice again in (13H-3) that the phrase *tonari no gotoo ni sa* is used. Because this phrase was used, the only possible grammatical completion of the utterance would be something similar to (17) in which the verbal *osiete moratta* occurs. The use of this compound verbal, however, implies that the recipient of the information, the NP *ga*, or *ore* 'I,' had initiated the request for the answers to the test, and that therefore *ore* is guilty of initiating the cheating incident. Because H begins this episode by marking *gotoo* with *ni*, it is impossible for him to continue with an expression like *osiete kureta* 'he told me' since the NP *ni* for this verbal must refer to the speaker. Had H begun his utterance with something like *tonari no gotoo ga ne* 'this guy Goto who sits next to me,' he could have continued using *osiete kureta* and the blame for initiating the cheating incident could be 'properly' placed on Goto.

The conflict for H is that he wishes to appear a victim of circumstance, yet in reality he is as guilty as Goto. The fact that H does not restart his utterance reflects this conflict. The verbals *miro* 'look!,' *iu* 'say,' and *yokosu* 'pass over (to me)' all require Goto to be their grammatical subjects in this context. However, H has already marked Goto with an oblique case marker and has, by implication, put himself into the position of subject. Since none of these verbals makes any sense in this context with *ore* 'I' as the subject, the only other potential referent is *gotoo*. The addressee is thus forced to juggle the noun phrases *gotoo* and *ore* in order to interpret the instances of ellipted noun phrases properly.

Thus, if we imagine what H could have said in this context to indicate that he is a complete victim of circumstance, as he overtly states in (13H-4) and (13H-5), we can construct (20), identical to (13H-3) in all respects but two: one, it is grammatical; and two, *gotoo* is marked by *ga* instead of *ni*.

(20) kono mae no sikeN de ne, anoo, *tonari no gotoo ga sa, koo tira tto miro tte iu wake de yokosita N da yo.*

During the last exam, *Goto who was sitting next to me said look, and then passed me his test paper.*

The differences in interpretation are striking. In (20) H is seen as a true victim of circumstance, a posture he would like his addressee to believe. According to his actual utterance (13H-3), however, his *desire* to look like a victim of circumstance comes through, although he may be accurately judged to be less than innocent.

CONCLUDING REMARK

In brief conclusion, I wish to reiterate the major points of this paper. First, the examination of utterances in isolation, or in the laboratory, will often lead to incorrect generalizations about language use. The examples I have presented are only representative of the abuses the exclusive reliance on isolated intuitions of biased judges. Second, the examination of actual language data in a natural context will uncover facets of language use not known to exist. Native speaker, beware the new breed of linguist!

NOTE

* I would like to thank Danny Steinberg for reading an earlier version of this paper and for offering substantial aid. I remain responsible for errors of fact or judgment.

REFERENCES

Bates, E., W. Kintsch, and G. Masling (1978). 'Recognition memory for aspects of dialogue.' *Journal of Experimental Psychology: Human Learning and Memory* 4: 187-97.
Beattie, G. (1979). 'Planning units in spontaneous speech: Some evidence from hesitation in speech and speaker gaze direction in conversation.' *Linguistics* 17:61-78.
Chomsky, N. (1957). *Syntactic Structures.* The Hague: Mouton.
Chomsky, N. (1965). *Aspects of the Theory of Syntax.* Cambridge: MIT Press.
Hinds, J. (1976). 'Postponing in Japanese.' *Eoneo* (The Journal of the Linguistic Society of Korea) 1:113-25.
Hinds, J. (1979). *Ellipsis in Japanese Discourse.* Unpublished paper: University of Hawaii.
Hinds, J. (In preparation). *Japanese conversational narratives.* University of Hawaii.
Keenan, E., B. MacWhinney, and B. Mayhew (1977). 'Pragmatics in memory: A study of natural conversation.' *Journal of Verbal Learning and Verbal Behavior* 16:549-60.
Kintsch, W. and E. Bates (1977). 'Recognition memory for statements from a classroom lecture.' *Journal of Experimental Psychology: Human Learning and Memory* 3: 50-9.
Kuno, S. (1973). *The Structure of the Japanese Language.* Cambridge: MIT Press.

Kuno, S. (1978). 'Theoretical perspectives on Japanese linguistics.' *Problems in Japanese Syntax and Semantics,* ed. by J. Hinds and I. Howard, pp. 213-85. Tokyo: Kaitakusha.
Kuno, S. (1979) 'Japanese: A characteristic OV language.' *Syntactic Typologies,* ed. by W. Lehmann, pp. 61-138. Austin: University of Texas Press.
Kuroda, S.-Y. (1978). 'Case marking, canonical sentence patterns, and counter-equi in Japanese (A preliminary survey).' *Problems in Japanese Syntax and Semantics,* ed. by J. Hinds and I. Howard, pp. 30-51. Tokyo: Kaitakusha.
Labov, W. (1978). 'Sociolinguistics.' *A Survey of Linguistic Science,* ed. by W. Dingwall, pp. 339-75. Stanford: Greylock Publishers.
Minsky, M. (1975). 'A framework for representing knowledge.' *The Psychology of Computer Vision,* ed. by P. Winston, pp. 211-77. NY: McGraw-Hill.
Muraki, M. (1974). *Presupposition and Thematization.* Tokyo: Kaitakusha.
Nagatomo, K. (1978). ''NP-*ni* Vi-potential' in Japanese.' Unpublished paper: University of Hawaii.
Sagan, C. (1973). 'Extraterrestrial life.' *Communication with Extraterrestrial Intelligence,* ed. by C. Sagan, pp. 42-67. Cambridge: MIT Press.
Schlegloff, E. (1979). 'The relevance of repair to syntax-for-conversation.' *Syntax and Semantics 12: Discourse and Syntax,* ed. by T. Givon, pp. 261-86. NY: Academic Press.
Shibatani, M. (1977). 'Grammatical relations and surface cases.' *Language* 53:789-809.
Spencer, N. (1973). 'Differences between linguists' and nonlinguists' intuitions of grammaticality-acceptability.' *Journal of Psycholinguistic Research* 2:83-98.
Tamori, I. (1977). 'NP and particle deletion in Japanese.' *Discourse Across Time and Space,* ed. by E.O. Keenan and T. Bennett, pp. 243-63. Los Angeles: Southern California Occasional Papers in Linguistics No. 5.
Tonike, S. (1975/6). 'The case ordering hypothesis.' *Papers in Japanese Linguistics* 4: 191-208.

ADAM MAKKAI

What Does a Native Speaker Know about the Verb KILL?

ABSTRACT

The author searches in vain for a reliable Native Speaker to discuss the intracacies of the verb *kill* but is unable to find one single eligible soul – Winnebagos, truck drivers, – every one is out to lunch. In desperation he latches on to Jerome Q. Nemportky, the resident poet and polymath on campus, professor of comparative literature. JQN, in turn, instead of instructing the author about *kill*, performs an act of intellectual sadism on his would-be-interviewer by outperforming both his own, and the interviewer's competence. The result is truly amazing and, to everyone's genuine surprise, replete with various and sundry arboreal excretions with roots and crowns and foliage dashing away in a variety of unexpected directions this abstract cannot even possibly hint at. Warning: *Curiosity killed the cat*. Fasten your seat belt and start reading.

My problem was a genuinely acute one. For as my colleagues and friends know, I am no native speaker of ANY language. I have now lived the longer half of my life in the English-speaking world (23 years), but I was already 21 when I arrived here from Hungary. Optimistically, one could call me a 'bilingual', but I am not so sure about that. Thus I really had no choice: introspection was out of the question. I just had to find an ideal Native Speaker and fast. I tried all the tricks in the book and called, first of all, the local chapter of the Teamsters' Union. Truck drivers, you see, make excellent native speaker informants, as I have found out when adding the *C*(itizens) *B* (and) jargon to our *Dictionary of American Idioms* (Boatner, Gates, and Makkai 1975). However, there was a strike, and no one would inform me about anything, let alone the verb *kill*. In desperation I tried the Bureau of American Indian Affairs, remembering that top notch native informants used to be available among the Winnebagos of Wisconsin. Not one soul volunteered. "We're civilized, you know" Chief Whirling Thunder, also known as Mr. Johnson, indignantly declared. "You wouldn't be working for the CIA or something? . . . I used to do this for a fellow from up Canada way . . . way back in the thirties . . . Ed . . . Ed . . . S . . . something." "Do you mean Edward Sapir?," I asked with my mouth wide open. "That's the one" the Chief assured me, "he was nice though . . . He never asked us about *killing* people."

Utterly defeated, I tried stopping women in the street and I even called up the local television station and several radio stations that host talk shows in the larger Chicago Metropolitan Area. No luck at all. I got extremely depressed.

As I was walking the UICC campus to lunch, exuding sadness, gloom, and diffidence, a familiar voice addressed me from behind: "Hello there, Makkai my man, methinks you are suffering from the linguistics blues . . . . Have I not warned you before that a man of your caliber belongs with us in comparative literature . . . ?"

It was Professor Jean Nemportky, himself a former refugee immigrant in the United States. The Nemportkys were half French and half Polish and as is commonly known in Chicago, this particular ethnic combination produces extraordinarily high IQs in that subset of the population who are fortunate enough to have descended from such lineage. Jean barely misses being the Mezzofanti of the last quarter of the 20th century. Why, the man is simply PANGLOTTIC and OMNISCIENT. Hurriedly and as best as I could, I told him about my pressing problems to which he replied in more than paternal tones:

"It is not true that Native Speakers abound in every bush, highrise, suburban house, or urban tenement, my friend . . . Native Speakers are extremely rare specimens these days . . . And it is even less true that they know anything about their language at all . . . You have to spend a lot of time and exert a great effort in order to find any Native Speaker at all, and once you found one, you have to be ever so careful in determining whether his Language Acquisition Device was operating normally before puberty." I groaned: "But what am I going to do? My paper is due in Düsseldorf honoring the Native Speaker, and all you can tell me is that I won't even find one?" Lunch was nearly over, and Prof. Nemportky generously insisted that we continue the conversation in his apartment, only a short ten minute walk from campus. I was now admiringly sitting at his feet, full of newly rekindled confidence. Jean was comfortably reclining in his hand-carved African arm chair, lined with a most unusual looking black-and-white skin. "Is that an oversized skunk?," I asked naively. "Your ignorance kills me," Dr. Nemportky said. This is a *Colubus* monkey. No, no, not *Columbus*, kill the *m* in the middle . . ." "Got you," I said, and added half-apologetically: "nice way to kill time, these etymologies, don't you agree?" "That depends on who it is you're talking to" – he replied. "Take Dr. Quasimodo, my neighbor, for instance. He is the biggest bore in the world. He thinks of himself as an etymologist and keeps bursting in on me with his ideas. He's in the real estate game, you know, big guns, one huge, fat kill after another, but he is unsatisfied with his life. All he wants is more and more etymologies. I start asking him about safe investments, and the kill-joy turns right around and hits me with yet another harebrained etymological derivation. Worse yet, sometimes he borrows money from me, a poor comparative literature man at an upstart third rate state university, where rampant inflation kills the value of every raise we get . . . This guy is absolutely killing me with his nervy demands on my time and on my purse." "Surely he pays you back, perhaps even with a meaningful interest, doesn't he?" — I timidly tried to mollify Nemportky's wrath. "I wouldn't accept a penny of interest from a neighbor, not even that creep" — Nemportky thundered, "the embarrassment would just about kill me."

"Not to change the subject" — I said, "but is it true that your family name derives from the French *n'importe qui?*"

Nemportky's glassy stare practically rendered me lifeless. "We have an old mansion in the Kills, you know, between Staten Island and Bergen Neck, I am sure some of the old family records are still there in the attic . . . My aunt Mathilda, whom you met last year, may have taken lots of them to the hunting lodge in the Catskill Mountains where she lives these days, so if you're that keen on the subject you could go there and burn up some of your excess energy by digging into the records."

"I'm not sure I could manage that right now" — I said, "I have a terrible tooth ache that's been killing me for well over a week, and I have an unalterable dentist's appointment for later this afternoon and also one tomorrow morning."

"How about some 96 proof Jack Daniels Sippin' Whiskey," Jean asked benevolently, "it will kill the pain instantly". "Gee — how nice of you," I murmured. "Many thanks . . . But I really came up here to ask you about the verb *kill* which is of great linguistic . . . uh . . . pardon me, I mean LITERARY interest to me. I was just on the verge of giving up on the entire project in lack of a Native Speaker when you suddenly materialized on campus . . . You have been perceptive enough to identify my problem immediately and you were kind enough to invite me up here to talk about *kill.* This is a free gift from Heaven: you are a scholar, a poet, a general polymath. Could we please get on with it?"

"Yes, yes, I remember now, you poor linguistician," Nemportky continued to patronize me, "that's why you looked so gloomy before lunch. The trouble is, you see, that I am fresh out of ideas on that one . . . Actually, Makkai, I am under considerable time pressure myself. You see, that State legislature in Lincolnville killed Congressman Zolotorechny's proposed tax bill regarding the faculty merit raises, and I was caught right in the middle of the verbal slaughter . . . The legislature, as you may know, is heavily populated by spokesmen of the farm interest, and as you may also have heard, the farmers just won't kill more beef unless and until they're subsidized . . . So the subsidy has to be their first priority. Here is what happened: I got a phone call urgently requesting that I drive 300 miles from Great Lakes City to Lincolnville — by the way, the driving conditions were killingly hazardous; freezing rain, snow, mud, bottle-necks, you name it — so that I, as president of the

Academic Senate, could bolster Zolotorechny's position. So my car stalls on me right in the middle of all this mud and slosh. I almost managed to restart it once, but as it turns out I kept killing the engine by flooding it . . . Finally the AAA came after 3 hours of waiting and got me out of the mess . . . I finally got there. I just caught the last critical half-hour session. But just when I was ready to move in for the kill . . ."

"Don't tell me," I exclaimed excitedly, "let me guess what happened . . . They had to shut the power off in the Capitol . . . I heard there was some major electric disturbance there that day . . ." "Yeah, you've got it," Nemportky groaned, "the sergeant at arms rushed into the Assembly Hall and shouted: '*Kill the current!!! Kill the current!!!*' and then suddenly all the lights went dead.

"So what did you do then?," I asked. "Well," Nemportky mused, "we went down into the basement, lit some candles, and tried to play some ping-pong in the semi-darkness not to kill but just to mark time, you know." "How did it go?," I asked, always the table tennis fan. "Were you guys able to see at all?" "Well, I hate mediocre players, you know," Nemportky continued somewhat self-praisingly, "I kind'o feel sorry for guys who always lose . . . There was this middle-aged spinster who was absolutely mortified whenever she lost a point . . . " "Oh yeah?," I egged him on admiringly. "Well, first I deliberately killed every ball she served with my legendary back-hand twist – you just can't return those, remember?" – the bastard was grinning, "but soon enough I discovered that I had to be extra generous to this lady. I find womens' tears mortiferous . . . So I changed tactics and deliberately started killing a few balls not by smashing them, but by hitting them into the net, which enabled her to score a few points and save face." "That was very nice of you," I said. In fact I was ready to kill the loquacious bastard, to strangle him to death with my bare hands, or hit him on the head with the poker near the fire place, a hammer, a string – give me anything! My eyes were avidly searching the room.

"By the way and not to change the subject," Nemportky said, "this old Colubus monkey here I am sitting on must have killed well over one hundred pounds, guessing from the uncommon size of the skin, don't you think?"

By this time I was good and determined to get even with him and asked in an urgent voice: "Did you hear that plaintive and penetrating cry just now . . . ? What could it have been?," and I rushed to the half-open window. After a minute's watchful gaze I said: "I didn't know you had killdeer in this part of the country, enough of them to have a couple of *habitués* representing the whole breed right here in your own backyard." Nemportky's voice stabbed back in quick repartee, "you will see a bird feeder slightly to the right of it. Can you see that bucket next to it?" "Yeah, I can see it all right. How about the bucket?," I asked. "That's where I keep the killfish for bait,"

Nemportky said all too knowingly, as he squinted with his left eye, adding: "Killfish or killdeer . . . I bet most of your silly linguist colleagues wouldn't even know whether they're talking about fish or fowl." "Well now, Jean," I protested mildly, "that was literary overkill . . . My colleagues, you see, may indeed not be the brightest people in the world, but after all . . ."

"Come off it, Makkai," Nemportky sneered, "your crazy colleagues are so firmly entrenched in killing the goose that lays the golden egg that they don't even notice how they unwittingly wind up cutting the very branches of the trees they sit on! Is this some kind of collective death-wish? More and more pseudo-arboreal irrelevance about less and less? It kills the point of your whole silly profession man, I tell you, if you guys don't watch out, they'll keep torturing the speakers, the informants, the data — the language, in short — until some day they succeed in killing it good and dead."

"Well now," I interjected in great agitation, "you sounded now almost like a native born Appalachian . . . But seriously, Jean, whereas no one denies that there has been a gradual killing back, an atrophying, if you will, of actual field work in recent linguistics, you still cannot say that . . ."

"Don't kill the punch line, Makkai," Nemportky intoned thunderously, "and try to remember your historical linguistics!"

"My WHAT?," I asked with genuine horror in my voice and no little indignation. "What has historical linguistics got to do with the description of the verb *kill* about which, by the way, you still haven't said a word to me."

"Makkai, du quälst mich, lieber Mensch . . . Du langweilst und quälst mich immer . . . Don't you remember?" Nemportky was a notorious user of foreign words and phrases in the midst of English conversations, especially when he got emotionally involved. "OK — I have to fog your memory . . . Come on, let's kill this bottle here, you have barely touched your glass!"

"Wait . . . Wait," I said in great excitement. "Are you by any chance referring to stuff like the Old English þa het se cwellere þæs caseres cempan from *cweljan* 'torture, torment' and later also 'kill'?"

"No, no, no! A thousand times no!," Nemportky cried angrily. "You are the naivest creature in the world! Are you some kind of REACTIONARY or something? I say 'history' and right away, like a good little robot that has been pre-programmed, you turn to the sermon of Æ lfric as if 'history' could only be interpreted historically!!! Where on earth have you been these past few decades? Don't you know anything about the DERIVATIONAL HISTORIES of surface verbs? We do this sort of thing in mathematical botany, musicology, creative writing, comparative plot analysis and new criticism all the time!." He furiously grabbed a wrinkled napkin and scribbled with feindish speed: "This is what you do Makkai, pay attention!"

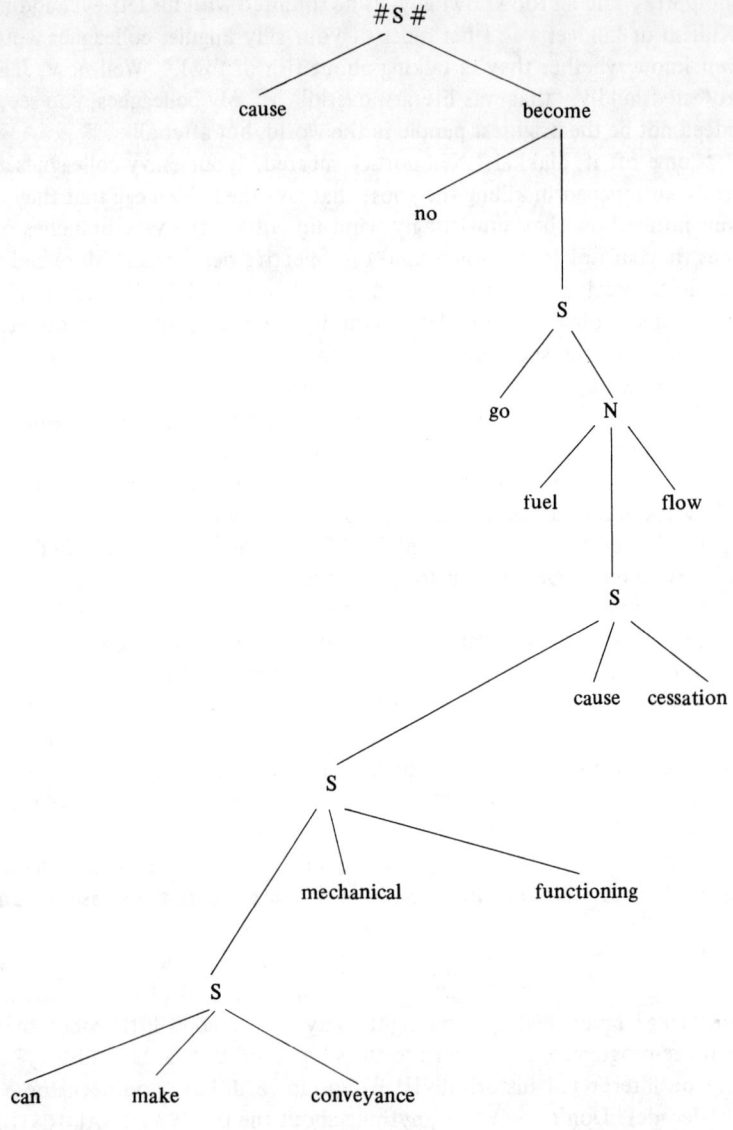

My eyes were about to jump out of my skull. But here was no stopping him now. "And certainly don't overlook this one!," he cried, as if in a trance: "... since this is one of my favorites. This one really cuts down the tree ... I mean it really goes to town."

KILL

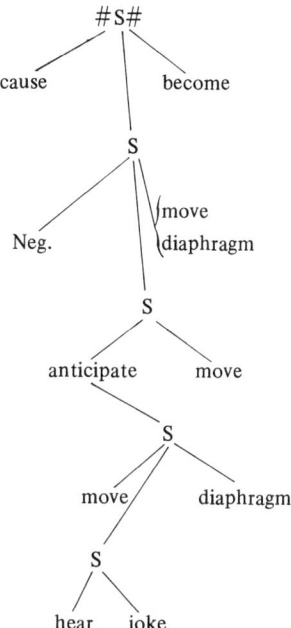

I was flabbergasted. "But where do you get all this amazing intuitive information?," I asked, hemming and hawing. "Jean, you are absolutely brilliant . . . I feel I can't hold a candle to you! You . . . you, a literary scholar, a poet, a multiple native speaker! Why, man you do this almost better than . . ."

"*Nomina sunt odiosa*, mein lieber Freund!," Nemportky pulled one of his superior Europeanisms on me. "By the way, – and I do not mean to kill the subject by innuendo –," he grinned maliciously, "but as a poet I ought to tell you that your precious *kill* is far more than just a verb, whether transitive or intrasitive, or some sort of nominalization of one of those underlying nouns!"

"How do you mean?," I asked, always the straight man, mesmerized by this sadistic joker.

"Well, Adam my boy, it's like this: part of the meaning of your precious verb *kill* derives from the fact that it associates with *bill, Bill, chill, dill, fil, Phil, gill, Gil, Jill, hill, mill, nil, sill, quill,* and *will* . . . are you following me?"

"Ah the rhymes," I muttered, "the associative counterpart to morphological paradigms, as already de Saussure, and later qua 'Gesamtbedeutungen' Jakobson . . ."

Nemportky rudely interrupted: "Rhymes, rhymes, what's a rhyme? Go home, Makkai, don't be a pill."

I was livid with anger.

Standing by the door, my fists clenched, I was talking more to myself than to him: "Associations . . . associations . . . and what if I choose not to rhyme but instead invoke a fixed piece of text in some other manner? Wouldn't I be killing two birds with one stone if, instead of beating up Professor Nemportky, I forgave him? After all, he is only a comparative literature man. I, on the other hand, am a real linguist. To lift a finger against this gentle savant would be like killing a mockingbird."

He must have heard me, or must have read my mind (maybe my lips, come to think of it) because I could hear him say as I was shutting the door behind me: "By the way, Adam my boy, just because I do playfully enjoy word games I am no mockingbird . . . I am the real McCoy . . . sort of like a false killer whale . . . Cross my heart and hope to cause me to be minus alive!"

REFERENCE

Boatner, M.T., Gates, E.J., and Makkai, A., eds. (1975). *A Dictionary of American Idioms*. Woodbury, N.Y.: Barron's Educational Series.

BJARNE ULVESTAD

On the Precariousness of Linguistic Introspection

> Denn je gröber der Irrtum, desto kürzer
> der gerade Weg zur Wahrheit, dahingegen
> der verfeinerte Irrtum uns auf ewig von der
> Wahrheit entfernt halten kann, je schwerer
> es einleuchtet, dass er Irrtum ist.
>
> (Lessing in *Berengarius Turonensis*)

ABSTRACT

For more than a quarter of a century, the allegedly primary problem of distinguishing between grammatical and ungrammatical constructions and sentences has been continuously engendering centrifugal processes in syntactical theory and practice. In consequence, syntax has in a very real sense become a linguistic-boundary science in which presumably crucial intra- and extrasystematic "facts" must of necessity depend on the native-speaker linguist's introspectional creativity for their very occurrence and subsequent analysis and description. Linguists of various schools have, in part for reasons of convenience, ultimately come to accept themselves as ideal research machines for the investigation of their native languages. This apotheosis of the native-speaker linguist, coupled with scholarly decorum and a prevalent abstinence from data-centered or "nontheoretical" discussion, has generated a plethora of in the final analysis supposititious "facts" and rules that must to an increasing degree bewilder serious students whose aim is to investigate and describe normal language, i.e., language as spoken or written by nonlinguists. The resulting confusion is particularly detrimental to the discipline of contrastive or pedagogical linguistics, the practitioners of which are confronted with virtually insolvable questions with respect to choice between contradictory published statements. In this article, a number of concrete examples are adduced in illustration of what must be regarded as harmful practices. A return to the study of actually spoken or written language, time-consuming though it may be, would at least tend to retard promiscuous creativity, especially the manufacture of indiscriminate rules and frivolous distinctions (in the Baconian sense), which makes the line-drawing between scientific and nonscientific methodology the fundamental problem in current syntactical work.

THE CORPUS ANALYTIC METHOD

There can hardly be any doubt that, from the point of view of the majority of scholars whose concern is the investigation of language, the most powerful research machine imaginable is the trained linguist who is also a native speaker of the object language. He is the ideal linguist par excellence; only he can be in possession of those "flashes of insight, those perceptions of pattern, which mark off the brilliant scientist from the dull cataloger of data" (Lees, 1957, p.380). Typical of the assessment of the capacities of the native-speaker linguist (NSL) are statements like this one: "Your are a native speaker of English; in ten minutes you can produce more illustrations on any point in English grammar than you will find in many millions of words of random text" (Francis, 1979, p.110). Another great advantage pertains to the fact that the NSL is "in der bequemen Situation, seine eigene Versuchsperson zu sein" (Bierwisch, 1966, p.10): the ideal research machine is not only eminently efficient but also economical in use. Nobody who has struggled with vast collections of recalcitrant linguistic data will fail to appreciate the *iuvat vivere* spirit that reveals itself in the following words: "Zu den wohltuenden Einsichten moderner Linguistik gehört die Erkenntnis, dass man nicht . . . für die grammatische oder semantische Analyse der Gegenwartssprache unbedingt von einem . . . Corpus von Belegen ausgehen muss" (Hermodsson, 1978, p.10).

However, the protagonists of the NSL do not only plead avowed advantages like efficiency, frugality, and convenience. A number of allegedly cogent reasons have been adduced in support of the virtual *sine qua non* position of the NSL, and such cumbersome tasks as gathering and analysing and describing a corpus of data have consequently been reduced to the status of a superfluous ceremony (Itkonen, 1976, p.65). Thus Engel (1970, p.23f.) concludes his *pro et contra* discussion of traditional empirical-linguistic methodology with the following apodictic statement:

Untersuchungen der Muttersprache (als langue) haben sich in erster Linie auf das Sprachgefühl des Untersuchenden zu gründen, dieses ist bis zu einem gewissen Grade auch Corpus und Informant. Man mag einwenden, dass auf diese Art nur Aussagen über die Sprache des Untersuchenden gewonnen würden. Das trifft zu, impliziert aber Aussagen über die Gemeinsprache, weil eben die Sprache des Untersuchenden den Anspruch erheben muss, zugleich Gemeinsprache zu sein: wie wäre sonst Kommunikation in einer Sprachgemeinschaft möglich?

Also, the following often-referred-to arguments propounded by Bierwisch are of interest in this context:

Es bleibt die Frage, wie die Beobachtungsdaten, die durch eine Grammatik erklärt werden sollen, zu gewinnen sind. Eine weit verbreitete Ansicht ist die, dass eine sichere Materialgrundlage durch Sammlung einer möglichst grossen Menge von Texten oder Textstellen, die die zu studierenden Erscheinungen enthalten, zu gewinnen sei. . . . Wir haben zu begründen versucht, dass eine solche Sammlung von Texten aus zwei Gründen nicht die Datengrundlage einer wirklich erklärenden Grammatik sein kann. Einmal kann

On the Precariousness of Linguistic Introspection 247

sie unkontrolliert nebeneinander ganz unterschiedliche Erscheinungen enthalten: grammatische und ungrammatische Sätze, grammatische Abweichungen der verschiedensten Art, die zu einer ganz wertlosen Grammatik führen würden, wenn man sie alle berücksichtiget (1966, p.9).

In consequence, Bierwisch repeatedly avails himself of "intuitive Evidenz" (1966, p.10), as do many others, for instance Wunderlich: "Heuristisch wird das Korpus ersetzt durch gezielte Intuition oder durch gezielte Suche nach charakteristischen Text- oder Äusserungsbeispielen" (1970, p.14). Needless to say, a large group of present-day linguists, no matter what "schools" they are associated with, more or less overtly subscribe to the methodological principles that these statements advocate.

In this paper, I shall endeavor to demonstrate some of the salient sources of error to which predominantly introspectional data production with subsequent analysis and description is exposed. The object language from which my illustrations are taken is standard German (Hochsprache), and the corpus I refer to consists of excerpts from printed German texts of various types. Furthermore, I shall be concerned with what may be called rock-bottom syntactical data, and I attempt to make my discussion substantially nonsensitive to, or independent of, particular theories, i.e. maximally understandable for all brands of linguists and Germanists. It may be added that my critical demonstrations of NSL practices are what I consider typical instances, that I could have chosen scores of other equally revealing illustrations.

The regrettable situation described by Rauch and Scott thirteen years ago has, in my opinion, hardly changed for the better so far:

In fact, there appears to be a gradual but increasing erosion of objectivity. . . . Equally serious has been a noticeable disdain of 'mere facts' and a certain amount of unpardonable inaccuracy that has accompanied some recent example of generative statement (1967, pp. VII, 4f.).

Today, the specific reference to generativist practices is far too narrow, as will be seen below. Fifteen years ago, a similar warning was issued by Winter:

There is no need for a revision of basic work techniques if one finds that virtually every published paper concerned with the production of sequences of rules contains some outright mistakes which evidently are there because the author just did not happen to think of the right thing at the right moment. It makes criticism very easy, and a little cheap, if all a reader has to do is outintrospect the author: patience and a slightly devious mind will normally do the trick (1965, p.489).

Now, if the situation with respect to the currently widely accepted empirical basis for the elaboration of object-language grammars is as described, one would reasonably expect a lively scholarly discussion bearing on such fact-related statements as grammatical/non-grammatical, acceptable/unacceptable and the like (cf. Matzel et al., 1976, 1978, Ulvestad, 1967, 1971, 1972a, 1972b, 1973, 1975, 1979, Ulvestad et al., 1979, forthcoming). In reality, however, such discussion is but rarely encountered, to cite Engel's very appropriate pronouncement:

> Wo Grammatiker im Streit miteinander liegen, geht es selten um Richtigkeit, fast immer jedoch um die bessere Grammatik. *Quot linguistici, tot grammaticae*: ein Alptraum? Eher ein Wunschtraum (1977, p.15).

To me, *yes* would seem to be a more suitable answer.

SOME CONTROVERSIAL CASES IN GERMAN SYNTAX

In a recent article, Beneš subjects to examination the choice of infinitival vs. *dass*-introduced object clauses dependent on certain "content verbs" (e.g. *Er glaubte, nach Hause gehen zu müssen* vs. *Er glaubte, dass er nach Hause gehen müsse*). He demonstrates, with the governing verb *sagen* as an example, that statements as to whether the infinitival clause can be used range from assertions of impossibility to claims of full acceptability: "Bei Kaufmann ist die IF/Infinitivfügung/im Satz: *Er sagte, damit einverstanden zu sein* ausdrücklich als unzulässig gekennzeichnet," whereas Brinkmann "*sagen* ohne Einschränkung unter den Verben nennt, die eine IF zulassen" (1979, p.377f.). In fact, Kaufmann's rule of exclusion does not refer only to the concrete sentence quoted above; he makes the general assertion that "das Verb *sagen* . . . nur mit einer indirekten Rede verbunden werden kann" (1976, p.142). After noting that apart from Brinkmann also Paul and Engelen accept *sagen* plus infinitival object clause (p.378), Beneš goes on to formulate sort of a verb-semantic rule for the choice of such clauses:

> Nach meiner Meinung verhält sich die Sache so, dass die IF bei *sagen* . . . möglich ist, weil *sagen* in der Bedeutung 'behaupten' bzw. 'jm. etw. auftragen' verwendet wird und weil der Kontext eben diese Bedeutungskomponenten deutlich zum Ausdruck bringt. . . . Derartige Fälle kommen allerdings selten vor (p.378).

His general conclusion contains an implicit methodological warning:

> Bei der künftigen gründlichen Untersuchung der Konkurrenz zwischen beiden . . . Typen [infinitive-clause and *dass*-clause] wird eine Kombination der Informantenbefragung mit der Datenerhebung aus gesprochenen und geschriebenen Texten unentbehrlich und schon deshalb vorteilhaft sein, weil der Untersuchende aufgrund dieser Daten die Tests aussagekräftiger konstruieren und ausserdem die Bewertungen der Informanten mit ihrem tatsächlichen Sprachgebrauch vergleichen kann (p. 382).

On the Precariousness of Linguistic Introspection 249

Here, another kind of native speaker is introduced, namely the native speaker as informant (NSI) for the professional linguist. Though the NSI is, as a rule, relatively harmless in comparison with the NSL, especially if his linguistic judgment is tested together with that of several other NSIs, he should be employed with more caution and circumspection than has been the case hitherto. Here, I am primarily concerned with the actual function of the NSL in the investigation of natural languages.

One may well raise the question as to whether it is worth our while to discuss phenomena that must admittedly be regarded as syntactical minutiae. Considering the way in which synchronic linguistics has been cultivated for the past twentyfive years, the answer must be yes, to quote Schachter:

'The fundamental aim in the linguistic analysis of a language L,' according to Chomsky . . . 'is to separate the GRAMMATICAL sequences which are the sentences of L from the UNGRAMMATICAL sequences which are not sentences of L, and to study the structure of the grammatical sequences.' While this aim is obviously somewhat utopian, the research results of recent years have shown that even a limited achievement of it, in connection with some small subset of the sentences of a language, may be of considerable interest both in itself and in its consequences for general linguistic theory (1977, p.86).

Schachter might have added that also with regard to the field of applied linguistics (e.g. for application in foreign language instruction) such results may be of great importance, dependent of course on the fidelity with which the correspondent statements reflect linguistic reality. The fidelity is usually measured by the number of counter-examples that can be mustered on the basis of critical examination of the language which the statements are supposed to describe. It is a matter of deplorable fact that seemingly innocuous erroneous assertions of possibility/impossibility of occurrence and contradictory rules of usage in more or less serious theoretical publications have a way of creeping into contrastive and ultimately pedagogical-linguistic restatements, which must necessarily bring about vexing difficulties for both teachers and students of foreign languages (cf. Ulvestad et al., 1979).

We have seen that Beneš, in his assessment of published rules, finds Kaufmann in error, whereas Engelen is listed among those who do justice to linguistic reality. On closer inspection, however, one will discover that also the latter's rule formulation is demonstrably inadequate and in need of revision. Engelen, whose well-known work is based on his own "Kompetenz der deutschen Sprache der Gegenwart" (1975a, p.17), gives for the governing verb *sagen* the part-formula "2($\frac{a}{a}$)" (1975b, p.144), the symbols of which carry the following usage information: 2 = "das Satzglied [dependent structure] hat die Form eines Gliedsatzes ohne Korrelat im übergeordneten Satz" (that the statement regarding the correlate is wrong, is of no consequence in this context); (å) = 1. an infinitival clause, 2. the implicit subject of the infinitival clause is identical to that of the governing clause, and 3. "Diese Möglichkeit ist in Norm und Rede nur sehr selten realisiert." One acceptable realization of the formula (taken from Beneš, 1979, p.378) is: *Und ich darf ohne Übertreibung sagen, in diesen Dingen etwas Erfahrung zu haben* (S. Zweig), in which the speaker is also the subject of the infinitive phrase.

However, the formula is on the one hand too open, in that it does not block questionable sentences, i.e., sentences that do not occur in my corpus, like **Er sagt zu Hause zu sein, *Er sagte auf mich zu warten, *Sagt er Beamter zu sein*? I have not submitted these three examples to the judgment of NSIs; all I can say is that my corpus does not include sentences of this type (the admittedly subtle difference between these and the just cited Zweig example need not concern us here). On the other hand, and this is a more serious drawback, the formula as stated excludes the by far most frequently encountered sentences of the form *sagen* (etc.) with the infinitive phrase following it. Engelen would use the following formula to describe them: 2(å) = the implicit subject of the infinitival clause is identical to the dative object of the governing clause. Well over ninety percent of the relevant sentences found in my corpus are generated by this formula. The most frequently found verb is *sagen*, but also verbs like *rufen* and *schreiben* are found: " . . . wie oft habe ich dir gesagt, nicht so wild zu reiten!" (v. Percha, 1976, p.133). "Mutti schrieb ihm, sich zu schonen" (Böll, 1962, p.74). Indeed, sentences of this type are rather often to be registered also in German translations of English prose, cf. the following from *Casino Royale*: "Er wollte ihr nur sagen, nicht weich zu werden" ('He just wanted to tell her not to give in', Fleming, 1965, p.105); "Dann sagte man mir, mich im Kasino nicht hinter Dich zu stellen" ('Then I was told not to stand behind you in the Casino,' Fleming, 1965, p.169). The current translation, *to tell one to do something = jemand sagen, etwas zu tun,* furnishes us with a clue as to the meaning in which the verbs involved are used. E.g., the sentence "Ich werde Fritz sagen, schnellere Fahrt zu laufen" (Fleming, 1967, p.126) contains an admonishment that would seem to be less insistent or emphatic than the one residing in *befehlen* and less imploratory than the meaning of *bitten*. Indubitably, a complete account of this syntactical construction would also include a third type, extremely rare though it is, one in which there is a dative object in the governing clause correlating with an oblique case object of the infinitival clause, e.g. "Einst sagte die Hexe dem Mädchen, es entlassen zu wollen, wenn es drei Bedingungen erfülle" (Kapfhammer, 1971, p.129).

As we have seen, the corpus-analytical method of syntactical research enables one to push forward to the establishment of constructional and semantical, not to speak of statistical, regularities that no NSL or NSI can be expected to supply. I do not doubt that we still have a long way to go before

On the Precariousness of Linguistic Introspection 251

we shall be able to formalize Engelen's rule in a scientifically satisfactory and pedagogically useful manner. As long as the fundamental job of data gathering and rough provisional classification remains largely undone, suspension of judgment seems preferable to the intuition-based elaboration and presentation of at best half-true rules.

Before proceeding to the next confrontation of NSL rules with language as it really is, a problem of considerable importance must be posed: what does it mean to test NSL statements against linguistic reality? What are the facts to be considered?

RULES AND REALITY

In the discussion following a lecture on the "grammatically impossible" though textually recurrent main clauses with the negation *nicht* as the first (preverbal) element, e.g., *Nicht wusste er aber, dass sein Vater schon tot und begraben war,* the following critical question was asked by a colleague: "How would you meet the objection that you have only collected a fair number of ungrammatical sentences? Such sentences are after all present in all kinds of linguistic texts." This question bears on the type of text descriptions that I have already cited (Bierwisch, 1966). Another member of the audience suggested that I failed to distinguish between data and facts, and kindly refered me to an important article by Chomsky (1961; my lecture was held at the University of Hamburg in 1975). Both objections are still often raised in linguistic debate, so it may be useful to examine them for a while and see if they can be accorded any validity with respect to the choice between textual and introspectional data.

Bierwisch' statement to the effect that texts, also the written ones, may contain ungrammatical sentences, is of course irrefutable but of scant scientific significance (in so far as written or printed texts are concerned, a point I want to make clear). The following argument deserves to be mentioned here:

Würde man die beobachtbaren Sätze nicht in grammatische und ungrammatische einteilen, so müsste die Grammatik ganz unterschiedslos die folgenden Sätze behandeln: *Als im weissen Mutterschosse aufwuchs Baal, war der Himmel schon so gross und still und fahl* und *Und der Himmel blieb in Lust und Kummer da.* Beide kommen im gleichen Gedicht ... von Brecht vor (1966, p.61).

It is hard to see any real obstacle here. Prose is prose and poetry is quaint. To my knowledge, no linguist has ever chosen synchronic poetic texts to be used as material for syntactical analysis of normal language. Brecht's poetry may be well worth studying, but not as a specimen of natural German. More important, there seems to be little reason to believe that prose texts, whether in original German or in German translated from other languages by competent NSs are marred by ungrammatical sentences and the like to the extent that a clean-up job by an NSL is needed before they are admitted as reliable data collections. Storytellers and dramatists may of course insert monologues and dialogues that are signalled in some way or other as spoken and the language of which is clearly not identical to that of the writers. Thus the language of the village idiot or that of the floundering linguist ejecting would-be ungrammatical utterances, the Lessingian Damis in reverse, interesting though it may be, would not be registered as data-yielding specimens of normal German. A linguist must be allowed to describe the syntax of modern prose as found, e.g., in novels by Heinrich, Konsalik, and Simmel, without worrying about some NSL's condemnation or rejection of a very small number of sequences. One must on the whole be careful not to reject sentences that have a certain measure of recurrence, though one may be tempted to brand them as ungrammatical. In Hockett's words, "the basic uniformity in language is the mere recurrence of forms and constructions" (1968, p.90), and there is no reason for expecting a writer of recreative or expository prose to deliberately produce ungrammatical or otherwise deviating or unacceptable sentences. And, finally, I cannot see why one should trust the *Sprachgefühl* of the NSL in cases where it conflicts with that of the native novelist or journalist. Bierwisch's eloquent description of the sad result to which syntactical analysis based on texts would lead has, strangely enough, proved to be of adequately persuasive power to convince hundreds of linguists. As far as I am aware, nobody has bothered to test his hypothesis of basic text unreliability by finding and listing all the (seemingly) ungrammatical sentences found in, say, one thousand pages of "clean" prose (that is, exclusive of sentences belonging to represented speech). My non-NS hypothesis, for what it is worth, is that the number of such sentences will represent considerably less than one per cent. It would therefore seem to make good sense to rely on the texts and describe their syntax as a set of patterns against which the patterns encountered in represented mono- or dialogical speech could be projected and contrastively described, also in statistical terms.

The second question is of a more difficult nature. Chomsky's famous dichotomy of data vs. facts (1961, pp.219ff.) turns out to be very hard to follow; yet it is constantly invoked in discussions of the problems involved in establishing grammaticality and nongrammaticality. He starts out as follows:

It is useful, at the outset, to make a distinction between *data* and *facts*. The linguist's data consist of certain observations about the form and use of utterances. The facts of linguistic structure that he hopes to discover go well beyond these observations (1961, p.219).

This seems clear enough. The problem arises when one is made aware of the

On the Precariousness of Linguistic Introspection 253

fact that most of the data are said to be JUDGMENTS of one kind or another, e.g., "judgments of well-formedness" (p.223). In order to get an impression as to the nature of data of this description, let us consider two sequences of German words:

(1) *Der alte Pfarrer ist nicht krank*
(2) *Krank nicht ist Pfarrer alte der*

In traditional terminological usage, these sentences stand on the page or are registered by the ear as things given and are called data or facts. Now, it would seem sensible enough to distinguish between the two sequences in such a way that (1) is accepted as a genuine German sentences, while (2) is rejected as ungrammatical. Sequence (1) then enters the collection of data on the basis of which a syntactical description can be worked out. We are consequently confronted with data on two levels, a. (rock-bottom data) (1) and (2); b. (second-level data), (1) alone. On the rock-bottom level, (2) is a datum, but for the next level it is adjudged to be a nondatum.

On the other hand, Chomsky's data are the very judgments as to well-formedness and the like, not the sequences evaluated. But if the linguist's judgments are data, then his data ultimately reside in his own mind; they are his opinions regarding grammaticality, not the forms or constructions on which judgment is passed. One may go along with this definition of data as judgments, opinions, only to get into logical trouble as soon as one tries to keep the *data* definitionally distinct from the *facts*. For instance, Chomsky describes as a *fact* the observation that the sequence *Colorless green ideas sleep furiously* is well-formed "in a sense in which [its well-known counterpart] is not" (p.224). Thus it is a *fact* that the sequence *Furiously sleep ideas green colorless* is ungrammatical, and the judgment that it is ungrammatical is a *datum*. Consequently, Chomsky's *facts* appear to be merely the verbal expressions of the judgments termed *data*. Thus the judgment that "(1) is well-formed, (2) is not" is the *datum* for the *fact* here stated between quotation-marks. Later on, in the same article Chomsky writes about "attempts to discover and state the facts that underlie and account for the observed data" (p.225), i.e., the judgments of well-formedness etc. that one has observed oneself making are accounted for by reference to the facts that the judgments establish. It seems to me that the article does not succeed in making clear the presumably crucial distinction between data and facts. If this is so, it would seem advisable to term entities that are immediately observable (e.g. sentences appearing in print) *data* and to abstain from using the term *fact* except as a synonym of *datum*. It follows that recurrential syntactical sequences that are observed in texts are in themselves legitimate data or facts that may be confronted with existing rule statements, whether the latter be based on introspection or on other kinds of alleged evidence. Thus a few hundred sentences of the form *Nicht* + verb fin. + subj. + XYZ that have been observed in standard prose cannot reasonably be called ungrammatical, if our aim is to construct an adequate and exhaustive rule apparatus for the German language. In other words, it is not safe to rely one hundred per cent on ones own *Sprachgefühl*. Especially dangerous is it to state that certain observed sentences are ungrammatical or impossible or whatever epithets one may choose for characterizing them, if they turn out to be diachronically and synchronic-diatopically recurrent. A couple of examples of introspectional rules or statements of regularities may serve to illustrate this point.

"Es"

The first one exemplifies what in Lessing's phraseology is a "grober Irrtum," from which the road to truth is short. It is taken from the conglomerate of irreconcilable statements that are found in recent descriptions regarding the use of the object-clause correlate *es* in sentences like: *Sie liebt es nicht, allein im alten Hause zu sein*. Here, the transitive verb *lieben* selects so to speak a preliminary object *es*, which stands in correlate function to the object clause *allein im alten Hause zu sein*. The problem as to whether *es* is obligatory (e.g. Engel et al., 1978, p.218) or "kommt . . . weniger häufig vor" (Schade, 1975, p.241) does not concern us here. According to König, there are but "sehr wenige Verben, nach denen vor Objektsätzen das Element *es* auftauchen kann" (1973, p.303). In this statement, the pseudoterm *sehr wenige* is rather vague: "dieses 'sehr wenige' bleibt solange völlig subjektiv, wie nicht verlässliche Zahlen vorliegen" (Seiffert, 1973, p.234). Still, few readers would conclude from König's assertion that *sehr wenige* stands for well over four hundred verbs, not counting a large number of combination verbs (*es darauf ankommen lassen*, etc.), and not a few would be inclined to speak of a large number of verbs rather than of very few. Then one reads: "Nach all den Verben, die wir Verben des Sagens und Denkens genannt haben, also zum Beispiel *vermuten, meinen, vorschlagen* etc., kann nie das Element *es* vor Objektsätzen eintreten" (p.304). This *fact,* as Chomsky would call it, is patently erroneous. In my corpus, I have come across a large number of sentences of the allegedly impossible type, sentences like:

Er hat es schon gestern gesagt, dass . . .
Ich hätte es nicht gedacht, dass . . .
Er glaubte es ganz einfach nicht, dass . . .
Ich will es wohl meinen, dass . . .
Ich habe es bereits vermutet, dass . . .
Er hat es ja selbst vorgeschlagen, dass . . .

On the Precariousness of Linguistic Introspection 255

For further examples, see Ulvestad et al., 1979, pp. 107ff.). Now, König's generalized exclusion rule (and he is by no means alone in stating it) can scarcely do any harm in a German-speaking country. It is different when it reappears in slightly changed wording in grammars that are to be used in teaching German to foreigners. Just one example of this, taken from a Norwegian grammar of German: "Especially problematic is perhaps . . . the fact that certain verbs ('verbs of saying or thinking'), such as *vermuten, meinen, sagen* etc. *cannot* occur with the correlate (*es*)" (Askedal, 1976, p.264); translation mine).

It may be good, clean fun to play around with introspectional data in theoretical discussions, and I do not doubt that many linguists find it wrong to discourage it. However, there are theoretical as well as pedagogical reasons for finding it inadvisable to generalize rules for an important natural language in the easy way that I have exemplified. It must be added that a goodly number of the grammaticality discussions which take place among foreign teachers of German could have been avoided if German, Austrian, and Swiss linguists were a little more careful with the information that they pass on to colleagues who are not NSL. More than twenty years ago, Sledd, in noting a similar disregard for easily available data for English usage, issued the following warning: "Though concern for the theoretical foundations of linguistics is all to the good, linguists must also take proper care for the adequacy of their data" (1962, p.15).

The reason why I think König's statement an example of a "grober Irrtum," pertains to the fact that counterexamples are so easy to find, in spoken as well as written texts, and in a sense my falsification is in itself but an insignificant correction, an introduction of a "little truth" into the scholarly discussion. But all too frequently the importance of the "little truths," truths that are often merely convincing corrections of demonstrably false spot hypotheses (Chomsky's *facts*), is overlooked. The ultimate top of the truth-about-German pyramid, the "ideal grammar," may some day in the distant future be cut off from its massive substructure and stand on its own as a maximally compact deductive apparatus or super-algorithm. But that ultimate set of rules cannot be properly discussed even in terms of heuristic models, as long as linguists keep on disagreeing as to what data constitute the language under investigation. Thus one has to take into account not only the truth that the formula **sagen + es* . . . is false, but also the truth regarding the corrected formula, i.e. the restrictions on the use of *es*. The formula will state that *es* can be used after *sagen* etc. if certain semantic or pragmatic factors are present. This formula will generate sentences like: *Ich kann es noch nicht sagen, dass ich seit Jahren übermässig trinke,* but block sentences like: **Man kann es nicht sagen, dass er eine grosse Leuchte ist.* In my opinion, the fact that the elaboration of a given set of rules may prove difficult, does not justify denying the grammaticality or acceptability of the constructions involved.

Subjunctive in German

My last illustration of the precariousness of NSL-introspectional data is more complicated, and the composite statement under discussion is of the type that Lessing would characterize as a "verfeinerter Irrtum." In a book containing recommendations for the use of the subjunctive in German one reads:

> Auch in den Fällen, in denen der Indikativ für den Konjunktiv I eintreten kann, ist mit einer Änderung der Information des Satzes zu rechnen . . . Bei zukünftiger Situierung des Geschehens . . . wird der Unterschied greifbar. Vgl. (11) *Er sagte mir vor drei Wochen, dass er gestern kommen werde.* (12) *Er sagte mir vor drei Wochen, dass er gestern kommen wird.* Satz (12) wird als ungrammatisch empfunden (Jäger, 1971a, p. 47).

This is a curious syntactical statement: changing *werde* in (11) to *wird* brings about a change of information, and the new information is that the carrier sentence is ungrammatical. It would probably be better not to discuss ungrammatical sentences in terms of their content. The same argument is found in Jäger (1971b, p.111f.), now with the adverb series *vorgestern . . . gestern* instead of *vor drei Wochen . . . gestern*. In this case, Jäger reports that informants have confirmed his conclusion, but he does not describe his testing procedure (p.289). Let us consider a few supposedly acceptable sentences of this kind:

> *Er sagte mir vorgestern, dass er gestern kommen werde.*
> *Er sagte mir vorgestern, er besuche mich gestern.*
> *Er sagte mir vorgestern, er komme vielleicht erst gestern.*
> *Er sagte mir vor fünf Jahren, dass er vor vier Jahren komme.*
> *Er wusste vor drei Monaten, dass er vor zwei Monaten kommen werde.*
> *Er ahnte vor einer Woche, dass er vor drei Tagen krank werde.*

The sentences may be high on grammaticality, but certainly low on acceptability, for a reason that doesn't seem to be connected with lack of understandability. Eighteen out of twenty German students (Univ. of Essen) found all of them unacceptable; nobody found all acceptable. My questionnaire asked only for judgments about acceptability (Yes: no-answers). It is interesting that Jäger, whose *magnum opus* (1971b) is based on corpus analysis, did not find *vorgestern . . . gestern*-sentences in his material, but produced them through introspection. Still more interesting is that Wunderlich finds

On the Precariousness of Linguistic Introspection 257

"dass pragmatisch vielleicht korrekte Sätze [like the ones listed above] dennoch nicht akzeptiert werden" (1970, p.207), whether the subjunctive or the indicative is used. His example is: *Fritz erzählte mir vorgestern, dass er gestern ins Kino gehen wird* (*werde/würde*), and he forwards the following explanation: "Da diese Adverbien durch ihre Merkmale bestimmte Tempusmorpheme implizieren, werden auch diese nur in Bezug auf die oberste Sprechsituation verstanden" (p.206f.). I don't want to take sides on this issue, but I do find it noticeable that not a single example of this sentence type was to be found in a text-corpus of more than twenty million words. One should not spend too much time debating semantic niceties in sentences that one has never heard, and perhaps never will.

Jäger does, however, offer testable rules for sentences that are related to the ones above. He writes, with a glance back at these:

Der Unterschied [in information] lässt sich auch an weniger extremen Beispielen zeigen. Vgl.: *Er sagte mir, dass er kommen werde. Er sagte mir, dass er kommen wird.* ...Im zweiten Beispiel kann das Kommen für den Berichtenden nur ein Zukünftiges sein (1971b, p. 112).

whereas in the first sentence the act of coming can take place before or after the reporter's time of speaking (writing). This rule is not quite new. Jäger, who rarely points to earlier statements that support his own results, might for instance have quoted a similar formulation by Wilmanns three-quarter century ago for sentences like *Sie sagte, vermutete, wusste, dass er bald zurückkehren würde* (*werde*): "*zurückkehren wird* könnte nur gesagt werden, wenn die Handlung auch für den Redenden zukünftig ist" (1906, p. 244). Again, Jäger does not give examples taken from his corpus, but, as noted above, his (and Wilmann's) rule can be tested against examples found in modern texts.

It turns out that the rule governing the use of *wird* as against *werde* (*würde*), in the formulation proposed by Jäger and Wilmanns, can be satisfactorily falsified on the basis of the corpus of the former scholar, and one does not have to peruse the texts to establish this fact. In a description of grammatical/syntactical methods, Glinz has chosen a text that overlaps with Jäger's corpus (Glinz, 1970, pp. 129 ff.), namely Frisch's novel *Homo Faber*. Glinz cites a number of pertinent examples from this novel, and he states with reference to its language: "Zunächst fällt auf, dass wir den Indikativ sehr oft in Inhaltssätzen finden" (p.133). He also generalizes formulaic or paradigmatic examples like (p.137):

A sagte um x Uhr, dass B um y Uhr kommen würde (werde, wird) and (*ibid.*):

Jemand *wusste* (schon) in der Zeit a genau, wie ein zu erwartender Prozess

in der (späteren, aber auch als vergangen betrachteten) Zeit b
verlaufen würde
verlaufen werde
verlaufen wird
verlaufe
verläuft

As if he were taking his stand against Jäger's rule, he writes: "Bei all diesen Fragen kommt es offensichtlich *nicht* darauf an, ob der erst erwartete . . . Aussage-Inhalt auch in Wirklichkeit noch nicht eingetreten ist oder ob er längst eingetreten ist" (p. 136). In fact, counter-examples to the rule in question are to be found throughout the novel, right down to the very last sentence (Frisch, 1969, p.252, emphasis mine): "Hanna hat immer schon gewusst, dass ihr Kind sie einmal verlassen *wird*; aber auch Hanna hat nicht ahnen können, dass Sabeth auf dieser Reise gerade ihrem Vater *begegnet*, der alles *zerstört*" (Hanna's daughter Sabeth did leave her, and is now dead, and her meeting with her father obviously lies in the past, thus: act time before report time).

DISCUSSION

As seems clear from this discussion, the NSL Jäger has employed his introspectional faculties for generating rule statements that are falsified by the text-corpus on which his investigation is based. Thanks to Glinz, who, due to temporal coincidence, could not refer to Jäger, (1971a) and (1971b), Germanists interested in syntactical problems are made aware of the manifest contradiction between asserted rule and linguistic reality. And the contradiction can hardly be explained by reference to stylistic idiosyncrasies on the part of the Swiss novelist, as similar sentences appear also in modern German texts, e.g., (emphasis mine):

Du hast wohl selber gewusst, dass das nicht immer so weitergehen konnte, und ich hab dir's auch gesagt, dass Strafe kommen *wird* . . . . Gott . . . hat dir eine milde Strafe geschickt (Feuchtwanger, 1977, p. 471).
Das hat sie nicht überraschen können: 'Ahnte ich doch, dass noch irgendwas, so'n Extrafurz *kommt*' (Grass, 1979, p. 151).
Ich habe es versäumt; es tut mir leid.' 'Du hast es nicht versehentlich versäumt,' sagte sie. 'Als ich dich gestern mit diesem Mädchen reden sah, hatte ich gleich das Gefühl, dass etwas dazwischen kommen *wird* (Heinrich, 1978, p. 153).
Ich habe es dumpf geahnt, dass es einmal so kommen *wird*. Jetzt ist es soweit (Siegl, 1978, p. 159).

It would seem to be unnecessary to adduce further instances of contra-rule usage. Jäger has, however, followed the advice implicit in so many introductions to linguistics etc. over the last twenty-five years, for which he cannot be blamed: He has tacitly discarded an unknown number of text instances that he has found ungrammatical, i.e., he has separated the ungrammatical sentences from the grammatical, which is a legitimate and indeed essential practice, according to Chomsky, Bierwisch et al. Yet I think I have shown that this practice is pernicious: it leads to hasty, opinionated premature judgments of grammaticality etc. that run counter to scientific methodology in general. The readers of a linguistic description have a right to know, not only what data were found worthy of inclusion in the basismaterial from which rules were generalized, but also what data (in the traditional sense of the term) were thrown out, and for what reasons. Presumably ungrammatical sentences whose recurrence is unquestioned, are certainly worth reconsidering, as in this case.

With regard to Wilmann's rule, one cannot be certain that it does not correctly reflect usage in the language toward the end of the nineteenth century. The well-known fact that the indicative today is found with increasing frequency in constructions in which the subjunctive reigned almost supreme a few generations ago, would serve in partial explanation of a syntactical innovation here. At least Curme sees it this way. He discusses the phenomenon under the heading "The Indicative in Indirect Discourse" and gives examples like: *Ich hab' nicht gewusst, dass Herr Olten kommt* (Villinger) and *ich hätt' nicht geglaubt, dass du dies Jahr noch fertig wirst* (Hesse), in which *kommt* and *wirst* are explicitly described as having the time reference "future to the subject of the main verb at the moment in question, but *past at the time of utterance*" (Curme, 1952, p.242).

There may be "kein Ende der Abenteuer innerhalb der syntaktischen Grenzen und eben an ihnen" (Kraus, 1956, p.437), but the evidence obtained through goal-directed intuition is always in danger of being tenuous and unreliable, and the exclusive use of such evidence represents a research practice that is, in my opinion, inimical to sound scientific methodoly. At least in the complex field of natural-language syntax, the general precariousness of NSL-produced data and of the syntactical rules proposed to describe them should be constantly kept in mind.

REFERENCES

Askedal, J.O. (1976). *Inføring i tysk grammatikk*. Oslo, Bergen, Tromsø: Universitetsforlaget.
Beneš, E. (1979). 'Zur Konkurrenz von Infinitivfügungen und *dass*-Sätzen.' *Wirkendes Wort* 29: 374–384.

Bierwisch, M. (1966). *Grammatik des deutschen Verbs*, 3rd. ed. Berlin: Akademie-Verlag.
Böll, H. (1962). *Wo warst du, Adam?* Frankfurt am Main: Ullstein Taschenbücher Verlag.
Chomsky, N. (1961). 'Some methodological remarks on generative grammar.' *Word* 17: 219-239.
Curme, G.O. *A Grammar of the German Language*, 2nd ed. New York: Frederick Ungar.
Engel, U. (1970). 'Regeln zur Wortstellung.' *Forschungsberichte des Instituts für deutsche Sprache* 5: 3-148.
Engel, U. (1977). *Syntax der deutschen Gegenwartssprache*. Berlin: Erich Schmidt Verlag.
Engel, U., and H. Schumacher (1978). *Kleines Valenzlexikon deutscher Verben*, 2nd ed. Tübingen: TBL Verlag Gunter Narr.
Engelen, B. (1975a). *Untersuchungen zu Satzbauplan und Wortfeld in der geschriebenen deutschen Sprache der Gegenwart*, Teilband 1. München: Max Hueber Verlag.
Engelen, B. (1975b). *Untersuchungen zu Satzbauplan und Wortfeld in der geschriebenen deutschen Sprache der Gegenwart*, Teilband 2. München: Max Hueber Verlag.
Feuchtwanger, L. (1977). *Goya oder Der arge Weg der Erkenntnis*. Frankfurt am Main: Fischer Taschenbuch Verlag.
Fleming, I. (1965). *Casino Royale*, transl. by G. Eichel. Frankfurt am Main and Berlin: Verlag Ullstein.
Fleming, I. (1967). *Tod im Rückspiegel*, transl. by W. Thaler. Bern and München: F. Polakovics, N. Wölfl, and M. Meinert, Scherz Verlag.
Francis, W. Nelson (1979). 'Problems of Assembling and Computerizing Large Corpora.' In H. Bergenholtz, and B. Schaeder, eds., *Empirische Textwissenschaft*. Königstein/Ts.: Scriptor Verlag, 1979, pp. 110-123.
Frisch, M. (1969). *Homo Faber*. Frankfurt am Main: Suhrkamp Verlag.
Glinz, H. (1970). Deutsche Grammatik I. Bad Homburg v. d. H: Athenäum Verlag.
Grass, G. (1979). *Der Butt*. Frankfurt am Main: Fischer Taschenbuch Verlag.
Heinrich, W. (1978). *So long, Archie*, 3rd. ed., München: W. Heyne Verlag.
Hermodsson, L. (1978). *Semantische Strukturen der Satzgefüge im kausalen und konditionalen Bereich*. Stockholm: Almquist & Wiksell International.
Hockett, C.F. (1968). *The State of the Art*. The Hague: Mouton.
Itkonen, E. (1976). 'Was für eine Wissenschaft ist die Linguistik eigentlich?.' In D. Wunderlich, ed. *Wissenschaftstheorie der Linguistik*. Kronberg/TS: Athenäum Verlag, 1976, pp. 56-76.
Jäger, S. (1971a). *Empfehlungen zum Gebrauch des Konjunktivs in der geschriebenen deutschen Hochsprache*, 2nd ed., Düsseldorf: Pädagogischer Verlag Schwann.
Jäger, S. (1971b). *Der Konjunktiv in der deutschen Sprache der Gegenwart*. München: Max Hueber Verlag, Düsseldorf: Pädagogischer Verlag Schwann.
Kapfhammer, G. ed. (1971). *Bayerische Sagen: Sagen aus Altbayern, Schwaben und Franken*. Düsseldorf and Köln: E. Diederichs Verlag.
Kaufmann, G. (1976). *Die indirekte Rede und mit ihr konkurrierende Formen der Redeerwähnung*. München: Max Hueber Verlag.
König, E. (1973). 'Transformationsprozesse II.' In M. Gerhardt, ed., *Funk-Kolleg Sprache*, Band 1. Frankfurt am Main: Fischer Taschenbuch Verlag, 1973, pp. 299-312.
Kraus, K. (1956). *Die Sprache*, 3rd ed., München: Kösel-Verlag.
Lees, R.B. (1957). Review of N. Chomsky, *Syntactic Structures*. In *Language* 33: 375-408.

Matzel, K., and B. Ulvestad (1976). 'Asymmetrie im syntaktischen Regelwerk.' *Sprachwissenschaft* 1: 73–107.
Matzel, K., and B. Ulvestad (1978). 'Zum Adhortativ und *SIE*-Imperativ.' *Sprachwissenschaft* 2: 146–183.
Percha, I. von (1976). *Der König soll sterben*, 2nd ed. München: W. Heyne Verlag.
Rauch, I., and C.T. Scott, eds. (1967). *Approaches to Linguistic Methodology*. Madison, Milwaukee, and London: University of Wisconsin Press.
Schachter, P. (1977). 'Constraints on Coördination.' *Language* 53: 86–103.
Schade, G. (1975). *Einführung in die deutsche Sprache der Wissenschaften*, 5th ed. Berlin: Erich Schmidt Verlag.
Seiffert, H. (1973). *Einführung in die Wissenschaftstheorie*. Erster Band, 6th ed. München: Verlag C.H. Beck.
Siegl, I. (1978). *Die Schuld der Sonnhoferin*. Hamburg: M. Kelter Verlag.
Sledd, J. (1962). 'Prufrock among the syntacticians.' In A.A. Hill, ed., *Third Texas Conference on Problems of Linguistic Analysis of English*. Austin: University of Texas, 1962, pp. 1–15.
Ulvestad, B. (1967). 'Die Fügung *werden* + Part. Präs. im Bairischen.' *Zeitschrift für Mundartforschung* 34: 258–280.
Ulvestad, B. (1971). 'Die logische Struktur grammatischer Regeln.' *Sprache der Gegenwart* 20: 156–173.
Ulvestad, B. (1972a). 'Zum postpositiven Attribut im Deutschen.' *Sprache der Gegenwart* 22: 165–180.
Ulvestad, B. (1972b). 'Das pränukleare Adverbialattribut bei Nominalen im Deutschen.' *Sprache der Gegenwart* 26: 267–282.
Ulvestad, B. (1973). 'Zur Rettung des Temporalrelativums *als.*' *Sprache der Gegenwart* 24: 226–237.
Ulvestad, B. (1975). '*Nicht* im Vorfeld.' *Sprache der Gegenwart* 34: 373–393.
Ulvestad, B., and H. Bergenholtz (1979). '*Es* als "Vorgreifer" eines Objektsatzes.' *Deutsche Sprache* 2: 97–116.
Ulvestad, B. (1979). 'Corpus *vs.* Intuition in Syntactical Research.' In H. Bergenholtz, and B. Schaeder, eds., *Empirische Textwissenschaft*. Königstein/Ts.: Scriptor Verlag, 1979, pp. 89–108.
Ulvestad, B., and H. Bergenholtz: forthcoming, '*Es* als "Vorgreifer" II' (*Deutsche Sprache*).
Wilmanns, W. (1906). *Deutsche Grammatik* III. Strassburg: J. Trübner Verlag.
Winter, W. (1965). 'Transforms Without Kernels?.' *Language* 41: 484–489.
Wunderlich, D. (1970). *Tempus und Zeitreferenz im Deutschen*. München: Max Hueber Verlag.

D.H. WHALEN

The Native Speaker and Indeterminacy

ABSTRACT

Most modern theories of language tacitly assume that every structure of language is determinate. However, lack of agreement (especially on the status of sentences with complex syntax), among linguists and native speakers, is, in some cases, evidence of *indeterminacy* in language. In addition to the variations which occur within each individual's speech and which are best described by variable rules (as proposed by Labov), there are also constructions which are indeterminate in the speaker's dialect considered as a system, but which are treated consistently by individuals. It is proposed that future descriptions of languages strive specifically to outline those portions of a language which show such conflicting consistencies within dialects, to describe the differing personal resolutions of the indeterminacy, and to show which rule systems will both account for the determinate core of the language and one or more of the personal systems as well. Such descriptions will necessarily be more complex than those that assume determinacy, but they will avoid vacuous controversies over conflicting data, be inherently more accurate, and emphasize the importance of the native speaker as both a learner and user of his language.

INTRODUCTION

Variation has long been the bane of grammarians. If one is to give a coherent description of something, that something must itself be fairly coherent. Variation at the lowest level of linguistic substance is no particular problem; it can be called "free variation" and deemed of no linguistic significance. However, integrating variation at higher levels and, more importantly, variation between structures rather than elements has always caused more trouble. Since the levels above phonetics begin to signify, it is irresistable to assume that a change in form results in a change in meaning (Bolinger (1977) makes this the theme of his book), and meanings must be incorporated into a complete linguistic description. (Even a theorist who doggedly excluded meaning from his description would find indeterminacies, but I will not go into the sticky question of just how he would find them. Suffice it to say that it would be about as difficult as deciding whether such a theory has any data at all.) Many of the aspects of meaning that Bolinger treats have been attributed to style, implicature, etc., and thus have been excluded as evidence for the linguistic rules involved. However, the examples in this paper which depend on meaning data will deal with core, denotational meaning, that meaning which is used directly for communication of propositions. This type of meaning is included in all linguistic theories which include meaning at all. Thus, certain troublesome questions about what a description of the language's semantics should include will be irrelevant to the analysis of indeterminacy.

Variation between dialects of the same language is best accounted for as differences between independent, yet quite similar, linguistic systems. Such an approach leads the linguist to capture all those regularities which can be used for communicative purposes within a speech community; it may not be the best approach when we wish to consider, say, a conversation between speakers of different dialects. (A dialect is a variant of a language which has noticeable, consistent deviations from other variants of the language and which is spoken by a group which intercommunicates by means of that language variant.) Since dialects can follow geographical, social and generational lines, one is almost certain to find dialects within any language with a nontrivial number of speakers. Some variation within a dialect is presumably due to "style", although the recognition of socially defined dialects makes the recognition of styles much more problematic. Even with style described separately, there is still, in every dialect, a residue of intra-dialectal variation which is symptomatic of indeterminacy in the language. That such indeterminacy exists and has important consequences for grammatical analysis is the thesis of this paper.

INCONSISTENCY AND STATISTICALLY GROUNDED VARIATION

There are two main types of indeterminacy in language: that where each speaker of the language is so in doubt about the status of a particular construction that he simply does not have a judgement about it, and will change his mind about it freely (= individual *inconsistency*); and that where different segments of the population (not constituting dialect groups) have made the determination in conflicting ways (= intradialectal *conflicting consistencies*). The latter type will occupy most of the discussion, but I want to dismiss the former as being much less interesting, although still not deserving of the official silence that has accompanied it through linguistic theorizing. That dismissal is contained in the remainder of this section.

The variability found by Labov and other sociolinguists is not, in one sense, an indication of inconsistency. If each of two pronunciations, for example, is allowed, the fact that a speaker does not always choose just one

Indeterminacy 265

of them is not quite an inconsistency, but more of a choosing between alternates. What the addition of variable rules (c.f. Labov 1972a:93-101, Bickerton 1971, Cedergren and Sankoff 1974) does is to make the precise nature of the variation an object of study. It does not make the behavior of the individuals involved inconsistent in the above stated negative sense. Or, if we do decide to call this statistically grounded variation inconsistency as well, then we will have to recognize that the second type is more interesting than the first, and each has different implications for linguistic theory. Here, "inconsistency" will be reserved for those cases where the native speaker has conflicting tendencies, cannot decide on the status of a construction, and tends not to use the construction himself. For the implications of the other type of variation for linguistics, the reader is referred to the papers mentioned above; I am in general agreement with the position indicated there, and need not pursue the matter further here.

Personal inconsistency is very difficult to determine. And, since inconsistency for a dialect or for the language is the result of all its speakers behaving inconsistently, attested cases of language inconsistency are quite rare. The main trouble in eliciting inconsistency is that there is almost always the possibility that there has been some shift in register or style that makes the change in language behavior determinate despite its contradictory appearance. The style-switch explanation may eventually seem untenable, but it is very hard to get good evidence against. Similarly, even when the conflicting forms come out in quick succession, we still cannot tell for certain whether the speaker was confused over the forms themselves or was rather having difficulty imagining a coherent context for the elicited sentences.

For the linguist who wants to show that such inconsistencies are a part of every language and not just occasional accidents, there is an added difficulty. To the extent that linguists have been willing to talk about inconsistent behavior, they have ranged in their comments from treating it as evidence of loss of language ability (Bloomfield (1927) 1964:395) to evidence that we cannot construct a theory based on everything the native speaker does but must instead rely on "clear cases" (Chomsky 1965:3-24). The linguistic literature contains few statements such as, "After extensive research, it was found that none of my thirty-four informants could decide on the grammaticality of sentences containing subjunctives in relative clauses." Much less will one find the conclusion "Thus such constructions are indeterminate in this language." We might expect such statements in attempts at complete grammars, but there is always more than enough determinate material in a language to keep dozens of linguists working a lifetime. Our next expectation might be that specialists examining, say, subjunctives in relative clauses would report such instances of indeterminacy. But most linguists see such negative results as non-results, and thus not worth reporting. Even if the investigator thought the results should be known, it is doubtful that an editor would agree. While there is less that one can say straightforwardly about the constructions found to be inconsistent than about determinate or statistically grounded ones, such indeterminacies can, potentially, shed light on other parts of the grammar, to the extent that they can show cases where the rules ought to fail. If the rules one has devised make definite predictions about what are in fact indeterminate, inconsistent constructions, then one's rules are incorrect. However, at present, it is more than difficult to find documented cases of inconsistency in natural languages, so I will not attempt to argue their existence convincingly. Their existence is assumed and defined as a counterpoint to the indeterminacy caused by conflicting consistencies.

CONFLICTING CONSISTENCIES

A more important type of indeterminacy in language is that of internally consistent determinations about some portion of language, which differ for large groups of speakers who cannot be divided into inter-communicating dialects. Such areas of the language are not strictly coded. While there will certainly be some easily recognized parts of the constructions under consideration (else we would not hesitate to call it outside the language), nothing definite can be communicated by that part of the construction which is indeterminate. The most interesting cases occur when it is clear that the language *ought* to say which of a number of possibilities is the actual one, but doesn't. This can happen, for example, when two or three basic rules, learned fairly early in first language acquisition, interact, but the situation described by the sentences showing the interaction does not come up very often, especially in the topics of childhood and youth. Thus by the time the relevant data begins to come in, the native speaker must already have come to a decision about the interaction, and will perhaps be more willing to reject the sentences that contradict his grammar than to change that grammar. There are, of course, other possible origins of conflicting consistencies, but this example is meant to introduce the concept as conceivable. The next three sections will discuss examples.

Phonology

Although there is a great deal of room for personal variation and divergent determinations on the phonetic level, there is much less of a possibility for conflicting phonologies. Since the phonetic data does not lend itself to structural analysis, I will leave the phonetic level as an untried case. Since

Indeterminacy 267

there is an extremely limited inventory of phonemes in any language, and since all signs and sentences of a language make use of the phonology, there is a great deal of evidence for every phonemic distinction, most phonotactic combinations, and most morphophonemic processes. This is not to say that only one phonological analysis is ever feasible for a language, but only that most analyses will make the same prediction in every case, and thus be functionally equivalent. There are examples (such as that of English 'adze,' which is the only instance of a morpheme-final voiced obstruent cluster) in which the relevant evidence may come late in life, or never at all. But the differences between a system which allows the combination and one which doesn't are exceedingly trivial. More compelling examples come, not unreasonably, from the incorporation of loan words into the native language, a process which is likely to occur late in the native speaker's language history. A similar example is the evidence that Latinate vocabulary in English provides for morphophonemic processes (cf. Chomsky and Halle 1968).

Unfortunately, it is also the case with treatment of loan words that there is almost always a stylistic judgement that accompanies any of the possible alternatives. So even if one speaker were to use foreign words as a reason for establishing new phonemic distinctions, and another assimilated all the words into his previous phonology, we would not be very likely to have conflicting consistencies so much as coexisting styles, with corresponding systems. Bloch's analyses of Japanese (1948, 1950) provide a good example. He found that there was a simple, coherent phonology of Japanese if one ignored English loan words. In the later paper, he decided that such an exclusion was arbitrary and that each system should be analyzed on its own, forcing him to conclude that "standard colloquial Japanese is not one dialect but several, which differ from each other, greatly or little, in their treatment of English loans" (1950: 88). He went on to describe the two extreme dialects, that with fully assimilated loans and that with restructured phonology. These are not the most interesting dialects from the viewpoint of the present discussion; rather we are concerned with the intermediate dialects which have some assimilation of English loans, but presumably also have some restructuring of the phonology. Speakers of such dialects could have indeterminate reactions to English loans. More importantly, if we could prove that speakers from all points on the continuum spoke the same dialect (as defined by other features), we would have to conclude that that dialect of Japanese was indeterminate in its treatment of English loans. Such proof is not forthcoming from (nor attempted in) Bloch's articles, and it is difficult to imagine proof that would satisfy a majority of linguists. However, the existence of indeterminate dialects is still a problem if we wanted to say that each of the treatments (naturalizing or non-) of the loans was a separate style, for then speakers of the intermediate dialects would have to be seen as constituting a completely separate style, or to vacillate between two styles in any one conversation. The formalization of the intuitive notion of "style" here is quite problematic, and cannot be dealt with at length. It should be noted, though, that Labov finds similar problems in trying to describe Black English as a "style." In one short passage spoken in Black English vernacular (1972b:189), he found Black English features alternating with Standard English features, each surrounded by forms occurring in both. "Without any clear way of categorizing this behavior, we are forced to speak of 'stylistic variants,' and we are then left with no fixed relation at all to our notion of linguistic structure" (ibid.). The "stylistic" analysis has the greatest intuitive appeal, but the "stylistic" solution is not really a part of linguistic description as presently practiced and defined. Features which communicate some aspects of social status, education, etc., by virtue of belonging to a separate system ("style") but which can be used outside the system are indeed a problem. However, it is a different problem from the one addressed in the present paper.

Differences which can be analyzed in terms of rule order have been proposed for certain instances of dialect variation (e.g. Bailey 1973b), and some of his examples might be within a dialect as well. If more such studies appear, it may be possible to document indeterminacy in phonology as shown by conflicting rule orders. There is at least a greater chance for discrepancies of this sort than for those between simple phonemic inventories. For now, in view of the present examples and their small numbers, it appears more likely that phonology is not subject to large-scale indeterminacy, which is no doubt a factor in the relative success of linguistic analysis on the phonological level.

Lexicon

Most lexical items learned early in life denote objects and actions with well-established cultural relevance. To the extent that objects of indeterminate cultural status may be ignored completely, there may never be occasion to see if individual speakers differ in their conception of the meaning of various words. With rare words, which are seen in few environments, more mistaken conclusions could conceivably be drawn about the meaning, but it also seems to be the case that fewer speakers use such words, and thus there is more of a chance that such speakers will share views and background which will lead them to similar conclusions. It may well be that there are few words in the lexicon which have a completely indeterminate status in the language. The only examples seem to be words which occur only in idioms (such as English 'kith' (in 'kith and kin')), but it is arguable that such words do not have lexical entries apart from the idioms.

However, with every lexeme in the language comes a realm of indeterminacy.

Indeterminacy 269

This is the "fuzziness" of the boundaries of the meanings of lexemes. Since indeterminacy of this sort is so pervasive and so hard to deal with, it has received some attention. Reactions have ranged from assuming such fuzziness irrelevant to linguistic theory (Katz and Fodor (1963) 1964:498) to envisioning new logics based on it (e.g. Lakoff 1973). The most important study of word-meaning boundaries, however, is Labov (1973).

In that study, Labov found that subjects would label objects ranging from cup-like shapes to vase-like shapes, and others, fairly consistently; and that the boundaries between categories could be shifted by asking the subjects to imagine various substances (coffee, potatoes, flowers, etc.) in the containers. From the data, Labov concludes that all the subjects utilized a definition that contained elements both of form, material and size, and of function. Such uniformity across subjects would indicate that, while the objects intermediate on the scale might be indeterminate in their relation to the language (and the culture as well), the words themselves would have a determinate status since all speakers seemed to share the same boundaries. However, Labov's method of classing responses may have obscured significant variation. For his test, the main word used in the description was counted as the label; thus one person saying "It's a cup" and one saying "It's sort of like a cup" would be counted as giving the same label ("cup") to the object (Labov 1973:355). Yet such responses can show distinct differences in the denotation of words for different speakers; the core of clear cases may be analyzed into, say, different features by different speakers. If, for example, having a handle is not criterial for 'cup' for one speaker but is for another, they might give the responses mentioned above, and be assumed by Labov's method to have the same definition of 'cup' when in fact they do not. We do not see direct evidence of this in the data Labov puts in his report. However, such differences would mean that there is an allowable amount of variation in the definition of 'cup,' and by labelling objects in the indeterminate range, speakers may show that they have chosen one option rather than another. Consistent and non-dialectally-determined disagreement about whether a term literally applies indicates both that the object being described has an indeterminate relation to the denotative words of the language and that the meanings of the words have indeterminate parts. Attempts to communicate in the regions of indeterminacy have less than optimal chances of succeeding, but can also show existing variation within the analysis of core meaning.

Syntax

Conflict of judgements in syntax began to be treated seriously by American linguists in the late 1960's. Fundamental concerns about grammaticality judgements per se were expressed by Bolinger (1968) and others. The phenomena of English which displayed variation to investigators include compound nouns (Gleitman and Gleitman 1970), deletion in subordinate clauses and 'do so' verb phrases (Elliott, Legum and Thompson 1969; on the former, see also Greenbaum 1973), "missing readings" for passives (Katz and Postal 1964), transformations of idioms (Fraser 1970), "backward" pronominalization (Cole 1974), contraction of 'to' across deletion sites (Pullum and Postal 1979, and previous articles cited there), and many others. Elliott et al. conclude that "the regularities we have observed indicate that variation needs to be accounted for by grammatical theory" (1969:58), but linguists have not, in general, come to the same conclusion or attempted to incorporate variation into their grammars. (The exclusion of "unclear" cases would lead to the rejection of more sentences than linguists would like, as shown by Spencer's (1973) discovery of uncertainty about sentences which received unequivocal judgements in the transformational literature.) In addition, the status of such variation is unclear, even if some condition on the grammar might "account" for it. The following detailed example will show that describing (generating) the variable data is only the first step in accounting for the variation, and that variable data is outside the determinate part of language and thus requires a modified view of linguistic description.

The example I will now present in detail is based on Carden's (1970, 1973a,b) analysis of the interaction of negative and quantifier words, 'until,' and tag questions in English. These phenomena are common in English, and have no reason not to interact. Yet even so, sentences displaying the interaction, such as (1) and (2),

(1) (*)All the boys didn't leave until midnight,
(2) (*)All the boys didn't leave, did they?

have an indeterminate status in the language. While individual speakers usually have a consistent opinion about these sentences, speakers from the same dialect often disagree about just what that opinion ought to be. It is probably significant that systematic negation is learned late in the early stages of language acquisition (Bowerman 1973:221), tag questions quite late (Brown and Hanlon 1970), and (to make a tentative conclusion based on Bowerman's and Brown's (1973) silence) quantifiers rather late as well. It may be that once such rules are incorporated into the grammar, speakers are more willing to interpret sentences displaying the interaction pragmatically, by the context and probable meaning, rather than accepting such late evidence as reason for changing their already developed systems.

Basically, Carden found that speakers divided into three main groups according to their interpretation of sentence (3):

Indeterminacy 271

(3) All the boys didn't leave.

Some got only the reading

(4) Not all the boys left,

Where the quantifier was negated (the NEG-Q group). Others got only a reading

(5) All the boys (didn't leave) (=All the boys stayed),

where the verb was negated (NEG-V group). The third group got both readings (the Ambiguous group). "These groups, however, seem to be randomly distributed with respect to the sociological characteristics of the informants, with members of the same nuclear family falling into two or even three of the dialects" (Carden 1973b:6-7). He goes on to propose an analysis based on differing placements of the negative and different rule orders which can account for the different judgements noted.

Carden's analysis, with quantifiers as higher predicates and with extrinsic rule ordering, may not be the best possible; it is certainly rejected out of hand by many linguists with different theoretical frameworks. But in any framework, saying that the method of producing and interpreting such sentences is in tripartite free variation misses the point: Different groups behave in consistent yet conflicting ways. Some are consistently NEG-Q, others NEG-V, and others consistently ambiguous. A single grammar with free variation, even if constructable, does not account for such consistencies. Yet the consistencies are in clear conflict. While different dialects often give us instances of conflict, it is not proper to assume, with Carden, that every conflicting consistency produces a dialect split. No one of the three treatments of sentence (3) has a communicative basis. Although sentences like (3) can be used to communicate, they cannot be depended on to convey one or the other or both of the interpretations on the basis of linguistic conventions alone. Speakers of the ambiguous "dialect" will depend on disambiguating context, but for the wrong reason — they think that the construction is determinately ambiguous, when in fact it is indeterminate. Speakers from the NEG-V and NEG-Q groups, unless they recognize but do not imitate the other groups, will act as if the construction is determinate and stand greater chances of being misunderstood. Since they do not consider the context important for deciding between the two conceivable readings, they will not pay as much attention to making it decisive. Thus indeterminacy can cause problems which are not so large as to make communication impossible, but large enough to cause misunderstandings.

It is important to note, in this respect, that "standing a chance of being misunderstood" does not place our discussion in the statistical realm. The "chance" here does not depend on some (arbitrary or empirically derived) percentage, but simply on who is listening to which type of speaker. A listener who speaks the same "dialect" will have a 100% chance of understanding – or as near to 100% as is possible in natural language. If, say, a NEG-Q speaker talks to a NEG-V speaker, he stands a 100% chance of being *mis*-understood; and ignoring context, he has (somewhat arbitrarily) a 50% chance of being understood by an ambiguous speaker. The sort of percentages that Hockett (1952) discusses in his article on semantic noise are appropriate only to systems considered as wholes. If we look at the semantic noise computed for specific messages, the situation looks much more like what I have just described. Of course, the percentages I derived apply only to the one aspect of the sentence that is indeterminate, i.e., the scope of the negative. While a more realistic measure of semantic noise for individual sentences could be derived by considering the determinacy of each of the constructions and words involved, the result would still be irrelevant to the indeterminacy I am describing. For I am not saying that a sentence containing an indeterminate structure necessarily has 0, 50 or 100% codability; rather I am saying that, as far as that construction is concerned, when we abstract away from other communicative factors, there is an indeterminate communicative effect of this construction for the dialect as a whole. An indeterminate sentence may communicate, much the same as an ungrammatical sentence sometimes communicates; but the method for analyzing both those exceptional cases is different from that for the determinate core of the language.

Another type of objection to Carden's analysis, and indirectly to mine, appears in Baltin's (1977) study. He found a large and statistically significant correlation between subjects' narrow or broad interpretation of quantifier-negative sentences and restrictive/non-restrictive adjectives (e.g. "The *industrious* Chinese will prosper," where the sentence can indicate that all Chinese are industrious, or that only those who are industrious will prosper.) Although this is an interesting result, it does not make much difference to my analysis (and no necessary difference to Carden's). While speakers *prefer* one reading to another (as the test showed), they still must deal with an indeterminate phenomenon in the negative-quantifier interaction and a determinately ambiguous one with the restrictive/non-restrictive adjective situation. In English, most adjectives (and certainly the ones Baltin used in his experiment) are simply ambiguous between these two readings in the prenominal position. Thus the grammar will have to deal with these constructions differently, regardless of this correlation between the preferred reading of the one and the only reading of the other. If we were to try to explain the preferred readings in this case, we would be obliged to do so in all cases – a much different task from that usually undertaken in linguistic analysis.

IMPLICATIONS OF INDETERMINACY FOR LINGUISTICS

The admission of indeterminacy does not change the structure of linguistics as much as it might appear. Its main effect is to end some endless debates about data by showing that there can be no answer, or, rather, that there must be more than one answer. If two theories make different predictions about a sentence yet that sentence is indeterminate, then there is no decision between the two systems that will be supported by the language, for the language as a whole. It may well be that each of the two is a possible personal resolution of the indeterminacy, and that there are native speakers in both camps. Since there would not have been any conflict unless there were cases where the two disagreed, it will also be the case that there is potential for a change to occur, and that one system or the other will win out (or one in one dialect and the other in another). But it is fruitless to insist that because such a sentence would decide between two systems it must be determined one way or the other. Linguistic analyses must make room for alternate analyses, which the native speaker is as likely to discover (unconsciously) as the linguist (consciously). This approach should certainly not be taken to be claiming that any system that describes part of a language but not others is a legitimate analysis; on the contrary, an analysis that makes wrong predictions about determinate areas of a language is still wrong.

Thus, a complete description of a language is theoretically possible. However, it would look quite different from what recent linguistic theory would lead us to expect. In particular, indeterminate sentences will either have to be underdetermined by the description, or they will have to be defined as outside the language. The latter approach is not only unpalatable, it also makes the necessary indeterminacy of some portion of language seem to be anomalous rather than a source of insight into the structures underlying the determinate part and a probable force in language change. Descriptions should include details of possible variation (ultimately with occurring percentages; cf. Labov 1972b), and the extent to which native speakers control (both in production and reception) more than one variation (as in polylectal grammar; cf. Bailey 1973a:23-29). This calls for a great deal more information to be collected and described than is usually assumed to be needed (or wanted) for linguistic analysis; but it should be recognized that there is simply more data which can be described than has normally been described. There is still value in grammars which do not deal much outside the determinate parts of language, but that should not be taken as an indication that they are the most that linguistics (and linguists) can do.

The notion that the idiolect is the proper object of linguistic research (as seen from Bloch (1950) through the present) can now be seen to be untenable for yet another reason. First, to mention the main previously given reason for rejecting the idiolect, Labov has noted that "it is doubtful whether anyone has found within such an 'idiolect' the homogeneous data which Bloch hoped for" (1972b:192). Now, in addition, we have the complication that all consistencies of the individual are not of equal communicative consequence. There can be personal consistencies whose lack of communicative determinacy can only be discovered by the examination of the language systems of the people that the native speaker communicates with. Here again, the social side of language regains prominence.

So far, I have talked of proven indeterminacies as indeterminate for a dialect. If it could be shown (as I think it could for the quantifier-negative sentences of section 2.3) that the construction in question was indeterminate for all the dialects of a language, then we would be quite justified in saying that the construction was indeterminate for the language as a whole. On the other hand, another possibility, somewhat at variance with the previous discussion, is to say that every construction that is variable within *or* across dialects was indeterminate for the language. In a resolution similar to that proposed above for conflicting consistencies, we could propose that all possible variants be described, thus leaving a certain determinate core intact. The addition in this case would be that certain of the variants would have communicative reliability. While there would be some interest in discovering just how much overlap there was between dialects (and perhaps incidentally a measure of how justified certain classifications of variants as dialects rather than as separate languages were), treating the two types of variation at the same time would obscure the very distinction that the classification of "indeterminacy" rests upon, namely the lack of communicative effectiveness for *any* of the decisions concerning the construction. However, in those cases where speakers of different dialects talk to each other, then the speakers must depend on the communicative capacity of the language, not of their own dialects, and so the indeterminacy becomes a real factor. Here, the native speakers will treat the language as a system, not as a set of closely related systems. And the linguist should be prepared to do the same, and to admit that dialectal differences can introduce communicative indeterminacy of a somewhat different sort that, but of the same effect as, that described in section 2.

RECOMMENDATIONS FOR LINGUISTIC RESEARCH

There are some changes in research tactics that are immediate consequences of accepting indeterminacy as a linguistic phenomenon. The first is the unacceptability of intuitive judgements of one speaker as the sole source of data. If even sentences about which the linguist has sure judgements can be indeterminate for the language, it is clear that the resulting grammar would be misleading in proportion to the number of indeterminate constructions described as determinate. (Intuition itself has come under attack, but indeterminacy does not bear directly on that issue.) It might be that the determinacy of a sentence is in direct proportion to the stability of introspection about it, but that remains to be tested. In any event, getting a number of speaker judgements about any but the most trivially determinate sentences is requisite.

When no single solution is the only one possible, it is better to outline all of the possible solutions than to arbitrarily adopt one. Doing so avoids Lamb's (1975:546) complaint that we forget that arbitary decisions are arbitrary; it also acknowledges the possibility that changes elsewhere in the language may eventually mean that the decision is no longer arbitrary. Thus, to take Wells' (1979:26) example but not his solution, we can define English 'all' in terms of 'some' and 'not,' or 'some' in terms of 'all' and 'not,' or each independently. Although the last is less economic than the others, it should not be excluded as a possibility in a human language. It is clear that a semantic change in 'not' could affect the three systems differently, leading to possible dialect splits. In fact, there are more possible systems, if we assume that the words can be defined not only in relation to other words, but in terms of semantic features as well. If all reasonable possibilities are explicitly mentioned, such effects will be easier to understand.

The label "indeterminate" should not be used to avoid thorough data collection and analysis. The limits and features of indeterminacy are not well known — this paper depends on lengthy studies of quite well-known languages. Again, the present remarks in no way lead to the conclusion that only indeterminacy should be studied, only that it should not be excluded. If the means of data collection are limited, there is the possibility that spurious variation will appear. This is a danger with relying on intuitive judgements — especially when it is not clear that everyone is passing judgement on the same thing (see Bolinger 1968). Studies of indeterminacy require more solid data than studies of determinate phenomena; but we cannot tell from small data bases which is which.

CONCLUSION

As the native speaker learns his language, he must make decisions about various constructions and how they are used. In some cases, it seems, he must make independent decisions about constructions that could interact but do not very often. Thus competing systems can arise that force sentences which show the interaction into a communicative limbo, that make the constructions indeterminate for a dialect and potentially for a language. If he is linguistically sensitive, a native speaker may discover the indeterminacies of his language and seek to avoid them or to use them in disambiguating contexts; it is probably seldom the case that an indeterminate construction cannot be fairly easily paraphrased in a determinate construction.

Formal, structural systems do not handle indeterminacy very well. To do so, some readjustment is necessary, probably the addition of statements about the distribution of constructions and elements rather than a drastic change in theory. The arguments in this paper are compatible with a large range of theories, and point towards fundamental uncertainties about data (especially in syntax) that linguists can ill afford to continue to ignore.

ACKNOWLEDGEMENTS

This paper was presented, in a much different form, at a Linguistics Workshop, Yale University, October, 1979. Rulon Wells, Leon Serafim, Charles Hoequist, Guy Carden and Judith Aissen all provided useful comments on earlier drafts. They are not responsible for the residue of opinion.

REFERENCES

Bailey, C.-J. N. (1973a). *Variation and Linguistic Theory.* Arlington, VA: Center for Applied Linguistics.
- (1973b). 'Variation Resulting from Different Rule Orderings in English Phonology.' In C.-J. N. Bailey and R. Shuy, eds., *New Ways of Analyzing Variation in English.* Washington, DC: Georgetown University Press, pp. 211-252.
Baltin, M. (1977). 'Quantifier Negative Interaction.' In R. Fasold and R. Shuy, eds., *Studies in Language Variation.* Washington, DC: Georgetown University Press, pp. 30-36.
Bickerton, D. (1971). 'Inherent variability and variable rules.' *Foundations of Language* 7: 457-492.
Bloch, B. (1948). 'A Set of Postulates for Phonemic Analysis.' *Language* 24: 3-46.
- (1950). 'Studies in Colloquial Japanese IV. Phonemics.' *Language* 26: 86-125.
Bloomfield, L. ((1927) 1964). 'Literate and Illiterate Speech.' In D. Hymes, ed., *Language in Culture and Society.* New York: Harper and Row, pp. 391-396. (Originally *American Speech* 10: 432-439.)
Bolinger, D. (1968). 'Judgements of Grammaticality.' *Lingua* 21: 31-40.
- (1977). *Meaning and Form.* New York, London: Longmans.
Bowerman, M. (1973). *Early Syntactic Development.* Cambridge: Cambridge University Press.
Brown, R. (1973). *A First Language.* Cambridge, MA: Harvard University Press.
Brown, R., and C. Hanlon (1970). 'Derivational Complexity and Order of Acquisition in Child Speech.' In J.R. Hayes, ed., *Cognition and the Development of Language.* New York: John Wiley and Sons, pp. 11-53.
Carden, G. (1970). 'A Note on Conflicting Idiolects.' *Linguistic Inquiry* 1: 281-290.
- (1973a). 'Dialect Variation and Abstract Syntax.' In R. Shuy, ed., *Some New Directions in Linguistics.* Washington, DC: Georgetown University Press, pp. 1-34.
- (1973b). *English Quantifiers: Logical Structure and Linguistic Variation.* Tokyo: Taishukan.

Cedergren, H., and D. Sankoff (1974). 'Variable Rules: Performance as a Statistical Reflection of Competence.' *Language* 50: 333-355.
Chomsky, N. (1965). *Aspects of the Theory of Syntax.* Cambridge, MA: MIT Press.
Chomsky, N., and M. Halle (1968). *The Sound Pattern of English.* New York: Harper and Row.
Cole, P. (1974). 'Backward Pronominalization and Analogy.' *Linguistic Inquiry* 5: 425-443.
Elliott, D., S. Legum and S. Thompson (1969), 'Syntactic Variation as Linguistic Data.' In R. Binnick, A. Davison, G. Green, and J. Morgan, eds., *Papers from the Fifth Regional Meeting,* Chicago: Chicago Linguistics Society.
Fraser, B. (1970). 'Idioms within a Transformational Grammar.' *Foundations of Language* 6: 22-42.
Gleitman, L.R., and H. Gleitman (1970). *Phrase and Paraphrase.* New York: Norton.
Greenbaum, S. (1973). 'Informant Elicitation of Data on Syntactic Variation.' *Lingua* 31: 201-212.
Hockett, C.H. (1952). 'An Approach to the Quantification of Semantic Noise.' *Philosophy of Science* 19: 257-260.
Katz, J., and J. Fodor ((1963) 1964). 'The Structure of a Semantic Theory.' In J. Fodor and J. Katz, eds., *The Structure of Language.* Englewood Cliffs, NJ: Prentice Hall, pp. 479-518. (Originally *Language* 39: 170-210).
Katz, J. and P. Postal (1964). *An Integrated Theory of Linguistic Descriptions.* Cambridge, MA: MIT.
Labov, W. (1972a). *Language in the Inner City.* Philadelphia: University of Pennsylvania.
- (1972b). *Sociolinguistic Patterns.* Philadelphia: University of Pennsylvania.
- (1973). 'The Boundaries of Words and their Meanings.' In C.-J. N. Bailey and R. Shuy, eds., *New Ways of Analyzing Variation in English.* Washington, DC: Georgetown University Press, pp. 340-373.
Lakoff, G. (1973). 'Fuzzy Grammar and the Performance/Competence Terminology Game.' In C. Corum, T. Smith-Stark, and A. Weiser, eds., *Papers from the Ninth Regional Meeting,* Chicago: Chicago Linguistics Society.
Lamb, S. (1975). 'Mutations and Relations.' In A. Makkai and V. Makkai, eds. *The First LACUS Forum.* Columbia, SC: Hornbeam, pp. 540-557.
Pullum, G.K., and P. Postal (1979). 'On an Inadequate Defense of "Trace Theory".' *Linguistic Inquiry* 10: 689-706.
Spencer, N.J. (1973). 'Differences Between Linguists and Non-Linguists in Intuitions of Grammaticality-Acceptability.' *Journal of Psycholinguistic Research* 2: 83-98.
Wells, R. (1979). 'Semantics in a Linguistic Framework.' In W. Woelck and P. Garvin, eds., *The Fifth LACUS Forum,* Columbia, SC: Hornbeam, pp. 21-36.

DIETER WUNDERLICH

Linguistic Strategies

ABSTRACT

The native speaker as well as the native informant is permanently faced with the task to choose between verbal alternatives. Some of the more specific strategies behind such a selection are here considered. These strategies can be stated either in grammatical or in referential or in functional terms. The question is posed of whether there is a hierarchical ordering of strategies of different kinds. In addition, the relationship of grammatical rules, rule conflicts, and strategies is discussed.

INTRODUCTION

Whenever I said to my little daughter, *"Du hast da noch etwas vom Essen hängen"* ('You've got something there at your mouth'), thereby pointing at the right side of *my* mouth, she tried to remove something from the *left* side of *her* mouth, which, in almost every case, was the wrong side. What was the source of this misunderstanding: did I behave wrongly, or did she?

In a way, I translated her perspective into mine. If I meant her right side, I used my right side to show this (cf. figure 1). My daughter, however, looked at me as a mirror-image of herself (cf. figure 2). My right side was taken by her as corresponding to her left side from which she, accordingly, tried to remove the bread crumb, or whatever it was. Or, in other words, while I tried to convey my message on the basis of adopting an intrinsic perspective, using not my body, but my addressee's body as the point of orientation, she decoded my message by adopting a deictic perspective. She was just as right as I was. If, however, I had known more about children's behavior, I could have avoided the mistake.

In a little test we exposed a number of subjects of different age groups, to the situation described above. Children below the age of 10 almost always (up to 95%) behaved as my daughter did, i.e., they conformed to the behavior illustrated in figure 2. The age group above 10 was equally divided (50% each) in conforming to figure 2 and figure 1.

For adults there seems to be a conflict of two strategies: should they

Figure 1   Figure 2

decode the message by adopting an intrinsic or a deictic perspective? Some of our informants commented upon their first, i.e., deictically oriented reaction as being 'illogical,' and corrected themselves by switching to the intrinsic perspective. This never happened the other way round. What has all this to do with linguistic strategies employed by a native speaker?

Although in the situation described above no use was made of the words 'right' and 'left,' it shows us something about the understanding of the concepts 'right' and 'left.' These expressions or concepts, as many others, can be used either deictically (related to the speaker's, or, more generally, to the user's body) or intrinsically (related to other bodies or objects). Which of these perspectives has prominence above the other? Which factors are responsible for the use of the one or the other? How can conflicts of the underlying strategies be solved?

We may also look at the situation described above as revealing some features which are typical for informant situations. We put the informant into a situation where he has to fulfil a certain task, verbally or nonverbally. Every task of this sort is perspective-bound. How can we be certain that the informant conforms to the perspective we have in mind? What, after all, is it that determines the relevant perspective? And if, as in the test described above, 50% (or, even 70%) of the informants behave in one way, and the rest in another, what do we have to conclude from this? At first glance, the answer might be that we have two different groups of the whole population (say, groups with different sociolects or dialects). But nobody has ever heard of one dialect which is prominently deictically oriented, and another which is intrinsically oriented. We could interpret these different orientations as personality features. But this would be even more problematic of informant situations, for the question must then arise of how we can control the specific interferences with the personality features of our informants. The only

Linguistic Strategies

rational answer seems to be that the task has not been determined univocally, or, in other words, there are no strict rules to be followed. However little our experience with linguistic testing may be, this seems to be what happens more often than not. If there are no strict rules to be followed, the informant has to conform to some strategies. But his choice of the appropriate strategy can hardly be accidental. Rather, it would be more plausible to assume that his strategies follow certain principles. Hence all our testing would only be sound if we tried to control as best we can the components that determine the linguistic strategies of our informants.

The remainder of this article is concerned with this question. However, I have to warn the reader that I have no real results. Even the reported tests were implemented somewhat naively.

DEICTIC VERSUS INTRINSIC PERSPECTIVE

The situation described above was clearly underdetermined. If, instead of saying *"Du hast da noch etwas vom Essen hängen,"* I had said *"Du hast da rechts am Mund noch etwas vom Essen hängen"* ('There is a bread crumb at the right side of your mouth') – my daughter had very probably done the right thing, provided she knew what the words 'left' and 'right' mean when referring to parts of her body. If someone asks us "raise your right hand," we can follow this command without doubt or hesitation. Is there, thus, any problem at all?

Suppose the doctor asks us "please, turn right." Quite probably, we will turn our body to the right in our perspective. We assume that the doctor took the intrinsic perspective not arbitrarily. But when I asked my students in a lecture hall to move 'a little more to the right,' up to 30% of them moved in my right direction. Obviously, in the context of a lecture a student may assume that he has, in every instance, to take the perspective of the lecturer, regardless of whether or not the respective movements are his own. Hence, the functional context of the movement may be important.

In a little experiment we tried to control the influence of movement. The subjects were presented figure 3 and two possible instructions that A gives B:

Figure 3

(1) *"Die Lampe soll rechts neben das Sofa gestellt werden."*
('The lamp is to be put to the right of the sofa')

(2) *"Die Lampe soll rechts neben dem Sofa stehen."*
('The lamp is to stand right of the sofa')

The question to the informant then was: Wohin stellt B die Lampe? ('Where does B put the lamp?') With respect to (1), 46% of the informants chose the deictic perspective of B, while with respect to (2) only 28% did that (out of a total of 68 informants). This means that 72% of the informants understood 'right of the sofa' in connection with a static verb as related to the sofa, which is a rather fixed object. The intrinsic perspective of a sofa is that one has when sitting on the sofa.

Let us consider a last example. During an excursion to Paris we make an appointment to meet 'right of Notre Dame'. Would any rational person try to meet his date left of Notre Dame which happens to be right of Notre Dame according to his incidental deictic perspective? I think not.

These observations lead to the following conclusion. Rather than having in all instances a clear-cut decision between the deictic and the intrinsic perspective we arrive at a continuum between these two:

deictic perspective regarding P — parts of the body of P
— movements of the body of P
— movement of unrelated objects by P
intrinsic perspective regarding Q — relations to a fixed object Q.

This hierarchy is influenced by further circumstances such as the local relationship between speaker and P, or between speaker and Q, and the functional contexts in which speaker, P, and Q are involved.

In another test we sought further evidence for the above hierarchy, concerning the deictic or intrinsic use of *vor* and *hinter* ('in front of' and 'behind'). The questions were these: If you were in A's position, what would you prefer to say, concerning figure 4:

Figure 4

Linguistic Strategies 283

(3) *Oh, jetzt ist der Ball vor/hinter das Haus gefallen.*
('Oh, the ball dropped in front of/behind the house')

(4) *Siehst du den Baum dort vor/hinter dem Haus?*
('Do you see that tree over there in front of/behind the house?')

(5) *Die Bank steht vor/hinter dem Haus.*
('The bench is in front of/behind the house')

Concerning figure 5:
(6) *Die Diskothek befindet sich vor/hinter dem Rathaus.*
('The discothec is in front of/behind the town hall')

(7) *Die Diskothek kommt vor/hinter dem Rathaus.*
(lit. 'The discothec comes in front of/behind the town hall')

(8) *Die Jakobikirche ist vor/hinter dem Rathaus.*
('The church is in front of/behind the town hall')

Figure 5

Concerning figure 6:

(9) *Hol mir doch mal eben den Eimer, er steht vor/hinter dem Auto.*
('Please get me the bucket, it is in front of/behind the car')

Figure 6

(10) *Hol mir doch mal eben die Bürste, sie liegt vor/hinter dem Auto.*
('Please get me the brush, it is in front of/behind the car')

We received the following results, by asking 54 informants:

	vor ('in front of')	*hinter* ('behind')
(3)	39 % i	61 % d
(4)	48 % i	52 % d
(5)	76 % i	24 % d
(6)	69 % d	31 % i
(7)	93 % d	7 % i
(8)	35 % i	65 % d
(9)	69 % i	31 % d
(10)	44 % d	56 % i

The letters 'd' and 'i' indicate the deictic and the intrinsic perspective respectively.
What can we conclude from this?
We can assume some underlying strategies determining the choice between the two perspectives.

(11) If a movement with respect to the speaker's (and/or hearer's) position is involved, then the deictic perspective is preferred.

This strategy is effective in cases (3), (6) and (7). The throwing of a ball induces a movement which starts at the place where A and B are. (6) and (7) can be considered as part of a route information. This route would constitute a movement starting at the place where A and B are. (7) is the only clearly preferred case of *vor* ('in front of'), here the word *kommen* ('come') makes the deictic perspective grammatical. For if we say *A kommt vor/hinter B*, it is implied that both objects are considered as destinations of a movement. This can be a bodily movement or an imaginary movement, i.e. gaze direction. If no other source of movement is indicated, it is also implied that the movement starts at the place where the speaker (or hearer) is.

Linguistic Strategies

(12) If a fixed object related to another fixed object with a prominent front side is involved, then the intrinsic perspective is preferred.

This strategy is effective in cases (5) and (8). A town house with an outside staircase and a front garden has a prominent front side as well as a residence facing the street. Every movement which passes the prominent front side would pass the related fixed object nearly simultaneously, hence there is no evident reason for choosing strategy (11).

In case (4), however, the deictic and the intrinsic perspectives are equally probable. This indicates that there is a conflict between two strategies involved. The tree is a fixed object related to the front side of the house, but it is also within the visual field of A and B and therefore object to a sight 'movement.'

(13) If an object with a prominent internal or use-perspective is involved, then the intrinsic perspective is preferred.

This strategy is effective in case (9). A car constitutes such a use-perspective either by its normal direction of movement or by the perspective of the driver. Case (10), however, again indicates a conflict between the prominence of a car and the prominence of a sight.

These considerations seem to support the assumption of a continuum in the choice between the deictic and the intrinsic perspective such as the one proposed above. However, there are clearly further determining functional considerations which we did not control in detail.

There is still another aspect of our experiment to be considered. With respect to questions (3)–(10), four out of 25 informants behaved purely deictically and four mostly deictically (except to one question), whereas one behaved purely intrinsically and five behaved mostly intrinsically (except for one question). This corresponds to the fact that the strategies described above (11)–(13) are not strictly followed. It indicates that in addition a personality factor must be involved. It is not clear, however, whether there was a biasing factor determining the experimental situation, or whether the informants were inclined to stick to the strategy once chosen for some other reason.

If we refrain from assuming two different populations concerning the choice between the deictic and the intrinsic perspective, then we have to accept the fact that our task was somewhat underdetermined. This seems to be quite typical of informant situations. Generally, the informant is given too much freedom in choosing an interpretation of the task. Very often, however, we are unable to discover (and hence to control) the conditions determining the interpretation at which he arrives. Does he fix some variables we did not control, or are there other latent conflicts of strategies involved?

INDETERMINACIES AND RULE CONFLICTS

In the experiment described above some situations could simultaneously be subject to two different strategies, leading to opposite results. Thus the strategies were conflicting with each other.

Another case of conflict can arise if we have different external reference systems. On normal geographical maps 'up' is North, and 'down' is South. But the up-direction is also related to geographical height, or to the source of a river. Possible conflicts are easily conceivable. Do I go from Düsseldorf up to the Alps, or down to the Alps? If I think of the river Rhine as the means of transportation or simply as a reference object, I will very probably say 'up'. If my focus is on the Alps as being situated further in the South, I may, however, disregard the height of the mountains. This I would not do if the proper purpose of my travel was mountaineering.

I shall be concerned here with still another type of conflict. It arises out of the extension of certain grammatical rules. Consider the following examples.

(14) *Hol mir den Eimer.* ('Get me the bucket')
(15) *Bring mir den Eimer.* ('Bring me the bucket')
(16) *Hol dir den Eimer.* ('Get yourself the bucket')
(17) **Bring dir den Eimer.* ('Bring yourself the bucket')

(17) is strictly ungrammatical, whereas (14)–(16) are grammatical. Owing to the particular nature of the verbs involved, (14)–(16) can, however, only be uttered in certain situations. A proper utterance situation may be thought to fulfil the following conditions (S = speaker, H = addressee):

(14′) The bucket is neither near to S nor near to H; H is near to S.
(15′) The bucket is not near to S.
(16′) The bucket is not near to H.

According to this analysis, (14) is more specific than (15): in any situation where (14) can be used (15) can be used but not vice versa. This analysis does, however, not show why (17) is ungrammatical.

We may now go on to complete the condition for (15):

(15″) The bucket is not near to S but it is near to H.

According to this analysis there is no situation where both (14) and (15) can be used, since the bucket must be near to H to fulfil the condition for (15), and it must be distant from H to fulfil the condition for (14). And (17) turns out to be ungrammatical, because we would get

Linguistic Strategies 287

(17″) The bucket is not near to H but it is near to H, which is contradictory.

Whenever (14) is appropriate, we can also use

(18) *Geh und hol mir den Eimer.* ('Go and get me the bucket')

as well as

(19) *Geh und bring mir den Eimer.*

(19) could be read as follows:
'Go to the place where the bucket is. Then you are near the bucket and condition (15″) holds. Hence: bring it to me'. The interchangeability of (18) and (19) may account for the fact that some informants claim that (15) can be used instead of (14).

Notice now that *holen* and *bringen* can also be used with 3rd person subjects.

(20) *Peter bringt die Post.* ('Peter brings the mail')
(21) *Peter holt die Post.* ('Peter fetches the mail')

Therefore we may generalize the following use conditions:

(22) Use *bringen* if the object is near the carrier's place but meant to be elsewhere.
(23) Use *holen* if the object is not near the carrier's place but meant to be there.

Further, we may observe that *bringen* needs a directional NP and *holen* a source NP. This corresponds to the use conditions (22) and (23).

(24) *Peter bringt die Briefe zur Post.*
('Peter brings the letters to the post office')
(25) *Peter holt die Briefe von der Post.*
('Peter goes to get the letters from the post office')

But (26) and (27) are somewhat odd:

(26) ?*Peter bringt die Briefe von der Post.*
(27) ?*Peter holt die Briefe zur Post.*

Accordingly, we may state the rules:

(28) Use *bringen* only with a directional NP.
(29) Use *holen* only with a source NP.

Now, I will try to show where the conflict arises. 12 informants were asked to complete the following situation.

S and H are either in the house or in the courtyard, the bucket is in the courtyard. Which of the following sentences can be used, and where are the respective positions of S and H?

(30) *Holst du mal den Eimer herein?*
(31) *Holst du mal den Eimer hinein?*
(32) *Bringst du mal den Eimer herein?*
(33) *Bringst du mal den Eimer hinein?*
('Could you bring the bucket into the house?')

The answers were these (number of informants):

	cannot be said	S is inside	S is outside	H is inside	H is outside
(30)		12		10	2
(31)	6	4	2	4	2
(32)	1	11		6	5
(33)	2	3	7	1	9

In (30)–(31) *holen* has a directional NP, which violates rule (29). There is, however, the complex verb *reinholen*. Hence, (30) seems to be considered grammatical throughout. But half of the informants reject (31), presumably based upon rule (29). The other half of the informants try to extend rule (29). Four of them conform to rule (23) – they construe H's position inside the house, but they also conform to (15') since they construe S's position inside the house as well. The answers to (32) show that for (31) and (32) similar situations are assumed. These informants thus claim the interchangeability of *holen* und *bringen* regardless of the different forms *hinein* und *herein*. Other informants construe identical situations for (30) and (32). Since the results showed a considerable difficulty in carrying out the task, I added another test. My hypothesis was that a sound extension of (29) could follow the rules (22) and (23) throughout. This would predict the following results:

	S is inside	S is outside	H is inside	H is outside
(30)	X		X	
(31)		X	X	
(32)	X			X
(33)		X		X

Linguistic Strategies 289

Moreover, I assumed that the situations with H being outside could suitably only be verbalized by means of *bringen*. The test was then reduced to the following question.

S intends that H carries the bucket, which is in the courtyard, into the house.

Situation 1 (cf. figure 7)
Both S and H are inside.
What would S say?

(32)   1
(30)   21 (95%)
other   -

Situation 2 (cf. figure 8)
S is outside, H is inside.
What would S say?

(33)   4
(31)   14 (65%)
other   4

The answers are indicated in the right column.

Figure 7   Figure 8

The results show that with respect to (30) the answers are as unanimous as in the first test. The percentage of informants who reject (31) as well as the percentage of those who interchange with the use of *bringen* has, however, been reduced drastically.

The informants in the first test were given too much freedom. They had to decide between 4 alternative situations. As a consequence of this they extended rule (29) in a more or less accidental way, their way of solving the conflict could not be controlled. On the other hand, the informants in the second test were given a fixed situation, they had to decide between two alternative utterances.

What is the moral of these considerations?

One moral is this. The informant cannot analyze the whole problem. On the basis of a foregoing analysis and a clear hypothesis the linguist must present to him only a few alternatives not confronting him with too many conflicts at a time. Another moral is this. Informants find it much easier to react verbally to a given situation than to contextualize a given sentence. Only the former task, however, corresponds to his daily practice.

Let us briefly consider another type of conflict which arises if the rule of number and gender agreement in German cannot consistently be followed. This rule is given in (34):

(34) The finite verb agrees in number and gender with the subject NP.

In sentences like (35)–(36), the native speaker of German has to decide between two competing forms of the verb, or he has to rule out the sentences as being ungrammatical.

(35) *Nicht er, sondern du* $\begin{Bmatrix} mu\beta \\ mu\beta t \end{Bmatrix}$ *mich besuchen.*
('Not he but you must visit me')

(36) *Nicht seine Fähigkeiten, sondern seine Ausdauer*
$\begin{Bmatrix} haben \\ hat \end{Bmatrix}$ *ihm geholfen.*
('Not his skills but his persistence $\begin{Bmatrix} has \\ have \end{Bmatrix}$ helped him')

Most speakers choose the second alternative, *mußt* or *hat* respectively, which agrees with the second subject NP. Only very few (less than 15%) consider the sentences as being ungrammatical or even problematic.

What was the strategy to solve the conflict with rule (34)? The German Grammar of Helbig-Buscha (1972, p.32f.) states the following strategy:

(37) If there are different subject NPs, partly affirmative and partly negative, then the finite verb agrees with the affirmative subject NP.

This strategy is semantically based, as the predicate is rejected for the negative subject but asserted for the affirmative subject. The strategy seems to be effective for (35)–(36).

In order to examine the validity of (37) some informants were presented (38) and (39).

Linguistic Strategies

(38) *Seine Ausdauer, nicht seine Fähigkeiten* $\left\{\begin{array}{l}hat\\haben\end{array}\right\}$ *ihm geholfen.*

('His persistence not his skills $\left\{\begin{array}{l}\text{has}\\\text{have}\end{array}\right\}$ helped him')

(39) *Für ihn* $\left\{\begin{array}{l}steht\\stehen\end{array}\right\}$ *nicht der Beruf, sondern die Freunde im Vordergrund.*

('For him, not his job but his friends $\left\{\begin{array}{l}\text{is}\\\text{are}\end{array}\right\}$ important')

The subjects had to choose one of the alternatives by stating their degree of certainty (50, 75, or 100%). In (38), *hat* got a total of 10% and *haben* a total of 45%, while in (39) *steht* got 35% and *stehen* 15%.

These results clearly rule out (37) as a valid strategy. This strategy can only be effective if it is supported by the position of the NPs. Otherwise we have both a high degree of unacceptability (conforming to the former rule (34)) and some other superseding strategy. This strategy concerns the relative position of the NPs:

(40) If there are more than one subject NPs, the finite verb agrees with the most adjacent one.

This strategy may be based on a structural consideration. We can look at (35), (36), (38) and (39) as elliptical sentences. There may be a deletion rule for a second finite verb operating even when the forms of the verbs do not correspond.

(32') *Nicht er muß mich besuchen, sondern du mußt mich besuchen.*
         ↓   ↓
         φ   φ

Strategy (40) is effective for (35)–(36) *and* for (38)–(39). But it cannot be the only strategy at work, because (35)–(36) are much more acceptable than (38)–(39). We are thus forced to conclude that besides (40) also (34) is effective. Whenever (40) and (34) complement each other the respective sentence will be almost fully acceptable, but if (34) conflicts with (40) the effectiveness of (40) is weakened, and the resulting sentence will only be partly acceptable.

In cases such as (41)–(44) still another strategy is at work.

(41) *Eine Dose Erbsen* $\left\{\begin{array}{l}kann\\können\end{array}\right\}$ *zubereitet werden.*

('A tin of peas can be prepared')

(42) Eine Handvoll Männer $\begin{Bmatrix} \text{erreicht} \\ \text{erreichen} \end{Bmatrix}$ das Meer.
 ('A handful of men $\begin{Bmatrix} \text{arrives} \\ \text{arrive} \end{Bmatrix}$ at the sea shore')

(43) Eine Menge Kohlen $\begin{Bmatrix} \text{wird} \\ \text{werden} \end{Bmatrix}$ gekauft.
 ('A lot of coal will be bought')

(44) Eine Reihe Bücher $\begin{Bmatrix} \text{wird} \\ \text{werden} \end{Bmatrix}$ gekauft.
 ('A number of books will be bought')

The results are shown in the following chart.

	singular	plural
(41)	93 %	–
(42)	55 %	25 %
(43)	45 %	35 %
(44)	20%	50 %

The conflict is between the quantity NP in the singular and the quantified N in the plural. Obviously, the options for singular or plural in the finite verb range on a continuum. The following semantic-pragmatic strategy seems to work here:

(45) If you can give the predicate with respect to the subject an undivided reading choose the singular, if you can give a divided reading choose the plural.

All informants seem to consider the preparing of a tin meal as a single, undivided activity, whereas the majority of informants consider the buying of books as an iterative, divided activity. If singular and plural get about the same percentages we can conclude that the informants are equally divided between those who conceive of a single activity and those who conceive of a divided activity. This seems to constitute a fact about possible experiences in our society. (45) is thus an experience-based strategy.

However, two points should be added.

(i) In every particular instance of using (43) or (44) we can assume a certain knowledge of the contextual background. If the informant was put into a situation where a number of books is bought at once or a

Linguistic Strategies 293

lot of coal is bought piece by piece, he would presumably control his choice by such an information.

(ii) The choice of number agreement is sensitive to the type of construction. When we presented the informants (46),

(46) *Eine Reihe von Büchern* $\begin{Bmatrix} wird \\ werden \end{Bmatrix}$ *gekauft.*

instead of (44), about 80% of them chose the singular. Besides the variation due to the background knowledge, we thus find another variation due to the specific verbal means of a language.

CONCLUSIONS

We have had strategies relying on an experiential background (e.g., (45)), on general functional properties of objects (e.g., (13)), on semantic features (e.g., (11), (37)), or on syntactic considerations (e.g., (29), (40)). Are there any general principles governing such strategies? Is there, for instance, some hierarchy of syntactically, semantically and functionally based strategies? Is it the case that a conflict with a syntactical rule can be solved in either way, but a conflict with a semantical rule only by semantically or functionally based strategies, not by syntactically based strategies? It seems to me that we are far away from answering those questions. The gap between detailed investigation and broad generalization is still far too large. I shall, therefore, restrict myself to a couple of further comments.

Let us first take another look at the problems considered so far. What was the relevant task structure of the respective informant situations? In the section 'Deictic versus intrinsic perspective' I considered the situational (referential, pragmatic and functional) components determining the choice of the deictic or the intrinsic perspective. At first I presented a comprehension task simulating an instruction situation. The informants had to follow the instruction within a fixed context, ((1)–(2)). Next, I presented a production task. The informants had, again within a fixed context, to select a verbal utterance matching the context ((3)–(10)). In both tests, there were only two alternatives. In some of the examples the selection strategies conflicted with each other. But as the informant had only to make an arbitrary decision, no procedures to solve such a conflict could be determined. The selection strategies constituted a continuum between the two perspectives but did not seem to be hierarchically organized.

In 'Indeterminacies and rule conflicts', I was concerned with two different kinds of rule extension. First I considered the movement verb *holen*, the grammatical frame of which had to be extended ((30)-(33)). One solution was to replace it by another verb, *bringen*, which happens to require just that frame. Another strategy was based on a thorough application of a referential use-condition obtained from preceding analysis. The informants were first given a contextualization task. They had to select the proper referential conditions for a given utterance. There were more than two alternatives, and only few of them produced an analysis to be required for a consistent extension of the rule in question. Therefore, a considerable number of informants were not ready to extend the grammatical rule; either they rejected the sentence or they produced a context predicting the exchangeability with *bringen*. Then I presented a reduced production task. The informants had to select the proper utterance for a given context. Only two alternatives were given. This simplified test seems to have enabled the informants to extend the rule. In this case a contextual or referential strategy determined the frame extension.

Finally, I considered possible extensions of the number and gender agreement rule ((38)-(39)), ((41)-(44)). In one case the strategy was syntactically motivated but semantically controlled. In the other case the extension led to a continuum which was seemingly controlled exclusively by an experiential strategy. In both cases I presented a production task. The informants had to choose between two alternatives in gender or number. The experiential strategy just mentioned could, however, be more strictly fixed by presenting appropriate contexts. Then the strategy would turn into a referential or contextual one. If we speak of experience with regard to linguistic tasks, what we mean is often only the ability to produce contexts relative to which the utterance is appropriate or true.

We can demonstrate the dependence on experience by another test. The informants were presented sentence fragments with an empty space for either *und* ('and') or *aber* ('but').

(47) *Das Bier ist gut – kühl.*
('The beer is good – cold')

(48) *Max ist klein – schwach.*
('Max is short – weak')

(49) *Wir sitzen hier eng – unbequem.*
('We are sitting here close – inconvenient')

(50) *Das Klima ist warm – angenehm.*
('The climate is warm – pleasant')

(51) *Der Aufsatz ist kurz – interessant.*
('The article is short – interesting')

For these items and the corresponding items containing the respective antonyms, I received the following results.

	und	aber
(47)	100 %	–
(48)	93 %	7 %
(49)	89 %	11 %
(50)	79 %	21 %
(51)	57 %	43 %

What is the strategy guiding the solution of this task? If a good beer is considered to be a cold one, we cannot use *aber*. The use of *aber* implies that the opposite of some feature which could be expected (normally, under certain conditions) holds. Thus, the results indicate that the majority of subjects think that a warm climate is pleasant. Although the strategy of choosing between *und* and *aber* is linguistically controlled, it is based on nonlinguistic experiences, or preference, or even association. This might be of interest to the psychologist but not to the linguist.

We can, however, change the task as follows. We present some of the defining or inducing contexts verbally, e.g.,

– Beer is only good, if it is cold.
– If the climate is warm, it is pleasant.

and then present the informants with the task of filling in the gaps. The strategy of selecting between *und* and *aber* will now be semantically based. We will not get any results about individual preferences, which are of little interest, but results about inferences which are very interesting. In a way, it is a truism to speak of experientially based linguistic strategies. Every case of this sort indicates that the informant was allowed too much freedom, or, to put it differently, that our experimental design was not specific enough. Tests of the kind discussed in this paper can only lead to interesting results if the informant is restricted with respect to the freedom of the choice he is supposed to make, or even more importantly, with respect to the strategies he may apply.

Let us finally ask: what *are* these strategies I have discussed so far? Every native speaker has at his disposal a set of grammatical rules, which enable him to compose or to decompose sentences of his language. In every verbal situation, he (or she) must make use of these rules in order to produce or to comprehend an utterance, or to judge possible utterances. This is determined by certain strategies. These strategies have a much clearer psychological nature than grammatical rules. It is those strategies that relate the utterance with a situational (referential and functional) or with an experiential background.

Linguistic strategies are, however, not arbitrary. They are acquired during the global process of language acquisition. They have certain features, they are based, for instance, on syntactical, referential or functional properties.

The strategies I have discussed here fall into three groups, at least: one kind of strategies relates to the respective orientation in space and time; another kind of strategies governs the possible extension of grammatical frames; and a third kind serves to solve a latent rule conflict which arises when a grammatical pattern has been produced which is not straightforwardly continuable.

In a way, linguistic strategies are the essence of verbal behavior, whereas grammatical rules are only their sediments. Typologically, grammatical rules of different languages can be compared by the strategies which lie behind these rules. Strategies do not only extend rules or solve rule conflicts, they can also be subject to grammaticalization in a particular language. With the verb *reinholen,* for instance, a certain spatial orientation has been lexicalized in German. And with the difference of *eine Reihe Bücher, eine Reihe von Büchern,* and *eine Reihe dieser Bücher,* a certain individuation strategy has been put into a scale of grammatical patterns of German.

The ultimate hope is that a thorough study of linguistic strategies will not only shed new light upon the native speaker's real behavior but also give an explanatory background for language typology and, at the same time, for the proper individuation of particular languages.

ACKNOWLEDGEMENTS

I thank Florian Coulmas for his initiative and his generous advice. I also thank the students who performed some of the tests, especially Harald Mispelkamp. I was inspired in this chapter by works of H. Seiler, M. Reis, G. A. Miller and P. N. Johnson-Laird.

REFERENCE

Helbig, G., Buscha, J. (1972). Deutsche Grammatik. Ein Handbuch für den Ausländerunterricht. Leipzig: Verlag Enzyklopädie.

PART FIVE

Aspects of Language Acquisition and Use

WALBURGA VON RAFFLER-ENGEL

The Native Speaker in his New Found Body

ABSTRACT

In the past, linguists transcribed what a male native speaker said. If they jotted down notes on any behavior that was not strictly verbal they did this only for a prop for the time they would get down to the real business of analyzing the verbal transcript. Then they proceeded to analyze these transcripts as if they had been written to begin with. Eventually linguists no longer even transcribed anything, they only generated well-formed sentences and the linguist became his own native speaker. This approach is criticised on the grounds that the native speaker may be male or female and that face-to-face interaction is pluri-modal, its meaning consisting of the sum of the verbal and the nonverbal component plus the shared presuppositions, the social situation, and the inter-personal relationship.

When presenting scientific findings dealing with human behavior it is customary to inform the reader about one's research design, one's subjects, and the statistical evidence for one's conclusions. Most journal articles and books in linguistics present the data as a given, then develop an *ad hoc* methodology and come to conclusions that can easily be challenged. In the past most challenges have centered around the methodology. It is time now for a vital challenge of the subject population.

Subject population, that is a euphemism. Most of the time the lonely subject was one mystical native speaker who could even be the author himself. In the latter case the data were produced through introspection. This paper will concentrate on the concept of the native speaker, the informant who was generally defined as an average speaker. What was not defined was what qualified the speaker to be average. Eventually, linguistic theoreticians produced the fully perfect average native speaker and called him the ideal speaker-hearer. The ideal this mythical creature conformed to was that of the linguistic theoretician. It was tacitly assumed that to be an ideal speaker automatically qualified for being an ideal hearer. Production and perception were considered mirror processes by stated definition. Linguists knew intuitively how the ideal speaker-hearer programmed his speech. The informant had been a bit removed from his patronizing analyst but the ideal speaker-hearer shared a common innate competence with his analyst. Differences among speakers and between the speaker and the analyst were more trifle performance and unworthy of linguistic investigation.

Anthropological linguists were aware of the fact that speech communities are not homegeneous but did not worry about increasing their subject population for statistical purposes. They simply layered their data according to one average old informant, one average middle aged informant, and one average young informant.

The sociolinguists divided native speakers by social class and even realized that each social class had more than one speaker. Eventually, the native speaker was also endowed with a cultural background which manifested itself in the ethnography of speaking.

The average native speaker was always male. The average woman entered the subject pool only recently. She is generally still so average that be she young and middle class or old and lower class she can be compared to any type of average man. She is also so average that her verbal behavior can be examined without regard to the social situation in which it takes place. Women's language and men's language about women were scrutinized for their relationship to power politics. The native speaker had finally acquired sex albeit very little of it was biological. Except for his or her pitch all differences were culturally induced.

The early informant spoke in the monologue. When he was not limited to short answers he was asked to recount a story. It remained to the ethnomethodologist to go beyond such highly unnatural language samples. They also realized that the interpersonal relationship between subjects had its impact on the language used by the conversation partners. The native speaker was no longer so lonely and now we have interacting native speakers, mostly in the dyad. Groups are difficult to analyze and treated more rarely. Having someone to speak to and to listen to in the natural give and take of human discourse showed to the linguist that there were certain shared presuppositions between the interactants. The native speaker had 'feedforward' and feedback, both of which are extremely difficult to simulate in artificial intelligence. Interactional behavior was quite different from the simple answering behavior of the earlier informant. The native speaker was finally speaking rather than merely providing elicited responses. The gap widened between the native speaker and the computer. The native speaker was happy. He had less memory but a more complex comprehension than the computer. He had become human. The question now was to see how he differed from the higher animals. Does he differ in kind or in degree? The native speaker now was joined by the native chimp.

Through the interactional approach the robot-like informant had finally become a native speaker not in name only. What he still did not have was a

The Native Speaker in His New Found Body

body. He had a mouth of which the lips, spread or rounded, were visible; and he had a well explored oral cavity and speech organs down to the lungs. But his mouth was not in a face. He neither smiled or frowned. The native speaker was strictly verbal. His 'yes' and his 'no' were recorded but if he nodded or shook his head this was not a legitimate part of his expression. He had to state clearly that he did not understand if his eyes roving aimlessly were to be credited with some communication problem. Deictics were surface manifestations derived from lengthy deep structures and understood through a series of back transformations. A pointing finger was no part of that surface, nor was it in the deep. If someone only had invented an ordered set of deictic movement transformations the native speaker might have been endowed with hands, or at least with a finger or with a lower lip. But as nobody did, all the native speaker could move were his articulatory organs.

The stern informant did produce modulated speech. Stress was analyzed and found morphologically significant. Intonation contours became part of syntax. Paralanguage started to gain recognition. But this wild behavior did not last for long and the native speaker was soon redimensioned within his well formed verbality. Even little children were innately deprived of melody. To compensate, the native speaker gained a new part inside, the language acquisition device.

The structural linguists had transcribed what they heard from their informants and then analyzed their transcripts as if they were the real thing. They did not acknowledge that spoken language and written language are different modes of communication, not simply stylistic version of an identical mode. In the sixties the linguists who then called themselves modern went one step further. They no longer analyzed the transcripts of what they heard. That would have been trivial. They analyzed what was revealed to them from the native speaker's psyche — or was it their own? The ideal speaker-hearer had become a true idea.

Somehow going to the height (or depths?) or nirvana did regenerate the native speaker. In the nineteen seventies the native speaker resurrected as if he were new. He had a real body for the kinesicist to analyse. It was an orgy of body language. Over 90% of the native speaker's message was said to be communicated nonverbally. Women speakers had more of a body than men speakers. They were biologically more atuned to nonverbal cues. While women's verbal language had been all culturally conditioned her nonverbal sensitivity was all nature. If this sounds paradoxical, the native speaker was able to cope with it.

Even when the native speaker had no body he had always been healthy in mind and body. Pathological cases were treated more as a general phenomenon where speakers were just plain subjects and not necessarily native. Psychologists liked schizophrenic language, educators favored the retarded long before either discipline had established from what norm their data were deviant. Eventually, the language of the deaf was to be considered an alternate but basically normal form of communication. Sign language and the gesticulation of the native speaker were a bit confused. It took a while to notice that signers had gesticulation too.

There he was, the native speaker, normal, healthy, and equipped with a body. The two hemispheres of the brain cooperated through electrical circuits so that his hand and his mouth would not act in dyssynchrony. Linguists could no longer handle him by themselves. The native speaker no longer spoke, he communicated. The study of his communicative competence needed teamwork and multidisciplinary grant applications. Interdisciplinary researchers looked at the native speaker and called him man, then person, and finally human being. He communicated within his group and cross-culturally. Those native speakers who had been bilingual before now were bilingual-and-bicultural. Children in such societies had to learn not only two languages but also two kinesic systems. Researchers started looking at humans in real life situations. Child language specialists also looked at living children and discovered that children had mothers, fathers, siblings, and peers.

Researchers in linguistics, psychology, anthropology, sociology, and communication science listened and looked. The tape recorder gave way to film and tape. Was it the need for a look at total man that increasingly necessitated the use of the portable videopack or was it the development of affordable and manageable video equipment that generated kinesic research? Was it the general diffusion of television that convinced researchers that spoken and written language have to be analyzed with different approaches? Or was it the ever growing problem of children that could speak and understand but were unable to learn to read and write that shook linguists out of their lethargies?

Writing has to supply what in face-to-face communication is expressed nonverbally. By analyzing verbal transcripts as if they had originally been intended for writing linguists had been forced to find a way to supply all the information that in face-to-face interaction is provided nonverbally. They found it by creating theories of psycholinguistics that made verbal language more powerful than it is in reality positing all sorts of covert entities. When the native speaker acquired his body he overcame the theories that made his language so powerful. Having a body he was also able to step out of the lab.

The native speaker began as a robot like informant, he went on to an even more confining existence as a judge of grammaticality and collapsed inside the lab of the psycholinguist. But the native speaker is strong, he underwent an apotheosis and during the era of natural food and pure woollen fabrics he emerged in the naturalness condition. This writer is constantly skirting the borders of legality concealing her video equipment, and constantly harrassed

The Native Speaker in His New Found Body 303

by poor lighting, native speakers that move out of the range of the camera, or speak all at once. But the lack of continuity can be made up by extending the hours of tape and increasing the number of subjects, not to mention the time and energy it takes to evaluate the material. Except for tearing eyes the fatigue is rarely felt because the thought of studying human behavior in its raw state created genuine excitement between professor and students. The native speaker could provide great excitement in the past too, like when the linguist was able to fill the hole in phonemic symmetry. But it is quite a different type of exhiliration. Since the native speaker has adorned himself with a body he has become more mysterious. The analyst no longer has a clear idea of what to look for. Sometimes his first task is to figure out where to start at all.

The results of the research no longer have to be elegant. What counts is that they be true. Induction has superceded deduction. A great deal of time is spent in analyzing the surface manifestation, to use a term that has almost become obsolete. One now speaks again of just plain data. The native speaker by gaining his body has lost his split personality. In evaluating video taped performances the overt behavior of each interactant can be devided into three categories: the referential (informative) category, the regulatory (interactional) category, and the affective (emotional) category. All three categories can be expressed and perceived verbally as well as nonverbally, and frequently in both modalities at the same time. The latter multi-modal manifestation does not necessarily increase the amount of emphasis or of redundancy contained in the message because it may parallel a decrease in emphasis and/or redundancy in the overall pattern of either the vocal or the kinesic mode. Paralanguage and kinesics are particularly close and supposed to be together in the brain as opposed to language even though this writer does not fully understand how this happens given that kinesics can function as both language and paralanguage. Even before the native speaker acquired his body he had gotten a brain. The poor native speaker has been in a constant state of fever brain research still being very hot.

Even if he leaves the brain in medical school the linguist has come to realize that to analyze spoken language without its non-spoken concomitant is to misinterpret it. The verbal and the nonverbal component of the communicative interaction are produced and perceived interdependently. Their separation is an artifact of the analysis. We are all doing a lot of partial analysis because we know how to break down the components. To examine the native speaker in his entirety is still beyond our reach as we are yet not fully capable of reassembling the parts into their original whole. The native speaker, not having had his body for very long, feels a bit scattered and can't quite put himself together.

Since the native speaker acquired his body he has been able to venture outside academy where he has been man-watching and can be read like a book. The popular belief is that kinesics fulfills primarily the affective and the regulatory function while the referential message is conveyed mainly by verbal language. This is not so and it is not even possible to determine the precise percentage of importance of each of the three components in reference to the three functions. Such overlapping would have been extremely disturbing to the linguist of the past who worshipped neatness beginning from the separation of levels and ending with the lexicologists. The native speaker revolted against all this tidiness. And he is finally having a good laugh at his analyst. He laughs with sound (paralanguage), with a twinkle in his eyes (kinesics) and he even says how funny we all are (language). This is his considerate opinion (informational), and by it he regulates the conversation we have with him (interactional). We stop and think and don't quite know what to do. It's very depressing for us (emotional) but it is sheer vengeance for the native speaker. He orients his posture a bit away from the analyst, leans back on his chair in the typical gesture of dominance. "You studied me for so long" he says "and you know so little about me."

JOHN O. REGAN and ALAN L. ZIAJKA

Observing the Native Doer: Prelinguistic Behavior among Infants and Young Children

ABSTRACT

Preverbal action can be quite complex and is not always an imperfect substitution for speech. The observations presented in this paper show than nonverbal behavior of preverbal infants may follow a sequence of structured steps. Moreover, the communicative behavior prior to language is an important prerequisite of becoming a native speaker. The authors document, systematically describe, and assess the modes of communication that the preverbal child has at his disposal: the proxemic, the kinesic, the gestural, the ocular, the proprioceptive, and the vocal mode.

INTRODUCTION

The native speaker is first a native nonspeaker, an actor on the world, a preverbal communicator. He is first a doer, then a speaker. Our purposes here are to describe the modes of communication available to the preverbal child and to demonstrate the importance of the study of preverbal communication to researchers in linguistics and other disciplines.
  The history of human development is marked by the discovery of the value of previously unrecognized directions of study. Through sudden insights or a gradual shift in perspective, a topic once easily disregarded often becomes the pearl of great price. So it is that in research, what one generation of scientists by-passes as of little consequence becomes for another the object of great investment of resources.
  Until very recently the study of human communicative behavior has centered almost exclusively on the verbal-vocal mode.
  First, the history of language, then its nature, structure, and composition, dominated scholarship, and the methods and categories for phonological, morphological, and syntactical analysis were precisely defined and well established in the literature. This tradition and these firmly established tools helped perpetuate the focus of rigorous communication study on the verbal realm, and nonlinguistic communication data and preverbal subjects were

infrequently studied. Insufficient research data and insubstantial categories and procedures made even the limited study of nonlinguistic behavior problematical.

For various reasons, including recent interest in the nonverbal accompaniments of speech, or paralinguistic features, and the schools' efforts to adapt to pupils' learning/communication styles, the study of communication has been broadened to include all strategies, including non-linguistic ones, used to convey meaning. It is now generally recognized that during their first months of life, young children begin to learn the communication options at their disposal, what these modes can be used for, and how the use of these tools defines the individual as a social being, a member of a culture. Young children learn to use socially understood nonverbal communication modes long before they utter their first words.

Parents, like professional linguists, recognize that considerable communicative behavior takes place in the months before the child first utters a two-word sentence that can be understood by the native speaker. The nature and extent of this preverbal communication ability has not, however, traditionally been acknowledged. Typically, the nonverbal modes have been considered to be simply preliminaries to linguistic modes, limited in scope and power and incapable of sophisticated function; they have been considered viaducts only for imprecise, unintentional messages conveying auxiliary, emotional overtones. Pointing, crying, smiling, laughing, cooing behaviors as well as throwing, grabbing, pulling, for example, are generally regarded as immature efforts to do what will later be accomplished by language. Although for some such actions this judgment is appropriate, preverbal action is not always so simple, nor is it simply a substitution for speech. As the following observations demonstrate, nonverbal behavior may follow a sequence of architecturally sophisticated steps, and, indeed, in some cases (see, for example, Observations 8, 12, 15), it is difficult to construct verbal sequences as effective as nonverbal ones.

The remainder of this paper will describe these communication choices available to the young child prior to language.

THE STUDIES

The following observations are drawn from two studies involving a total of five observers who reported on the preverbal efforts of nine children to communicate with significant others. The preverbal modes through which these infants and young children communicated have been organized into six broad categories: (1) the proxemic mode, which includes the location, arrangement, and positioning of individuals in a communication context; (2)

the kinesic mode, which includes the finger, facial, and other small-muscle movements occurring in communication; (3) the gestural mode, which includes the distinctive hand and arm motions made by individuals in a communication context; (4) the ocular mode, which includes the nonverbal communication that takes place during eye contact; (5) the tactile-kinesthetic (proprioceptive) mode, which includes the nonverbal communication that occurs between individuals through the sense of touch and the sensation of movement; and (6) the vocal mode, which includes the communication that occurs between individuals through the use of the voice.

The Proxemic Mode

Anthropologist Edward Hall (1959, 1966, 1968, 1976) proposed throughout his writings that the various communication patterns through which people interact are at the core of culture. Although spoken language is one of the most significant of these culturally learned patterns, Hall stressed the importance of other forms of social interaction, such as *proxemic* behavior: the location, arrangement, and positioning of individuals in a communication context.

Hall's major concern was to identify and describe the ways in which people send nonverbal messages through the spatial relationships they create. He maintained that, like other nonverbal forms of communication, spatial messages are learned through cultural contact and, hence, vary among cultures and subcultures.

The ability to achieve communicative ends through nonverbal means appears very early in the child's life. By the end of their first year infants already know a great deal about the ways in which proxemic options can be used to maintain contact or distance, to interact with others, and to communicate nonverbally.

The three observations presented here illustrate how some infants use their proxemic tools to achieve ends. These observations also illustrate how in the real world communicative options cannot be isolated from one another. In a given context, several modes may be used simultaneously.

Observation 1. Joey's mother was sitting in a living room chair reading the morning newspaper. Her legs were crossed, and she slowly moved the foot that was off the floor in short, rhythmic arcs. Eight-month-old Joey, who was on the other side of the room over 10 feet away, intently watched this moving foot for approximately 2 minutes. He then crawled across the room, reached for the dangling foot with his hand, positioned it near his mouth, and started to chew on one of the laces on his mother's shoe. Joey's mother stopped reading, looked down, and moved her foot to one side, though with the lace still in Joey's mouth, her shoe came untied. She gently extracted the lace from her son's mouth, retied it, and went back to reading the paper. Within a few seconds, however, Joey had the lace back in his mouth. His mother again reached down and pulled the lace away, although this time it remained tied. This sequence of events was repeated once more before Joey's mother picked him up, placed him on her lap, and together they "read" the front page of the newspaper.

Observation 2. An observer briefly visited Alan's parents. Twenty-month-old Alan entered the kitchen where final preparations were being made for the family meal, and, as general conversation continued, went into the kitchen alcove and began pulling a chair towards the visitor. Seeing this action, Alan's parents began adding such words to the actions as "You're bringing him a chair to sit on." "Good boy, Alan, bringing a chair."

Observation 3. Twelve-month-old Natasha and her mother were at opposite ends of the living room, over 10 feet away from each other. Natasha's mother looked at her daughter, smiled, reached out her arms, and said, "Walk to mama." Natasha looked at her mother, toddled a few steps toward her, fell to her knees, crawled about 3 more feet, got up, took another few unsteady steps, and fell the last 2 feet into her mother's outstretched arms, making a high-pitched screeching sound as she was caught.

The Kinesic Mode

Anthropologist Ray Birdwhistell (1962, 1968, 1970) first employed the term *kinesics* to describe the study of the small muscle movements of the body and face that occur during communication. He maintained that kinesic behaviors such as body motion and facial expression are relative to a given culture and are therefore learned. As children develop, they learn the patterns of subtle communication movements – such as head nods, smiles, frowns, lid closures, brow movements, and nose and mouth positions – of their culture, much as they learn language. Learning these kinesic movements helps children become communicative participants in their culture.

Smiling was one of the most salient kinesic options used by the young children in the sample. Observations 4 and 5 illustrate how this mode, in conjunction with other tools, was used in natural settings.

Observation 4. Nine-month-old Ann and her mother were on the patio; Ann was at the edge of the cement pulling pieces of grass out of the lawn while her mother was 5 feet away, sitting in a chair, sipping ice tea. After a few minutes of alternately pulling grass and watching her mother drink tea, Ann crawled to her mother, pulled herself to a standing position by holding on to her mother's leg, and reached for the coffee mug her mother had placed near the edge of the table. Ann couldn't quite reach the mug, however, so her mother brought it to her daughter's lips. After the first gulp, part of which rolled down Ann's chin, Ann looked at her mother's face and gave her a broad smile which was immediately returned by her mother. For the next 60 seconds mother and child engaged in a sequential pattern of tea drinking and smiling.

Observation 5. One of ten-month-old Joey's playthings was a large plastic tube, about

3 feet in length and a foot in diameter. One afternoon, Joey's mother placed this object on the living room rug, lay down facing one end, looked through it as if it were a telescope, and said, "Where's Joey?" When her son bent down to look through the other end, she smiled at him, and both engaged in a 30-second bout of sustained smiling.

The Gestural Mode

Birdwhistell (1970) included gestures in his study as forms of kinesic behavior. Large, distinctive motions such as the "Okay" sign made with the hand, the "Victory" sign made with outstretched arms, and specific reading and pointing gestures are considered here, however, as a separate set of options. The antecedents of many of these nonverbal forms of communication can be seen in infant-adult interaction.

Recent studies of infant-adult interaction reveal the early age at which children begin to put gestures to work as communicative options. Bower (1977), for example, found that infants as young as 4 months use distinctive gestures such as reaching to achieve physical closeness with significant adults. Similarly, Rheingold (1969) observed 6-month-old infants using reaching gestures to initiate contact with others. Bowlby (1969) noted that the gesture of raised arms can be seen in infants of about 6 months when they crawl to their mothers and when their mothers approach them.

The young child's use of nonverbal gestures such as reaching and pointing are reported in observations 6 through 8.

Observation 6. Eight-month-old Ann was playing on the floor of the family room with some toy animals when her mother returned from the kitchen. Ann and her mother looked at each other for a moment from a distance of 5 feet, Ann's mother extended her hand to her child, and Ann responded by reaching her hand toward her mother in an almost exact imitative fashion. The mother walked to Ann, grasped both her child's hands, pulled Ann to a standing position, and held the child's arms as mother and daughter jointly walked – infant toddling more than walking – through the open sliding glass door into the backyard.

Observation 7. Heather's mother was talking on the phone while her 9-month-old daughter was playing with scraps of paper on the coffee table 2 feet away. Heather crumpled one piece of paper into a small ball, looked at her mother, and handed the ball to her. Heather's mother continued to talk on the phone but glanced at her daughter's proffered gift. She took the ball of paper from her daughter, held it a moment, and then gave it back. Heather took the ball of paper, put it in her mouth for a few seconds, and then again handed it to her mother. During the next 3 minutes, Heather sustained contact with her mother, who remained talking on the phone, through the exchange of a crumpled, and increasingly wet, ball of paper.

Observation 8. When Alan was 17 months old, he and his parents visited Steven's house to meet a house guest. After introductions, Alan and the eight other people that formed the group sat down at a table. The host sat across from Alan. As a social entertainment, one person introduced the familiar activity of asking Alan to point to a person when a name was given.

"Where is Sarah?" Alan pointed to the relevant person. "Where is Steven?" Alan pointed. As the game continued, Alan was asked to point to John. Alan unexpectedly pointed not at the host, the intended person, but to the visitor, who it had been forgotten was also called John. Alan apparently had heard his name during the introduction. "That's not the real John," the host in mock indignation said. Humorous comments ensued.

As the conversation topic shifted, Alan slipped down from his high chair and passed behind the four people between him and the other end of the table. He went directly to the host, took hold of his arm, and tugged. His next action was to sustain the tug until the host rose and followed him to a clearing on the floor. There Alan flopped down, sat with legs astride. As a final action, he picked up a toy car and pushed it along the floor to the now similarly seated John.

The Ocular Mode

Although the major focus of his work is on proxemic behavior, Hall (1959, 1966, 1968, 1976) also examined eye contact as a form of nonverbal communication that reveals important cross-cultural differences. He noted that English, French, and American men and women, for example, all make different "use of the eyes" when interacting in communication contexts (1966, pp. 143–145). The integration of eye contact with verbalization during conversations between adults provides another example of the way in which various options are used jointly in social interaction. People do not gaze randomly at one another in the course of a conversation; rather, they look at each other in orderly patterns, and their gazes play a significant part in synchronizing the flow of interaction.

Eye-to-eye contact is initiated and maintained between mother and preverbal child throughout a wide range of daily activities. Not infrequently, it is just a playful game that involves other modes as well, as observation 9 illustrates.

Observation 9. Nine-month-old Billy was sitting in his mother's lap when she reached down to retrieve a blanket on the floor. She lifted the blanket to her face, held it in front of her eyes for a few moments, and then jerked it below her chin line while simultaneously yelling, "Peek-a-boo!" Billy, who had been watching this sequence of events, loudly laughed when his mother's face was back in sight. Mother and child maintained eye contact for a few moments, smiled at each other, and the game was repeated several times, each time the mother holding the blanket a little longer in front of her face, assured that an expectant pair of infant eyes would be ready to meet hers when the blanket was pulled away.

A caretaker and infant may combine eye contact with mutual looking at the same object. Observation 10 illustrates how the ocular mode can be used by mother and child to maintain contact while simultaneously "discussing" an object with the eyes.

Observation 10. Nine-month-old Billy and his mother were in Billy's room. Billy's mother took a large toy train from a shelf, wound it up, placed it on the floor, and together she and her son watched it traverse an uneven circular pattern, occasionally running into other objects and stopping. Whenever this happened, Billy immediately looked at his mother, she returned the look, and then they simultaneously glanced down at the train. If his mother did not immediately remove the obstruction, Billy again looked at his mother, a glance she often awaited before starting the train once more.

The Tactile-Kinesthetic (Proprioceptive) Mode

In his book *The Hidden Dimension* (1966), Hall posited that the individual's relationship to the surrounding environment is mediated to a considerable degree by the tactile-kinesthetic mode. The sense of touch and the sensation of movement, according to Hall, are part of an "intimate transaction" with the surrounding world. Touch, for instance, "is the most personally experienced of all sensations" (1966, p.62). Hall also maintained that some cultures tend to inhibit and some cultures tend to encourage these sensory capacities. Japanese, for instance, according to Hall, emphasize the tactile-kinesthetic options more than do most urban Americans. These cross-cultural differences are communicated in interpersonal relationships, in art forms, and in the ambience of the home, as well as in many other ways (1966, p.62-63).

The young children in the sample frequently took the initiative in interacting with others through the tactile-kinesthetic mode. Observations 11 and 12 illustrate the use of these tools by preverbal children.

Observation 11. Joey's mother occasionally wore an old pair of shoes around the house, one of which had a hole in its bottom. One afternoon while she was sitting on the couch reading a book, 12-month-old Joey toddled over to her, holding onto the couch along the way for support. When he reached her, he got down on his knees and poked his finger through the hole in his mother's shoe, touching the exposed foot. His mother looked down, asked, "What's inside my shoe?" and both partners smiled and laughed at each other.

Observation 12. When he was 16 months old, Alan went over to Steven who was seated in a chair. Alan first touched Steven's hands, then took both of Steven's hands and, holding on, walked slowly backwards to an open place on the floor, and sat steadily looking at Steven, inviting him to play. Three times in the next weeks Alan was observed following this pattern, pulling people to places by taking their hands and moving them to a space on the floor.

The Vocal Mode

A major focus of the work of anthropological linguist Michael Halliday (1973, 1975, 1978a, 1978b, 1978c) is upon how children learn a social semiotic, an increasingly complex system of cultural meanings and social functions. Learning a language "consists of mastering certain basic functions of language and in developing a meaning potential in respect of each" (1975, p. 33).

Young children, however, convey meanings before they speak their first words. This, according to Halliday, is a "proto-language" composed of vocalizations that are used for instrumental, regulatory, interactional, and personal functions. Halliday defined this proto-language in terms of two criteria: systematicity and functionality. To be systematic, a consistent relationship must exist between meaning and the sound used to express that meaning; to be functional, the vocalization must have uses in the life of the child. As soon as systematic and functional expressions are present, according to Halliday, proto-language exists. Children learn in infancy that vocalizations can achieve certain ends for them, that vocalizations have meaning in the functions they serve. According to Halliday, for the preverbal infant "using [the] voice is doing something . . . a form of action . . . which soon develops its own patterns and its own significant contexts (1975, p.10). Thus, the investigator can begin to study a child's communication options at a time "before words and structures have evolved to take over the burden of realization" (1975, p.6).

Much of the communicative interaction between young children and the significant others in their lives takes place through the vocal mode. Observations 13 through 15 illustrate how vocal tools are often combined with other, nonverbal options.

Observation 13. Joey's mother pushed a large toy car in front of her eleven-month-old son while simultaneously making "rumm!" engine noises. Joey emitted a "tata" sound, reached for the car as it passed by, and together he and his mother pushed the car around the living room. Joey's mother alternately made the engine sounds and spoke the word "car" and Joey contributed his "tata" vocalizations as mother and child navigated the hair-pin turns on the highway leading around the dining room table, behind an overstuffed chair, and between a lamppost and the couch.

Observation 14. Eleven-month-old Heather was in the living room alternately taking the phone off its hook and then putting it back. Her mother, sitting in a chair 5 feet away, stopped reading the newspaper, looked up, and said, "Hello, Heather," just as her daughter picked up the phone for the fifth time. Heather paused briefly, looked at her mother, waved the phone in her hand, and emitted a long string of sounds – "Ya, yi, ya! Da, da, do! Yi . . . yi?" – vocalizations punctuated by pauses, stress, and rising intonation.

Observation 15. Marilyn, at 16 months was sure of sound. She made noises in a sophisticated way that called for interaction. The other person was supposed to either talk or

Observing the Native Doer 313

make noise back. Although Marilyn's communication did not contain a single word from the dictionary, the inflectional, gestural foundation was there; she knew when and where to stop for the others to speak and her voice rose into a question, fell in reply. At her door, one night, Marilyn engaged the observer in what sounded like an adult conversation. She leaned forward, looked through the screen door, and pointed in the direction her mother had just gone. Then she uttered a string of her own near words. Of these, not a syllable could be understood, but their general drift was clearly comprehensible, for the structure of conversation, its blueprint, was present. Marilyn went through preliminaries, made assertive and negative statements. She asked a question with its whole shape, intonation, pauses, emphasis, rhythm, body position. The adult nodded and said "Yes" in reply, and the child went on with another string of sounds as response. The adult nodded and responded again. This was followed by another question accompanied by a couple of steps down the hall, arm and finger pointing in the direction of where everyone was. "You stay; I'll get the person," it could have meant, or, "You want Steven? He's down there," or "Wait on, they won't be long." Again she waited for a response. When one was given she was satisfied and the conversation moved on.

CONCLUSION

The young child possesses many options for communicating with others prior to the development of language. These include various proxemic, kinesic, gestural, ocular, tactile-kinesthetic, and vocal tools. Some of these, such as the vocal options, crying, are present from birth, whereas others make their appearance during the child's first year of life. Gestures such as reaching and pointing, proxemic movements such as crawling, ocular skills such as the ability to follow an adult's look visually, and vocalizations of increasing sophistication all appear before words do and are used in various combinations in complex social interactions. Thus, in the course of the first months of life numerous options begin to function, often simultaneously, to promote interaction between the young child and other individuals.

The communicative interaction that takes place between infants and adults during the child's first months of life also is the precursor of later, adult linguistic behavior, and the communication options used by the young child for this interaction are the harbingers of adult verbal and nonverbal interactive modes. Before their first birthday, infants learn, for example, how to initiate and sustain interaction and become experts at modulating the flow of social exchange. Infants and adults come to share a code of nonverbal conduct long before they share a linguistic one, and the former provides the underpinning for the latter. What infants learn about nonverbal communication prior to language helps them later to acquire adult verbal and nonverbal choices.

The exchange that occurs during reciprocal looking, the give-and-take dialogue of preverbal vocalization and the gradual use by the infant of gestures and adult sounds are but a few examples of early antecedents of adult communicative patterns. Before employing their first words, for instance, young children combine vocal options such as stress, pitch, and juncture with gestures, arm motions, and finger movements to form the inflectional gestural foundation of language. Likewise, the exchange of looks between caretaker and infant is a kind of proto-conversation between parent and child, a powerful sign of communicative growth. The antecedents of what will later become a sophisticated interactional pattern involving language and various nonverbal modes can be seen in the visual exchange between infants and the significant adults in their lives. Further, many of the linguistic forms used by the older child and adult are derived from gestures that occur in infancy. Demonstrative sentences ("There is the cat"), for example, have their antecedents in the attempts by infants and young children to initiate social interaction by pointing to an object in the presence of an adult or older child. The use of specific gestures such as pointing is a major milestone on the road to language. Nonverbal gestural tools, however, do not cease to function when language appears. The gestures used by infants to interact with the significant human beings of their world continue to serve important functions throughout the life span.

Increasingly, the widening interests of linguists in the study of communication is providing impetus towards establishing workable systems of analysis. The broader dimensions of linguistic research will increasingly be found within the study of the verbal and nonverbal behavior of the native speaker. Until recently, a lacuna has existed in the plotting of this native speaker's development. This was a result of scholarship's disregard for children's preverbal experiences as a source of valued data. This disregard produced both a gap in theoretical knowledge and a paucity of information that could be applied to child rearing and educational practices.

To grapple with the nonverbal modes such that the communication of a child is studied as a whole, it is first necessary to establish in the discipline a recognition of the value of this area as a source of information. To this end we have presented examples from a series of participant observation studies aimed at establishing profiles of individual native doers – the precursors of our most favored informant, the native speaker.

REFERENCES

Birdwhistell, R. (1962). An approach to communication. *Family processes* 1: 194–201.
Birdwhistell, R. (1968). Communication. *International Encyclopedia of the Social Sciences*, Vol. III. New York: Macmillan.
Birdwhistell, R. (1970). *Kinesics and context: Essays on body motion communication.* Philadelphia: University of Pennsylvania Press.
Bower, T.G. (1977). *A primer of infant development.* San Francisco: Freeman.

Bowlby, J. (1969). *Attachment and loss,* Vol. I. London: Hogarth.
Hall, E. (1959). *The silent language.* New York: Doubleday.
Hall, E. (1966). *The hidden dimension.* Garden City, New York: Doubleday.
Hall, E. (1968). Proxemics. *Current Anthropology* 9: 83-108.
Hall, E. (1976). *Beyond culture.* Garden City, New York: Anchor Press.
Halliday, M.A.K. (1973). *Explorations in the functions of language.* London: Arnold.
Halliday, M.A.K. (1975). *Learning how to mean.* London: Arnold.
Halliday, M.A.K. (1978a). A sociosemiotic perspective on language development. In L. Bloom, ed., *Readings in language development.* New York: Wiley, 1978.
Halliday, M.A.K. (1978b). *Language as social semiotic.* London: Arnold, 1978.
Halliday, M.A.K. (1978c). Meaning and the construction of reality in early childhood. In H. Pick and E. Saltzman, eds., *Modes of perceiving and processing information.* Hillsdale, New Jersey: Lawrence Erlbaum, 1978.
Rheingold, H.L. (1969). The social and socializing infant. In D.A. Goslin, ed., *Handbook of socialization theory and research.* Chicago: Rand McNally, 1969, pp. 779-790.

TON VAN DER GEEST

How to Become a Native Speaker: One Simple Way

ABSTRACT

In the first part of the paper some general characteristics of the native speaker concept are discussed. The questionable objectivity with respect to linguistic intuitions is worked out in some detail: schooling, cultural influences, logical considerations vs. linguistic judgement, pedagogical practice etc. Finally, some methodological aspects and problems when working with the native speaker concept will be dealt with, and we conclude that this concept should be accepted at the idiolectical level, as linguistics is principally interested in the detection of the linguistic system and not so much in the question as to what degree native speakers' judgments correspond with each other.
In the second part of the paper we will characterize the native speaker as the ultimate state at which first and second language learners may arrive and as the ultimate goal in language pedagogy. Five different approaches in LA research will be discussed briefly with respect to semantic, syntactic, and interactive development. It will be argued (and demonstrated) that an interactive approach, in which both the child and the adult are assumed to be actively engaged in the developmental process explains most validly what is going on in first and second language learning.

INTRODUCTION

The first time I met the native speaker he was introduced to me as being a kind of lightning authority in the troublesome world of linguistic inquiry with its intuitions and judgements, a world that was full of trials, errors and uncertainties. Let me relate my experiences of him in a first chapter before dealing in a main chapter with the actual objective of this paper: the acquisition of a first and (or) second language to the level of a native language user. I will restrict my remarks to syntactic matters, although they all apply also to other linguistic areas, such as pragmatics.

In this first chapter I will first deal with the questionable objectivity of linguistic intuitions and with some aspects of the native speaker as an instrument to determine the correctness or incorrectness of a speech act. Finally we will discuss briefly some methodological difficulties when working with the native speaker concept, and we conclude that this concept should be accepted at the idiolectical level.

In the second chapter we will accept the native speaker as the ultimate state at which first and second language learners may arrive, and as the ultimate goal in language pedagogy. The main question may be how human beings may arrive at a full mastery of a language, as I am convinced that, by knowledge of the development processes, we learn a lot of the psychological processes and mechanisms as they occur in adult behavior.

SOME RELEVANT FEATURES OF THE NATIVE SPEAKER CONCEPT

The native speaker was presented to me as a man with a one hundred or more percent knowledge of the language under investigation. As such he was to be considered as a relative of the ideal speaker-hearer as far as the linguist's daily practice is concerned. (This ideal speaker-hearer is a man I have never met, but, on the basis of all kinds of rumours, I do not feel any affinity to him.) His daily task can be characterized as both to investigate the nature of language and to describe specific languages with the aid of our knowledge about the nature of human languages. In this field of linguistic activities the ideal speaker-hearer's role can be described as Chomsky (1965) did: "Linguistic theory is concerned primarily with an ideal speaker-listener in a completely homogeneous speech community who knows its language perfectly and is unaffected by such grammatically irrelevant conditions as memory limitations, distractions, shifts of attention and interest, and errors (random on characteristic) in applying his knowledge of the language in actual performance." Thus the ideal speaker-hearer is the linguist's projective concept of the perfect state of the linguistic system, with practically only one but rather important restriction, viz. our own understanding of this system since we are not ideal speaker-hearers and (or) linguists ourselves. This restriction implies that the linguist's capacity, his intuitions and judgements, are taken in practice as approximations of the ideal linguistic conception, and furthermore it implies that our intuition is not directly related to competence as it is highly determined by performance factors. As the problems and uncertainties in these kinds of linguistic activities can, under certain circumstances, be extremely great, some guarantees for correctness and restrictions ought to be built in. We shall return to this behavioral aspect of linguistic judgement later. One of the guarantees could perhaps be the native speaker: the linguist should either restrict his observations to his mother-tongue (linguist = native speaker), or he has to rely on judgements of one or more informants who are native speakers of the language he is dealing with.

How to Become a Native Speaker

Linguistic Intuitions

Chomsky (1957) emphasizes with respect to linguistic intuitions that only clear cases of grammaticality should be used to test the adequacy of a grammar, and that we should be prepared to let the grammar itself decide on the many intermediate cases. This standpoint led to the notion of semigrammaticalness (Chomsky, 1964) which could be handled and described by grammar itself. This idea, however, was to be rejected in standard-theory (Chomsky, 1965), so that we are at the mercy of our own linguistic intuitions again since then. In order to illustrate the danger of relying on one's own linguistic intuitions exclusively, I can mention the case from my own experience in grammatical investigation. As I wanted to be completely certain about the grammaticality of certain types of sentences on a certain occasion I asked some of my colleagues and a relative (my mother) to judge whether the sentences I presented to them were correct. The question I was dealing with was the synonymy between certain 'to+infinitive' and 'that–clause' complement sentences in Dutch. Furthermore I wanted to prove that if a sentence had an object complement, the pronominal dative could not be subjectivized in the passive sentence (which may be interesting when comparing these aspects with German and English). In table 1 the three types of judgements are represented for some crucial sentences (see also Van der Geest, 1968,ms).

From these judgements it could be hypothesized that if a verb has an obligatory complement clause (with '*to* + infinitive' most probably) then the 'that-sentence' is possible and the pronominal dative as subject is to be rejected. We cannot be certain about these possibilities, however, as the judgements contrasted with each other in the most crucial sentences. It is therefore obvious that both the criterion 'native speaker' (all three types of judgements) and the combination 'native speaker + linguist' (both I and my colleagues, which are presented in the table by a mean judgement) are insufficient, as they were contradictory on many occasions. Although it is self-evident to me after all these years that I was right in my judgements (after all of linguistics is normative by nature), I cannot definitely determine whether my mother's linguistic judgements were better or worse than those of the other native speaker-linguists, my colleagues, if we realized that my family, living close to the German border and speaking a low saxon dialect, could have problems with judging the *he* or *him* in these cases. On other occasions, however, my mother's judgements were more decisive. Now that the dialect as a disturbing factor in linguistic judgements is at issue, I remember a clause that one frequently would pick up on such occasions where linguistic intuitions were manifold but at the same time crucial and contradictory: "In my dialect . . ." in which *dialect* in my opinion almost got the status of *idiolect*.

Table 1: Three types of judgement with respect to 'to + infinitive' sentences; '+' = grammatical, etc.

Sentences	I	mother	colleague
Ik adviseerde hem te gaan (I advised him to go)	+	+	+
Hij werd geadviseerd te gaan (He was advised to go)	−	?	?
Hem werd geadviseerd te gaan (Him was advised to go)	+	+	+
Hij werd geadviseerd (He was advised)	+	+	+
Ik adviseerde hem dat hij zou gaan (I advised him that he should go)	−	−	+
Ik raade hem aan te gaan (I advised him to go)	+	+	+
Hij werd aangeraden te gaan	−	?	−
Hem werd aangeraden te gaan	+	+	+
Hij werd aangeraden	−	−	−
Ik raadde hem aan dat hij zou gaan	+	+	−

I will return to the inclusion of naive informants later. Now I will restrict myself to the remark that it often occurs that such observations of accepting or rejecting borderline sentences by referring to one's own dialect, play a crucial role in the proposed solutions and descriptions of the linguistic problems at issue. That this is not actually recommended was emphasized more than once by leading linguistic methodologists e.g. Chomsky (see Levelt, 1971 for discussion).

Normative Linguistics

As an outsider one could get the impression that such intuitive linguistic methods as sketched in the foregoing may lead to a rather normative viewpoint of language and its description. By over-emphasizing in their research the appropriate language form, whether it is syntactic or pragmatic, linguists neglect, in my opinion, the essential function of language to communicate meanings (or, in other words, mutual understanding), which often appears to be rather independent of formal matters. An example may clarify my point. It is a kind of unwritten rule — at least in American linguistics — in syntactic investigations to consider a grammatical or well-formed sentence as consisting of at least a subject and a predicate in the surface structure. Elliptical sentences, therefore, are often not considered as belonging to the set of sentences the language consist of. In this sense linguistics is as normative as, e.g., the standpoint of Bereiter and Engelman (1966) and of other compensatory educationalists who refuse(d) to accept such utterances as "In the tree" or "There" as the appropriate answer to the question "Where is the squirrel?" (see Labov, 1970), or such exclamations as "Into the dungeon with him!" that cannot immediately be traced back to so-called well-formed sentences. Linguists (with a few exceptions; e.g., Shopen, 1972; see Van der Geest, 1975 for discussion) neglect such kinds of sentences, although they can be described most of the time with similar kinds of rules such as equi-NP-deletion in complex sentences. Furthermore their contextual dependency is not greater than contextual phenomena, like deixis, anaphora, and other substitutions (e.g., the verb *do* in tags), which are all accepted by linguists.

Cultural Influences on Linguistic Intuitions

It seems to me that the linguistic behavior described above goes back to American/Anglo-Saxon pedagogical tradition in which the emphasis on 'subject-predicate' well-formedness plays an essential role (Bernard T. Tervoort, pers. communication): "Make a nice sentence, Johnny". This implies, that culture may determine to a certain extent what is grammatical or acceptable and that the school may play an interesting role in this respect.

Schooling

The role of the school (amount of schooling, linguistic or compensatory training, and so on) may determine to a large extent which is the appropriate way for a child to express himself verbally. Its role can hardly be overestimated. In Holland, for example, where 'subject-predicate' fetishism hardly played any role (at least until recently), thousands of children from age 3;0 onwards were trained linguistically in the late sixties with translations and adaptations of American compensatory programs. Once I observed that eight children had to answer one after the other the question: "Where is Tessa's bead?" (no girl with the name Tessa was in the group actually, nor did any child know a girl of that name). The answer was defined as: "Het kraaltje van Tessa *is* op de plank in de kast." (Tessa's bead is on the shelf in the cupboard.) Answers like "There." or "On the shelf." were not accepted. The eight literal repetitions of the sentence made clear that the children's actual achievement was only a better trained memory and not a more complex language use. If other compensation programs (see von Raffler-Engel et al., 1975) mention that children make fewer mistakes, then we can imagine that the characterization of mistakes is crucial for the judgement of this result. Anyhow the psycholinguist's translation of the program was without any doubt false, as the English verb of location 'to be' has to be translated with 'liggen' (to lie) as in German (liegen). Thus it happened to be that the native speaker psycholinguist was able to accept eight repetitions of an ungrammatical sentence in a language compensation program where a non-Dutch phenomenon of American tradition was trained intensively. A remarkable world.

Foreign Language Teaching

The last observation brings us to second language teaching. Are second language teachers and authors of second language course books afraid of the native speaker? Not the man who wrote a coursebook on Dutch as a second language for Germans (Huisman, 1974, 2nd edition). Apart from the facts that his linguistic explanations of phenomena which only exist in his own mind (1) are most of the time amusing and (2) illustrate the possibility of learning a second language in spite of the application of didactic institutional resources, he prescribes the German people how to use the rules of Dutch grammar. As an illustration consider the following instructive rule: Dutch has two possible comparative prepositions, viz. *dan* (than) and *als* (as) that are not interchangeable as *als* is only used with numerals: "12 is more *als* 10" and as *dan* on all other occasions is mandatory (I am discussing the second revised edition, wondering what the first edition may be like.) This rule I never found in a Dutch grammar, nor in Dutch speech. Older more conservative and normative grammars prescribe that *dan* is used in comparatives (John is bigger *dan* Peter) and *als* is used in structures like 'Peter is as small *als* Rudolf.' Many people, especially educated and older people will agree with this prescription. Other more progressive and descriptive approaches to grammar will have to admit that both words are mutually interchangeable, which reflects the daily practice of both the man in the street and many authors and poets who set the tone. This is only one of a number of instances in which foreign language instructors and their coursebooks present remarkable observations of the target language.

Another type of prescription one can find in idioms. Here, for whatever reasons, similarities between the first and second language are often either neglected or rejected and contrastive aspects are mentioned or introduced as the only appropriate translation or expression. For example, consider the following lexical entries in a Dutch-German idiom book:

How to Become a Native Speaker

vegen (to sweep) ≠ fegen; but = kehren
keren (to turn) = wenden
meer of minder (more or less) = mehr oder weniger ≠ mehr oder minder
verstaan (to hear) = verstehen
begrijpen (to understand) = verstehen
begrijpen ≠ begreifen
wijs maken (to make a person believe something) ≠ weiss machen; but = Geschichten erzählen

I restricted myself here to the level of the lexicon. It could, however, easily be expanded to examples from other linguistic areas, such as syntax and pragmatics, which would all confirm the experiences of people who initially learned a foreign language at school and afterwards in the natural situation, that they had to relearn their lessons. All kinds of forbidden things are actually practised and function apparently as a kind of *shibboleth* for the native speaker. We can only guess what the reasons for this type of didactic behavior are. It can be found in almost all kinds of pedagogical situations where an additional problem has to be taken into consideration: either in compensatory education for disadvantaged children, children with hearing loss, aphasic patients, etc., or in second language learning situations in the school. An international example can be taken from the education of the deaf in which one applies one of two conflicting methods: the free or maternal reflective method or the tied method in which a restricted part of the language is taught and trained in artificial educational settings which disregard the actual situation and experiences of the children. In this method the so-called Fitzgerald Key is applied, by which is meant a set of basic structures, which the child should learn to handle. Object-subject-verb word order is neglected (two apples I ate) and the passive construction, the topicalized structures, (pseudo) cleft sentences, adverb initial structures, etc. are widely neglected in this key, although it is obvious that these structures are frequently used in daily speech and also in conversations with language learning children. We may fear that children educated by this method have large difficulties in understanding the speech of the environment, as the Fitzgerald Key adaptations with respect to the situation of special education does not necessarily correspond with the adult speaker's natural language adaptation when he is talking with a person who is learning his language. We will return to the role of adaptation in language acquisition below in (Ch. 2.).

Foreign Language Informants

Closely related to the problem discussed above is the information one gets about a language one does not speak as a native speaker. Take, for example, the case that we are studying prominence in interpretation. In such a study one could expect the hypothesis to occur that in elliptical sentences without context one reading is more prominent than the other ones. So one can imagine that in languages in which the verb 'to be' is used in order to speak about one's age the expected and therefore prominent specification '*years (old)*' can be omitted, e.g.

(1) *She is forty*
(2) *Sie ist vierzig*
(3) *Zij is veertig*

in contrast with for example

(4) **Elle a quarante*

but:

(5) *Elle a quarante ans*

Unfortunately, however, when native speaker informants are asked whether such sentences are grammatical they often reject (2) and (3) on whatever grounds, although one can observe such utterances in daily conversation more than just occasionally. This means that there is no reason to trust the judgements of (naive or professional) informants more than one's linguistic intuitions with respect to one's mother-tongue. The same disturbing factors could play their role, in school, for example.

Logical Considerations in Linguistic Judgements.

A last disturbing factor to be mentioned with respect to the native speaker's judgements of grammatical correctness is that a language form is considered to be of a fully logical nature. Labov discusses this topic in some detail and presents a number of examples of remarkable conclusions to which the identification of logical and linguistic considerations may lead. Quite exemplificatory is the double negation in nonstandard black English, which is rejected by compensatory educationalists as this would be the converse meaning of what actually was meant, and had to be substituted therefore by the single negation of standard English. However, several other languages, such as French, Old English, and some Dutch dialects, all show this phenomenon.

Also the *als*(*as*)-*dan*(*than*) mentioned in the preceding section can be traced back to this phenomenon, as it was introduced by men of letters artificially in the seventeenth century. Another striking example is the probably common opinion among Dutch linguists that one has to say:

(6) *Ik ken Engels*
    (I know English)

in spite of the fact that the capacity of speaking and understanding is meant. The linguistic (pre- or descriptive) rule is: *kunnen* (*can*) is to be used with verbs, *kennen* (*to know*) is to be used with nouns. The man in the street and many dialects in Holland have a different usage in this respect. That the proposed solution is linguistically fully arbitrary, seems obvious to me, as the two languages that are most related to Dutch have opposite solutions:

(7) I know some English (English)
(8) Ich kann Englisch (German)

Also French does not present us evidence in this matter because in this language one has to say:

(9) Je parle anglais
    (I speak English)

The problem in such cases as presented here is that frequently one cannot determine whether one's intuitions rest on logical considerations or on linguistic reasoning, if this latter reasoning is something different from the simple statement that a certain linguistic phenomenon is actually used.

This applies to many tests used to judge grammaticality as, e.g., the 'do so' test in which one sometimes cannot decide between the logical conclusion that only action verbs are 'do so' verbs and the intuitive linguistic feeling that 'John went to New York and so did Peter' is grammatical and acceptable. First of all paraphrases often sound artificial as they are long winded in comparison with the more natural 'John and Peter went to New York.' Secondly in other languages (e.g. Dutch and German) 'do' — substitution is not so frequently used as in English and, what is more important, it is used differently in these languages.

The above examples demonstrate that linguistic solutions with respect to syntax are often intermingled with logico-semantic considerations. The problem of accepting borderline sentences is again at stake here. In the next section we will deal with this problem from a psychological viewpoint.

Some Psychological Considerations with Respect to Linguistic Intuitions

I know of only a few psycholinguistic studies on the reliability of linguistic and native speaker judgements and intuitions with respect to grammatical correctness.

First of all Bever (1970) should be mentioned. He worried about the fact that linguists emphasize that speaking and hearing are affected by disturbing performance factors whereas they treat judgements about sentences for some reason as exempt from the influence of performance variables. He suggests furthermore that if we would take sentences from several linguistic articles these sentences would receive the same judgements as in the original papers if we would present them in the original order and context, but probably very different judgements if we would present them mixed with each other. Finally he suspects that a linguist's grammar might differ from a performance grammar with respect to the accepted rules.

Levelt (1971) repeats Bever's complaints and offers some evidence. Fourteen sentences from a volume edited by Jacobs and Rosenbaum (1970) were judged by 24 trained linguists, anglicists, but actually all were non-native speakers of English. It appeared that the ungrammatical cases had less chance (4.2 judgements) of being judged ungrammatical than grammatical sentences (8.6 judgements). Furthermore, he found (see also Bever, 1970) that judgements in isolation are very different from judgements by contrast, and his conclusions could easily be reformulated to hints for obscure linguists: "If a linguist wants a borderline sentence to be grammatical, he should place it at the end of the list of very ungrammatical examples." or "If many grammatical examples are given, one slightly less grammatical case will be judged 'ungrammatical'."

Finally Levelt presents some precautions which are interesting in the light of the present discussion:

1. Any unnecessary loading (of short term memory and (or) distracting semantic loading) should be avoided.
2. The linguist should not rely only on his judgements nor on those of other linguists but should check them against those of at least a few native speaking linguists.
3. If he cannot restrict himself to the use of clear cases, then the linguist should confine himself to judgements about the rank order of grammaticality, and should present his informant a pair of sentences and ask him which one is more (or less) grammatical.

Snow (1975) accepts Levelt's suggestions for an improved methodology of testing linguistic intuitions. The two experiments she reported firstly confirm

Levelt's findings, but now with native non-linguist speakers. Her data consisted of twenty unclear sentences from Kraak and Klooster (1968) and 20 equivalent forms. It appeared that judgements of the sentence pairs differ widely with respect to acceptability and in reliability, which means that the subjects changed their judgements considerably (20-40%) within a few weeks. Furthermore, she found in the second experiment that acceptability largely depends on the context in the test, as already suggested by Levelt.

In conclusion she suggests a kind of methodology of testing linguistic intuition that can easily be characterized as originating from experimental psychology, e.g.,

1. test naive subjects, not linguists;
2. select subjects (by using pre-tests) who can give reliable judgements;
3. test enough subjects in order to determine dialectal and idiolectal variation;
4. present one or more alternative forms, etc.

It is clear that in such a test all kinds of performance factors, and subject features like sex, educational background, etc. can be controlled. Such an approach would, however, deny the independent and deductive status of linguistics. Furthermore, it would force a method upon a linguist which cannot solve adequately the problems of experimental psychology itself (see Wottawa, 1977, 1979, for an interesting discussion on fundamental errors in psychological methodology).

CONCLUDING REMARKS

I have made some remarks about the concept of the 'native speaker' as it was conceived in linguistic and psycholinguistic methodology during the last two decades. As it is most often applied explicitly in transformational (psycho) linguistics, and therefore in the first place functions in syntactically oriented investigations, I have restricted these remarks to current syntactic ideas and working methods of American linguistics.

Also in data oriented analyses or in semantic or pragmatic investigations we are permanently dealing with the 'native speaker' idea as long as we base our research fundamentally on our own judgements of utterances, speech acts, meanings or sentences, or on those of colleagues or incidental informants, and not on the systematic experimental investigation of reliable, average, and consistent linguistic judgements.

By accepting in principle our capability to judge linguistic cases, we accept both the native speaker concept and also the ethnomethodological starting point that we are allowed to interpret and capable of interpreting social behavior occuring in a given culture as long as we are members of that culture (Garfinkel, 1967). In fact, I think that almost all scholars accepting this starting point for their research are convinced nowadays of the many risks that are involved in this type of deductive reasoning. It is all just a matter of choice and of being practical, because the alternative is not without risks either.

On the one hand, we can restrict ourselves to time-consuming linguistic tests as is proposed by Snow (1975). Let us accept for a while the correctness of this methodological standpoint. Such a standpoint leads to an intensive data gathering activity which could ultimately bring results, if correct, that were clear anyway. If we restrict ourselves to clear grammatical or ungrammatical cases (the overwhelming majority of all cases) we may assume that almost complete agreement between linguists can be achieved. All experimental evidence against native speaker consistency and reliability concern the so-called unclear cases and can be neglected as such in the present discussion. Furthermore, there are a lot of disturbing factors in experimental testing – as Levelt (1971) and Snow (1975) not only admit but actually demonstrate with their data – that could possibly lead to results that are intuitively incorrect. Incidentally we know of many experimental studies in psychology showing that such results only rarely lead to the rejection of a theory or a subtheory, but to a refinement of the experimental testing design, to reinvestigate the phenomenon at issue. Apparently intuition ultimately determines the progress in research in the field of experimental psychology too. First of all, this is apparent from the fact that the experimenter's common sense is (happily?) stronger than his methodological shackles. That this is after all reasonable may become evident from the growing resistance to Spearman-statistically oriented methodology in which the status of the null-hypothesis and the 'population'-concept are in the centre of discussion (see Wottawa, 1977, 1979). Secondly, as ethnomethodologically oriented investigators emphasize, it is not so much the method of data gathering or the results that ultimately play a crucial role in research but most of all the interpretation of the results that gives direction to future research. This interpretation, however, will always remain a kind of art, at least in the social sciences, and underlies the rules of ethnomethodological reasoning (Garfinkel, 1967; Turner, 1974).

If we finally take linguistics to be a branch of experimental psychology, we accept at the same time that system research is a kind of behavior-research. However, the incorrectness of this assumption is apparent from the widely accepted standpoint in system research that if one counter-example against the hypothesized rule can be found, then this rule has to be reformulated such that this exception can be accounted for. Such a standpoint contrasts

How to Become a Native Speaker

sharply with psychological research that always operates with statistical evidence, and explains exceptions as being caused by intervening variables or uncontrolled disturbing factors. Psychology tries to describe regularities in human behavior as it takes place in *all* human beings. Linguistics is interested in the system as such, and possibly how this system is actualized within one person or another. This person's idiolect can serve as a kind of illustration of how systems may function. System research is not a behavioral discipline but should describe the members of a system (e.g. words, sentences, speech events, speech acts, utterances, and the system's process.) as adequately and as simply as possible, and should detect an automatism to exclude those elements of the inventory that do not belong to the system. The same holds true for research in physics and mathematics (in contrast with psychology), as in these disciplines it is also impossible to arrive at valid solutions to the problems by accepting the average opinion of informants. In sum, linguistics is not a behavioral science, but it is concerned with problems of systems. Its subjects are not human beings but linguistic units like utterances and speech acts. The linguistic task is to find a general system to describe its subjects adequately and as such one can say that the differentiation between deductive and inductive aspects and between population and sample and the like is artificial and trivial.

On the other hand, however, if we accept the linguist's task as detecting the system of a natural language there are a number of difficulties we have to cope with. First of all, we have to take into consideration the unreliability of certain judgements (especially as far as unclear cases are concerned or the more hidden pragmatic aspects). I think that the restriction to clear cases solves this problem to a large extent. To ask naive informants or trained linguists will only lead to new problems like those dealt with in connection with experimental testing, as we lack any sound criteria to decide on whose judgements (e.g. mine, my mother's or my colleagues' judgements) are right or wrong. I would suggest relying completely on one's own judgements and, methodologically, I would provisionally reject all unclear cases as ungrammatical in order to let the system decide on the unclear cases later. A last possibility in this respect could be to observe how such cases are handled by speaker and hearer in actual situations.

A standpoint as sketched above implies methodologically that (a) the native speaker concept is strictly speaking narrowed down to the informant's idiolect and (b) that the detected system as such is in principle not an intersubjective one that holds necessarily for the whole speech community. Practically this latter point implies that the results thus obtained may not immediately be applied in scoring systems, in remedial and pathological practice, etc. as we are uncertain about the reliability amongst persons. What we need in addition is experience about what kinds of judgements we may generalize. The problems that may appear in the generalization process are dealt with in some detail in the first part of this chapter: they refer to amount of schooling, cultural norms, norms of the school, logical vs. linguistic considerations, dialectical and idiolectical variation, second language experience and the like. The problem in linguistics is that one deals with the development of a system that, strictly speaking, holds only for one's own idiolect but of which one assumes at the same time that it holds for all speakers of a language. The system is actually defined as referring to languages (Chomsky, 1957, 1965; Searle, 1969; Wunderlich, 1976). This is also illustrated by the discussion of intention as opposed to illocution in speech act theory. It seems to be common sense nowadays that intention should be regarded as belonging to the domain of research as far as it is systematic, in the sense that it is explicitly expressed by means of the language, and is (automatically) accepted and interpreted by the hearer and also by the 'native speaker' − investigator with this intention. In other words an intention can only be accepted if language is organized in such a way that speaker, hearer, and observer have the same interpretation in mind. That this is not so simple to decide can be illustrated with some observations.

Firstly, a teacher says: "Marion is allowed to answer this question." Four possible intentions come to mind: (1) Marion is requested to answer the question; (2) the other pupils are requested to keep quiet; (3) the cameraman gets the information that he has to switch to Marion; (4) the teacher tries to redirect the children's attention to the lesson again. Which ones have to be accepted as belonging to the system? Secondly, what can be considered as systematic intention when the omniscient author creates tension by informing the reader that he knows a lot more than the main character of the story. If now someone tells something to the main person it is very likely that the reader and the person in the book come to different interpretations, and both the author and the reader know that. What is the author's intention with the 'someone's' intention with respect to the two addressees (mainperson and reader?).

Thirdly what is systematic in the following story? In 'Spring in Fialta' Nabokov talks about a meeting with Nina in Fialta. This meeting is interwoven narratively with all other meetings he has had with her before. About the second meeting he writes the following:

As I entered the room I caught sight of her at once (. . .). She was sitting in the corner of a couch, her feet pulled up, her small comfortable body folded in the form of a Z; an ash tray stood aslant on the couch near one of her heels; and, having squinted at me and listened to my name, she removed her stalklike cigarette holder from her lips and proceeded to utter slowly and joyfully, 'Well, of all people −'.

The last meeting before the actual one is described as follows:

How to Become a Native Speaker 331

... and led me to Nina, who sat in the corner of a couch, her body folded Z-wise, with an ash tray at her heel, and she took a long turqoise cigarette holder from her lips and joyfully, slowly exclaimed, 'Well, of all people –'.

Why this repetition in the meetings with Nina? Does it function as a kind of special information? In other words what is the author's intention with this repetition of information? If we realize that (1) at the second and the last but one meeting the same kinds of things happen, and (2) such information as given above often functions as a kind of extra signal in Nabokov's composition technique, it is reasonable to assume that the actual meeting has to be the last meeting with Nina. It is not so astonishing, therefore, that the story ends in the following way:

... and I stood on the station platform of Mlech with a freshly bought newspaper, which told me that the yellow car I had seen under the plane trees had suffered a crash beyond Fialta, having run at full speed into a truck of a travelling circus entering the town (...) while Nina (...) had turned out after all to be mortal.

Can this type of information be considered to be systematic, or does it only belong to Nabakov's idiolect of constructing texts? The problem is that the reader, if he is trained in Nabakov's peculiarities, is able to detect his intentions in this respect, although the interpretation of individual peculiarities is not systematic in a strict sense. Should we leave such aspects out of consideration on the ground that they are unsystematic in the sense that they do not regard shared knowledge?

The restriction of the term 'intention' as discussed above is generally accepted although I know of no systematic research with experimental subjects on this matter nor of an indication that such an investigation is mandatory. I have also the sad feeling that the restriction of the terms leads to the neglection of large parts of the communication process that are essential for a correct understanding of what is going on in actual communication. In the first place, this is our capacity to judge idiosyncratic aspects of communicative behavior, as they are not used systematically in the same way by all speakers of a language. Secondly the nonverbal aspects of language have to be mentioned, as far as they concern the analogous (Watzlawick, 1967) or intentional and attitudinal (Van der Geest, 1975) or '*Appell*' and '*Auslösung*' (Bühler, 1934) aspects of language use. Actually these two points are closely related inasfar as they are often expressed systematically only within individuals, and as they can or ought to be used in order to arrive at the correct and valid interpretation. An example from phonetic research may illustrate that this communicative aspect is in no way restricted to the intentional aspects of language.

It is well-known that every vowel can physically be regarded as a combination of two different tones: the first and second formant. Each vowel covers a certain area determined by the f_1- and f_2-axis. If we take the data of vowels of more than one subject into consideration we will see that there is a lot of overlap between the areas of different vowels. Taking only the vowel system of one person into account one will find such an overlap generally not to exist. Thus is appears that the vowel system is furnished rather individually in the sense that, e.g., if the first formant of a vowel is larger or smaller than average, this apparently goes more or less for all first formants in the individual vowel system, as contrast between the individual vowels has to be guaranteed. The interpretation whether someone says 'wet' or 'wit,' is, therefore, determined to a certain extent by the interpreter's knowledge of the speaker's phonetic-phonological system. If even such an exact and physically determined system like the vowel system exhibits such a remarkable degree of individual but systemic variation, it is not surprising that in the nonreferential analogous aspects of communication such individual shifts will take place more intensively. The native speaker, in spite of current linguistic standpoints, ought to (and is able to) deal with these problems in actual communication.

In sum, by accepting the concept of the native speaker as an informant with respect to language instead of idiolects (1) we will make errors by generalizing individual phenomena to the community and by applying such knowledge in socially relevant areas, without being aware of these (small?) errors; (2) we narrow down the field of linguistics more than can be accepted by neglecting the individual differences every language user is aware of in daily communication and that play an essential part in perception and interpretation of speech acts; (3) we deny that there are many other branches in linguistics deserving of our attention.

THE NATIVE SPEAKER CONCEPT IN LANGUAGE ACQUISITION RESEARCH

Introduction

After all considerations about the native speaker concept in the foregoing I have to admit that this concept is not very attractive to me. Firstly, as I try to restrict this concept to a kind of justification not to jeopardize my own linguistic intuitions and judgements (in cooperation with the restriction 'as far as the clear cases are concerned'), the native speaker is by definition identical with my own or my colleague's linguistic ability. Secondly, because of its unrealiability, the concept is not to be used in cases where we most urgently need it viz. in cases of doubt. Thirdly, because its usage is practically restricted to judgements of formal correctness, of syntactic, semantic, and pragmatic interpretation, with neglect of individual manifestation of the

How to Become a Native Speaker

system, and of adequacy and appropriateness of form and content in actual situations, of social valuation, in short of differentiation of linguistic phenomena, the concept is also disappointing in its application. Nevertheless, the 'native speaker' does not play an unimportant role in my research on the analysis of conversation although it does not substantially influence its content and directions. First of all, there is the practical point that I accept the ethnomethodological starting point that I — as a member of the culture — am able to describe every speech act with respect to all kinds of linguistic variables that are used in the investigation.

Secondly and more interestingly the concept of the native speaker may serve as a kind of ultimate goal with respect to the kinds of processes I investigate. Research in language acquisition has as its superordinate question: How does the child come to a full mastery of his language? As such the present concept may be characterized as his being equipped with a full mastery of his language. What is meant by this full mastery cannot be summed up so easily. At least all rules of grammar belong to it, both productively and perceptively. These rules of grammar, however, are dependent on the kinds of semantic contents that are spoken to and by the persons who are being investigated. It appears namely that the frequency of occurence of certain grammatical phenomena in speech styles are often in agreement with their corresponding semantic phenomena in these samples (see Van der Geest et al., 1973 and Van der Geest, 1978a). Thus semantics has to be included also. Thirdly the pragmatic aspects, such as the attitudinal and intentional aspects. the social rules how to use language in certain situations, Hymes' (1971) notion of appropriateness, conversational rules like those of turn giving and taking (Sacks et al., 1974; Duncan, 1972/3), have to be taken into account. Finally the vocabulary should be sufficiently large.

I could only make a grab at some of the many aspects of the native speaker as the ultimate goal and perspective in language acquisition. Many relevant aspects had to be omitted. One of the points that is relevant in this latter respect is Hymes' (1971) notion of social valuation as it appears to be very difficult to valuate people in a second language. In short, we may characterize the native speaker as the ultimate state one may arrive at in one's mother tongue of being able (1) to express indefinitely many thoughts, wishes, requests, and the like and to react appropriately in an indefinite range of (new) situations (compare Chomsky, 1965: 'the creative aspect of language use'; Campbell & Wales, 1970; Hymes, 1971); (2) to maintain contact, to build up new relations and the like; (3) to steer other persons' (verbal and nonverbal) behavior. The ultimate state of the three aspects mentioned above may be characterized such that one is not hindered by language difficulties, if we accept the 'native speaker' concept as the child's (and the researcher's) ultimate perspective in the process of language acquisition.

The question may be relevant of how a human being may arrive at this ultimate state of language capacity. This question can be subdivided into (a) the child learning his mother-tongue; (b) the child learning a second language (either simultaneously or shortly after each other); (c) a person learning his first language retardedly due to (deafness, child aphasia, isolation, etc.); (d) a person, not in the age one normally acquires one's first language, learning a second language in natural settings; (e) as (d) but now in an artificial institutional setting: foreign language learning.

In two separate sections we will restrict ourselves to answering speculatively questions (a), (b), and (d). The other questions will be dealt with only incidentally.

The function of these chapters with respect to the native speaker can be justified with one general assumption from the field of developmental psychology, namely, that by investigating the developmental processes we learn a lot of the psychological processes and mechanisms as they occur in adult behavior. In our case the adult is the native speaker. A last introductory remark is that the contents of the two sections will be rather speculative and will sometimes reflect rather personal opinions which is partly due to the fact that I concentrate on the discussion of my own investigations in the first place.

First Language Acquisition

If we leave older assumptions out of consideration and act as if many of the modern assumptions, theoretical standpoints and results could not already be found before American (psycho) linguists became interested in language acquisition (see e.g. Wundt, 1900; Stern, 1907/1917; Preyer, 1889; Gregoire, 1937) than we can say that child language research started in the early sixties. Since that time the following theoretical standpoints were – roughly speaking – chronologically introduced, were worked with, and many times already abandoned again.

1. *The innateness theory* accepts an innate linguistic (= syntactic) theory in which universal expectations about language are formulated. Language acquisition in this sense is nothing more than actualization of this theory by the child for a specific language. Semantics does not play an intrinsic role but only a motivational one (Chomsky, 1965; McNeill, 1966/1970; Gruber, 1967; Menuyk, 1969; Bloom, 1970). Initially this theory was accepted but actually behavioristic and Bloomfieldian methods and explanations were applied (Braine, 1963; Miller & Ervin, 1963; Brown & Fraser, 1963; Jenkins & Palermo, 1963; Slobin, 1970).

2. *The semantic approach*; long before semantics became relevant in American

linguistics, Schlesinger (1967) proposed a semantic model for language perception and language acquisition (but this model was neglected). Later after Chafe (1970), Fillmore (1968), and McCawley (1968) had worked out semantically based approaches in linguistics, semantic explanations for language acquisitional results were introduced. Most of the time, case approaches are applied (Bowerman, 1972; Brown, 1973; Miller, 1975; Snow, 1977), but incidentally also generative semantic approaches (Antinucci & Parisi, 1973; Van der Geest, 1975; et al., 1973). Generally the innateness hypothesis is rejected and language acquisition is considered to be dependent on cognitive development (Bruner, 1975; Van der Geest, 1974; Levelt, 1975).

3. *The input approach* considers the primary linguistic data as of central interest. It was found that, in contrast with general assumptions hitherto about the clumsiness of language input, it can be characterized as ideally preprogrammed and adapted to the child's linguistic progress (Smith, 1970; Snow, 1972; Snow & Ferguson ed., 1977; Beheydt, 1979). Although the theoretical starting point and implications often remain vague and implicit, it seems to be that the present approach has to be characterized as a reaction to Chomsky's innateness hypothesis and the overemphasis on the study of children's linguistic output data as a consequence thereof by the initial language acquisition researchers e.g., McNeill and Menyuk. It can also be regarded as an empirical approach as it emphasizes the relevance of input data (stimulus material) and as such it is working within the field of learning theory. The child's role in the developmental process is widely neglected.

4. *The interactive approach.* In this approach neither the child nor the environment alone plays the crucial role in language acquisition. It is assumed, however, that a cooperative and complementary role of both the language learning child and the language teaching adult is mandatory in order to arrive at a prosperous language development. Cooperative, in this context, means to influence each other's behavior in such a way that data in language acquisition are ordered optimally in order to be applied in the developmental process (Snow, 1972; Van der Geest, 1974, '75, '77; Cross, 1977).

5. *Universals in first and second language acquisition.* This approach can actually be regarded as a kind of 'innateness-revival'. But in contrast with Chomsky's more technically and theoretically oriented theory and the simple acceptance of this hypothesis by its investigators, this approach concentrates on remarkable findings with respect to universal aspects in language acquisition: (a) in all languages, as far as we know, consistent sequences are passed through at the phonological and structural level; (b) the sequences mentioned under (a) appear also in second language acquisition, regardless of which

language is the first or the second language; (c) in language acquisition some processes can be observed which are — as far as we know at present — unequalled in other developmental processes (Wode, H. & Felix, 1979).

It is essential to mention at this point that all approaches, as characterized here, concentrate on the acquisition of semantic, syntactic and morphological phenomena. All aspects concerning the problems of how to learn to communicate appropriately — the crucial phenomena with respect to the native speaker concept — are widely left out of consideration by these approaches, with perhaps one exception: the interactive approach. In the following sections we will first concentrate on the acquisition of new features and then on the acquisition of style/register.

The Acquisition of New Linguistic Features

The child's active role. It is astonishing to notice how the role of the child's perspective skills — a very relevant native speaker aspect — in the process of language acquisition is neglected in research. Either one concentrated on the child's linguistic productions to investigate the language acquisition device, that is (was) assumed to be innate and therefore to be relatively free from performance restrictions in the child's linguistic perceptions, or one concentrated on input data and assumed that these are gradually incorporated by the child in one way or other. Brown & Bellugi (1964), however, found that there was a correlation between understressing words in otherwise caracatural language use of parents with respect to pitch and stress and omissions of these words in children's utterances. As this evidence was, however, restricted to rather peculiar parts of mother–child conversation (child utterance — parent expansion; parent utterance — child imitation) a control study (Van der Geest, 1972, '74, '75) was undertaken in which paraphrases of spontaneous child utterances (equivalent to adult expansion) were compared with these child utterances for 5 different children. The results of the study confirmed Brown and Bellugi's findings: (1) the stressed words of the adult utterances are also stressed in the child's utterance; (2) the understressed units (morphemes and words) tend to be omitted by the child.

To explain these facts I worked out (Van der Geest, 1972, '74, '75) a theory in which the child's perceptual capacity functions as a kind of filter that allows only the prominent information to get through. If e.g. the adult would say:

(10,a) Co$\overset{3}{u}$ld you thr$\overset{2}{o}$w me the b$\overset{1}{a}$ll?

it can be hypothesized that the child in the initial stage of development would perceive

How to Become a Native Speaker   337

(10,b) // noise//   bȧ́ll?

and later

(10,c) // noise// thr̂ow // noise//   bȧ́ll?
(10,d) Coȗ̇ld// noise // thr̂ow //noise// bȧ́ll?

This filtering function is apparently caused by limitations of memory span, that are not only effective in speech production but also in speech perception and probably has a neuropsychological correlate (see also R. Clark, 1978, for similar kinds of evidence). If we accept now, in contrast with Chomsky (1965), that the primary linguistic data, or better: the primary linguistic input, has to be ordered in accordance with language acquisitional strategies, then we see that the child himself — or his neuropsychological maturation — is able to order his input to a large extent (see also Levelt, 1975). This conclusion does not necessarily confirm the innateness hypothesis as it is not specifically formulated with respect to language acquisition. It emphasizes, however, the child's active role in the acquisitional process. We will see furthermore that the child is also actively engaged in this process as far as he is able to steer the adult with respect to the input data.

The role of semantics. Chomsky (1965) does not attribute an inherent role to the semantic aspects in the process of language acquisition. Schlesinger (1971), Bowerman (1972), Brown (1973), Slobin (1973), and Bruner (1974) give some indication that the semantic aspects could play a more substantial role in the sense that they are necessary prerequisites for the development of language. Slobin formulates this semantic primacy as follows: "New forms express old functions, and new functions are first expressed by old forms." Bruner's findings may indicate that prelinguistic play routines between mother and child may function as training procedures for the cognitive prerequisites of the basic syntactic/semantic relations. Schlesinger, Brown, and Bowerman present indications that a kind of case approach may describe the child's initial linguistic development more adequately than a syntactic approach. Recently I (Van der Geest, 1977, '78b, '79) have presented some observations making plausible (1) the assumption that, although the semantic base of language development generally may hold, there are a number of observations that, for more difficult structures that do not regard the predicate-argument system or the case system (e.g. the passive, comparative, if-then constructions and the past perfect), the opposite may occur, viz. that syntactic forms develop before the corresponding semantic cognitive structure; (2) that, incidentally, children may take other routes than that of semantic primacy; and (3) that children in a later stage (age 6;0-8;0) concentrate fully on syntactic forms, as may appear from a number of investigations on children's perception. Apart from these few restrictions we may conclude that semantic theories explain the language development processes more adequately than syntactic theories do. The general assumption is that language in its syntactic aspects does not develop on the basis of innate syntactic knowledge but on the basis of prior cognitive knowledge and some kind of a nonspecifically linguistic learning theory. Whether semantics develops according to innate principles remains an open question, although Bruner's findings may suggest the contrary. Another advantage of the semantic theory is that it allows for the study of communicative development as the integrated study of how children learn to utter their thoughts and feelings by means of both nonverbal aspects (developing kinesics, intonation patterns, gesturing as in sign language, mimicry, etc.), and verbal aspects, rather than assuming (without any kind of systematic evidence) that linguistics is an autonomous part of communication and its development.

In this sense I would accept Dore's (1979) standpoint only as a kind of working program to investigate how linguistic and nonlinguistic aspects influence each other in the process of the acquisition of a communicative system, but not as a theory on how communication develops because language is in reality just an undeniable insoluble subpart (but an essential one) of the human communication system. We may ignore this fact in our investigations but should always be aware that we are doing so.

The child's interaction with his environment. As already mentioned, a lot of research has been done to characterize the linguistic input for LA. Although the implicit and motivational assumption of this type of research apparently is that the input plays an essential role in LA it is seldom investigated with respect to this role. One of the possibilities to do this is to compare mothers' speech to children with child speech or with the child's linguistic capacity. As far as I know, Brown & Hanlon (1970) were the first to do this systematically. It appeared from their data that both cumulative derivational complexity (innateness theory) and mother's speech (environment) could explain equally well the child's linguistic progress. In the end, it seems that the author decided on complexity as the valid explanation at issue. They overlooked that there were two alternative explanations to be examined; (1) derivational complexity explains the children's route. In that case, however, one ought to explain why the parents restrict themselves to the same kind of complexity in their speech with the children, although it is actually assumed that their speech is irrelevant for the child. (2) the environment determines the child's speech development. In that case one should explain why the children's speech can be described with derivational complexity.

With respect to (1) I have to admit that I can find no other explanation than 'accident'. In (2), however, the complexity of child's speech must be traced back to the adult's application of complexity in their speech with the children which means that the adults' speech functions as a kind of filter or is organized as a kind of curriculum for language. In other words one may hypothesize that adults have a kind of systematic knowledge of linguistic complexity, which they apply in adult-child speech. In several experiments (see Snow, 1972) it is shown that adults are able to adapt their speech with respect to complexity to the child's level.

In our investigation of parental influences on LA we cannot restrict ourselves to data that are not longitudinal for both the child and the parent, as Brown & Hanlon (1970), Brown (1973), Cross (1977), and Newport et al. (1977) actually did, because we have to answer the question of who takes the initiative for a new linguistic structure in the mother-child conversation. In order to examine this question we have investigated 8 mother-child pairs monthly for 6 months with respect to semantic and syntactic new features. Furthermore, it was controlled whether the utterance was an initiative (spontaneous) or a reaction and whether the utterance was reacted to or not. The results of this investigation are represented in Table 2.

Table 2: The role of the investigated aspects of the mother child dyad (for explanation see the text)

Variables	total scores	expected scores	
mother speech (syntax)	86	112	A
mother speech nonspontaneous (syntax)	59	56	B
mother speech not reacted to	51	172	C
mother speech nonspontaneous	45	176	D
mother speech spontaneous (syntax)	37	56	E
child speech spontaneous	35	168	F
child speech nonspontaneous	21	176	G
mother speech spontaneous	14	168	H
mother speech reacted to	8	172	I
mother speech nonspontaneous (semantics)	−4	120	J
mother speech spontaneous (semantics)	−23	112	K
mother speech (semantics)	−27	232	L

The score +86 (mother speech: syntax) means that it happened 86 times in one of the dyads that a syntactic variable occured earlier in the speech of the mother than in that of the child (expected was + 112). Furthermore, I made some statistical calculations as presented in Table 3, from which it appears that in conversation (1) the mother is normally more progressive with respect to syntax than the child (2); the child is more progressive in semantic respect,

Table 3: Statistic results of the investigated aspects.

		Chi-Quadrat	p <
B > E			
D > H	nonspontaneous vs. spontaneous	33.6	.001
J > K			
C > I	not reacted to vs. reacted to	28.9	.001
B > J			
E > K	Syntax vs. Semantics	76.4	.001
A > L			

at least in spontaneous utterances; (3) the decrease of the semantic differences in the nonspontaneous setting may be an indication that it is not so much that the mother and the child should differ in semantic terms but that she has to be aware that she has to manipulate her input utterances within the limits of the child's cognitive semantic development.

Thus it seems that the child has the initiative semantically and that the mother takes the opportunity to feed the child with the appropriate linguistic material for the content for which the child is motivated. (4) The other results indicate that the interactive conversation steering aspects of communication are relevant with respect to semantics and syntax. It can be stated e.g. that a conversation starts rather simply (spontaneous utterances) and that thereafter more complex material can be introduced. The child can apparently present cues that mother utterances are too complex by not reacting. Snow (1972) presents evidence that mothers actually interpret such nonreactions as cues to repeat the utterances in a more simple fashion (for further details see: Van der Geest, et al., 1973a; Van der Geest, 1974, '77, '79; for a defense of this interactive viewpoint against some criticisms of Brown (1977) and McTear (1978) I refer to my 1979 paper).

If our observations are correct then one of the features of the native speaker must be that he becomes able to adapt his speech in a flexible way to the state of semantic and syntactic knowledge of the addressee. Studies which deal with the development of this aspect in children found that young children (from 3;0 onwards) already possess this capacity. Until the age of 6 or 7 children do not, however, apply this capacity in a flexible way. I actually observed a 24 months old child applying separate registers when talking with her dog (with complete adult morphology, but rather catechism-like) and another one for daily usage in the family (elliptical, without morphology but creative). At the age of 7 a child begins to be able to use certain strategies of adaptation, by which he can continue his conversation with a language learning child, like action supporting communication, partner centered communication, and anticipatory instead of reactive communicative adaptation. Flexible adaptation is the essential condition for being a competent language teacher in daily settings (Heckhausen, 1979; Van der Geest & Heckhausen, 1979).

On the other hand, the child is already at the beginning of his linguistic career a competent language learner, as he is able to steer the conversation with his mother such that it makes sense to him with respect to the contact function, information, and language development. Snow (1975) presents evidence that large parts of interactive communication steering is learned by the child in interactive interplay between mother and child, before the first word is learned.

The social rules for conversation such as those formulated by Sacks et al. (1974), and Duncan (1972/3) on giving and taking turns are learned this way. This steering capacity of children is a central issue of the native speaker's behavioral pattern and determines to a large extent content and form of his speech and his partner's speech.

The Acquisition of Communicative Competence

If we define the study of language acquisition as the study that is concerned with the acquisition of new semantic and syntactic structures by the child, then communicative competence can best be regarded as dealing with:

1. the acquisition of the illoculionary or pragmatic aspects of communication;
2. communicative adequacy and appropriateness with respect to context and situation;
3. the aspect whether and to what extent something is done and what its being done entails in terms of social valuation.

The development of the first aspect can probably be explained in the same way as semantic and syntactic development, i.e., as a result of intensive parent-child interaction (see Van der Geest, 1975, ch.X, for evidence). That the acquisition of pragmatics is to be described separately from semantics and syntax is clear if one realizes that pragmatically correct and unequivocal utterances may accidentally have an underdeveloped syntactic form and (or) an anomalous content, and that syntactically correct utterances now and then do not express the children's intention. As an illustration consider the fact that the child is not aware initially of typical role differences in communication between both participants, e.g. *come* and *go, here* and *there, thanks* and *please, I* and *you* and *have* and *get* have particular functions that depend on the conversational role. As an example may serve the utterance of Mark (2;2):

(11) *Ik krijg niets meer* (I don't get anything more)

with the meaning:

(11,a) *Ik wil niks meer hebben* (I don't want to have anything more)

where the parental example sentence with identical reference (Mark will not have more of x) but different intention (the denial of x that M. wants to have) was:

(11,b) *Jij krijgt niets meer* (you don't get anything more)

When we are dealing with the third and also second point mentioned above and when we contrast these aspects against acquisition of new structures then we are dealing (according to Dore, 1979) with development rather than acquisition, with frequencies rather than single occurences. It appears (Van der Geest, 1977, '78a,b, and id. et al. 1973a and b) that what was stated for the acquisition of linguistic structures also goes for frequencies. This is not so surprising if we realize that one can hardly imagine that a child can learn something with only a single presentation of a linguistic feature, and without frequent training of the variable at issue.

Although the developmental and acquisitional processes may be identical, there is a noticeable difference between syntactically defined linguistic competence and a general communicative competence in which the appropriate use of linguistic knowledge is a central point. Children may, generally speaking, not differ in terms of linguistic competence but actually do differ in terms of communicative competence.

The ideas about which a person prefers to speak, the kind of acts for which language is the instrument, determine to a large extent what kinds of speech forms he prefers to use. The ideas about which the speaker generally talks agree with the contents preferably used in the environment's linguistic input to the child; they are culture- or class-specific. This could mean that the ideas discussed in the child's environment and the instrumental usage of language in his environment may lead to the development of some specific communicative habits.

From the foregoing discussion on communicative development it may have become clear that the rules of communication and the process of communicative development are inseparably related. I regard this revamped 'correspondence'-hypothesis as a hidden curriculum for language acquisition, since the actual task in a parent-child dyad is to communicate, and successful communication leads to growth of communicative competence. In another study (Van der Geest, 1978) it is not only stated that communication is a necessary prerequisite for language learning, but that, furthermore, communication is a learning process in itself. Inasfar as the participants are concerned we may speak of mental changes with respect to context and these changes, essential for the communicational process itself, may be considered as learning effects. These effects concern, among other things, the topic spoken about, the participants, the situation, and, not least, the code.

The basis for such an assumption are the results of a longitudinal investigation of the communicational processes of a group of children and their teacher from kindergarten to the end of the first grade. The following results are relevant for the present exposition. Initially the four groups of children (lower vs. middle class; boys vs. girls) did not differ qualitatively but only quantitatively (more utterances, more words, etc.) in classroom interaction. These quantitative differences initially occured only in the children's verbal productions and were only hesitatingly taken over by the teacher, with respect to whom she spoke. Probably this adaptation of hers was against her assumption of equal participation of the children. Later the children's participation in classroom interaction also differed qualitatively. In this case, however, it was the teacher who initiated this difference: it was in her speech with the children that such differences first came to the surface. The same kind of, or complementary qualitative, differences accordingly appeared later in the speech of these groups of children. We may explain this remarkable communicative phenomenon as follows: the quantitative differences functioned for the teacher (erroneously?) as a signal that there were differences among the children in the classroom. Talking less apparently means for the teacher: talking differently.

Initially we may expect the following to occur:

Teacher: Nora you may give the answer
Nora: (hesitates)
Paul: In the autumn
Teacher: Paul wait for your turn! Nora?

And now you may guess who gets the next turn. The same type of children who cannot wait for their turns initially are exactly the children the teacher later preferably talks to. And because of the interpretation 'talking much is talking differently' she talks with qualitatively different contents, intentions and structures to the several groups of children. Ultimately the groups of children develop different registers, namely those that fit into the registers that are directed to them. The children become different native speakers, at least in the different school settings, as the result of an interactive play with the teacher that can be described as a hidden curriculum. Middle class children and boys preferably used an informative and more abstract speech style, and participated most often in the classical conversation of more cognitively oriented lessons. Lower class children on the contrary used a more concrete and more instructional speech style, especially during classical conversation and instruction. The differences were most pronounced in the calculus lessons. The interaction of the teacher with girls and lower class children was concerned with very concrete action describing instructions of how to solve a mathematical problem. Boys and middle class children, however, got rather abstract, problem oriented and explanatory contents. One can imagine that such conversational practice not only leads to differences in communicative competence but also, little by little, to different curricula for mathematics, namely a concrete problem solving oriented one and one that is concerned with more abstract understanding of mathematical problems. It is this latter point that illustrates the close relationship between communication and learning. Figure 1 represents my idea of communication, learning, and communicative development. The double arrows in this diagram indicate an interaction between the components they are pointing at. If such an arrow consists of a dotted line then the interaction takes place between the situ-

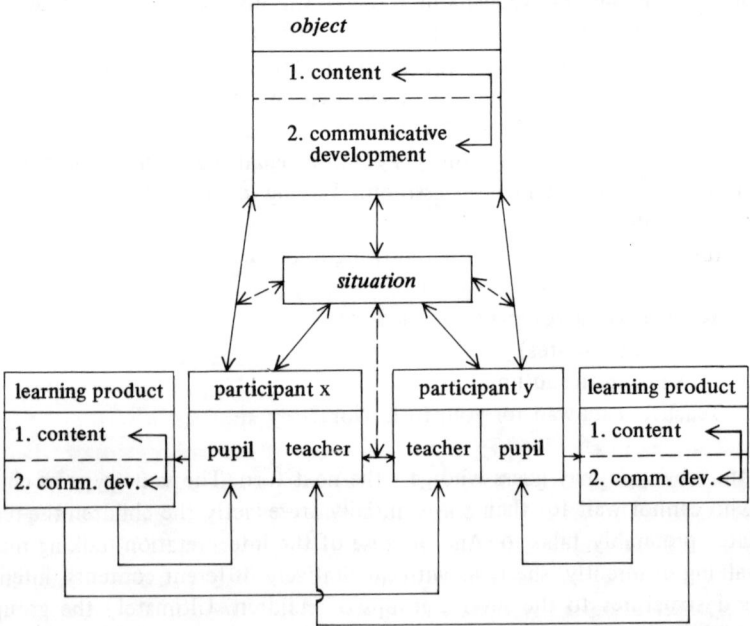

Figure 1: Learning as a communication process (for explanation see the text).

ation and an interaction between two other blocks of the diagram. A single arrow means that the influence takes place only in the indicated direction. In the two blocks *learning product* and *object* the double function of communication is represented, namely the mental change with respect to both the communicative content and to communicative development.

A last point to be mentioned concerns the double arrows in the blocks *learning product* and *object*. After the preceding discussion it will be clear that the communicative object and product not only refer to its content but also to the capability to communicate about these contents. It seems, therefore, reasonable to accept the assumption that the communicative competence of the participants restricts or at least influences the contents and vice versa, and that people who developed a different communicative competence with respect to the content will discuss the conversational topics differently.

The Acquisition of a Second Language

Only recently has the field of second language acquisition been rediscovered (see Marcussen Hatch (ed.), 1978). A number of hypotheses have been developed which are almost all relevant for first language acquisition (L1A) too, and therefore need some consideration in discussions of language acquisition and the native speaker concept.

The first hypothesis is derived from contrastive analysis and assumes that L2 is learned through the screen of L1. It would predict and explain errors and learning problems in the L2A process. As this actually appeared not to be completely the case (Dulay & Burt, 1973), this hypothesis was abandoned in its strong form.

Another hypothesis claims that 'errors' are reflections of a provisional grammar developed by the child (Corder, 1967; Richards, 1971; Selinker, 1972). Wode (1978) accepts that L2A in a natural setting proceeds according to an ordered sequence of stages but expresses some doubt about Hatch's claim that a language is acquired in the same sequence, irrespective of whether it is acquired as L1 or L2.

Wode & Felix (1979) seem to favor the assumption that there are certain regularities in the developmental sequences of LA irrespective of whether it concerns L1 or 2 or whatever L. They even assume that these regularities occur both in natural L1A and L2A and in L2A in classical settings. They accept these findings, finally, as indications of innate processes of LA. Although I agree that one can observe many regularities in L2A, I disagree that this observation is the alpha and omega of LA. One can list a number of recurring regularities in LA but also a number of phenomena that are either idiosyncratic for an individual, or are specific to a specific language or to a specific L2 after a specific L1 (e.g. the 'l-r' substitution is specific to Chinese as L1 and every L2 with an r-phoneme).

Secondly one is not allowed to deduce from such kinds of observations, even if one does not accept the former criticisms, that LA is innate. The same holds for L2 as we have stated for L1, that one has to examine whether or not these regularities occuring in the data can be traced back to the input. If not, we could, for instance, ask ourselves by what circumstances a particular error could be caused. Is it systematically or at least frequently done or is it the communication pressure or, for example, a kind of nonchalance in speaking that causes the error? My sons Mark and Joost, for example, differed with respect to a certain error that one could expect to occur on the basis of the contrastive hypothesis between Dutch and German.

Joost (5;2-7;6) produced from the onset in L2 errors like

(16) *Er sagt, daß er es hat getan.

instead of

(16a) Er sagt, daß er es getan hat.

In Dutch one preferably says 'Hij zegt, dat hij het heeft gedaan.' Mark (6;10-9;2), however, did not produce this error until recently and only incidentally. For both children the interference between L1 and L2 may be the cause of this error. By testing perceptively it was clear to me that for Joost this error is still in his provisional grammar and thus L1 is still a disturbing factor for L2. The same goes for my daughter Frederiek (2;0-4;4) who learned L1 and L2 at almost the same time. For Mark, however, this error is not in his L2 grammar, if we define it in Chomskyan terms, but is only part of it in Labov's sense, as an alternative choice in a variable rule. Because of its contextual dependency the error has to be accounted for also in a communicative competence approach, as characterized by Hymes (1971). This difference between Mark (L1 is hardly a disturbing factor for L2) and the younger children can probably be explained by age differences, along the lines of Snow & Hoefnagel (1978) who found that L2A is more prosperous in older children, and adults except for the phonetic system.

For the above mentioned reasons it can hardly be maintained that L2 and L1 are necessarily learned according to the same principles or that they necessarily follow the same kinds of sequences in their acquisition. Before answering the question of whether development in natural L2A is organized by innate principles or by systematic variations of the input by the environment, one has to admit that L2A, in comparison with L1A, is more complicated because of interference. Although we are uncertain about the particular

How to Become a Native Speaker

influence of L1 and whether this influence is always of the same kind for every L2-learner, its influences cannot be denied, like Dulay & Burt (1973) tend to do. Thus, the important question is whether L2A can be explained more adequately by 'L1 + environment' or by 'L1 + innate principles.'

In order to get some insight into this question, we (Van der Geest & Heckhausen, 1979; Heckhausen, 1979) made a longitudinal study of conversations of my three children with peers from another German family (see figure 2):

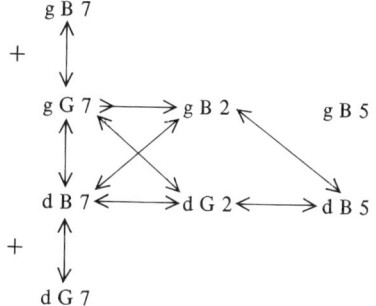

Figure 2: The investigated dyads; B = boy, G = girl, d = Dutch, g = German, 2,5,7 = years of age; '+' are control dyads.

The results from this investigation generally confirm the hypothesis that the environment adapts linguistic complexity with respect to the addressee's language development whether the child is 5 or 7 years old and whether it concerns L1 or L2.

Table 4 shows the syntactic, semantic and interactive variables that have been investigated, and how they differ between dyads with homogeneous age (5 or 7 years old) and dyads of the 5 or 7 year old children with the younger ones.

Table 4: The investigated variables and their discriminative qualities with respect to language adapation.

Variables:	differentiating:			total
	well	moderately	badly	
syntactic	9	1	2	12
semantic	14	2	3	19
interactive	13	1	2	16
	36	4	7	47

It appears that almost 80% of the variables are adapted by the more capable children with respect to L as used in the dyad. It also appears that the German 5 and 7 year old children reduced the complexity of their speech when talking to the Dutch children of the same age. Most interesting for our purpose are the dyads with the two year old children. As can be deduced from table 5, the Dutch girl in L1 was far more advanced in language acquisition than the German boy and she was far more eager to communicate. In the dyads of gG7 with the younger children we can therefore investigate the problem of whether communicative competence or same L1 is more profitable for language learning. In the dyads with gG2, G7 has to cope with two problems: (a) the partner is younger than G7 is; and (b) the partner has a different L1.

Table 5: The investigated variables insofar as they discriminate sharply between the two year old children

Variables:	diff. positively between		total
	dG2	gB2	
syntactic	4	0	4
semantic	5	0	5
interactive	4	1	5
	13	1	14

Comparison of the dyads in the first data collection made clear that the L2 problem with G2 was easier to overcome than the small communicative capacity with identical L1 in the dyad with B2 (see table 6).

Table 6: Variables discriminating positively between the two dyads with respect to adaptation.

dyad with	syntax	semantics	interaction	total
gB2	6	3	0	9
dG2	5	8	6	19
	11	11	6	−28

Except for syntactic complexity the speech of G7 to G2 is more advanced than that to B2. This could mean that the communicative capacity of the language learning child (being attentive and reacting) leads to more complex contents in the speech of G7 and is, therefore, more attractive for the child. It is not surprising for this reason that in the data collection two months later, G7's speech in the dyad with dG2 was also syntactically more complex than her speech to her brother B2.

How to Become a Native Speaker

The development as sketched in the preceding should be accepted as an indication that the same kinds of interactional processes as are assumed to operate in L1A are also active in L2A. This way we can agree with the hypothesis that in L1A and L2A the same kinds of principles are working. Another observation may support this hypothesis. A correlational study on sentence stress assignment (Van der Geest, 1974) shows that English-speaking adults learning Dutch in a natural setting were better able to assign stress in a test situation to Dutch than to English sentences, and, furthermore, that this effect was stronger for the less advanced L2 learners. This could mean that (1) sentence stress is stronger when less advanced learners are addressed, and that it is stronger in L2 than L1 when more advanced learners are addressed; and (2) that (less advanced) learners are relatively more dependent on stress than on, e.g., syntactic means to interpret utterances. It may be hypothesized, in other words, that the stress strategy for language learners works in both L1A and L2A.

Finally, when I observe my children and when I ask myself whether they will arrive at a native level, some observations make clear to me that L2 gradually interferes more with L1 than the other way round. To give some of the many examples:

Dutch:	verkopen (sell)	verkocht (sold)
	kopen (buy)	kocht (bought)
	koken (cook)	kookte (cooked)
German:	(ver) kaufen	(ver) kaufte (English: buy and (sell))
	kochen (cook)	kochte (cooked)

Recently all three children have preferably used *koopte instead of kocht but not *verkoopte instead of verkocht; and when they are corrected they comment that kocht means cooked.

Furthermore, they used words like *tweedens (zweitens; secondly), *eerstens (erstens; firstly) instead of ten eerste or ten tweede, of which they assumed that they were false.

Such observations make clear that the concept of 'native speaker' is also of limited usefulness in the field of L2A.

REFERENCES

Antinucci, F. & D. Parisi (1973). *Early language acquisition.* In Ch. Ferguson & D. Slobin, eds., pp. 607–619.
Beheydt, L. (1979). '*Variatie in Taalaanbod*' Ph.D. Thesis Leuven.
Bellugi, U. & C. Brown, eds. (1964). *The acquisition of language.* Monographs in Child Development Ser. 92. Chicago: University of Chicago Press.

Bereiter, C. & S. Engelmann (1966). *'Teaching disadvantaged children in the preschool.'* Englewood Cliffs, N.J.; Prentice Hall.
Bever, T. (1970). *'The cognitive basis for linguistic structures.'* In J. Hayes, eds., pp. 279-362.
Bloom, L. (1970). *Language development, form and function in emerging grammars.* Cambridge (Mass.): MIT.
Bowerman, M. (1973). *'Early syntactic development.'* Cambridge: Cambridge University Press.
Braine, M. (1963). 'The ontogeny of English phrase structure.' *Language* 39: 1-13.
Brown, R. (1973). *'A first language.'* Harmondsworth.
Brown, R. (1977). *'Introduction.'* In C. Snow & Ch. Ferguson, eds., pp. 1-27.
Brown, R. & U. Bellugi (1964). 'Three processes in the child's acquisition of syntax.' In E. Lenneberg, ed., *New directions in the study of language.* Cambridge Mass: MIT Press.
Brown, R. & C. Fraser (1963). 'The acquisition of syntax.' In C. Cofer & B. Musgrave, eds., *Verbal behavior and learning.* N.Y.: McGraw Hill.
Brown, R. & C. Hanlon (1970). 'Derivational complexity and order of acquisition.' In J. Hayes, eds., *Cognition and the development of language.* N.Y.: Wiley & Sons, pp. 11-53.
Bruner, J. (1975). 'The ontogenesis of speech acts.' *Journal of child language* 2: 1-19.
Bühler, K. (1934). *'Sprachtheorie.'* Jena: G. Fischer Verlag.
Campbell, R. & R. Wales (1970). The study of language acquisition. In J. Lyons, ed., *New horizons in linguistics.* Harmondsworth: Penguin pp. 242-260.
Chafe, W. (1970). 'Meaning and the structure of language.' Chicago: University of Chicago Press.
Chomsky, N. (1957). *'Syntactic structures.'* The Hauge: Mouton.
Chomsky, N. (1964). *'Current issues in linguistic theory.'* The Hague: Mouton.
Chomsky, N. (1965). *'Aspects of the theory of syntax.'* Cambridge (Mass.): MIT Press.
Clark, R. (1978). *'Some even simpler ways to learn to talk.'* In N. Waterson & C. Snow, eds., *The development of communication.* Chichester: John Wiley.
Corder, P. (1967). 'The significance of learners' errors.' *IRAL* 5: 161-169.
Cross, T. (1977). *'Mothers' speech adjustments.'* In C. Snow & Ch. Ferguson, eds. pp. 151-188.
Dore, J. (1979). 'What's so conceptual about the acquisition of linguistic structures?' *Journal of Child language* 6: 129-137.
Dulay, H. & M. Burt (1973). 'Should we teach children syntax?' *Language Learning* 22: 235-252.
Duncan, S. (1972). 'Some signals and rules for taking speaking turns' *Journal of personal and social psychology* 23: 29-46.
Duncan, S. (1973). 'Toward a grammar of dyadic conversation.' *Semiotica* 9: 29-46.
Fillmore, Ch. (1968). 'The case for case.' In E. Bach & R. Harms, eds., *Universals in linguistic theory.* New York: pp. 1-88.
Ferguson, Ch. & D. Slobin, eds. (1973). *'Studies in child language development.'* New York: Holt Rinehart & Winston.
Garfinkel, H. (1967). *'Studies in ethnomethodology.'* Englewood Cliffs N.J.: Prentice Hall.
Gregoire, A. (1937). *'L'apprentissage du language.'* Liege-Paris: Broz.
Gruber, J. (1967). 'Topicalization in child language.' *Foundations of language* 3: 37-65.
Hayes, J.R., ed. (1970). *'Cognition and the development of language.'* New York: Wiley.
Heckhausen, J. (1979). *'Linguistische, kognitive und interaktive Anpassung.'* Ruhr-Universität Bochum, ms.

Huisman, C. (1974). 'Niederländisch für Angänger.' Wuppertal: Putty-Verlag.
Hymes, D. (1971). 'Competence and performance in linguistic theory.' In R. Huxley & E. Ingram, eds., *Language acquisition, models and methods.* London, pp. 3-23.
Jacobs, R. & P. Rosenbaum, eds. (1970). *'Readings in English transformational grammar.* Waltham, Mass: Ginn.
Jenkins, J. & D. Palermo (1964). *'Mediation processes and the acquisition of linguistic structure.'* In U. Bellugi & R. Brown, eds.
Kraak, A. & W. Klooster (1968). *'Syntaxis.'* Culemborg: Stam-Kemperman.
Labov, W. (1970). 'The logic of nonstandard English.' In Williams, F., ed., *'Language and poverty,'* Chicago: Markham Publishers, pp. 153-187.
Levelt, W.J.M. (1971). 'Some psychological aspects of linguistic data.' *Linguistische Berichte* 17: 18-30.
Levelt, W. (1975). *'What became of LAD.'* Lisse: P. de Ridder Press.
Marcussen Hatch, E., ed. (1978). *'Second language acquisition.'* Rowley (Mass.): Newbury House.
McCawley, J. (1968). *'Lexical insertion in a transformational grammar without deep structure'* (mimeo).
McNeill, D. (1966). 'Developmental psycholinguistics.' In F. Smith & G. Miller, eds., *The genesis of language.* Cambridge (Mass.): MIT Press.
McNeill, D. (1970). *'The acquisition of language.'* New York: Harper and Row.
McTear, M. (1978). Review of Snow/Ferguson, eds., 'Talking to children.' *Journal of child language* 5: 521-530.
Menyuk, P. (1969). *'Sentences children use.'* Cambridge (Mass.): MIT Press.
Miller, M. (1975). *'Zur Logik der frühen Sprachentwicklung.'* Doktorarbeit, Frankfurt/Main, 1975.
Miller, W. & S. Ervin (1963). *'The development of grammar.'* In U. Bellugi & R. Brown, eds., 1964, pp. 35-39.
Nabokov, V. (1958). *'Spring in Fialta.'* N.Y: Popular Library.
Newport, E. et al. (1977). 'Mother I'd rather do it myself.' In C. Snow & Ch. Ferguson, eds., *Talking to Children,* pp. 109-149.
Preyer, W. (1889). *'The mind of the child.'* N.Y.: Appleton-Century Crofts.
Richards, J. (1971). 'A non-contrastive approach to error analysis.' *English language teaching* 25: 204-219.
Sacks, H. et al. (1974). 'A simplest systematics for the organization of turn taking in conversation.' *Language* 50: 696-735.
Schlesinger, J. (1967). *'Production of utterances.'* Unpublished version of Schlesinger (1971).
Schlesinger, J. (1971). 'Production of utterances and language acquisition.' In D. Slobin, ed., *The ontogenesis of grammar,* N.Y.: Academic Press, pp. 63-101.
Searle, J. (1969). *'Speech acts.'* Cambridge: Cambridge University Press.
Selinker, L. (1972). 'Interlanguage.' *IRAL* 10: 201-231.
Shopen, T. (1972). *'A generative theory of ellipsis.'* Unpubl. Ph. D. Thesis.
Slobin, D. (1971). 'Universals of grammatical development in children.' In G. Flores d'Arcais & W. Levelt, eds., *Advances in psycholinguistics,* Amsterdam: North Holland, pp. 174-186.
Slobin, D. (1973). *'Cognitive prerequisites for the development of grammar.'* In Ch. Ferguson & D. Slobin, eds., pp. 175-208.
Smith, C. (1970). *'An experimental approach to children's linguistic competence.'* In J.R. Hayes, eds., pp. 109-136.
Snow, C. (1972). 'Mothers' speech to children.' *Child Development* 43: 549-565.

Snow, C. (1975). 'The development of conversation between mother and baby.' *Journal of child language*, 1977. In press.
Snow, C. (1975). 'Linguistics as behavioral scientists; toward a methodology for testing linguistic intuitions.' In A. Kraak, ed., *Linguistics in the Netherlands*, Assen: Van Gorcum, 1975.
Snow, C. & Ch. Ferguson, eds. (1977). *'Talking to children.'* Cambridge: Cambridge University Press.
Snow, C. (1977). *'Mothers' speech research.'* In C. Snow & Ch. Ferguson, eds., pp. 31-50.
Snow, C. & J.M. Hoefnagel (1978). *'Age differences in second language acquisition.'* In E. Macussen Hatch, eds., pp. 333-346.
Stern, C. & W. (1907). *'Die Kindersprache, eine psychologische und sprachtheoretische Untersuchung.'* Leipzig: Barth.
Turner, R., ed. (1974). *'Ethnomethodology; selected readings.'* Harmondsworth: Penguin.
Van der Geest, T. (1968). *'Te+ infinitief constructies.'* University of Amsterdam, ms.
Van der Geest, T. (1972). 'Hoofdstuk II.' In B. Tervoort et al. *Psycholinguistiek*, Aula reeks, Utrecht.
Van der Geest, T. (1974). 'A stress strategy for language learners.' In A. van Essen & J. Menting, eds., *In the context of language learning*. Assen: Van Gorcum.
Van der Geest, T. (1974). 'Language acquisition as a hidden curriculum.' *Communication & Cognition* 7: 169-190.
Van der Geest, T. (1975). *'Some aspects of communicative competence and their implications for language acquisition.'* Assen: Van Gorcum.
Van der Geest, T. (1977). 'Some interactional aspects of language acquisition.' In C. Snow & Ch. Ferguson, eds., pp. 89-108.
Van der Geest, T. (1978). 'Sprachentwicklung in semantischer und interaktionistischer Sicht.' In *Zeitschrift für Entwicklungspsychologie und pädagogische Psychologie*, pp. 286-304.
Van der Geest, T. (1978). *'Entwicklung der Kommunikation.'* Bochum: Kamp Verlag.
Van der Geest, T. (1978b). 'Towards a functional analysis system.' In J. Regan, ed., *The analysis of discourse*. In press.
Van der Geest, T. (1979). 'Mother-child interaction and their researchers.' In *Grazer Linguistische Studien* 10: 46-69.
Van der Geest, T. (1979). 'Language acquisition in different developmental stages.' In W. von Raffler-Engel & R. St. Clair, eds., *Language & cognitive styles*, Amsterdam: Swets & Zeitlinger, in press.
Van der Geest, T. et al. (1973a). *'The child's communicative competence.'* The Hague: Mouton.
Van der Geest, T. et al. (1973b). *'Developmental aspects of mother-child conversation.'* University of Amsterdam, ms.
Van der Geest, T. & J. Heckhausen (1979). *'Sprachliche Anpassung in alters- und erstsprachheterogenen Spielsituationen.'* Bochum, ms.
Von Raffler-Engel, W. & R. Hutcheson (1975). *'Language intervention programs in the United States 1960-1974.'* Assen: Van Gorcum.
Watzlawick, P. et al. (1967). *'Pragmatics of human communication.'* N.Y.: Norton.
Wode, H. (1978). *'Developmental sequences in naturalistic L2 acquisition.'* In E. Marcussen-Hatch, ed., pp. 101-117.
Wode, H. & S. Felix (1979). 'Vortrag zum Spracherwerb in L1 und L2.' Oktober 1979, Anglistentagung, Berlin.

Wottawa, H. (1977). *'Psychologische Methodenlehre.'* Juventa München.
Wottawa, H. (1979). *'Grundlagen und Probleme von Dimensionen in der Psychologie.'* Meisenheim/Glan: Verlag Anton Hain.
Wunderlich, D. (1976). *'Studien zur Sprechakttheorie.'* Frankfurt: Suhrkamp.
Wundt, W. (1900). *'Völkerpsychologie, 1. Die Sprache.'* Stuttgart: A. Kröner Verlag.

FLORIAN COULMAS

Spies and Native Speakers*

> At once, with contemptuous perversity, Mr. Vladimir changed the language, and began to speak idiomatic English without the slightest trace of a foreign accent.
>
> (Joseph Conrad, The Secret Agent)

ABSTRACT

This chapter is concerned with a particular kind of non-native speakers of a language: spies. Intelligence agents who are bilingual from early childhood as well as those who spy on their own country are not considered in this article. Our interest is focused solely on those spies who, in spite of their non-nativeness, try to adapt to their "host" country, linguistically and otherwise. What does it take to acquire native-like proficiency in a language? Our intention will not be to offer a finished or comprehensive proposal but rather to characterize a number of particular problems beyond grammar and phonology. It is shown that, among others, linguistic awareness and language routines play a critical role.

THE IDEAL SPY

Mey (this volume) points out that "there is, of course, no doubt that insufficient command of the language of the host country can be a serious obstacle to finding and holding down a job" (p. 79). He goes on to state that "this principle is applied very selectively" (*ibid.*): While it may serve to deprive unskilled immigrants of proper jobs, highly qualified staff are hardly judged by this criterion. There are of course exceptions, and it cannot be overlooked that the standards as to what is considered "insufficient command" are job specific.

To the personnel under consideration here, the said principle is applied most rigidly, to be sure. If a non-native spy wants to be successful in his profession and avoid the transformation into a *persona non grata* he must be able to make himself understood in his host country. But, this is evidently a far cry from the requirements he must meet. For spies, there is a greater need to adapt to their host countries than for most guest workers. To be able to make oneself understood in a foreign idiom does not imply any extraordinary linguistic skills, and in many branches of business life it is exactly this that is required of a foreigner. For spies, however, things are different, because they have to conceal themselves in their host country as best they can. While for most guest workers there is no existential need to deny their foreign origin, spies have an eminent interest in camouflaging their identity as agents of a foreign power. It is a widely held belief and an element of many espionage stories that a perfect command of the language of the host country is a necessary prerequisite.

This belief is, of course, well founded, as language serves a variety of functions aside from conveying messages, one of them being that it indicates (or reveals) membership in a group. Searle (1969:44) has constructed an example where the propositional function of language is completely superseded by the group-membership-indicating function: A captured American soldier in World War II addresses his Italian captors with the sentence: *Kennst du das Land, wo die Zitronen blühen*? His only intention in uttering this sentence is to make believe that he is German, not American. He is not at all interested in communicating with his captors on a propositional basis. If he succeeds in deceiving them into thinking that he *is* German it is only due to the fact that they don't know German but can tell the difference between American English and German, and furthermore that they accept his one German sentence as sufficient evidence of his (make-believe) nationality.

Under regular circumstances, linguistic functions do not come alone as in this extraordinary example. Rather, in performing speech acts whole clusters of functions are realized simultaneously (cf. Hymes 1961; Jakobson 1960). Hence, the non-native spy's situation is much more complicated than that of the fictitious American captive whose tricky maneuver it was to isolate an individual function. The spy cannot concentrate on linguistically manifesting his faked identity while disregarding the content of what he says. Neither can he confine his efforts to the unequivocal expression of whatever he has to say. It is not enough that he takes care *what* he says, he must also be on his guard with his accent and, more generally, *how* he says what to whom. His nefarious profession requires him to do all this at the same time, and if he is not able to perform this feat, he surely isn't an ideal spy and hence of little interest for our present discussion.

I am concerned here, primarily, with an ideal spy who lives and works in a heterogeneous speech community and knows its language perfectly. He is affected, on occasion, by such grammatically irrelevant conditions as memory limitations, distractions, shifts of attention and interest, and errors . . . in applying his knowledge of the language. He is, however, not affected by intereferential mistakes induced by the regularities of his mother tongue. The distractions, errors, etc., that occasionally mar his performance do not differ in a characteristic manner from those that creep in when native speakers of that language converse. He is the perfect chameleon.

THE TASK

Part of making believe that one is not a spy is commonly believed to be making believe that one is a native speaker of the language in one's environment. It is not easy to figure out the reasons for this belief, because, as everybody knows, not every non-native speaker is a spy. Yet there is no doubt that it is a very strong belief among spies and spy trainers, and to do justice to this belief is a formidable task indeed.[1]

When in Rome do as the Romans do is a maxim followed by many residents and visitors of foreign countries, lest they give offence to their hosts by disregarding their conventions. Spies honor this principle, too, if for less respectable reasons. To operate within the foreign milieu without behavioral uncertainty and without attracting too much attention is vitally important for them. The linguistic behavior is only part of this, though a crucial one, and I shall concentrate on it here.

In job advertisements for foreign language teachers one can often read requirements such as these:

– "near native-level proficiency in French"
– "near native proficiency in Russian"
– "near native fluency in Peking Chinese," etc.

Intelligence agencies do not usually announce their vacancies publicly, but if they did, these requirements wouldn't do. With foreign language teachers, one is ready to make concessions. An approximation to native like competence is usually considered sufficient on the grounds that native fluency is unattainable and, maybe, undesirable for non-native speakers anyway. One can always tell a foreigner, and there is no harm in that – unless, that is, one is a spy. "Near native-level proficiency" in the language of his host country is not enough, hence, in this regard, his job is somewhat more demanding than that of a foreign language teacher.

If he decides to conceal his identity as a foreigner, he must be able to play his role perfectly and without a prompter. Absolute familiarity with an integrated set of speech habits, social conventions, and cultural customs that enable the members of his host community to interact with one another is a *sine qua non*. In every conceivable situation, he must be able to react *as if he* were *a native* of his host country. The issue, I think, is that the spy must not be merely simulating reactions, he must reach a degree of matter-of-factness beyond mimicry. Spontaneous reactions within the range of "normal" anticipations must be second nature to him. In brief, his task is not to perform on a *near native* level but on a *native-like* level of proficiency that makes him indistinguishable from genuine natives.

A number of linguistic prerequisites are plain enough. First of all, the ideal spy's pronunciation must be natural. A slight regional accent may even be more desirable than a "received" or standard pronunciation. If he thus identifies manifestly with a particular region of his host country, the spy must however be prepared to give an answer if questioned about his "native land." Next, he must of course have a perfect command of the grammar of his second language. It must be at his disposal freely and without reflection. His performance must reflect and follow a variety of grammatical norms and never confuse the differences between the vernacular and the standard language or between spoken and written language (cf. Vachek, 1973). Thus native like fluency implies perfect command of more than one grammatical variety, as well as the knowledge as to when which one is appropriate. Thirdly, there is the lexicon. An ideal spy has an above average vocabulary. If we come across a hitherto unfamiliar word of our mother tongue, we are usually self-confident enough to assume that we needn't have known it. If a native speaker of English doesn't know what, for instance, *kelson* or *nemoricale* means, he will hardly begin to doubt whether he knows his language well. Ignorance of a word in a foreign language, however, is often experienced as an indication of defective competence. Is it a word one should have known? Do most native speakers know it? These are the questions that come to mind more readily than when walking on the familiar territory of one's native language. An above average sized vocabulary will spare the spy uncertainties of this kind.

These three requirements, natural pronunciation, perfect grammar, and above average sized vocabulary, are clearly hard to fulfill for a non-native speaker. Yet, for the ideal spy, they merely constitute the groundwork on which he must build the sophisticated edifice of his non-native but nevertheless native-like linguistic behavior. In the following sections we shall attempt to point out some of the aspects of native-like linguistic competence beyond the three requirements just mentioned.

AUTOMATIZATION

If an ideal spy is required to have perfect command of his second language, what, then, is the difference between his linguistic competence and that of a native speaker? Or, to put the question differently, what does his non-nativeness amount to? The most obvious difference lies in the course of language learning.

It is, possibly, the most significant characteristic of a native speaker that he learns his language without instruction. According to Chomsky (1968), it is the structure of the mind that determines the course and result of language learning. Innate restrictions on the possible form of all languages enable him to select a hypothesis as to the grammar of his language on the basis of very limited experience. Whether or not Chomsky is right in claiming that the linguistic knowledge of the child extends immensely beyond his experience at a very early stage of his development is a hotly debated and, I think, as yet unresolved problem. I do not want to become embroiled in this issue here. One thing, however, is clear. The acquisition of one's native language does not require active instruction or conscious control, and the result, as Chomsky has been tirelessly pointing out, is not concious knowledge. The important point in the present connection is that command of one's native language does not presuppose a stage in the speaker's individual history where the regularities that constitute the grammar of his language were subject to conscious knowledge. To use Ryle's distinction: native competence of one's language is tantamount to *knowing how* but not to *knowing that*.[2] Learning one's mother tongue as a child does not result in knowing much about it.

By contrast, the ideal spy to be cannot dispense with instruction and hence *knowing that* if he wants to acquire native like proficiency in the language. He lacks the natural environment and the conditions of language socialization characteristic of native development. His language acquisition process therefore passes through a stage of conscious learning, and his *knowing how* is mediated, in large measure, by *knowing that*. In other words, his command of the language is based on a high degree of linguistic awareness.

The particular mental structure that constitutes knowledge of a language is thus established unconsciously in the case of the native speaker, while it is a result of conscious effort in the case of the ideal spy. This leads to the conclusion that lack of linguistic awareness is a characteristic part of native speakerhood.[3] Let me try to elaborate on this point a little.

The native speaker does not normally pay much attention to the activity of speaking. If he does, his attention is not focussed on matters of "correctness" but rather on the content of what he says, on refinement in formulating, personal style, etc. Under regular circumstances his language use is not encumbered by reflections on language as such. *To a large extent, native language use is automatized.* Whichever activity is automatized is removed from conscious control and hence it is a relief of conscious planning operations. Rather than reflecting on how we put which foot on the accelerator or the break we concentrate on the traffic around us and react automatically according to the demands of the situation, to take an obvious example.

Automatization in language is an important prerequisite of 'natural' and efficient performance as well. Graham Greene has an example:

> The young man spoke excellent English; only a certain caution and precision marked him as a foreigner. It was as if he had come from an old-fashioned family among whom it was important to speak clearly and use the correct words... (1963:45).

Our benign reader will not be too surprised to learn that the young man in Greene's story turns out to be a spy, although not an ideal one. He is too much aware of his performance to pass for a native, still lacking the necessary degree of automatization.

We can distinguish two levels of automatization in language. Grammatical structures functioning as general patterns are automatized on a very abstract level. They enable him to produce well-formed sentences.[4] On a less abstract level, actual expressions become automatized. By way of quasi-repetition[5] sequences of actions and reactions including recurrent expressions become part of one's automatized linguistic knowledge. Thus, grammatical structures settle onto an unconscious level of linguistic creativity, and standardized expressions form a part of our linguistic repertoire.

At this point, we come back to the lexicon. That an ideal spy must have an above average sized vocabulary is a very imprecise and abstract statement as long as the units of the vocabulary remain unspecified. Briefly put, the problem is this, and it is by no means trivial (cf. e.g. Bolinger 1976): How much is memorized and how much is put together? On the one hand we have the conception of theoretical grammars according to which rules operate on minimal units to synthesize larger units. Hence we don't need to include any units in the lexicon which can be construed by means of rules that operate on smaller units. On the other hand, it is indubitable that our mental repertoire of linguistic units contains not only elementary lexical items but also a great many expressions that display higher than word level grammatical structure. There is a variety of set expressions which the competent members of a speech community recognize as units and which are passed as such from one generation to the next:

> idioms of various sorts (Makkai 1972, this volume);
> routine formulae (Coulmas 1979; Ferguson 1976);
> gambits (Keller 1979);
> collocations (Mitchell 1971);

as well as some other, less readily classifiable kinds of phraseological items[6] all of which are part of the automatized linguistic knowledge. Phraseological items are linguistic units whose structure is transparent but whose make-up is automatized. They don't need to be construed anew every time they are used. To some extent, the automatization of these units is a consequence of their high frequency of occurrence.[7] Clearly, mastery of the phraseology of a language is an important component of its competent usage.

Phraseological expressions cannot be translated on a lexemic basis. Joseph Conrad, a non-native who achieved native like linguistic competence (at least in writing) to a most remarkable degree, was very much aware of the intricate problems involved:

> "Mr. Vladimir stopped and became guttural.
> 'What makes you say that?'
> 'I don't. It's Verloc who says that.'
> 'A lying dog of some sort', said Mr. Vladimir in somewhat Oriental phraseology.'"
> (Conrad 1967:184). (Vladimir, needless to say, is a spy.)

Hence in addition to grammar and basic vocabulary, the ideal spy must command a large stock of set expressions.

Storage of set expressions is a crucial component of native like proficiency for a variety of reasons. Many of them defy semantic decomposition. Their meanings cannot be told from the meanings of their parts (*big shot*). Others are not semantically anomalous, yet the high frequency of their occurrence has hollowed their meaning potential (*(my) pleasure!*). Many expressions are not only restricted in their contextual distribution but also with regard to social situation (*shut up!*). Some are associated, as a kind of metaphor, with typical situations (*this is where I get off*). Another important feature is the frozen syntax; for instance, the fixed order of bi-nominals or bi-verbials (*bits and pieces* vs *pieces and bits; flesh and blood* vs *blood and flesh; win or lose* vs. *lose or win*).

Children learn all of these properties by memorizing set expressions holistically rather than by penetrating their structure. It has been observed that set expressions play an important part in language learning (Wong-Fillmore forthcoming; Peters forthcoming). Apparently, memorization of chunks of complex linguistic material *before* internal grammatical analysis is a necessary stage. Children use complex units before they are able to break them down and isolate their individual parts. In many cases, awareness of internal structure is preceded by competent usage. Set expressions may, on occasion, remain unanalyzed until adult age simply because correct usage does not require analysis.

Adult learners, instead of trying to use the language, often try to understand it. The proportion of analytic and holistic learning is very different for them as compared to children. In a sense, the order of automatization and analysis is reversed. The analytic efforts of adult learners may thus be an obstacle to automatization.

As pointed out above, native command of a language is characterized by automatization on various levels. In the regular course of language acquisition, *analytic insight into the structure of the language is preceded by automatization.*[8] The difficult task of the ideal spy is to reach automatized performance through analytic learning. He must overcome linguistic awareness in order to achieve native like proficiency.

SPY TRAPS

In the present discussion, to have overcome linguistic awareness means to be able to perform in accordance with the conventions of the host community without self-observation. Let us assume now that there is such an animal as an ideal spy who has achieved this degree of perfection. Should there be no difference at all between those who were born into a culture and those who had to acquire at a much later age all of the habits and conventions that make up a culture. This is hard to imagine, and as spies cannot afford training on the job there should be some weak points that betray their non-nativeness.

One of the spy's problems is that unlike linguists and foreign language students he may never separate grammar from rules of usage and other aspects of culture. He must share with his hosts the same set of situational norms, and yet more important, he must be able to apply them in every possible role relationship. His utterances must be grammatically correct *and* communicatively appropriate relative to diversified social functions. In short, he must have what Fishman (1972) has called "socio-linguistic communicative competence." The factors that combine to form this sort of competence are very subtle.

The story is told of an almost ideal British spy in Crete during World War II, who spoke fluent Greek and dressed like a Greek.

Once (he was) sitting beside a road as an old woman approached. *Cherete* 'hello' he called out, but she walked on toward him with no reply. Passing him, she said in a low voice "God bless you, my son, and take you safe back to your native land." (Applegate 1975:276.)

This spy didn't have to say much to disclose his secret, but how did the native speaker know? It was as simple as this: He had ignored an interactional rule regulating the way people in Greece make transitions into (and out of) social encounters: *The stationary person never greets first.* Every speech community makes use of numerous rules and rituals of this kind. They serve to coordinate behavior in a particular way and thus serve to establish the identity of a group. A spy can only afford to ignore them at the risk of detection.

There are, of course, other traps into which spies can fall. Particularly dangerous are emotional expressions which many spy trainers and linguists fail to recognize as linguistic in nature, because their utterance lacks essential features of talk proper. As opposed to regular speech acts they are characterized by the absence of intentionality and semanticity. Expressions of this sort are typically emitted involuntarily when speakers experience unexpected sensations or sensations calling for some sort of emotional response. There is no ideational mediation involved. This is probably the reason why they are not considered linguistic objects. More problematic is the erroneous equation of *involuntary* and *natural.* The immediate vocal expression of emotions is too readily taken to be 'natural' and unaffected by convention. It may seem paradoxical, but it takes a lot of *conventional* knowledge to be able to show 'natural' emotional expression.

Quine introduces his argument for a stimulus-response conception of meaning with a detailed discussion of the "one-word sentence" *ouch. Ouch* is the "socially proper thing" to say in response to certain stimulations. Clearly, this expression is not independent of social conventions: "One has only to prick a foreigner to appreciate that it is an English word" (Quine 1960: 6f.). We don't find words of this sort in dictionaries because they don't 'mean' anything. Still, they are parts of individual languages. Their regular usage does not involve cognition or conscious control. Their utterance is part of a sensation rather than a designation of it. Nevertheless, they are arbitrary signs that differ markedly from one language to another.

In a recent article, Goffman (1978) has coined a very appropriate name for these words which are generally regarded as non-words: *response cries. Ouch,* for example, is a "pain cry," and there are many other kinds. A number of emotional sensations habitually provoke similar verbalizations: anger, shock, terror, strain, revulsion, surprise, etc. The interesting point about response cries is that, while they serve the non-propositional and seemingly unmediated expression of sensations, they are conventional, i.e., learned and patterned signs nevertheless. That they differ between languages is, after all, not very surprising.

Firstly, the phonological structure of every language induces a preference for certain sounds and sound combinations in its speakers. If we don't assume that *ouch* has some inherent pain property, there is no reason why a pain cry should not have a phonetically different form in other languages.[9] Secondly, it is important to note that socialization means habit formation beyond conscious control. Response cries are produced in accordance with largely unconscious habits. For spies they are very treacherous, as they may fail to notice their conventional character.

Again, automatization is crucially important. The native speaker, in a regular course of conversation, simply has no time to focus his attention on phonology and grammar. He is busy figuring out how to react and how to get the meaning of his message across. The act of speaking follows automatic speech habits. If this is so with voluntary, properly worded expressions, how much more with spontaneous exclamations. There is no time to think. Hence response cries must be properly ingrained into the ideal spy's subconscious reaction potential. He must never be shocked out of his automatized habits and relapse into uttering a response cry of his native language.

The two major reasons why spies must beware of response cries are the affective control of their (natural) production and the lack of meaning. Both of them make it particularly difficult to determine the proper range of their application, which is, of course, by no means random. Wittgenstein's maxim "to look for the use, not for the meaning" is not only one very good principle among others; in this case it is the only way, because there is no meaning. Hence, a dictionary entry could only consist in an elaborate description of the kinds of situations where spontaneous exclamations of anger, pain, or joy are appropriate. Pain, and anger, and joy are experienced as natural and uncontrolled sensations. They are, however, not independent of values, habits, and conventions. Accordingly, learning the response cries of a foreign community presupposes the internalization of some of its values.

Interestingly, there are also 'real' words which can only be properly described and learned by following the said Wittgensteinian principle, and which serve similar functions: swear words. In spite of their regular lexical status they are semantically almost as empty as interjections. More correctly, their utterance as affective imprecations does not usually fulfill a semantic function. The meaning proper of such words as *Fuck!* or *Jesus!* or *Hell!* does not allow any conclusions about their usage. A special danger lurks here for spies. Swear words of obscene or blasphemic content usually violate taboos. And these taboos have a psychological, unconscious reality for those who have grown up with them. Foreign language speakers are liable to underestimate the force of swear words as their taboos, even if they are similar in content, are not so intimately associated with the particular lexical forms. Hence the law of decreasing emotive meaning:

The worse one's practial knowledge of a language, the weaker the emotional reactions associated with its swear words.

The validity of this law can be tested quite easily by introspection. Obscenities have a different 'feel' if uttered in a foreign language. A foreign language speaker can say the most outrageous combinations of 'four-letter words' in public without blushing, unless he is completely at home in his host community and identifies with its values.

Swear words and response cries demonstrate the indissoluble link between language and culture. They also show that the behavioral adaption required of

Spies and Native Speakers

the ideal spy involves much more than fluency in the language. That language learning will affect one's personality should cause no surprise. However, the extent to which this is true varies on a large scale relative to purpose and individual aptitude and talent. Hence, not everyone can meet the demands for an ideal spy.

"When in Rome, do as the Romans do" is a handy cliché, and, maybe, a valuable piece of advice. But its succinctness cannot deceive us into believing that it is easily followed. Only some of the pitfalls which those who strive to reach this aim must take pains to avoid can be mentioned here. However, the demands that the ideal spy must be able to cope with suffice to demonstrate what it means to take it seriously. Nothing has been said about gestures, facial expressions, interpersonal proximity patterns and many other cultural features whose internalization allows a personality to identify with and to be recognized as a member of a group. Yet, the lesson the ideal spy teaches us is obvious enough. The price of becoming "a facsimile of a native" (Nostrand, 1966:4) is a change of one's personality. Everyone may not be ready to pay this price. And the answer to the question as to how strictly the above maxim should be adhered to depends on one's personal wants and the challenges of one's profession.

There is no need here to discuss the differences between learning a language and learning about a language. Despite the distinction between *knowing how* and *knowing that,* those patient readers who have followed us to this point will have come to realize how much the spy and the linguist have in common. It is not only that every scientist is something of an investigator. His cunning and capacity to attain knowledge should not be inferior to that of a spy. Clearly, knowing how to perform properly is what the spy is after. The linguist can be content to know that certain conditions must hold to warrant this result. Both linguist and spy aim to detect the secrets of the native; the spy in order to copy his skills, the linguist in order to explain them.

NOTES

*The title of this article was inspired by Charles Fillmore who in a public lecture during the 49th Linguistic Institute in Salzburg, 1979, observed that some of the phenomena under discussion here are particularly treacherous for spies.
1. All my efforts to contact spy schools on this were of no avail. Institutions of this kind are characterized by a great disproportion between acquiring and distributing information.
2. cf. Ryle, 1949 chapter 2.
3. Anttila makes a similar point emphasizing the difference between "'naive' speakers" and linguistically trained speakers. (cf. Anttila, 1972:349).
4. Harry Whitacker, in a public lecture of the Linguistic Institute 1979 in Salzburg,

reported neurological evidence that automatized grammatical patterns are stored and processed in morphologically different parts of the brain than other linguistic functions.
5. Repetition has always been a difficult topic in philosophy. Peirce's answer is his famous *type-token-distinction* which allows him to preserve sameness in difference. Repetition in the strict sense is logically impossible, because the identity relation holds only between an object and itself. "Quasi-repetition" alludes to Kierkegaard's notion of reiteration: " ... ich hatte entdeckt, dass es überhaupt keine Widerholung gab, und dessen hatte ich mich vergewissert, indem ich dies auf alle möglichen Weisen wiederholte" (Kierkegaard, 1961: 42).
6. For an overview see Coulmas forthcoming.
7. By the same token, one might argue, it is a precondition of their high occurrence frequency.
8. This is one possible reason why a psychologically real grammar may be very difficult to achieve through introspection.
9. cf. e.g. German *au*, Japanese *itai.*

REFERENCES

Anttila, R. (1972). *An Introduction to Historical and Comparative Linguistics.* New York: Macmillan.
Applegate, Richard B. (1975). The Language Teacher and the Rules of Speaking. *TESOL Quarterly* 9 (3): 271-281.
Bolinger, D. (1976). 'Meaning and Memory.' *Forum Linguisticum* 1(1): 1-14.
Chomsky, N. (1968). *Aspects of the Theory of Syntax.* M.I.T. Press.
Conrad, J. (1967 (1907)). *The Secret Agent.* Penguin Modern Classics. Harmondsworth: Penguin Books.
Coulmas, F. (1979). 'On the Sociolinguistic Relevance of Routine Formulae.' *Journal of Pragmatics* 3(3): 239-266.
Coulmas, F. (forthcoming). Introduction: Conversational Routine. In *Conversational Routine. Explorations in Standardized Communication Situations and Pre-patterned Speech.* Coulmas, F., ed., The Hague: Mouton.
Ferguson, C.A. (1976). 'The Structure and Use of Politeness Formulas.' *Language in Society* 5: 137-151.
Fishman, J. (1972). *The Sociology of Language.* Rowley, Mass.: Newbury House.
Goffman, E. (1978). 'Response Cries.' *Language* 54(4): 787-815.
Greene, G. (1963). *The Ministry of Fear.* Harmondsworth: Penguin Books.
Hymes, D. (1961). 'Functions of speech: an evolutionary approach.' *Anthropology and Education,* Fredric C. Gruber, ed., Philadelphia: University of Pennsylvania Press.
Jakobson, R. (1960). 'Linguistics and Poetics.' *Style in Language,* T.A. Sebeok, ed. Wiley, New York, pp. 350-377.
Keller, E. (1979). 'Gambits. Conversational Strategy Signals.' *Journal of Pragmatics* 3 (3): 219-238.
Kierkegaard, S. (1961). *Die Wiederholung. Ein Versuch in der experimentellen Psychologie.* Werke II, Reinbeck: Rowohlt.
Makkai, A. (1972). *Idiom Structure in English.* The Hague: Mouton.
Mey, J.L. (1980). "Right or wrong, my native speaker." This volume.
Mitchell, (1971). 'Linguistic "Goings On"; Collocations and other Lexical Matters Arising on the Syntactic Record.' *Archivum Linguisticum* 2 (new series): 35-69.

Nostrand, H.L. (1966). 'Describing and teaching the sociocultural context of a foreign language and literature.' A. Valdman, ed., *Trends in Language Teaching*, McGraw-Hill.
Peters, A. (forthcoming). 'The Units of Acquisition.' The University of Hawaii, mimeo.
Quine, W.V.O. (1960). *Word and Object*. M.I.T. Press.
Ryle, G. (1949). *The Concept of Mind*. London: Hutchinson.
Searle, J.R. (1969). *Speech Acts. An Essay in the Philosophy of Language*. Cambridge: Cambridge University Press.
Vachek, J. (1973). *Written Language. General Problems and Problems of English*. The Hague: Mouton.
Wong-Fillmore, L. (forthcoming). *The Second Time Around*. New York: Academic Press.

TOHRU KANEKO

On Translatability

ABSTRACT

Many a native speaker has a command of more than one language, and he can intuitively map well-formed expressions of one language onto those of another. Theoretically the intuitions underlying the process of translation are not at all easy to account for. It is argued in this paper that 'meaning equivalence' is the key notion calling for explication in this connection. In many cases lexical and structural correspondences help to establish meaning equivalence. However, where no structural correspondence can be found a direct semantic interpretation of sentences is necessary. This can be achieved by means of an interpretive meta-language some of whose features are discussed in this paper.

0. Translation is one of the most remarkable practical abilities of native speakers as well as one of the most intriguing theoretical problems of linguistics. Ideally, this ability is based on fully developed bilingual competence; and, also ideally, the problem is solved on the basis of a meta-linguistic representation of meaning which can be mapped on well-formed expressions of each one of the languages involved. A meta-linguistic representation of this sort would serve us as an instrument of inter-linguistic comparison and, at the same time, provide a model of the intuitions on which translations are based. The crucial question for me has always been how the theoretical basis for comparison can be construed. In other words, what kind of *tertium comparationis* do we need? Meaning equivalence has often been regarded as one such base for comparison, and it seems to be the one that actual translators and interpreters make use of most. However, meaning equivalence is nothing we can take for granted simply considering it as a means to an end. Rather, it is to be theoretically explained in its own right before it can be put to use in practical work.

1. In typological comparisons of languages, sets of pairs of formal structures are contrasted. In order to do this, the formal structure of the languages to be compared must be described in the same way. In other words, the structural descriptions of the languages must be written in the same meta-language. To take an example from the comparison of phonological structure, we can

compare the Japanese phoneme /r/ with German /r/ by means of their distributional values, phonotactic characteristics and substantial phonetic features which belong to the descriptive device of phonology in general.

For the comparison of formal structure of syntax, two sets of phrase structure rules must be contrasted. This is only possible if they are constructed in the same way. If the phrase structure of one language is constructed morphologically and that of the other is a type of Montague grammar we find no basis for comparison.

We assume that for the purpose of structural comparison the morphologically based categories are appropriate. They must first be established for each of the languages and then compared. Suppose that two sets of phrase structure rules have been made based on such categories. We get first two sets of the whole repertoire of the categories, second the rules of their possible concatenations and, therefore, their distributional values within the syntactic structure of the languages. For example, we can find that both languages have a syntactic device to assign a sentence to a noun phrase. In this case we need not rely on the meaning. It is sufficient to establish the mutual relationship of the categorial notions which are presupposed to be common to the languages in question. But here we encounter two serious problems: First, we must ask what categories can be supposed to correspond to each other and how this can be established, and second, we must be able to state the correspondence of the mutual relationship of the categories.

1.1. It is a truism that every language has its own set of grammatical categories. But such a statement can easily lead to a linguistic relativism of a very radical sort which will deny completely the possibility of translation and the effability hypothesis. We know empirically and intuitively that a set of functional equivalences can be found between the grammatical notions of totally different languages and that, therefore, at least in this restricted sense the extremely relativistic view of languages has to be revised.

By functional equivalence we mean the correspondence of grammatical categories in the following sense:

For the grammatical categories $X_1, X_2, \ldots, X_n$ of a natural language L_x, for $Y_1, Y_2, \ldots, Y_m$ of another natural language L_y, and for $Z_1, Z_2, \ldots, Z_n$ of a categorial language L_z, we say that X_i corresponds to Y_j functionally if X_i and Y_j can be translated into Z_k.

We assume that the categorial language L_z must be a sort of categorial grammar such as Montague's PTQ (1974, originally 1970) or Cresswell (1973). Because of the formal properties of the categorial language L_z, functional equivalence must be established from top to bottom of the categorial tree.

On Translatability

The initial symbol S or t must be postulated first and then the primary derivations such as noun phrase in the sense of Chomsky (1975) are established. Let us take an example from our Japanese-German contrastive research: Suppose that X_1 and Y_1 are noun phrases derived directly from the initial derivational rules. The functional notion of a predicate or the verb phrase in the sense of Chomsky (1975) is established in Japanese as the concatenations

$$\text{(Complement)} + \begin{cases} \text{one of the finite forms of a verb} \\ \text{one of the finite forms of an adjective} \\ \text{noun phrase or nominal adjective} + da \text{ or } datta \end{cases}$$

The German predicate, by contrast, has the following structure:

(Complement) + one of the finite forms of a verb.

Let us designate these complex notions as X_2 and Y_2, respectively. We can now define adnominal sentences in Japanese and relative sentences in German by means of X_1, X_2 and Y_1, Y_2 in the simplified way:

adnominal sentences in Japanese: $X_2 + X_1$

where noun phrase + *da* and nominal adjective + *da* must be changed into noun phrase + *no* and nominal adjective + *na*, respectively.

relative sentence in German: $Y_1 + Y_2$.

Moreover, we find another crucial difference in the adnominal structure: the coreferential noun phrase in the concatenation $Y_1 + Y_2$ must be changed into a demonstrative pronoun *der* or *welcher* in the appropriate case form. But in Japanese the coreferential noun phrase may not occur in the concatenation $X_2 + X_1$. In this way we can establish the functional equivalence of a type of adnominal sentence.

So far as the categorial grammar L_z is readily given it may not be difficult to establish the functional equivalence of the major categories. We may get a set of corresponding categories of the languages L_x, L_y and L_z and at the same time the correspondences of the major construction types such as the type of adnominal sentences $X_2 + X_1$ and $Y_1 + Y_2$. The correspondence of the phrase structure rules of the languages L_x and L_y may therefore be found for the major categories at least.

1.2. However, this procedure is inevitably accompanied by a more serious problem: most grammatical categories of natural languages are morphologically motivated, probably with the exception of the initial symbol S or Montague's t.

They are, therefore, not always in accordance with the functionally motivated categories of the language L_z. To take an example from Japanese-German contrastive research, Japanese nouns are defined by means of the following syntactic properties: they make a noun phrase in the concatenations N *no* N as well as *sono* N. Moreover, the case particle *o* must be able to follow nouns. German nouns, by comparison, are defined by means of the following three morphological properties: they are specified in case, gender and number, each of which must be able to be marked in some way. The correspondence between Japanese and German nouns can obviously be established only through functional equivalence. However, some grammatical categories have no correlates in other languages to be compared. They are so-called minor categories in most cases, but yield many difficult problems in language comparison. Typical examples are articles in some European languages and final particles in Japanese and other post-positional languages. For contrastive research such as that between Japanese and German, these categories show a zero-contrast in the sense of Schulte-Pelkum (in: Vergleichende Grammatik Japanisch-Deutsch in prep.), that is, they have no correspondence in the language to be contrasted. Formally, it is not difficult to assign a functional definition to them: articles belong to the category which makes noun phrases of the category noun, i.e., the category of determiners. And this does not exist in Japanese. The sentence final particles in Japanese represent a category which makes a sentence of a sentence. Except for the tag *nicht wahr?* this possibility does not exist in German.

As far as the formal comparison of languages is concerned there are practically three possibilities: (a) A direct functional equivalence can be established between two categories of different languages, e.g., Japanese and German nouns; (b) an indirect functional equivalence can be found, e.g., three categories of a language correspond to a subcategory of another language; auxiliary verbs in German to suffix verb or adjective in Japanese for example, and (c) there is no mutual correspondence, as is the case with the articles and sentence final particles mentioned above. The question is now, how we can continue to compare different structures of languages over and above functional equivalence. In case (c) we cannot go on if we confine ourselves to a purely formal comparison of structures. However, we know empirically that meaning equivalence plays a crucial role even if no functional correspondence can be found. Generally speaking, meaning equivalence or, in other words, translation correspondence must be introduced as a device of language comparison precisely at the stage where no functional equivalence can be established.

2. Translation presupposes meaning equivalence between two sentences belonging to different languages. Now, from the viewpoint of the compositional

hypothesis, the meaning of a sentence can be given as a compositional sum of the phrase structure of the sentence and the lexial terms assigned to the structure. For the sake of simplicity we assume that the meaning of a sentence is constructed by means of a set of amalgamation rules which run upwards from the lexical terms to the top of the structure tree of the sentence. Suppose that a sentence S_x of the language L_x has a phrase structure P_x with lexical terms $x_1, \ldots, x_m$ and a sentence S_y of the language L_y a phrase structure P_y with lexical terms $y_1, \ldots, y_n$. If the sentences S_x and S_y have the same meaning, then the sets of lexical terms must correspond to each other semantically and at the same time the structures P_x and P_y must be identical. This is also true when we take account of a transformational derivation of sentence meaning, if we assume that P_x and P_y must be identical on some level of the derivation. If this assumption holds, then the sentences S_x and S_y are different only in phonetic form. Therefore, translation would mean merely the substitution of the lexical terms of one language with the semantically corresponding lexical terms of another language. In other words, translation would change only the phonetic shape of sentences, not the meaning of lexical terms nor the phrase structure of the sentences.

However, we know empirically that this assumption holds only in marginal cases such as the sentences *Katzen fangen Mäuse* and *cats catch mice*. The majority of lexical terms of languages do not correspond to each other. Therefore, the phrase structures of semantically equivalent sentences cannot be identical. Suppose that one of the lexical terms x_i of the sentence S_x has no equivalent in the lexical terms of the sentence S_y, then the structures P_x and P_y must be different if S_x and S_y have the same meaning. Otherwise S_x and S_y cannot be equivalent semantically. We can thus conclude from the empirical assumption of the general difference of the meaning of lexical terms in different languages that the phrase structures of the sentences must be different if the sentences have the same meaning. On the face of it, this seems to be quite trivial. But it implies some interesting problems, if we consider the question of exactly how the structures differ. The difference can vary vastly in its extent. The minimal difference can be found in cases where a category node in P_x corresponds to two nodes in P_y, for instance:

$$P_x : X_i = P_y : \begin{array}{c} Y_k \\ \diagup \diagdown \\ Y_i \quad Y_j \\ | \quad | \\ y_i \quad Y_j \end{array}$$

$$\begin{array}{c} | \\ x_i \end{array}$$

In this case the lexical item x_i corresponds to $y_i + y_j$ semantically.

We can imagine the maximum difference in cases where the sets of formation rules of the languages have no corresponding categories other than the initial symbol S. In this case, the only thing the languages have in common is the fact that they have sentences. But the maximum difference in this sense is inconsistent with the hypothesis of language universals which claims that at least some formal universals can be established between major categories in most languages. It is most probable that language difference is found somewhere between this minimum and maximum, i.e., that the differences lie mainly in morphologically based categories while the formation rules are constructed in some universal way.

It is also common knowledge that every language has a set of morphologically based categories which are inevitably different from those of other languages. But if this statement is combined with our tentative conclusion that meaning equivalence between different languages can be established only through structural difference, then we can find evidence for translatability even in morphological differences of languages. This has some important implications for the typological comparison of languages: First, we must find different patterns of the categorial assignment of lexical terms. Lexical terms of the same meaning in different languages can be assigned to totally different categories. For example the negation markers of Japanese *Anai, n, Azu, mai, na* have very different syntactic properties and are assigned to the morphological categories suffixical adjective (*Anai*), verbal suffix (*n, Azu*) and sentence final particles (*mai, na*). On the other hand the negation markers in German are adverbs (*nicht, nie, niemals, nirgends, nirgend-, weder . . . noch*), nouns (*nichts, niemand*), or pronouns (*kein-*). This categorial difference obviously has a crucial influence on the syntactic behavior of the negation markers. Second, we must find different patterns of category combinations. The complement in Japanese is marked by case particles. In German, on the other hand, it takes very heterogeneous forms: inflected nouns and pronouns, preposition plus noun, adjectives and adverbs. Third, we must therefore pay attention to the different patterns of formation rules. This is merely the logical consequence of the facts stated above.

A translation mechanism that serves to establish the meaning equivalence between different languages changes not only the lexical terms but also the morphologically based categories of one language into those of another. We come back here to the problem mentioned in the previous paragraph: the functional categories $Z_1, \ldots, Z_n$ of the categorial language L_z serve to relate the morphological categories of different languages. The language L_z is regarded, therefore, as the so-called *tertium comparationis*. In our ordinary work of translation we carry out this procedure intuitively, almost without noticing what we are doing. Before we substitute lexical terms, we analyze the structure of the input sentence and try to find the corresponding structure in the target language. As far as the functional equivalence between the morphologically motivated categories of different languages can be established we get a solid base for translation. Where there is no functional equivalence to be found, we must assign a specific expression form of the output language directly to the meaning of the sentence of the input language. In this area, we have practically no formal device to verify the translation. It is important to grasp the referential meaning correctly and to render this crucial part of the meaning in the output language exactly. For this purpose we need another meta-language.

3. Let us call the essential part of a sentence meaning the referential or denotative meaning of the sentence if we are concerned with the state of affairs referred to by the sentence. We assume that the referential meaning of a sentence is properly given by the semantic interpretation of a sentence. Contextual information and situational framework serve to disambiguate the semantic interpretation but do not participate in forming the meaning proper.

It is a well-known fact that every language has a different pattern of meaning. This is true, regardless of whether we favor an effability or an extremely relativistic hypothesis. What we are concerned with here is, however, to find the linguistic procedure which enables us to make correspondences on the basis of what is essentially different. Referential meanings of lexical terms have generally no correspondence if considered in isolation. But it is not impossible and even probable that they can have the same reference when they are combined into a construction which is a constituent of a sentence. Let us take an example from Japanese-German contrastive research once again. The following pair of sentences has the same reference:

(1) *Kono too wa mukasi kaminari de kowasareta.*
(2) *Dieser Turm wurde einst durch einen Blitzschlag zerstört.*

The semantic correspondence can be easily found between the nouns: *too* and *Turm, kaminari* and *Blitzschlag*. It can be easily imagined, too, that temporal nouns such as *mukasi* correspond to temporal adverbs like *einst*. An actual comparison begins with the phrases *kono too wa* and *dieser Turm, kaminari de* and *durch einen Blitzschlag*. In Japanese the case is marked overtly with postpositions, of course with the exception of elliptical cases. German prepositions have the corresponding function in the case of *de* and *durch*. Cas marking in German is mainly by nominal inflection.

Besides this typological comparison, it is most interesting for our purpose to compare the verbal complexes: *kowas+are+ta* is agglutinative but *wurde ... zerstört* is analytic and discontinuous. These passive forms correspond to each other functionally as well as semantically. (cf. Kaneko "Passiv versus

Ukemi," in *Vergleichende Grammatik Japanisch-Deutsch.*) The sum of these partial correspondences shows that, inasfar as regular passive forms of Japanese and German are concerned, the functional and semantic correspondence can be established on some level of interpretative procedure of the sentence meaning.

However, things are not always so simple. An adversative passive sentence in Japanese cannot be translated into any German passive sentence:

(3) *Bokutati wa yama de hidoi ame ni hurareta.*
(4) *Wir hatten in den Bergen einen starken Regen.*
  *Wir wurden in den Bergen durch einen starken Regen geregnet.

Adversative passive sentences are characterized by an extra noun phrase as the theme of the sentence, i.e., the noun phrase which is not contained in the embedded sentence *yama de hidoi ame ga hutta* ('in the mountains it rained violently'). The extra noun phrase *bokutati wa* refers to the person who is adversely affected by the event referred to by the embedded sentence. However, German does not have this special type of passive construction. The adversative affectedness can be expressed in German only implicitly as shown in the translation above. Otherwise it must be expressend explicitly with a lexical term such as *leider*. In this case, the structural correspondence can be found merely on an abstract level of derivation.

Let us take one more example in order to show that where there is no structural correspondence we must construct first the meaning of the substructure of the sentence which will then be transferred appropriately into a construction of the target language. The sentence final particle *mai* conveys the meaning of negative supposition when the subject is the second or third person:

(5) *Kyoo kare wa kuru mai.*
(6) *Heute kommt er vielleicht nicht.*

The correspondence is found in *mai* and *vielleicht nicht*. The question is how this correspondence has been established. The meaning of *mai*, i.e. "negative supposition," has been translated into two German words. Here the meaning description "negative supposition" plays the role of an interpretative metalanguage which relates the expressions of different languages to each other. Therefore, it is part of the task of language comparison to postulate a set of semantic primitive predicates relevant to the languages to be compared.

Notice now that every language has a series of expression which cannot be translated literally. In such cases, a structural and lexical correspondence often leads to a fatal misunderstanding *although* the expressions are seemingly well-formed according to their own grammatical rules. Compare the following sentences:

(7) *Kuzira wa honyuurui da.*
(8) *Der Wal ist ein Säugetier.*   (Whales are mammals.)
(7') *Aki wa Arasi-yama da.*
(8') **Herbst ist Arasi-yama.*   (Autumn is Arasi-yama (place name).)

While sentences (7) and (8) correspond very nicely, (7') and (8') don't. This is due to the differences in the syntactic restrictions governing the application of the respective rules. The Japanese construction "X *wa* Y *da*" has a vast scope of application ranging from definitional sentences such as (7) to proverb-constructions such as (7'). The respective German rule cannot be extended in a similar fashion. Hence the ungrammaticality of (8').

4. A last point I want to touch upon briefly here concerns a class of expressions which constitute a particular problem for translation: idioms. In general, they cannot be translated into other languages literally. They are regarded in most cases as lexical units, and even within a language they can be substituted by other lexical terms which convey the corresponding – if not the same – meaning. For example, if the English expression *to turn out to be* is to be translated into German, the translation is only possible by means of the semantic interpretation of the entire syntactic segment. The meaning of the segment is then changed into a German expression, e.g., *sich ergeben, zustandekommen,* or the like. Structurally the translated expressions have nothing to do with the original one. In the field of idiomacity the semantic interpretation of the input language is the only possible approach to a correct translation.

Moreover, every language has a series of expressions which can only be interpreted by means of their habitual usage. Neither the literal nor the compositional meaning indicates their function directly. In this field of linguistic expressions the Wittgensteinian principle is fully applicable as Coulmas (1979) has pointed out. He calls them "routine formulae" and claims that in order to explain the meaning and usage of e.g. *congratulations!*, *bon appétite, sayonara*, etc., it is necessary to construct a set of contextual and situational frames in which they are used correctly with respect to social conventions. Here we will not go into the details of the problems any more, especially because we already have a promising attempt from Coulmas in this field of research.

Moreover, in language comparison stylistic difference of expressions must be considered. Languages with the lexical and syntactic device of Honorifics, such as, for instance, Japanese cannot be translated correctly if these socially conventionalized stylistic factors are disregarded. We must, therefore, compare expressions of different languages always on the same stylistic level, whatever type of expressions come in question, i.e., whether they are idioms or routine formulae.

5. To sum up, meaning equivalence between sentences of different languages can be established on the basis of lexical and structural correspondence of sentences. Structural correspondence can be shown by means of a functional meta-language, say the categorial language L_z mentioned above. Where no structural correspondence can be found the direct semantic interpretation of the sentence, or at least of one of the constituents, is necessary. This can be carried out by means of another meta-language of an interpretive or logical sort. In this case, we have to make practically a double translation: from the input language into the meta-language and from this into the output language.

In many cases lexical and structural correspondences do not suffice. They must be supported by the corresponding systematic values of the syntactic rules applied in order to form the expressions. Moreover, idiomatic expressions and routine formulae make it necessary to postulate a parameter which is crucial for correct translation, namely the correspondence in usage. There is also a further factor to be taken into consideration: stilistic correspondence, which must hold for all sorts of expressions. Translation, i.e., meaning equivalence between the expressions of different languages, must satisfy at least these claims we would like to make on the basis of our research on the structural comparison of languages.

REFERENCES

Chomsky, N. (1975). *The logical structure of linguistic theory*. London and New York.
Coulmas, F. (1979). 'On the sociolinguistic relevance of routine formulae. In *Journal of Pragmatics* 3: 239-266.
Cresswell, M.G. (1973). *Logics and Language*. London: Closhester and Beccles.
Guenther, F., Guenther-Reutter M., eds. (1978). *Meaning and Translation. Philosophical and linguistic approaches*. London.
Montague, R. (1974). *Formal Philosophy* (Selected Papers of R. Montague, ed. and with an introduction by R.H. Thomason), New Haven.
Vergleichende Grammatik Japanisch-Deutsch, Bibliographisches Institut Mannheim (in preparation).

DAVID R. OLSON

The Literate Native Speaker: Some Intellectual Consequences of the Language of Schooling

ABSTRACT

Literacy involves a specialized use of language which may be critical to the habits of mind produced by schooling. This paper is an attempt at assessing the changes in linguistic usage incalculated through formal schooling of written language. It is argued that literate skills profoundly affect Native Speaker's orientation to language. Most importantly, it is shown that the differentiation of "sentence meaning" and "speaker's meaning" is tied to literacy.

Education tried, inadequately and hopelessly, to make a European of me ... almost everything I got from books was either at odds with what I knew from experience or irrelevant to it or remote from it. Books didn't enlarge me; they dispersed me (Wallace Stegner, 1962).

Formal educational institutions are sustained by a public which believes that schooling imparts a distinctive set of characteristics to the language and cognitive processes of the children who attend them. These effects of schooling are conventionally described in terms of the acquisition of bodies of knowledge and mental skills embodied in the curriculum of the school.

This way of representing the consequences of schooling, although useful for formulating goals, curricula and modes of evaluation, may divert our attention from the practical competencies and informal knowledge that is acquired outside the school especially that acquired in the other primary social groups of family and peers. My concern here is with the relationship between this unschooled form of cognition, what we may call "commonsense," and the forms of cognition inculcated through schooling. Those changes in cognition, I shall try to show, reflect changes in the uses of language, changes associated historically with the invention of literacy and developmentally with the acquisition of literate skills.

Psychological research both of a cross-cultural and developmental sort has provided much evidence that the cognitive processes are influenced by schooling. It is well known that unschooled children perform abysmally on the sorts of tests our society uses to measure intelligence. They have difficulty defining words, solving verbal problems, formulating algorithms for solving classes of problems, devising mnemonic strategies for remembering word lists, deriving valid inferences from verbal propositions and so on.

More recent and more detailed research in anthropology and in cross-cultural psychology, such as that recently described by Scribner and Cole (1978), has cast grave doubts on the validity of these means of assessment of intelligence in traditional cultures. Indeed, rather minor modifications in the tasks often yield substantial changes in traditional subjects' performance on those problems. Thus if Liberian farmers are given varieties of rice and medicinal leaves to classify instead of pictures of geometric shapes, they do markedly better. Similarly, if the content of a syllogism is congruent with what they know to be true, uneducated subjects draw the correct inferences as well as do educated ones. They justified their answers differently, however, the uneducated ones on the basis of what they knew, the educated ones on the basis of the premises represented by the sentences.

This cross-cultural evidence is quite congruent with the developmental evidence my colleagues and I have obtained with children in our own society, changes that occur in the course of schooling. We have traced these intellectual changes to an important change in the structure and function of language — a voluntary and self-conscious use of the logical properties of language. We can describe this development by saying that children's encounters with "schooled" language produced a new awareness of what was, in fact, specifically "said" as opposed to what was generally "meant". With this new awareness children begin when the occasion warrants it, to confine interpretation to the meaning explicitly conventionalized "in the text." We may state the argument more formally by adopting a distinction advanced by the philosopher H.P. Grice, between what a sentence means, the "sentence meaning," and what a speaker means by a sentence, the "speaker's meaning." The two are often but not always congruent. When a teacher says "I hear talking" his sentence literally means that some vocal noises are being registered by his auditory apparatus. Yet what he, the teacher, means or intends is that the talking should stop. But the ability to relinquish that speaker's meaning and to pay attention to what the sentence *per se* means is an important effect of schooling, an effect we have traced to the development of literacy.

I shall describe this change in the child's orientation to language which occurs over the school years by means of a series of studies conducted by my colleagues Angela Hildyard and Nancy Nickerson and I at The Ontario Institute for Studies in Education.

We have known for some time that if you tell a child of say, 5 years of age, that "John has more than Mary," he is unable to answer the question "Does Mary have less than John?" Similarly, if you tell him "John hit Mary" he is unable to answer the question "Was Mary hit by John?" We interpret this finding as a demonstration that young children fail to see the implication of the statement *per se*. Nancy Nickerson and I (Olson & Nickerson, 1977) recently conducted an additional experiment that casts a new light on this particular competence. In this experiment we simply varied the degree to which the characters of the sentence were known to the children. In the pilot studies we used names of siblings and classmates. In the experiment we used the familiar Peanuts comic-strip characters, Snoopy, Lucy, and Charlie Brown. There were four conditions. In the first, we used the arbitrary names John and Mary that we had used in earlier studies; in the second, we used the familiar Peanuts' names; in the third, we used the Peanuts' names embedded in a meaningful story; and in the fourth, we used pictures.

Two findings emerged. The more well-known the characters the better able were children to draw the correct implications. That is, the more readily sentences could be assimilated to the child's prior commonsense knowledge of the world, the more successful was he in drawing a correct inference. Note, however, that the ultimate goal for the child in a schooled context is to draw those inferences even when common sense intuition fails to do its part.

The second finding is more surprising. By performing an analysis on the number of correct responses to the sentence-question pairs we were able to show that children, when successful, proceed in a manner different from that of adults: for adults True Passives are most difficult; for children False Passives are most difficult. To account for these differences, we have postulated different processing models for children and adults. Adults, in these experiments, operate directly on the logical form of the statements: If x hit y, then y was hit by x. Adults simply compare sequentially the constituents of the representations of the sentences keeping track of the mismatches by means of some truth index. Their reaction times reflect the number of these operations. For adults, we may say that the meaning operated on is the sentence meaning, the meaning in the text so to speak.

Children, on the other hand, cannot calculate the logical implications of the statements *per se*. Rather, they can compare a sentence *with what they know* to see if it agrees directly; if it does not, they can give a new description of what they know and see if this new description now agrees with the test sentence. This new description is identical in form to that generated logically by adults — hence, they often get the question correct, *but* they get it by assimilation and redescription of *known events*, as in a paraphrase, and not as the necessary logical implication of propositions. And that, of course, is the reason children can only answer the question when asked in a meaningful context. Writing turns utterances as descriptions of known events into formal propositions with logical implications. And the children here are doing what we literate adults frequently do in ordinary conventional language.

In a second experiment in our laboratory, Angela Hildyard (1976) tested children who had had three, five, or six years of schooling (roughly 9-, 11-, and 12-year-olds) on their ability to draw logical inferences from presented premises involving spatial and temporal relations. Statements were of the form $A > B$, $B > C$. The questions involved inferences of the form $A > C$. The independent variable was the nature of the material in which these logical relations were embedded: Formal statements, Counter Factual statements and Meaningful texts and some other conditions I cannot detail here. As in the Nickerson study, Hildyard found that children had little or no difficulty drawing logical inferences when they were compatible with what the child knew or believed but had great difficulty when the same relations were given formally but without a supporting knowledge base. To illustrate, if children hear that "The elephant is ahead of the giraffe and the camel is behind the giraffe" and they are subsequently asked if the camel is ahead of the elephant, they perform poorly in early grades and performance improves significantly with grade level.

If, however, they are told that "The elephant is ahead of the giraffe because the giraffe's long neck kept getting tangled in the tree" and "The camel is behind the giraffe because the camel frequently stopped to eat," the young children do very well in drawing the correct inference and, moreover, on such items there is little improvement with age. Hildyard concludes that children can indeed draw logical implications from stated relations if those relations can be represented in terms of the child's prior knowledge base. What grows with development, or with schooling, is the ability to draw logical inferences whose sole distinguishing quality is that they follow necessarily from the explicitly presented statements; they are learning to confine interpretation "to the text."

This developing ability to pay attention specifically to what was "said" as opposed to what was "meant" is clearly shown in a further experiment of Angela Hildyard's in which she constructed a series of ten short stories, read them to Junior Kindergarten (4 year old) and Grade 2 (7 year old) children and tested them for their recall of a critical sentence. Her hypothesis was that younger children would recall what the speaker had presumably "meant" by the sentence while older, schooled, children would recall what the sentence had actually stated — be aware of the meaning of the sentence *per se*. Here is one of the stories:

One day Susie and Kevin Jones went to the movies. Their mum gave them some money to buy some popcorn. Susie bought a large box and they shared it out. When Kevin looked at Susie's share he didn't feel too happy. "You've got more than me" he said.

The stories, which described social predicaments of this sort were followed by a recall test, e.g., "What did they buy to eat?" "What did Kevin say?"

The Literate Native Speaker 383

The most interesting results came from Kindergarten and Grade 2 children's reply to the second question. Junior kindergarten children, when asked what Kevin had said, would frequently recall what had been given as a declarative "You have more than me" as either a request or a command, "Can I have some?" or "Give me some popcorn". By the second grade, children tended to recall the statement verbatim: "You have more than me". When further queried as to why he said that, they replied, "Because he wanted more". These results are shown in Figure 1. The implication of these findings is that almost all of the children interpreted the statement, "you have more than

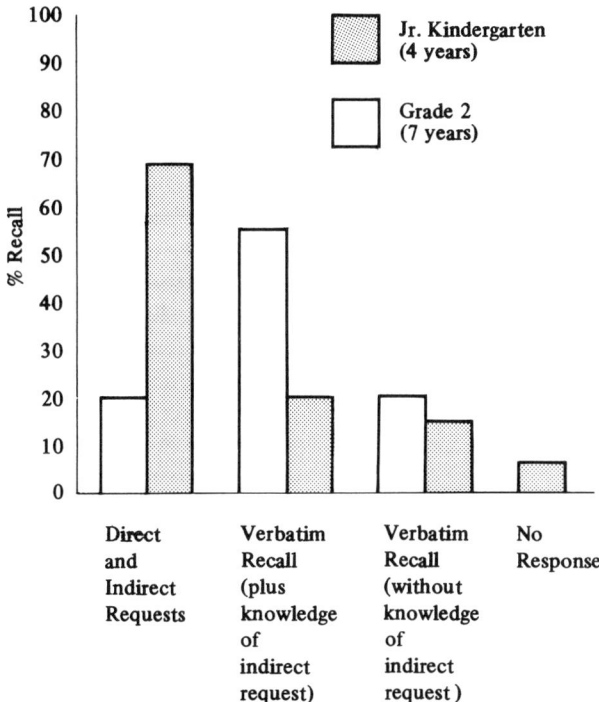

Figure 1. The recall of declarative statements as given (verbatim) and as direct and indirect requests by Junior Kindergarten and Grade 2 children.

me" not simply as a true statement but rather as an indirect request and that interpretation biased the recall of the younger subjects. Older subjects remembered both what was intended by the sentence and the means the speaker used to achieve it, (here a declarative, true statement). That is, the sentence was interpreted and evaluated not strictly or even primarily on what it said but rather on what the speaker presumably had meant by the sentence, what is sometimes called the pragmatic meaning. And the younger the children, the stronger the tendency to treat the sentence as a request and hence to report it as such.

These findings are similar to those we had obtained earlier in our studies of recall and inference from stories with children of different ages in which we showed that recall tends to be of "what was meant" rather than "what was said" and that with age (and schooling) children come to be able to differentiate the two.

In a fourth study of children's changing orientation to language, Beverly Wolfus gave Kindergarten and Grade 2 children a series of direct commands such as (Tell me what this is! Put the penny in the glass!) and ambiguous ability requests (Can you turn over the cup? Could you tell me the name of this?), while pointing to a cup or other objects and observed how children interpreted and responded to them. She was particularly interested in whether the children opted for the direct expressed "sentence meaning" or the indirect pragmatic "speaker's meaning" of the ambiguous expressions. Thus "Tell me if you can put the penny in the glass" could be answered by assent, Yes I can" — the direct meaning — or by compliance, by actually putting the penny in the glass — the indirect, or pragmatic meaning. When issued direct commands, both age groups complied extremely consistently. Told "Open the book," everyone opened the book. To "Tell me what this is" every one said, "A pen".

The differences in the responses to ambiguous questions and statements for the two age groups were striking. These differences occurred in response to the questions and statements which were ambiguous between a direct "sentence meaning" and an indirect "speaker's meaning" that is ambiguous in their call for *assent* as opposed to *compliance*. To the statement "Can you turn over the cup?" older children would say "Yes", that is, assent, younger children would silently turn it over, that is comply. To "Tell me if you can put the penny in the glass", older children would assent by saying "Yes" or "I can," younger children would comply by putting the penny in the cup. To "Do you know what this is?" while pointing at a penny or a cup, older children would assent by replying "Yes," young children would comply by replying "Penny" or "Cup". Even for the neutral statement, "The book is closed", young children would, more often than older children, silently open it, older children would not but rather await further information.

Overall, these data show that the younger children generally took utterances in terms of the expressed or implied "speaker's meaning" and complied with it, while older children tended to differentiate the direct sentence meaning from its indirect "speaker's meaning" and respond to the direct meaning. Ervin-Tripp (1977), observed a similar effect. When told to "Say why don't you stand up" the child said "Stand up!" and stood up — that is, they complied with the command rather than merely repeat it as it had in fact been stated. Again this indicates that the meaning of the statement is, at least at the beginning, not simply its direct sentence meaning, although that meaning may be calculated as part of its more pragmatic speaker's meaning. Rather, the sentences are scanned, in the attempt to recover the speaker's intention, and that is what the youngest children tended to respond to.

Again, with age or schooling, children begin to differentiate the propositional from the pragmatic meaning and to be able to respond to either of them. However, it appears that this propositional meaning is not primary but rather specialized out of an undifferentiated social speaker's meaning. All of these studies suggest that schooling is responsible for an important reorientation to language, the differentiation of what the sentence means, its direct or "sentence meaning." It is my conjecture that schooled competence, including competence on intelligence tests, is based on the ability to respond to the sentence meaning, the meaning in the syntactic and lexical structures of the sentence, or as I prefer to state it, to treat language as if the meaning were "in the text." The focus on language, on mastering and explicating the meanings in the language, takes many forms: formulating definitions of words, devising verbal rules, and drawing valid inferences. These are of course among the very intellectual effects associated with schooling.

It remains to show how this changed orientation to language and its associated forms of thought are tied to literacy. This relationship was first advanced on cultural-historical and literacy-critical bases; I shall briefly summarize these arguments and then add some of our more recent psychological evidence.

The assumption that sentences *per se* have a meaning which may be analyzed and formalized independently of what a particular speaker meant or intended by that sentence, is as we have seen above, a relatively late and relatively specialized "schooled" achievement; it was also a relatively late historical achievement that was tied to literacy.

The view that sentences and texts mean what they say is interestingly stated in Martin Luther's claim that scripture is *sui ipsius interpres* – scripture is its own interpreter (cited in Gadamer, *Truth and Method,* 1975, p.154). For Luther, the meaning of Scripture depended, not on the dogmas of the church, but upon a deeper reading of the text. That is, the meaning of the text is *in the text,* in the sentence meaning. The claim seems relatively straightforward but it indicates a profound change in the presumed autonomy of text which occurred early in the 16th century because of the invention and dissemination of a print literacy, as McLuhan (1962) and Ong (1971) have argued. Prior to Luther it was assumed that meaning could not be stated completely explicitly. Statements required the correct interpretation by the authorities – either scribes or clerics. Luther's claim and the assumption which guided it cut both ways: it was a milestone in the developing awareness that text could explicitly represent its meaning — and hence that it did not depend upon dogma or interpretive context; and it also indicated a milestone in the attempt, primarily in science and philosophy, to shape language to more explicitly represent its meanings. Thus, the Royal Society of London, according to its historian Spratt (1667/1966) was concerned not only with the advancement of science but also with "the improvement of the English language as a medium of prose" (p.56). The society demanded a mathematical plainness of language and rejected all digressions and swellings of style. But this reliance on explicit, autonomous text was merely a refinement of the process that had begun with the Greek invention of the alphabet as Havelock has shown.

The Greek alphabet, through its ability to make a permanent record of exactly what was said, provided a tool for the formulation and criticism of explicit meanings and was therefore critical to the evolution of Greek literacy. Writing systems which preceded the alphabet, such as syllabaries, tended to serve a somewhat limited purpose, primarily that of providing an aid to memory. In his *Prologue to Greek Literacy* (1973) Havelock wrote:

When it came to transcribing discursive speech, difficulties of interpretation would discourage the practice of using the script for novel or freely-invented discourse. The practice that would be encouraged would be to use the system as a reminder of something already familiar, so that recollection of its familiarity would aid the reader in getting the right interpretation . . . It would in short tend to be something — tale, proverb, parable, fable and the like — which already existed in oral form and had been composed according to oral rules. The syllabic system in short provided techniques for recall of what was already familiar, not instruments for formulating novel statements which could further the exploration of new experience (p. 238).

The Greek perfected the alphabetic system and developed a prose writing style which, greatly extended by the invention of printing and the form of extended texts it encouraged, resulted in both the belief in Luther and the aspiration in the members of the Royal Society that statement and text must be adequate, unambiguous and explicit representations of meaning. Those statements and texts, however, were no longer an ordinary language, a mother tongue, but rather a form of language specialized to serve the requirements of autonomous, written, formalized text. Indeed, this is the language into which children are progressively inducted during the school years. Thus, formal schooling, in the process of teaching children to deal with printed texts, fosters the ability as Patricia Greenfield (1972) has put it, to "speak a written language." It is the interpretation of written language which, I suggest, is responsible for developing the child's ability to operate on the sentence meanings rather than as he had done earlier, treating the sentences as a transparent cue to the speaker's meaning. It is an indication of the child's induction into a literate society.

Two of our recent studies of the children's acquisition of literacy skills tend to confirm this historical analysis by showing that written language is in fact the critical factor in word and sentence meaning. In the first Nancy Nickerson and Pat Cleland, following up some earlier research by Hazel Frances, found that pre-school children have no concept of a word as a unit of speech. When they do begin to form the concept, they apply it exclusively to the written form; for children *words* are units of print not units of speech. Hence the possibility of formulating word meanings and definitions would seem to be a by-product of the invention of a permanent artifact for preserving speech. Alfred Lord (1960) in his analysis of oral poetry in Yugoslavia made much the same observation. A word for these oral poets was a synonym for an utterance not for a grammatical constituent. Explicit awareness of and the ability to control word meaning is more a function of written than of oral language.

A second study, this one by Angela Hildyard, involved the comparison of reading with listening to texts. If as I have argued above, writing tends to change one's focus from speaker's meanings to sentence meanings, the written form should result in a better recall of what was said, that is, the "sentence meaning" while the oral form should result in better recall of what was meant that is the "speaker's meaning". This is what Hildyard, in fact, obtained. Verbatim recall of statements was better when both 5th Grade and Adult subjects read the stories than when they listened to them. Symmetrically, the tendency to accept plausible but unmentioned inferences as having been in the story was greater for those children and adults who listened to the story than for those who read them.

Both of these lines of evidence provide empirical support for the hypothesis that literal meaning, attention to the sentence meaning, to what the words, clauses and sentences conventionally mean, as opposed to conversational meaning, or what a speaker may mean by that sentence, is tied to the children's acquisition of literacy skills. That is, literate meaning commences with written language just as the original discovery of those meanings was tied to the invention of literacy in classical Greece.

Although the development of an artifact for making speech permanent was a decision factor in the development of western society and although children's exposure to and acquisition of literacy is a decisive factor in the specialization of the forms of competence we designate as "intelligence" it is important to notice that literate competence is merely one form of human competence. More than that, it is the form of competence that results from the explication of the linguistic and cognitive structures that are already implicit in our commonsense cognition and in our ordinary habits of speech. In that sense literacy is a derivative of and dependent upon those much more general and unschooled forms of language and cognition.

Written language, the language of schooling, is an instrument of great power for building an abstract, coherent, and explicit theory of reality and for managing a diverse heterogeneous and highly specialized society. It is the acquisition of this explicit formal system which accounts for some of the predominant features of Western culture and for the distinctive properties of the cognitive processes of educational adults.

Yet, the general theories and formal languages of science and philosophy provide a poor fit to daily, ordinary, practical and personally significant experience. Ordinary language with its breadth of resources, its nuances of meaning and its generality within a primary social group, while an instrument of limited utility for exploring abstract ideas, is a universal means for sharing our understanding of concrete situations and guiding practical actions. And it is the language which the child brings to school.

ACKNOWLEDGMENT

The research reported in this paper is part of a project on oral and written language development directed by the author and his colleagues Angela Hildyard and Nancy Nickerson. We are greatly indebted for financial support to the Canada Council and the Grants-in-Aid Program of the Ontario Ministry of Canada.

REFERENCES

Ervin-Tripp, S. (1977). 'Wait for me Roller Skate.' In S. Ervin-Tripp and C. Mitchell-Kernan, eds., *Child Discourse.* New York: Academic Press.
Gadamer, Hans-Georg (1975). *Truth and method.* The Seabury Press.
Greenfield, P.M. (1972). Oral or written language: The consequences for cognitive development in Africa, the United States and England. *Language and Speech,* 15: 169–178.
Grice, H.P. (1975). Logic and conversation. In P. Cole and J. Morgan, eds., *Syntax and Semantics: Speech Acts.* New York: Academic Press.
Havelock, E. (1963). Prologue to Greek literacy. *Lectures in memory of Louise Taft Semple, second series, 1966-1971.* Cincinnati: University of Oklahoma Press for the University of Cincinnati Press.
Havelock, E. (1976). *Origins of western literacy.* Toronto: Ontario Institute for Studies in Education.
Hildyard, A. (1976). Children's abilities to produce inferences from written and oral material. Unpublished doctoral dissertation. University of Toronto.
Lord, A.B. (1960). *The singer of tales.* Cambridge, Mass.: Harvard University Press.
McLuhan, M. (1962). *The Gutenberg galaxy.* Toronto: University of Toronto Press.
Olson, D.R. & Nickerson, N. (1977). The contexts of comprehension: On children's understanding of the relations between active and passive sentences. *Journal of Experimental Child Psychology,* 23: 402–414.

Ong, W. (1971). *Rhetoric, romance and technology: Studies in the interaction of expression and culture.* Ithaca: Cornell University Press.

Scribner, S. & Cole, M. (1978). Literacy without schooling: Testing for intellectual effects. *Harvard Educational Review,* 48 (4): 448–461.

Sprat, T. (1966). *History of the Royal Society of London for the improving of natural knowledge.* J.I. Cope and H.W. Jones, eds., St. Louis: Washington University Press (Originally published, London, 1667).

Stegner, Wallace (1962). *Wolf Willow.* New York: Viking Press.

List of Contributors

Thomas T Ballmer
Sprachwissenschaftliches Institut
Ruhr-Universität Bochum
D-4630 Bochum, FRG

Florian Coulmas
The National Language Research Institute
3-9-14 Nisigaoka, Kita-Ku
Tokyo 115, Japan

Konrad Ehlich
Seminar für Allgemeine Sprachwissenschaft
Universität Düsseldorf
D-4000 Düsseldorf, FRG

Bennison Gray
University of Indiana
Bloomington, IN 47402
P.O. BOX 2573
U.S.A.

Hartmut Haberland
Roskilde Universitetscenter
Roskilde, Denmark

John Hinds
Department of East-Asian Languages
University of Minnesota
Mineapolis, MN 55455
U.S.A.

Esa Itkonen
Department of General Linguistics
University of Helsinki
Helsinki
Finland

Tohru Kaneko
Jinbungakubu
Chiba University
281 Chiba, Japan

Asa Kasher
Department of Philosophy
Bar-Ilan University
Ramat-Gan, Israel

Werner Kummer
Fakultät für Linguistik und Literaturwissenschaft
Universität Bielefeld
D-4800 Bielefeld, FRG

Adam Makkai
Department of Linguistics
University of Illinois at Chicago Circle
Chicago, Ill. 60680 U.S.A.

Jacob Mey
Department of Linguistics
Odense University
Odense M., Denmark

Eugene A. Nida
American Bible Societies
1865 Broadway
New York, N.Y. 10023
U.S.A.

David R. Olson
Department of Applied Psychology
The Ontario Institute for Studies in Education
252 Bloor Street West
Toronto, Ontario M5S 1V6

Kenneth L. Pike
Summer Institute of Linguistics
Box 2550
Norman, Oklahoma 73070
U.S.A.

John O. Regan
Claremont Graduate School
Claremont, CA 91711
U.S.A.

Jon D. Ringen
Tingvein 15A
7000 Trondheim
Norway

H. Schnelle
Sprachwissenschaftliches Institut
Ruhr-Universität Bochum
D-4630 Bochum, FRG

Bjarne Ulvestad
Tysk Institutt
Universitetet Bergen
N-5001 Bergen
Norway

Ton van der Geest
Seminar für Psychologie
Ruhr-Universität Bochum
D-4630 Bochum, FRG

Walburga von Raffler-Engel
Vanderbilt University
Nashville, TN 37205
U.S.A.

D.H. Whalen
Department of Linguistics
Yale University
New Haven, CT 06520
U.S.A.

Dieter Wunderlich
Seminar für Allgemeine Sprachwissenschaft
Universität Düsseldorf
D-4000 Düsseldorf, FRG

Victor H. Yngve
Graduate Library School
The University of Chicago
Chicago, Ill. 60637
U.S.A.

Alan L. Ziajka
University of La Verne
La Verne, CA.
U.S.A.

Index of Names

(n. denotes footnote reference)

Achebe, C. 188
Aguilar, J. de 178
Aissen, J. 276
Akmajian, A. 148
Alisjahbana, S. T. 203-7, 209f., 218f.
Anjum, S. 196
Antinucci, F. 335
Anttila, R. 9, 164, 365
Applegate, R. B. 362
Arbib, M. 125 n. 15
Aristotle 31
Armbruster, F. E. 209 f.
Askedal, J. O. 255
Austin, J. L. 93, 99n.

Bach, E. 147
Bacon, F. 245
Bailey, L. J. N. 17, 268, 273
Baker, C. 147
Ballmer, T. 5
Baltin, M. 272
Bates, E. 223
Beattie, G. 230
Beheydt, L. 335
Bellugi, U. 336
Bendix, E. H. 2
Beneš, E. 248f.
Bereiter, C. 321
Bermann, T. 198
Bever, T. G. 15, 147, 149, 326
Bickerton, D. 265
Bierwisch, M. 246f., 251f., 259
Birdwhistell, R. 309
Bloch, B. 267, 273
Bloom, L. 334
Bloomfield, L. 16, 29, 37f., 41, 44f., 73, 129, 205-7, 219, 265, 334
Boas, F. 74
Boatner, M. T. 237
Böll, H. 250
Bohr, N. 87
Bolinger, D. 11f., 263, 270, 275, 360

Bopp, F. 33
Bothar, R. T. 65 n. 3, 133f., 147, 149
Bower, T. G. 309
Bowerman, M. 270, 335, 337
Bowlby, J. 309
Braine, M. 334
Brecht, B. 158, 251
Brentano, F. 149
Bridgman, P. W. 89f.
Brinkmann, H. 248
Brown, J. W. 121f.
Brown, R. 270, 334, 336, 338, 340
Brugmann, K. 29, 35
Bruner, J. 335, 337f.
Bühler, K. 156, 331
Burks, A. W. 125 n. 12
Burt, M. 345
Buscha, J. 290

Campbell, R. 333
Carden, G. 147, 150, 270-2, 276
Carnap, R. 133
Castillo, B. D. del 193
Cedergren, H. 17, 265
Chafe, W. 335
Chomsky, N. 2, 7, 9-11, 14, 16f., 19, 23 n. 4, 41f., 64, 69, 91, 109, 111-113, 115-118, 121, 125n., 129, 133, 142f., 147-149, 204, 206, 208, 219, 221, 249, 251-4, 259, 265, 267, 318-20, 330, 333f., 337, 359, 371
Cicourel, A. 195
Clark, R. 337
Cleland, T. 387
Cole, M. 380
Cole, P. 270
Collingwood, R. G. 97, 100n.
Columbus, C. 195, 197f., 238
Comrie, B. 218
Conrad, J. 355, 361
Cooper, W. S. 136-8
Corder, P. 345

Cortéz 178f.
Cresswell, M. 370
Coulmas, F. 65, 296, 260, 366, 377
Crosby, D. 73
Cross, T. 335
Curme, G. O. 259

Darnell, R. 196, 198
Davidson, D. 95, 150
Davis, S. 70
Delany, S. 61
Descartes, R. 197
Dickie, G. 100 n. 26
Dijk, T. A. van 12, 15, 23 n.6
Diogenes Laertius 48 n. 1
Dore, J. 338, 342
Dulay, H. 345
Dummett, M. 96, 99n.
Duncan, S. 333, 341
Durkheim, E. 204

Eccles, J. C. 119, 124 125n. 13
Ehlich, K. 159
Einstein, A. 85, 87, 89
Elliott, D. 270
Engel, U. 246, 248
Engelen, B. 248f., 251
Engelmann, S. 321
Ervin, S. 334
Ervin-Tripp, S. 384

Felix, S. 336, 345
Ferguson, C. A. 335, 360
Feyerabend, P. 23 n. 5
Fick, A. 34
Fillmore, C. J. 335, 365
Finke, P. 137f.
Fishman, J. 205, 362
Fleisch, P. 184
Fleming, I. 250
Fodor, J. 2, 147, 149, 269
Frances, H. 387
Francis, W. 246
Fraser, B. 270, 334
Frege, G. 96f., 99n.
Freire, P. 193
Friedrich, P. 48
Fries, C. C. 41
Frisch, M. 257f.

Gadamer, H.-G. 164, 385
Gardiner, A. 29, 39
Garfinkel, H. 328
Garret, M. 147, 149
Gates, E. J. 237
Gleason, H. A. 210
Gleitman, H. 270
Gleitman, L. R. 270
Glinz, H. 257
Goffman, E. 363
Goldsmith, J. 208
Graham, B. 180
Grass, G. 258
Gray, B. 3, 12, 16, 205, 208, 210, 218
Greenbaum, S. 6, 12f., 147, 270
Greene, G. 360
Greenfield, T. 386
Gregoire, A. 334
Grice, P. 98, 380
Grimes, J. A. 210
Gruber, J. 334
Gutzwiller, A. 198

Haberland, H. 74
Habermas, J. 130
Hall, E. 307, 310f.
Hall, R. A. jr. 208
Halle, M. 2, 208, 267
Halliday, M. A. K. 312
Hamp, E. 48n.
Hanlon, C. 270, 338
Hanzeli, V. E. 191f.
Harrah, D. 100 n. 16
Harris, Z. 41, 91
Havelock, E. 386
Healey, A. 156
Heckhausen, J. 341, 347
Hegel, G. W. F. 33
Heinämäki, O. 74
Heinrich, W. 252, 258
Helbig, G. 290
Henderson, L. J. 223
Heraclitus 85f., 88
Hermondson, L. 246
Hesse, H. 259
Hicks, R. D. 48 n. 1
Hildyard, A. 380, 382, 387f.
Hill, A. 6, 10
Hinds, J. 12, 228-31
Hirsch, E. D. 209

Index of Names

Hjelmslev, L. 205
Hockett, C. F. 170, 252, 272
Hoefnagel, J. M. 346
Hoequist, C. 276
Hoijer, H. 1
Hordhangen, E. 76
Huisman, C. 322
Hunter, J. F. M. 164
Husserl, E. 120
Hymes, D. 15, 17, 333, 346, 356

Inhelder, B. 66 n. 6
Itkonen, E. 12, 127, 129, 131-3, 136f., 148, 164, 246

Jacobs, R. 326
Jäcklein, K. J. 197
Jäger, S. 256-8
Jakobson, R. 29, 77, 205, 243, 356
Jaulin, R. 192
Jenkins, J. 334
Johnson-Laird, P. N. 296

Kaneko, T. 375
Kasher, A. 22, 99f., 135, 138
Kasher, N. 100 n. 26
Katz, J. 2, 11, 208, 269f.
Kaufmann, G. 248 f.
Keenan, E. 223
Keller, E. 360
Kibrik, A. 191
Kierkegaard, S. 366
Kintsch, W. 223
Klemke, E. D. 165
Klooster, W. 327
Köhler, W. 65 n. 4
König, E. 254
Kraak, A. 327
Kraus, K. 259
Kuhn, T. S. 217
Kummer, W. 157
Kuno, S. 224, 226, 228f.
Kuroda, S.-Y. 226

Labov, W. 9, 11f., 15, 17, 147, 150, 196, 222f., 263-5, 268f., 273, 321, 324
Lakatos, I. 134, 149
Lakoff, G. 17, 269
Lamb, S. 91, 275
Langer, S. K. 90

Langford, G. 100 n. 27
Lappin, S. 135, 138
Leclerc, G. 193
Lees, R. 246
Legum, S. 270
Lehmann, W. P. 35
Lehrer, T. 196
Leibniz, G. W. 116, 120
Lenneberg, E. 112
LePore, E. 147f.
Lessing, E. 245, 252, 254, 256
Levelt, W. 320, 326-8, 335, 337
Lieb, H. H. 125 n. 5
Linneaus, C. v. 33
Livingstone, D. 182
Lord, A. 387
Luther, M. 385f.
Lyons, J. 23 n. 2

Maclay, H. 6, 10
MacWhinney, B. 223
Makkai, A. 15, 237, 241, 244, 360
Malinowski, B. 29, 39
Manor, R. 100 n. 16
Marcussen Hatch, E. 345
Masling, G. 223
Mates, B. 48 n. 3
Matzel, K. 248
Mayhew, B. 223
McCawley, J. D. 48, 232, 335
McLuhan, M. 385
McNeill, D. 334
McTear, M. 340
Menuyk, P. 334
Mey, J. 198
Mey, J. L. 2, 74, 76, 81, 198, 355
Miller, G. A. 296
Miller, M. 334
Minsky, M. 228
Mispelkamp, H. 296
Mitchell 360
Moebus, J. 198
Montague, R. 370
Moore, G. E. 94, 99n.
Muraki, M. 227

Nabokov, V. 77, 330f.
Nagatomo, K. 226
Nagel, E. 90, 134
Nash, G. 73

Nemportky, J. Q. 237
Newport, E. 339
Newton, J. 32f., 134
Nickerson, N. 380-82, 387f.
Nida, E. 2, 6, 8, 13, 41, 70
Nostrand, H. L. 365

Olson, D. 381
Ong, W. 385
Osgood, C. E. 48 n. 6
Osherson, D. 137
Osthoff, H. 29, 35

Palermo, D. 334
Pap, A. 131
Parisi, D. 335
Patrick, G. T. W. 86
Paul, H. 29, 35, 37, 48
Pierce, C. S. 366
Percha, J. v. 250
Peters, A. 361
Piaget, J. 66 n. 5
Pike, E. G. 89
Pike, K. 22, 70, 88f.
Plato 90
Polanyi, M. 85, 90
Popper, K. 125 n., 132 f., 134
Post, E. L. 109, 116f.
Postal, P. 270
Powell, J. W. 196, 198
Preyer, W. 334
Pullum, G. K. 270
Putnam, H. 12, 23 n. 6
Pylyshyn, Z. 23 n. 7

Quasthoff, U. 198
Quine, W. V. 105-107, 110-112, 141-9, 363
Quirk, R. 10, 147

Rapaport, D. 121
Rask, R. 29, 33, 48 n. 4
Rauch, J. 247
Regan, J. 22
Reichel-Dolmatoff, G. 192
Reis, M. 296
Rekdal, O. 81
Rheingold, H. L. 309
Richards, J. 345
Ringen, J. D. 12, 147f., 150

Robins, R. H. 2
Root, M. 148
Rosenbaum, P. 326
Rosenberg, J. 148
Ross, J. 11, 17f.
Rubin, J. 205
Ryle, G. 359, 365

Sacks, H. 333, 341
Sagan, C. 222
Sahagún, F. B. de 295
Saint, R. 180
Samarin, W. J. 5, 23 n.2, 147, 156, 191
Samuel, H. L. 87
Sankoff, D. 17, 265
Şapir, E. 29, 38, 74, 172, 237
Saumjan, S. K. 91
Saussure de, F. 29, 36f., 43f., 205, 243
Schachter, P. 249
Schade, G. 254
Schatzmann, L. 198
Schegloff, E. 230
Schleicher, A. 29, 33f., 36, 43, 45, 48 n. 5
Schlesinger, J. 335, 337
Schnelle, H. 12, 14f., 125
Schütz, A. 156
Schulte-Pelkum, R. 372
Scott, C. T. 247
Scribner, S. 380
Searle, J. R. 330, 356
Sebeok, T. A. 48 n. 6
Seiffert, H. 254
Seiler, H. 296
Selinker, L. 345
Serafim, L. 276
Shibatani, M. 226
Shopen, T. 321
Shuy, R. 17
Siegl, I. 258
Simmel, G. 204
Skutnabb-Kangas, T. 74, 81, 198
Sleator, M. D. 6, 10
Sledd, J. 255
Slobin, D. 334, 337
Smith, C. 335
Smith, N. 218
Snow, C. 326, 328, 335, 339f., 346
Sokrates 49
Spencer, N. J. 10f., 223, 270
Spinoza, B. 116, 120

Index of Names

Spratt, T. 386
Stavenhagen, R. 193
Stegmüller, W. 130, 132
Stegner, W. 379
Steinberg, D. D. 234
Stern, C. 334
Stills, S. 73
Strauss, A. 198
Stravinsky, I. 77
Svartvik, J. 10

Tamori, I. 227
Tervoort, B. T. 321
Thomas, D. 77
Thompson, S. 270
Tonoike, S. 226
Toulmin, S. 21
Trevelyan, G. M. 84 n.
Turing, A. M. 109, 116f., 120, 125 n. 10
Turner, R. 328

Ulvestad, B. 10, 248f., 255

Vachek, J. 358
van der Geest, T. 20, 62, 65 n. 3, 321, 331, 333, 335, 340, 347
Voegelin, C. F. 4, 23 n. 1
Voegelin, F. M. 4, 23 n. 1
Voigt, G. 198
von Raffler-Engel, W. 22, 322

Wahlen, D. H. 15
Wales, R. 333
Warnock, G. J. 100 n. 25
Wasow, T. 148
Watzlawick, P. 331
Weinreich, U. 17
Wells, R. 41, 275f.
Whitaker, H. 19
Whitaker, H. A. 19, 365
Wilmanns, W. 257, 259
Winter, W. 247
Wittgenstein, L. 61, 109, 157, 364, 377
Wode, H. 336, 345
Wolfus, B. 384
Wong-Fillmore, L. 361
Wottawa, H. 327f.
Wright Mills, C. 81
Wunderlich, D. 21, 247, 256, 330
Wundt, W. 334

Yngve, V. 15, 41, 46
Young, L. 60
Young, N. 73

Zabeeh, F. 164
Ziajka, A. 22
Ziff, P. 17
Zweig, S. 250

Index of Subjects

acceptability 17f., 111, 154, 223, 248, 256, 327
acceptability judgements 10f., 13, 21, 108
acceptability of sentences 6
action, preverbal 305f.
action theory 156
adequacy of grammars 6
agreement 211, 290, 294
Algonquian 191, 206
alphabet 386
ambiguity 216
American English 80
American Indian languages 74
analysis of language 107
animal communication system 52
animal languages 58
applied linguistics 249
automata theory 110
automatization 358f., 361, 363
Aztec 197

behavior, communicative 32, 46
behavior, human 39
behavior, linguistic 127f.
behavior, nonlinguistic 306
behavior, observable 19
behavior, rule-governed 131
behaviorism 109f., 141, 146
belief 95f., 112
bilingualism 54
Black English 268, 324
body language 301ff.
brain 20f., 36, 40, 108f., 114, 118f., 121, 204, 302f.

case frame 228, 231f.
case marker 233
child language 58
Chinese 38, 52, 346, 357
class language 76
code 161, 343
cognition 387
cognitive act 127

colonial expansion 176ff.
colonization 178f., 181, 190
concepts 128
concept of a word 387
constituent structure 113, 141, 143
constituents, immediate 142
context 13, 23 n. 6, 170, 223, 270f., 281, 294, 341
context of situation 39
context, appropriate 93
context, coherent 265
context, colonial 179
context, defining 295
context, disambiguating 271, 276
context, fixed 293
context, interpretive 386
context, meaningful 381
context, natural 234
context, social 191
contrastive linguistics 245
convention 75
conversation 221, 230, 241, 268, 300, 310, 336, 339f., 344, 347, 363
conversation, analysis of 333
conversational interaction 230
conversational maxims 98, 100 n. 23
common sense 143, 379, 381, 387
communication 37, 54, 62, 90, 156, 219, 264, 271, 314, 331, 340
communication context 306
communication problem 301
communication, nonverbal forms of 307
communication, oral 67
communication, written 67
communicative behavior 32, 46
communicative interaction 303
communicative options 307, 309, 312f.
comparison of languages 35
comparative studies 34
competence 2, 14f., 17f., 21, 23 n. 7, 42, 56, 64, 72, 107, 118, 121, 157, 162f., 221, 237, 318, 381
competence in producing 82

Index of Subjects

competence in understanding 82
competence model 14
competence, analytic 61
competence, bilingual 369
competence, communicative 302, 341-6
competence, defective 358
competence, linguistic 94, 161, 342
competence, native 359
competence, native-like 357f., 361
competence, perfect linguistic 76
competence, pragmatic 93
competence, productive 61
competence, requirements of 56
competence, schooled 385
competence, socio-linguistic communicative 362
competence, theory of 10
comprehension 159, 163
computer 40, 53, 58, 112, 117, 300
computer, human 117
corpus 10, 44, 129, 164, 246, 250, 258
corpus, uniform 16
correctness 83, 326, 359
correct sentence 138
counter-examples 11f., 203, 208, 219, 223, 249, 255, 258
cultural change 186
cultural problems 88
culture 18, 88f., 157, 178, 186, 306f., 328, 333, 362, 364, 380
culture, destruction of 192
culture, science of 39
culture, semiotic system of 172
culture, Western 388
cybernetics 119, 123

Danish 79f.
data 1, 4-6, 8-11, 13, 21, 38, 41, 44, 47, 56, 72, 76, 83, 85, 120, 124, 130, 134, 141, 143, 147, 149, 154f., 157, 173, 195, 206, 218f., 222, 229, 234, 241, 248, 253, 263, 266, 273, 299, 328, 346
data collection 275
data of consciousness 87
data source 2
data, behavioral 2
data, conflicting 263
data, contradictory 172
data, distortion of 8

data, experiential 119,
data, empirical 135, 207
data, homogeneous 274
data, intuitional 129
data, intuitive 13
data, introspectional 12, 141, 150, 247, 251, 255f.
data, linguistic 29
data, nonlinguistic communication 305
data, phonetic 266
data, plain 303
data, primary linguistic 335, 337
data, standardized 203
data, syntactical 247
data, textual 251
data, uncertainties about 276
data, validity of 14
data, variable 270
deduction 303
deductive reasoning 19, 328
deep structure 208
deictic expressions 156
deictic perspective 279-82, 284, 293
deixis 279f., 301, 321
demarcation problem 133
description 90, 107, 209
description, grammatical 15
description, linguistic 263, 270
description, phonological 205
description, syntactical 253
descriptive adequacy 141, 143, 147
deviant sentences 12
dialect 14, 32, 55, 57, 61, 70, 154, 170, 187, 205, 222, 263-5, 267, 270, 274f., 280, 319f.
dialect split 271, 275
dialect variation 268
dialectology, social 76
dialects, intercommunicating 266
dictionary 15, 40, 364
discourse 210
discourse grammar 210
discourse structure 169, 172
distinctive features 38
Dschagga 185, 187
Dutch 319, 322, 324, 346f., 349

education 207, 323, 379
elicitation techniques 21
emic 85, 88f., 91

empirical 133ff.
empirical adequacy 14, 18
empirical argument 85
empirical evidence 163
empirical linguistics 51f., 57, 60, 164
empirical research 15, 18
empirical science 12, 133, 137
empirical studies 10
empirical test 57
empiricism 17, 42, 129
empiricity 62
English 4, 11, 16, 38, 41, 65, 77, 88, 93, 136, 203, 206f., 209, 219, 241, 246, 250, 255, 270, 272, 319, 325, 349, 355f., 363, 377, 386
English syntax 173
English, American 80
English, Black 268, 324
English, Middle 58
English, Old 241, 324
English, Oxford 82
epistemology 30, 42, 116
epistemology, behavioristic 110
epistemology, Gestalt 110
etic 88f.
experience 85, 87, 91, 114, 121, 128, 359
experience, internal 116
experiment 21, 57, 89, 121, 281, 285
experiment, linguistic 56
experimental psychology 35, 40
expert speakers 59
explanation 131
evidence 13, 96, 108, 134, 143f., 259, 264, 267, 282
evidence about language 46
evidence, cross-cultural 380
evidence, introspective 11, 16, 105, 109, 113, 122
evidence, linguistic 40
evidence, neurophysiological 114
evidence, phenomenological 113
evidence, statistical 299, 329

falsifiability 131
falsification 134
Finnish 136, 139
field linguist 16
field linguistics 5
field methods 162f.

field work 155ff., 163, 172, 179
foreign language 160, 162, 249, 364
frame 89f.
frame, grammatical 294, 296
frame, situational 377
French, 324, 357
function of speech 39
fuzzy grammar 18

German 88, 247f., 250, 252, 254f. 258, 290, 296, 319, 322, 346f., 349, 356, 366, 370-8
Gestalt 111
Gestalt epistemology 110
gesture 309, 319f. 365
grammar 7, 13, 29f., 32, 34, 38f., 136, 219, 246, 266, 270, 355, 359, 362
grammar of German 255
grammar, adequacy of 2, 6, 319
grammar, adequate 145
grammar, categorial 370f.
grammar, classical 36
grammar, complete 265
grammar, discriptively adequate 142
grammar, discourse 210
grammar, Dutch 322
grammar, English 210
grammar, form of 115
grammar, formal 17
grammar, fuzzy 18
grammar, generative 13, 111, 118
grammar, ideal 255
grammar, idiolect 16
grammar, limits of 6
grammar, Montague 370
grammar, normative 32, 42, 45
grammar, object language 247
grammar, observationally adequate 146
grammar, particular 112
grammar, performance 326
grammar, polylectal 273
grammar, procedural 108
grammar, provisional 345f.
grammar, psychological reality of 40, 42, 45, 112
grammar, psychologically real 366
grammar, recursive system of 142
grammar, scientific 9
grammar, sentence 12
grammar, theoretical 360

Index of Subjects

grammar, theory of 223
grammar, traditional 32, 36
grammar, transformational 14, 135
grammar, transformational generative 141
grammar, universal 108, 112
grammatical categories 370ff.
grammatical correctness 326
grammatical description 15
grammatical knowledge 143
grammatical model 14
grammatical research 13
grammatical rules 17
grammatical structure 35, 105, 360
grammatical system, discovery of 6
grammatical theory 40
grammaticality 17, 154, 252, 255f., 259, 265, 302, 319, 326
grammaticality judgement 7, 221, 223f., 269f.
grammaticality, degrees of 17
Greek 32, 35, 362

Haussa 53
hermeneutic circle 153, 162, 164
historical linguistics 241
historical reconstruction 33
history of linguistics 29, 175f., 196
Hittite 58
human behavior 39
Huron 191
hypotheses 86, 129, 255
hypothesis, grammatical 143

idealization 5, 7, 10, 13-6, 22, 40, 136f.
ideal native speaker 237
ideal speaker 98
ideal speaker-hearer 42, 47, 69, 136, 299, 301, 318
idiolect 13, 16f., 58, 61 n. 3, 70f., 154, 273, 319, 329, 331
idiom 268, 270, 322, 360, 377
idiomatic 215
idiomatic English 214
idiomatic usage 211
implicature 264
inconsistency 15, 203, 207f., 209f., 264, 266
inconsistency, formal 217
indeterminacy 15, 144, 146, 149, 263-5, 268, 273-5, 286

indeterminacy, communicative 274
induction 110, 303
inductive reasoning 19
informant 1, 4f., 7, 9f., 15, 23 n. 3, 38, 41, 52, 57, 59, 72, 136, 141, 143f., 146-8, 169-75, 178, 190f., 206, 237, 241, 246, 248f., 265, 271, 280, 282, 285, 287, 290, 294, 299, 314, 318, 326, 329
informant behavior 131
informant judgements 44
informant reactions 10
informant response 143
informant, average middle aged 300
informant, average old 300
informant, average young 300
informant, foreign language 323
informant, ideal 70
informant, naive 7, 320
informant, robot-like 300, 302
informant, sophisticated 8
informant, trained 173
initiation rites 186
innate competence 300
innate features of the human mind 99
innate ideas 19, 70
innateness 19
innateness hypothesis 335
innateness theory 20, 334, 338
intention 22, 149, 330f., 343, 356, 385
intentionality 146, 363
interaction 344
interjection 364
intonation 301, 338
introspection 9, 11f., 20, 56, 64, 105ff., 108f., 113ff., 118, 120f., 135, 141-5, 147f., 157, 161, 222, 237, 245, 275, 299, 364
introspection, phenomenological 105, 108
introspectional rules 254
introspective data 12
introspective evidence 11
introspective intuitionist method 163
introspective linguist 70
introspective methods 35
intuition 6f., 9-13, 15-17, 56, 64, 71, 77, 87, 108, 117, 128-30, 135, 138, 158, 208, 222f., 226, 229, 275, 318, 328, 369
intuition, goal-directed 259

intuition, isolated 234
intuition, linguistic 127ff., 135, 141, 317, 320, 324, 326, 332
intuition, rudimentary 162
intuitional science 127, 129, 131
intuitions, conflicting 132
intuitive judgements 13
investigator bias 12, 221
Iroquois 191

Japanese 53, 221, 223f., 228, 231, 366, 370-8
Juang 4
judgement 96f., 253
judgements over utterances 13
judgement, consistent linguistic 327
judgement, linguistic 317
judgement, unreliability of 329

kinesics 308
knowledge 382

language acquisition 161, 266, 270, 296, 317, 323, 332ff., 342, 348, 362
language acquisition device 238, 301
language acquisition strategies 337
language behavior 265
language community 61
language description 105
language education 16
language planning 203, 205
language policy 177
language problems 177
language processing 113
language structure 51, 191
language universals 374
language use 51, 72, 105ff., 234, 331, 333
language, biological conditions of 18
language, biological dimensions of 20
language, dead 58f.
language, first 4, 52, 54
language, foreign 160, 364
language, invariant features of 18
language, homogeneity of 59
language, innate nature of 19
language, neuro-physiological conditions of 19
language, pidgin 58
language, pragmatic demarcation of 95
language, private 61

language, second 4f.
language, universal properties of 20
language, unknown 155f.
language, variable features of 18
language, exotic 72
Latin 32, 58, 73, 136
learning theory 19f., 335, 338
Lebensform 157
lexical item 15, 65
lexicography 39
lexicon 268, 323, 358, 360
lexicon, mental 20
lingua franca 187
linguistic analysis 1, 4, 6, 12f., 20, 72, 157
linguistic argumentation 141
linguistic awareness 355, 359, 362
linguistic behavior 108, 127f.
linguistic change 34, 47
linguistic chaos 205
linguistic creativity 360
linguistic data 11, 47, 172
linguistic description 89
linguistic engineering 206
linguistic facts 51, 54
linguistic knowledge 9, 160, 162
linguistic problems 71, 88
linguistic reasoning 107
linguistic sign 36
linguistic structure 115
linguistic subdisciplines 3
linguistic theory 11, 14, 22, 34, 51, 54
linguistics, autonomous 129ff., 132f., 137
linguistics, empirical 51, 57, 155
linguistics, field 5
linguistics, introspective 155
linguistics, mentalist 7, 16
linguistics, normative 320
linguistics, prescriptive 207, 209
linguistics, scientific 42
linguistics, structural 7
linguistics, theoretical 5
literacy 207, 209f., 379f., 385, 387
literacy, acquisition of 387
literacy, Greek 386
logic, 30f., 97, 130, 136, 269
logic, deontic 133
logic, formal 137
logic, natural 137

Malay 203, 206

Index of Subjects

Maya 178
meaning 15, 31, 37f., 40, 44, 89, 98, 105, 107, 122, 144-6, 148, 203, 205, 211, 215-8, 243, 250, 263, 268, 320, 361, 364, 373, 376, 380, 382, 385f.
meaning, compositional 377
meaning, conversational 387
meaning, core 269
meaning, cultural 312
meaning, emotive 364
meaning equivalence 369, 372, 374, 378
meaning, explicit 386
meaning, intended 221
meaning, lack of 364
meaning, literal 377, 387
meaning, meta-linguistic representation of 369
meaning, pragmatic 384f.
meaning, probable 270
meaning, propositional 385
meaning, referential 375
meaning, sentence 379f., 384-6
meaning, speaker's 379f., 384-6
memory 20f., 65 n. 2, 110, 128, 223, 322, 326, 337, 356, 386
memory, working 41
meta-language 370
meta-linguistic judgement 141, 143, 146f.
meta-linguistic knowledge 52
mental conditions 95
mental entities 110
mental processes 14, 37
mental state 112
mental structures 15, 21, 118
mentalism 17, 110, 129
mentalist linguistics 7
metaphor 47, 361
method 39, 106, 116
method of introspection 141-4, 146-8
method of recursive definition 116
method of recursive description 108
method of sames and differences 44, 46
method, Bloomfieldian 334
method, comparative 33
method, conceptual 109
method, corpus analytic 245, 250
method, experimental 109, 130
method, fundamental 95f.
method, grammatical 36
method, grammatical/syntactical 257

method, intuitive linguistic 320
method, philological 164
method, psychological 36
method, relative 96
method, scientific 110
method, speculative 87
method, structural 125 n. 1
methodological conflicts 9
methodological problem 196
methodology 1, 130, 135, 153f., 161, 163f.
methodology of physics 131
methodology of testing linguistic intuition 327
methodology, *ad hoc* 299
methodology, black-box- 137
methodology, empirical linguistic 246
methodology, hypothetico-inductive 139
methodology, linguistic 146, 221, 327
methodology, neopositivist 196
methodology, nonscientific 245
methodology, philological 162
methodology, psycholinguistic 327
methodology, psychological 327
methodology, scientific 245, 259
methodology, statistically oriented 328
methods 130
methods of experimentation 136
methods, Alexandrian 38
methods, historical analysis of 176
methods, introspective 35
methods, nongrammatical 35
methods, objective 196
Middle English 58
mind 30, 87f., 90, 136, 359
mind-body problem 21
minimal pairs 169
morphology 33, 76, 105
mother tongue 386
Munda language 4

Nahuatl 170
naive informant 7
naming 88, 93f., 156
native chimp 300
native communicator 60f.
native doer 314
native experience 91
native fluency 357
native hearer 60

native informant 203, 207, 219, 279
native intuition 9
native insider 88
native language 54-6, 64, 88, 192, 245, 267, 358, 364
native language skills 80
native language user 317
native language, acquisition of 359
native non-linguistic speaker 327
native nonspeaker 53, 305
native novelist 252
native speaker 1, 3f., 5-8, 10, 13, 15-7, 19, 21, 29ff., 31, 34, 37, 40, 48, 62, 69f., 71, 85, 89, 93, 122, 127, 141, 153-8, 161-3, 169f., 173, 175, 178, 190-2, 195f., 198, 203, 206f., 211, 221f., 224, 234, 237f., 245f., 249, 263, 265f., 273, 275, 279f., 290, 295f., 299-305, 322, 327, 343, 357f. 369
native speakerhood 359
native speaker concept 317f., 327, 329, 332, 345
native speaker's death 160
native speaker judgement 7, 326
native speaker, actual 5
native speaker, concept of 2, 69
native speaker, definition of 54
native speaker, evidence about 38
native speaker, expert 6
native speaker, fluent 2
native speaker, good 55f.
native speaker, ideal 5, 14, 18, 237
native speaker, idealized 2, 10
native speaker, layman 9
native speaker, literate 379
native speaker, model of 40
native speaker, multiple 243
native speaker, naive 86
native speaker, normal 9
native speaker, notion of 59
native speaker, prototypical 66 n. 6
native speaker, real 18, 72
native speaker, reliable 9, 237
native speaker, sophisticated 8
native speaker, theory of 29ff.
native speaker, topology of 51ff.
native speaker, young 73
native speech 72
native tongue 206
nativeness 72, 77, 80, 88

natural speech 6, 8
near native speaker 164
neurophysiological processes 14
neurophysiology 106, 114, 125
nonnative speaker 32, 52, 77, 326, 355, 357-9
nonverbal behavior 305, 333
norm 62, 128, 134, 250, 302, 330
norm, grammatical 358
norms of usage 8
normative linguistics 320

objective science 198
objectivity in science 195
observation 5, 110, 121, 127-9, 132, 135, 138, 252
observer bias 38
observer component 86
observer relation 86
observer standpoint 89
Old English 241, 324
operative networks 122ff.
origo 156, 159f.
orthography 171
Oxford English 82

paradigmatic relations 170
paralanguage 303
parts of speech 31
perception 88f., 96, 110f., 119, 332, 335f.
performance 2, 15, 17, 19-21, 42, 64, 107, 118, 222, 318, 326, 357, 360
performance, automatized 362
performance, requirements of 56
performance, theory of 45
performatives, explicit 93
phenomenological analysis 110, 119
phenomenological experience 120
phenomenological introspection 105, 108
philological method 164
philological methodology 162
philology 33, 36, 153, 163, 176, 196
philosophy of language 32
philosophy of science 127, 130
phonemic system 205
phonology 33, 44, 76, 105, 129, 205, 266-8, 355, 370
phraseology 361
phrase structure rules 370
physics 130, 132, 135, 329

Index of Subjects 405

pidgin 58
Plains Miwok 4
positivism 130
Potawatomie 170
pragmatic demarcation of language 95
pragmatics 43, 76, 108, 129, 206, 323
prediction 10, 41, 89, 131, 267
prescriptive linguistics 207, 209
print 385
private language 61, 164
pronunciation 170, 264, 358
proposition 97
proto-language 312
proxemics 307
psycholinguistics 40, 47, 129f.
psychological reality 45, 112, (see also 'grammar')

radical translation 143f., 149
rational inquiry 16
rationality 7, 98, 129, 136
reality, linguistic 249f., 258
reality, theory of 388
rhetoric 30, 210, 219
routine 355
routine behavior 88
routine formula 360, 377f.
rule conflict 279, 286, 296
rule governed action 94
rule system 105, 109
rule, derivational 371
rule, grammatical 279, 286, 294f.
rule, interactional 362
rule, social 333, 341
rule, syntactical 293
rules 128, 251
rules of language 128
rules of usage 362
rules, sequences of 247
Russian 357

Sanskrit 33
second language 206, 317, 322, 333, 358
semantic ambiguity 216
semantic analysis 215
semantic change 275
semantics 40, 42, 76, 105f., 108f., 115, 118, 169, 172, 340
sentences deviant 12
setting 39

sign language 302, 338
simplicity 15, 20
social control 131
social dialectology 76
socialization 55, 75, 359, 363
society 83, 106, 178f., 186, 189f., 197, 380, 386
society, colonized 181
society, linguistic needs of 204
society, literate 386
society, traditional 186, 189f.
Spanish 178
speaker, ideal 98
speaker, minimal 93, 95, 97-9
speaker, native see native speaker
speech 30, 39, 61, 88, 128, 207, 252, 299, 305f., 338f., 348, 386
speech act 22, 93, 96, 98, 107f., 129, 158f., 317, 329, 332f., 356, 363
speech act theory 330
speech act, imaginary 130
speech act, kind of 94
speech act, necessary 93, 95
speech behavior 12
speech community 7, 11, 13f., 17f., 44, 59, 77, 264, 300, 318, 360
speech community, heterogeneous 356
speech data 175
speech disposition 145, 148
speech event 154
speech, norms, varying 82
speech situation 60, 155, 158-60
speech, function of 39
speech, power of 31
speech, received 82
speech, standard educated 55
speech, ungrammatical 71
Sprachgefühl 246, 252, 254
standardization 16, 203f., 206-8, 210, 219
statement, analytic 95
statement, synthetic 95
stimulus meaning 144-6, 148
Stoic logic 31
Stoic philosophy 30
strategies, linguistic 279ff., 296
strategy 279, 285f., 290, 306
strategy, contextual 294
strategy, experiential 294
strategy, functionally based 293
strategy, individuation 296

strategy, semantic-pragmatic 292
strategy, referential 294
strategy, semantically based 293
strategy, syntactically based 293
structural linguistics 7, 40, 69, 205
structuralism 36, 42, 109, 196, 208
structure of language 36, 144
study of language 1, 3, 22, 31, 33, 37, 44, 112, 218
style 33f., 264f., 267, 306, 336, 368
surface structure 208, 223
synchronic linguistics 249
syntactic research 10
syntagmatic relations 170
syntax 33f., 40, 42, 76, 105, 113, 115, 118, 122, 170, 173, 223, 245, 248, 252, 259, 269, 276, 323, 339f., 370
syntax, frozen 361
synthetic 134
system of rules 112

Tagalog 16, 206, 219
tagmemic 85
test 21, 279, 281, 327, 380
test, behavioral 195
test, experimental 129
test, theory independent 146
text 6, 36, 44, 154, 158f., 162f., 170, 251, 253, 331, 380, 382, 385
text corpus 258
text data 171
text, autonomy of 385
text, formalized 386
theoretical linguistics 5
theory 1, 5, 11, 42, 107, 134, 328
theory of automata 113
theory of grammar 223
theory of knowledge 30, 90, 97
theory of language 2, 5, 29, 36, 40, 43, 174, 217
theory of performance 45

theory of reality 388
theory of the sign 36
theory, competence 15
theory, empirical 134f.
theory, incomplete 41
theory, linguistic 11, 51, 265, 318, 338
theory, philosophical 132
theory, semantic 338
theory, syntactic 245, 338
time 109, 115, 128, 138, 296
tip-of-the-tongue phenomenon 20
translation 143, 250, 321, 369f., 372, 374f., 378
translation, radical 143f., 149
truth 30f., 33, 95f., 135, 146, 381
Turing-machine 105, 113, 120f.
typology 296

ungrammatical sentences 251f., 259
ungrammatical sequences 7
ungrammatical utterances 12, 221, 230, 252
ungrammaticality 377
universals in language acquisition 335
universals of language 2, 218, 374
universals, formal 374

variability 16, 18
variable rules 17, 263, 265
variants of language 52
variation 12, 16f., 207, 263-6, 269f., 273, 275, 330
variation, free 263, 271
variation, individual 34, 205
variation, linguistic 42, 47
varying speech norms 82
verbal behavior 296

well-formedness 13, 18, 121, 253
well-formed string 142
writing 171, 206f., 209, 302, 381, 387

LIBRARY OF DAVIDSON COLLEGE

Books on regular loan may be checked out for **two weeks**. Books must be presented at the Circulation Desk in order to be renewed.

A fine is charged after date due.

Special books are subject to special regulations at the discretion of the library staff.

MAY 0 6 1992			